Local Power in Old Babylonian Mesopotamia

Studies in Egyptology and the Ancient Near East
Edited by Professor John Baines, The Oriental Institute, University of Oxford

This interdisciplinary series publishes works on the ancient Near East in antiquity, including the Graeco-Roman period and is open to specialized studies as well as to works of synthesis or comparison.

Also published in the series

Myth and Politics in Ancient Near Eastern Historiography
Mario Liverani
Edited by: Zainab Bahrani and Marc Van De Mieroop

Poetry and Culture in Middle Kingdom Egypt: A Dark Side to Perfection
R.B. Parkinson

Local Power in Old Babylonian Mesopotamia

ANDREA SERI

equinox

SHEFFIELD UK BRISTOL CT

Published by Equinox Publishing Ltd.

UK: Unit S3, Kelham House, 3 Lancaster Street, Sheffield S3 8AF

USA: ISD, 70 Enterprise Drive, Bristol, CT 06010

www.equinoxpub.com

First published in hardback in 2006. This paperback edition published in 2013.

ISBN-13 978-1-84553-010-5 (hardback)

978-1-908049-00-1 (paperback)

British Library Cataloguing-in-Publication Data

A catalogue record for this book is available from the British Library.

Library of Congress Cataloging-in-Publication Data

Seri, Andrea.
Local power in old Babylonian Mesopotamia / Andrea Seri.
p. cm. -- (Studies in Egyptology and the ancient Near East)
Includes bibliographical references and index.
ISBN 1-84553-010-1 (hb)
1. Babylonia--Politics and government. 2. Community power--Iraq--Babylonia--History. 3. Local government--Iraq--Babylonia--History. 4. Central-local government relations--Iraq--History. 5. Iraq--History--To 634. 6. Iraq--Civilization--To 634. I. Title. II. Series.
JC61.S47 2005
320.8'0935--dc22

2005014322

Printed and bound in Great Britain by Lightning Source UK Ltd, Milton Keynes, and by Lightning Source Inc., La Vergne, TN

To Graciela Pilot and Víctor Seri

La historia, 'madre' de la verdad; la idea es asombrosa. Menard, contemporáneo de William James, no define la historia como una indagación de la realidad sino como su origen. La verdad histórica, para él, no es lo que sucedió; es lo que juzgamos que sucedió. Las cláusulas finales – 'ejemplo y aviso de lo presente, advertencia de lo por venir' – son descaradamente pragmáticas.

History, 'the mother' of truth; the idea is astounding. Menard, a contemporary of William James, defines history not as an inquiry into reality but as the very origin of reality. Historical truth, for Menard, is not what happened; it is what we believe happened. The final statements – 'example and signal of the present, warning of what is to come' – are brazenly pragmatic.

Jorge Luis Borges

Contents

List of Tables

Abbreviations

AbB	Altbabylonische Briefe
ABIM	Altbabylonische Briefe des Iraq Museum
Ad	Ammī-ditāna
Ae	Abī-ešuḫ
AfO	*Archiv für Orientforschung*
AHw	*Akkadisches Handwörterbuch*
AJSL	*American Journal of Semitic Languages and Literatures*
AnOr	*Analecta Orientalia*
AnSt	*Anatolian Studies*
AoF	*Altorientalische Forschungen*
AOAT	Alter Orient und Altes Testament
ARM	Archives royales de Mari
ARN	*Altbabylonische Rechtsurkunden aus Nippur*, F.R. Kraus *et al.*
ArOr	*Archiv orientální*
Aṣ	Ammī-ṣaduqa
AS	Assyriological Studies
A-S	Apil-Sîn
ASJ	*Acta Sumerologica Japan*
AuOr	*Aula Orientalis*
BaghMitt	*Baghdader Mitteilungen*
BAP	*Beiträge zum altbabylonischen Privatrecht*, B. Meissner
BB	*Babylonische Briefe aus der Zeit der Ḫammurapi-Dynastie*, A. Ungnad
BE	Babylonian Expedition of the University of Pennsylvania
BIN	Babylonian Inscriptions in the Collection of James B. Nies
BiOr	*Bibliotheca Orientalis*
Boyer *CHJ*	*Contribution à l'histoire juridique de la 1re. dynastie babylonienne*, G. Boyer
CAD	*The Assyrian Dictionary of the Oriental Institute of the University of Chicago*
CT	Cuneiform Texts from Babylonian Tablets... in the British Museum
CTMMA	*Cuneiform Texts in the Metropolitan Museum of Art*, I. Spar (ed.)

Dalley *Edinb.*	*A Catalogue of the Akkadian Cuneiform Tablets in the Collections of the Royal Scottish Museum*, S. Dalley
DCS	*Documents cunéiformes de Strasbourg conservés à la Bibliothèque Nationale et Universitaire*, D. Charpin and J.M. Durand
DN	Divine Name
ED	Early Dynastic
ED II	*Tell ed-Dēr II*, L. De Meyer (ed.)
FM	*Florilegium Marianum*
GAG	*Grundriss der akkadischen Grammatik*, W. von Soden
GN	Geographical Name
Ḫa	Hammurabi
Holma *ZATH*	*Zehn altbabylonische Tontafeln in Helsingfors*, H. Holma
HUCA	*Hebrew Union College Annual*
JANES	*Journal of the Ancient Near Eastern Society of Columbia University*
JAOS	*Journal of the American Oriental Society*
JCS	*Journal of Cuneiform Studies*
JESHO	*Journal of the Economic and Social History of the Orient*
JEOL	*Jaarbericht van het Vooraziatisch-Egyptisch Genootschap "Ex Oriente Lux"*
JNES	*Journal of Near Eastern Studies*
LFBD	*Letters of the First Babylonian Dynasty*, T. Fish
LH	Laws of Hammurabi
LIH	*The Letters and Inscriptions of Hammurabi*, L. W. King
MAH	Signature of the Musée d'Art et d'Histoire of Geneva
MAOG	*Mitteilungen der Altorientalischen Gesellschaft*
MARI	*Mari annales de recherches interdisciplinaires*
MDOG	*Mitteilungen der Deutschen Orient-Gesellschaft*
MHET	Mesopotamian History and Environment Series III: Texts
MLC	Signature of the Morgan Library Collection
MSL	Materialien zum sumerischen Lexikon
NBC	Signature of the Nies Babylonian Collection
Nippur Neigh.	*Nippur Neighborhoods*, E. Stone
NSGU	*Die neusumerischen Gerichtsurkunden*, A. Falkenstein
OA	Old Assyrian
OB	Old Babylonian
OBAT	*Old Babylonian Account Texts in the Horn Archaeological Museum*, M. Sigrist
OBO	Orbis Biblicus et Orientalis
OBTIV	*Old Babylonian Tablets from Ishchali and Vicinity*, S. Greengus
OBTTR	*The Old Babylonian Tablets from Tell al Rimah*, S. Dalley *et al.*

OECT	Oxford Editions of Cuneiform Texts
OIP	Oriental Institute Publications, University of Chicago
Or	*Orientalia*
OrNS	*Orientalia Nova Serie*
PAPS	*Proceedings of the American Philosophical Society*
PBS	Publications of the Babylonian Section, University Museum, University of Pennsylvania
PN	Personal Name
PSD	*The Sumerian Dictionary of the University of Pennsylvania*
RA	*Revue d'assyriologie et d'archéologie orientale*
RAI	Rencontre Assyriologique Internationale
RGTC III	Répertoire géographique des textes cuneiforms III, B. Groneberg
Riftin	*Staro-Vavilonskie iuridicheskie i administrativnye dokumenty v sobraniiakh SSSR*, A. Riftin
RIM	Royal Inscriptions from Mesopotamia, D. Frayne
RlA	*Reallexikon der Assyriologie*
RS	Rīm-Sîn
RSO	*Rivista degli studi orientali*
Sa	Sābium
Sd	Samsu-ditāna
Si	Samsu-iluna
Sl	Sūmû-la-el
SLB	Studia ad Tabulas Cuneiformes Collectas a F. M. Th. de Liagre Böhl Pertinentia
Sm	Sîn-muballiṭ
TCL	Textes cuneiforms, Musée du Louvre
TIM	Texts in the Iraq Museum
TJA	*Tablettes juridiques et administratives de la IIIe. dynastie d'Ur et de la Ire. dynastie de Babylone*, É. Szlechter
TJDB	*Tablettes juridiques de la 1re. dynastie de Babylone*, É. Szlechter
TLB	Tabulae cuneiforms a F. M. Th. de Liagre Böhl Collectae
TS	*Tell Sifr textes cuneiformes conserves au British Museum*, C. F. Jean
UCP	University of California Publications in Semitic Philology
UET	Ur Excavation Texts
VAB	Vorderasiatische Bibliothek
VAS	Vorderasiatische Schriftdenkmäler der Königlichen Museen zu Berlin
Waterman *BDHP*	*Business Documents of the Hammurapi Period*, L. Waterman
WO	*Die Welt des Orients*

YBC	Signature of the Yale Babylonian Collection
YOS	Yale Oriental Series
ZA	*Zeitschrift für Assyriologie*
ZL	Zimrī-Līm

A NOTE ON THE TRANSLITERATION OF AKKADIAN AND SUMERIAN

The syllabic divisions are those of the signs. Caps indicate that signs have been left without specific readings. Signs with accents or subscript numbers are homophones. Roman = Sumerian and italic = Akkadian.

Preface

This book is a revised version of my doctoral thesis submitted to the University of Michigan in 2003. I wish to thank the members of my dissertation committee, professors Norman Yoffee, Gary Beckman, Piotr Michalowski, and Tom Trautmann. Professor Yoffee encouraged me to publish this work and read and commented on several drafts. I owe Norm more than I can express. His views on the Old Babylonian period and on social theory were always, and will remain, a source of inspiration. I also wish to thank Professor John Baines from Oxford and the editors at Equinox publishing. Professor William Hallo has allowed me to study unpublished tablets from the Yale Babylonian Collection. Ulla Kasten was very cooperative during my visit to New Haven, and I appreciate her hands-on demonstration of how to bake clay tablets. Professor Martha Roth at the Oriental Institute of the University of Chicago kindly permitted me to use the files of the *Chicago Assyrian Dictionary*. Professor Roth read my dissertation and offered valuable suggestions. My gratitude also goes to Professor Piotr Steinkeller, Professor Matthew Stolper, Dr. JoAnn Scurlock, and Dr. Richard Beal for their comments. This research was possible thanks to fellowships I received from the Department of Near Eastern Studies, the Horace Rackham School of Graduate Studies, and the Institute for the Humanities of the University of Michigan. I am deeply grateful for their support to Dr Olga Gallego and Dr Dennis Pollard at the Department of Romance Languages and Literatures at the University of Michigan.

The affection and companionship of my friends are beyond recognition. Doris Fraker carefully read several manuscripts, and was always available when I needed help. Professor Charles Fraker lent me many books from his personal library and taught me a great deal of medieval historiography. Brad Crowell was unfailingly prompt when I wanted to discuss my interpretations. Laura Malaguzzi-Valeri willingly assisted me with her knowledge of technical issues. Marta Benetti has patiently answered my semantic and stylistic questions. The friendship of Ana María Ghio is invaluable. Professor María Inés Carzolio sent me bibliographic references every time I so requested. I have enormously benefited from the discussions I had with students and professors at various seminars in El Colegio de México, the Department of Near Eastern Studies, and the Institute for the Humanities. My studies in Argentina, Mexico, and the United States gave me the opportunity of having many good friends and teachers; I am exceedingly grateful to all of them.

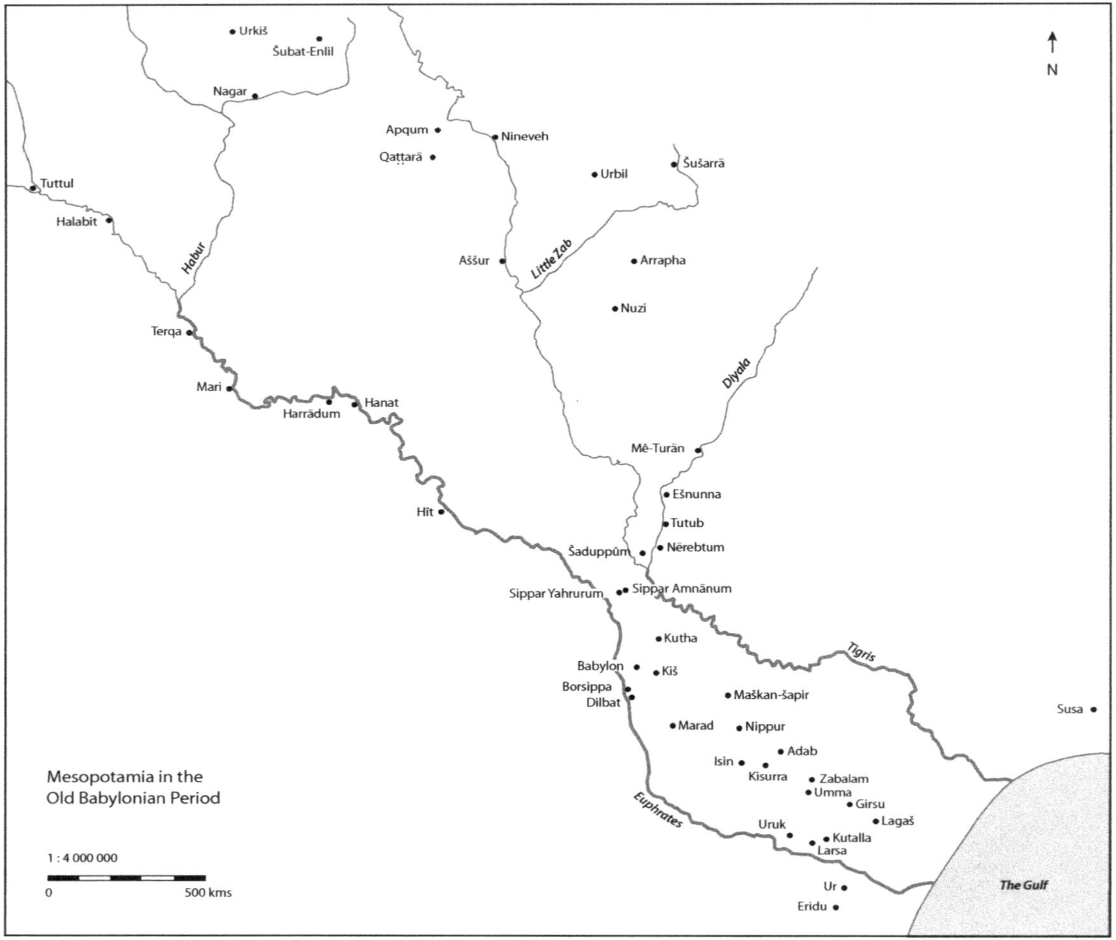
N
Urkiš
Šubat-Enlil
Nagar
Apqum
Nineveh
Qaṭṭarā
Urbil
Šušarrā
Tuttul
Halabit
Habur
Aššur
Little Zab
Arrapha
Nuzi
Terqa
Diyala
Mari
Hanat
Harrādum
Mê-Turān
Ešnunna
Hīt
Tutub
Šaduppûm
Nērebtum
Sippar Yahrurum
Sippar Amnānum
Kutha
Tigris
Babylon
Kiš
Borsippa
Dilbat
Maškan-šapir
Susa
Marad
Nippur
Adab
Isin
Kisurra
Zabalam
Umma
Girsu
Lagaš
Euphrates
Uruk
Kutalla
Larsa
Ur
Eridu
The Gulf
Mesopotamia in the
Old Babylonian Period
1 : 4 000 000
0
500 kms

Introduction

The structure and function of local institutions, their interaction, and their dealings with the state have seldom been systematically evaluated in Mesopotamia because studies have traditionally concentrated on the political and economic history of the state as well as on royal deeds and policies. The picture that emerges from state-centered approaches leaves little room for studying what happened in the interstices of the royal apparatus, and for seeking out conflicts and negotiation strategies between the state and other sectors of society. In this book I aim to show that researching these local authorities casts new light on the functioning of Old Babylonian society, for these institutions participated actively in judicial matters and economic affairs involving both the state and community members. I argue that local authorities acted as the hinge that articulated state and society. This perspective reveals mechanisms of collaboration between state and local powers, and it also reflects tensions concerning the control over local resources. By shifting the emphasis from the state to local authorities, this study depicts a complex network of traditional social and political relations embedded in the fabric of Old Babylonian cities, which not even the most centralized and efficient policies were able to suppress.

This book focuses on certain local powers in Old Babylonian Mesopotamia (c. 2000–1595 BC), namely the chief of the city (*rabiānum*), the elders, the 'city', and the assembly. I did not include other similar corporate bodies as for instance the *bābtum*, 'the city ward', the *kārum*, 'the port authority', and the local judges for several reasons. Thus, although the 'city ward' is probably a relatively independent authority, it very seldom interacts with the *rabiānum*, the elders, and the city. However, there are some examples in which the *kārum* acts in concert with the *rabiānum*, but its degree of independence from the state needs further investigation. The same remark applies to the local judges. Aside from this justification, exclusions also rest on a practical criterion: the incorporation of all those institutions would have rendered this project unmanageable, especially in view of the voluminous amount of Old Babylonian documents.

This approach to Old Babylonian history allows us to understand the constituency, activities, and sphere of influence of local institutions of authority, and the way they coped with state officials and royal policies. Focusing on local powers changes the traditional manner of looking at the state. Far from being a monolithic entity that unilaterally made decisions concerning people, water, land, and other resources, the state had to deal with local institutions that were not always willing to accept royal decisions passively. Due to this constraint, the state was usually unable to penetrate deeply into traditional social and economic practices that were accessible to local leaders, as is most apparent in the overlap of jurisdiction related to land distribution. I also take into account instances where the state surreptitiously co-opted local leaders into the royal domain. The methodology and conclusions of this case study of local authorities during a specific period are valuable for research on other ancient states and complex societies.

My work rests upon an exhaustive compilation and analysis of cuneiform documents encompassing economic, legal, and epistolary sources, royal inscriptions, as well as literary texts. Despite my attempts to be thorough in compiling data, I am aware of the fact that some attestations could have escaped my notice. One cannot but wait eagerly for the completion of the Old Babylonian electronic corpus, because such a valuable tool will prevent omissions and make the gathering of information easier. While I have also considered literary texts, my approach to interpretations that rely on literary compositions has been persistently critical. This is because I am skeptical about the use of literature for the reconstruction of political and social institutions. For similar methodological reasons, I have omitted omen texts mentioning the *rabiānum*, the elders, and the assembly. Including them was a temptation hard to resist, because omen literature refers to conflicts that are difficult to trace otherwise. Indeed, according to certain omens, local powers might challenge the royal authority and overthrow the king (see, e.g., Scheil 1930: 152 and Oppenheim 1936: 224–28). Nevertheless, it is worth emphasizing that, in spite of Jacob J. Finkelstein's (1963) claims, omens are hardly repositories of historical facts (see Michalowski 1999: 74–77).

In addition to published cuneiform documents, I include a number of unpublished tablets from the Yale Babylonian Collection. Information pertaining to local authorities can be drawn from texts regardless of their provenance. Thus, several royal letters in my corpus provide information valuable for understanding how the state related to local authorities. Since ancient scribes did not produce treatises discussing their institutions, I have studied documents and words. However, my study is not a decontextualized philological survey, but rather establishes the meaning of terms and approaches institutional practices through them. By means of a detailed cross-referential reading of sources, I ascertain the characteristics of these institutions and the way they operated. I further examine the interrelationship of the chief of the city, the elders, the 'city', and the assembly. Such an approach allows me to integrate local authorities within the broader context of Old Babylonian society. The new contribution of this work resides, therefore, in its analysis

Comparative chronology of Old Babylonian major dynasties

BC	Isin	Larsa	Ešnunna	Mari	Babylon
			Šū-ilīya	*šakkanakku*-period	
2025	Išbi-Erra (2019–1987)	Naplānum (2025–2005)	Nūr-aḫum (c. 2010)		
			Kirikiri		
2000	Šū-ilīšu (1986–1977)	Iemṣium (2004–1977)	Bilalama (c. 1995)		
1975	Iddin-Dagan (1976–1956)	Sāmium (1976–1942)	Išar-rāmāšu (n.d.)		
	Išme-Dagan (1955–1937)				
1950	Lipit-Ištar (1936–1926)	Zabāya (1941–1933)	Uṣur-awassu (c. 1950)		
		Gungunum (1932–1906)			
1925	Ur-Ninurta (1925–1896)		Azūzum (n.d.)		
1900		Abī-sarē (1905–1895)	Ur-Nin-MAR.KI (n.d.)		
	Būr-Sîn (1897–1876)	Sūmû-el (1894–1866)	Ur-Ningišzida (n.d.)		Sūmû-abum (1894–1881)
					Sūmû-la-el (1880–1845)
1875	Lipit-Enlil (1875–1871)		Ipiq-Adad I (n.d)		
			Šarrīya (n.d.)		
	Erra-imittī (1870–1863)		Warassa (n.d.)		
			Bēlakum (n.d.)		
	Enlil-bāni (1862–1837)	Nūr-Adad (1865–1850)	Ibāl-pî-el II (c. 1863?)		
			Ipiq-Adad II (c. 1863–1818)		
1850		Sîn-iddinam (1849–1843)			Sābium (1844–1831)
		Sîn-erībam (1842–1841)			
	Zambīya (1838–1836)	Sîn-iqīšam (1840–1836)			
	Itēr-pîša (1835–1832)	Ṣillī-Adad (1835)			
	Ur-dukuga (1831–1828)	Warad-Sîn (1834–1824)			
	Sîn-māgir (1827–1817)				Apil-Sîn (1830–1813)

BC	**Isin**	**Larsa**	**Ešnunna**	**Mari**	**Babylon**
1825		Rīm-Sîn I (1822–1763)		Yagīd-Līm ? (c. 1820)	
	Dāmiq-ilīšu (1816–1794)		Narām-Sîn (1818?)	Yaḫdum-Līm (c. 1810–1794)	Sîn-muballiṭ (1812–1793)
1800			Dannum-tāḫāz (n.d.)		
	1794: Annexed to Larsa		Iqīš-Tišpak (n.d.)	Sūmû-Yamam (c. 1793)	Hammurabi (1792–1750)
			Dāduša (?–1779)	Samsī-Addu / Yasmaḫ-Addu (c. 1792–1775)	
1775			Ibāl-pî-el II (1778–1765)	Zimrī-Līm (1775–1766)	
			1765: Elamite interregnum		
		1763: Annexed to Babylon	Ṣillī-Sîn (1764–1762)	1762: Destroyed by Babylon	
1750			Ilūni (n.d.)		Samsu-iluna (1749–1712)
		Rīm-Sîn II (1741)			
1725					
			Aḫušina (n.d.)		Abī-ešuḫ (1711–1684)
1700					
					Ammī-ditāna (1683–1647)
1675					
1650					Ammī-ṣaduqa (1646–1626)
1625					Samsu-ditāna (1625–1595)
1595					

of the articulation between state and local powers, and between local powers and society.

The motivations of this research project originated from my historiographical and methodological concerns regarding cuneiform sources and the writing of Old Babylonian history. Two questions helped shape this study. First, why is it that historians of ancient Mesopotamia concentrate on history of the state? Second, how is it possible with the available sources to go beyond the royal domain and study other spheres of society? The first chapter aims at exploring the ways in which Mesopotamian history has been written from the decipherment of cuneiform writing until the present. This is a survey of main currents and is not exhaustive. The evaluation of historiographic trends related to ancient Near Eastern history is relevant to explaining why certain research topics have been privileged over others. This examination is fundamental for understanding why the state occupies a predominant position in works dealing with Mesopotamian history. The centrality of the state is frequently attributed to the provenance of the extant sources. I argue, however, that the relation between facts and theory cannot be overlooked. Written documents answer the questions we ask them, but if the inquiry changes, the information that the sources provide will also be different.

The second chapter offers an outline of Old Babylonian political, economic, and social history that provides a framework for my research. This section is not merely a compilation of facts and events. Rather, I highlight the early political fragmentation of Mesopotamia into several kingdoms, the unification under Hammurabi, and the segmentation of the state already apparent under his successor Samsu-iluna. Political swings are important if we are to comprehend other domains of society. But political changes do not necessarily result in predictable autocratic governments, nor do they forcibly lead to the settlement of nomads and consequential changes in their institutions, as has been argued. For economic and social history, I examine three approaches that have influenced studies of the Old Babylonian period. First, I deal with theories proposing that the state had total control of economy and society. Second, I examine those studies that consider a bipartite division between state and communities. Finally, I consider the tripartite approach, which, besides state and community, also includes the private sector. I argue that debates about Old Babylonian economic and social history have reached stalemate, since any attempt to pursue these problems further seems to rely on accepting the general premises of one or another interpretation. The study of local power, then, offers an alternative way of looking at Old Babylonian society that has been neglected in previous works.

Chapter three examines the role of the *rabiānum*, a title attested only from the Old Babylonian period onwards. Previous interpretations maintain that the *rabiānum* was originally a tribal sheikh, and that when Amorites became fully settled the institution evolved into an urban office. I propose instead that the term *rabiānum* indicates two unrelated institutions. On the one hand, it was a royal title borne by several kings during the early Old Babylonian period. On the other hand, it was an urban office referring to the chief of the city. This interpretation rests upon the analysis of the extant *rabiānum* texts, which consist of economic and legal documents, letters, seal impressions, and royal inscriptions. The chapter is divided in two sections. The first deals with *rabiānum* as a royal title, usually combined with a gentilic. This is the case with the attestations *rabiān Amurrim* (chief of the Amorites), *rabiān Rababî* (chief of the Rababeans), *rabiān Amnānim* (chief of the Amnānums), *rabiān bābtīšu* (chief of his lineage group), and finally the alleged title *rabiān nārim* (chief of the river district). The second section deals with the *rabiānum* as a city authority, including the characteristics and jurisdiction of the office.

The fourth chapter studies the city elders. Interpretations of the role of the elders rely heavily on literary sources, and they depict the institution as a royal advisory body which lost power over the years to become a mere organ of the local administration. I reexamine all the published documents from Mari to show that the elders recorded in these archives were engaged in political, diplomatic, and military affairs and disputes involving kings, kinglets, and royal officials from the Mari region and northern Syria. The analysis includes not only the city elders, but also the elders of the district, the elders of the land, and the elders of ethnic groups. I propose that the elders from Mari sources are not identical in role and function to those acting in Babylonia. The second part of the chapter deals with the city elders in Babylonia. In this section I study the role and characteristics of the institution, its interaction with the *rabiānum*, and their joint role in legal disputes and economic affairs, including conflicts with royal representatives.

Chapter five focuses on the role of 'the city' as a local institution of authority similar to the elders. I argue that 'the city' was a collegiate body that presumably counterbalanced the role of the elders, and that this institution should not be regarded as a synonym for 'the assembly' or as an abbreviated form referring to local powers in general. This interpretation is based upon those cases where the interests and decisions of the city conflict with those of the elders and the *rabiānum*, and on documents where the city is mentioned together with those local powers that were allegedly part of the institution. The close reading of economic contracts makes it possible in certain cases to identify city members, showing that the chief of the city could have been part of this corporate body before or after he became a *rabiānun*. The chapter further explores the activities of the city in economic and legal issues as well as its interaction with other local authorities and royal officials.

The sixth chapter is devoted to the assembly. Literary sources and comparisons with Old Assyrian, Greek, and Roman assemblies underpin most interpretations of the Mesopotamian assembly. Such an approach is partially justified by the small amount of documents other than literary texts. The influence of interpretations entirely based on literary compositions was such that late in the 1940s the expression 'primitive democracy' was coined to characterize Mesopotamian government before the rise of monarchy. In this view, assemblies from later periods were the feeble survivors of their primitive ancestors. This chapter offers a critical approach to literary texts, and it also includes the analysis of legal contracts and letters. Based on this evidence, I examine the composition, activities and competence of the assembly. The conclusion shows that the Old Babylonian assembly was a mixed institution including royal officials and community representatives. Rather than a royal organ presided over by the king, the Old Babylonian assembly was the arena where different sectors of society came together to argue about their economic and legal problems.

The last chapter provides a synthesis of the problems discussed throughout the book. It summarizes those analytical approaches that stress the all-encompassing role of the state, those that emphasize the binary opposition between state and rural communities, and those that argue in favor of the existence of a private sector in Old Babylonian economy and society. These trends have led to an interpretive cul-de-sac, where the richness of historical facts and processes is lost in the maze of arguments to support a particular theory. Although Assyriologists have often been blamed for their positivist obsession, there is no doubt nowadays that not even the most positivist of scholars is theoretically *tabula rasa*. Since the early twentieth century and especially in recent decades, philosophers, sociologists, historians, anthropologists, and others have remarked on the unavoidable tyranny of interpretation and on the illusion of objectivity. Certain postmodern thinkers have overtly criticized the illusion of objectivity to the extent that they have undermined the relevance of collecting and analyzing data.

I maintain that an evaluation of the ways in which Mesopotamian history has been written together with a survey of certain historiographical analyses is fundamental if we are to pursue alternative ways of thinking about Old Babylonian society. My conclusion shows that the study of a number of relatively independent local authorities allows us to approach ancient history from a place other than the state or the communities. This perspective also permits us to trace a set of horizontal and vertical connections present in Old Babylonian society. Although I have dedicated a chapter to each institution for organizational reasons, the aim of the project is not to isolate local powers and study them in a vacuum. Rather I analyze local authorities to trace the ways in which the state, the elite members of the private sector, and the rest of society interacted. Therefore, the conclusions also summarize the results of my investigation concerning the activities and interaction of local powers, and the interaction between local powers and the state. This section seeks to reconstruct urban elites, and the ways in which these local leaders implemented, restricted, or overstepped state policies.

1

Is Mesopotamian History ... History?

HISTORY LOST

Ancient Mesopotamia entered the realm of history relatively late. Before the second half of the nineteenth century there was no book entirely devoted to the subject. Authors interested in this region and period drew their conclusions from the scattered references that appear in Herodotus and other Greek writers, in the Bible, and in what had survived of Berossos' work through secondary sources. Paradoxically, the region that gave birth to one of the earliest writing systems had been confined to the domain of 'the peoples without history', or to those societies which had no written records. This assessment could still be found in the early decades of the 1800s, as for instance in Hegel's *The Philosophy of History*. In the chapter dealing with Assyrians, Babylonians, Medes, and Persians, he states (1942: 182):

> Traditions respecting them ascend to the remotest periods of History; but in themselves they are obscure, and partly contradictory; and this contradiction is the less easy to be cleared up, as they have no canonical books or indigenous works.

This mention of the lack of written sources contrasts with Hegel's remark for the 'Zend people', whose history was poorly understood until the last third of the eighteenth century because their language was unknown to the Europeans. Although Hegel refers to travelers who sought to identify the ruins of the old tower of Babel, the existence of monumental inscriptions reported by adventurers like Pietro della Valle in the seventeenth century seems to have passed unnoticed.

The first samples of Mesopotamian writing brought to Europe in the 1600s had to wait until the next centuries, when the patient efforts of several scholars made texts intelligible. The decipherment of cuneiform writing was officially established in 1857, after the members of the Royal Asiatic Society compared four translations of the same inscription and agreed that the renderings were substantially alike. The British institution had submitted copies of a cylinder bearing the 'Annals of Tiglathpileser I' to Edward Hincks, Henry Rawlinson, Jules Oppert, and Fox Talbot, who translated the text similarly. The referees announced the decipherment in a report of the Royal Asiatic Society dated 29 May 1857, but of course this date is only a convention, for Rawlinson (1852) had already published his 'Outlines of Assyrian History Collected from the Cuneiform Inscriptions' five years earlier. The importance of this achievement was apparent not only for the philologist interested in ancient languages, but also for the historian. For the first time, the ancient kingdoms of Mesopotamia could be potentially studied by means of original texts written several thousand years ago. Nevertheless, there were still many gaps to be filled. The translation of the documents that came to light systematically since the middle 1860s was a slow process and the philological problems were far from being completely solved.

HISTORY REGAINED: THE EARLY ATTEMPTS AT WRITING MESOPOTAMIAN HISTORY FROM CUNEIFORM TEXTS

The decipherment of cuneiform writing and, therefore, the availability of Mesopotamian native sources took place during the apogee of positivism. A few decades earlier in Germany, Leopold von Ranke was developing his 'objective' historical method based on archival work, and his interpretations were generally focused on political history and the state. Ranke's first book (1824) *History of the Latin and Teutonic Nations 1494 – 1514*, voiced his criticism of contemporary historiography and its reliance on tradition. His tendency to concentrate on political history and the deeds of kings and leaders while ignoring economic and social forces is evident in the *History of the Popes during the 16th and 17th Centuries* published in 1834. Peter Burke (1992: 5–7) maintains that the reason why political history and the centrality of the state in historical works achieved a predominant position during the nineteenth century is narrowly associated with two main factors. On the one hand, European governments were viewing history as a means of spreading the national values of the recently created nation-states. On the other hand, the sources and methods of Ranke's school replaced chronicles by the use of government records housed in archives.

The influence of positivism on Assyriology was manifold, and initial interpretations usually followed other intellectual traditions rooted in both historiographic trends and religious principles. The field originally attracted scholars, theologians, and laymen whose motivations were, in many cases, led by religion instead of historical methods. The ancient inscriptions newly discovered offered the possibility of recovering the past, but they also provided an opportunity to test their information against the traditional knowledge coming from the Bible and Greek sources. This explains the huge amount of literature aimed at proving either that the Bible was right or that it was wrong. In the first decades of the twentieth century, the debate dubbed 'Babel/Bible' reached its zenith after a lecture delivered in 1902 by Friedrich Delitzsch. A series of even more controversial talks and articles followed, in which Delitzsch systematically questioned the Bible. The controversy was of such great interest to the public that even the emperor Wilhelm II took part in it (Larsen 1995).

The close ties between Assyriological themes and biblical stories also favored the general principles of universal history, a genre developed by influential churchmen such as Eusebius, Bede, James Ussher, and Jacques-Bénigne Bossuet (Kelley 1991: 16). The difference was that new versions of Mesopotamian history written under the auspices of universal history now included cuneiform and archaeological records. One of the last exponents of this school is François Lenormant, a professor of archaeology at the 'Bibliothèque Nationale' in France, who published his *Manuel d'histoire ancienne de l'Orient jusqu'aux guerres médiques* in 1868.[1] His work was welcomed in Assyriological circles to the extent that it is repeatedly quoted in the literature of the time. Lenormant stresses the importance of cuneiform sources and archaeology, and the aims of his project are clearly exposed from the beginning:

> En histoire, je suis de l'école de Bossuet. Je vois dans les annales de l'humanité le développement d'un plan providentiel qui se suit à travers tous les siècles et toutes les vicissitudes des sociétés. (…) Pour moi, comme pour tous les Chrétiens, l'histoire ancienne tout entière est la préparation, l'histoire moderne la conséquence du sacrifice divin du Golgotha. (Lenormant 1881: xi)

And indeed, the first volume of the *Manuel* mimics Bossuet's *Discours sur l'histoire universelle* written in 1681.

Lenormant organizes his work following the narrative sequence of the Bible: the creation of humankind, the antediluvian generation, the flood, and so forth. Lenormant's strategy is, first, to identify the cuneiform accounts with those in the Bible, and second to verify the biblical text in the light of Mesopotamian sources. He also resorts to a comparative approach considering different peoples and his examples go from ancient Mesopotamia to pre-Hispanic America. At several points, the book resembles more a study on comparative mythology than a historical work, and the mythical is often blended with the historical. To follow Bossuet in the late 1800s was somewhat anachronistic, because already in eighteenth-century historiography, the general tendency was to reject theological and providential interpretations in favor of the methods applied to the natural sciences. But Lenormant's approach was paradigmatic and it was generally adopted because biblical

1 Lenormant's project was ambitious and he was unable to finish it. The *Manuel d'histoire ancienne de l'Orient* was followed in 1881 by the publication of a three-volume set with the same title, only that the word 'Manuel' was omitted in the new edition. Of these three volumes, the first deals with The Origins and the two others with Egypt. After Lenormant's death three other volumes dealing with Mesopotamia were published in 1886. E. Babelon, one of Lenormant's students, completed the work. By 1886 the *Histoire ancienne* had turned into a massive publication.

narratives worked as a frame to hold and make sense of a wide range of examples collected from the ancient Near East.

Other studies were less programmatic than Lenormant's, even if they shared similar assumptions. The interplay between history and myth, for instance, also appears in *History of Babylonia* by George Smith (1877). This becomes clear from the beginning of the book, where there is a chronology divided into mythical and historical periods, while kings, gods, and fantastic beings alike populate the work's pages. Although Smith specifies that it is necessary, if not always possible, to separate stories from historical matters, he assigns a central place to the flood story. Following what was customary, he also emphasizes the importance of cuneiform documents to supplement the Bible. Naturally, Smith was fascinated with his own discovery of the Mesopotamian flood story and he had to grant it a place in history. Besides, the deluge fitted nicely into traditional narratives about ancient Mesopotamia. After his treatment of mythological times, however, Smith's history becomes more realistic, for he is able to follow the threads of political events primarily based on royal inscriptions. There were huge historical gaps and uncertainties because many of the documents that are available today were unknown; for example, the origins of Hammurabi[2] are unclear to Smith. In contrast, his descriptions of the first millennium are more detailed, and the biblical account is interwoven with information from cuneiform inscriptions and Greek authors. Consequently, Smith explains the fall of Babylon in the admonitory terms of the Bible: the decline was due to moral and mental decay. And he further traces the influence that ancient Mesopotamia had on Western civilization and human progress. As already mentioned, this linear evolution of human history was also one of Lenormant's starting points.

The exploration of a variety of subjects focused on social experiences soon accompanied the interest in religious and political themes. The end of the nineteenth century witnessed the edition of *Babylonians and Assyrians* by Archibald H. Sayce (1899), a clergyman and professor of Assyriology at Oxford. His work is not, strictly speaking, a book on ancient history. It rather focuses on Mesopotamian life and customs, and it is one of the forerunners of those studies dealing with everyday life that will appear later (e.g. Contenau 1954; Nemet-Nejat 1998; Bottéro 2001). According to the preface by James Craig, the editor of the series on Semitic handbooks, one of the aims of the work is to show how Semitic peoples influenced Western civilization. Sayce is not concerned with chronology or positivist methods. He refers to native sources, the Greeks, and the Bible without any critical remark. Despite the advances in philology, the information from cuneiform sources was

2 Following the editor's suggestion, I have written the name Hammurabi in the standard anglicized way.

still not sufficient to analyze certain topics. Therefore, Sayce has to resort to his imagination nurtured by his religious background. That is the case when he describes Mesopotamian government as a theocracy governed by a king-priest who was 'quite as much a pontiff as he was a king' (p. 168). When Sayce discusses education, it is difficult to avoid the impression that he is referring to Oxford and not to ancient Mesopotamia. He assumes that the library was attached to the school which 'in latter times developed into a university' (p. 56). He compares cuneiform tablets with modern books, whereas his Babylonian and Assyrian students who had to learn Sumerian and Aramaic resemble an Oxonian taking Latin and French.[3]

The histories by Smith and Sayce do not seem to follow any historical method. In that sense, they differ from Lenormant's proposal. Nevertheless, in the three cases the affinities between Assyriology and Biblical topics made it difficult to separate history from religion. It is in this respect that studies like those of Lenormant, Smith, and Sayce converge. The Bible functioned as a reference to interpret the dissimilar and fragmentary information coming from cuneiform sources, mainly mythological and literary accounts, and royal inscriptions. At the same time, it is possible to trace a selective appropriation of Mesopotamian tradition. On the one hand, these authors considered Mesopotamia to be the cradle of civilization; on the other, they questioned those religious beliefs and political practices related to polytheism and despotism. Obviously, these approaches did not follow Ranke's historical methods. They rather tend to mimic the writings of Herodotus, the 'Father of History', who had the 'habit of recording outlandish stories about giant ants and flying snakes', as Neville Morley (1999: 24) has put it.

Ranke's teachings, however, did not fall on arid soil, for during the same period other historians of the ancient Near East and Assyriologists adopted positivist methods, and those tenets will become a landmark of the field for the next years. George Rawlinson, for instance, wrote his *Manual of Ancient History* (1871) in tune with the general principles of positivism.[4] His definition of history highlights the centrality of states and nations in studying the past,

> The word 'History' (...) is attached in modern parlance pre-eminently and especially to accounts of the rise, progress, and affairs of nations. (...) History proper is the history of States or Nations, both in respect of their internal affairs, and in regard to their dealings with one another. (p. 13)

3 Sayce comments, 'But the dead language of Sumer was not all that the educated Babylonian or Assyrian gentleman of later times was called upon to know. (...) If Sumerian was the Latin of the Babylonian world, Aramaic was its French' (p. 56).

4 George Rawlinson was Camden professor of Ancient History at the University of Oxford and the brother of Sir Henry Rawlinson.

He further remarks on the importance of the sources of history, which he divides into two groups, written records and antiquities. The *Manual* is an example of the classical encyclopaedist handbook, positivist and yet fond of the eighteenth-century tradition, since it tries to summarize everything known about ancient history. The book was meticulously planned according to a geographical and chronological criterion, and it covers the history of the Near East, Africa, and Europe from the origin of early monarchies – around the year 2000 BC, according to the author – to the fall of the Roman empire. The section dealing with ancient Mesopotamia includes the Chaldean, Assyrian, Median, and Babylonian monarchies. All of them are characterized as despotic Asiatic kingdoms, and as such, different from European regimes.[5] The image of Asiatic despotism as opposed to Western democratic governments was not new. It had been circulating since the dawn of European political theory, from Aristotle and Montesquieu onwards. Even in the middle of the twentieth century Karl Wittfogel (1957) tried, with little success, to rescue the concept of 'oriental despotism' to fashion a universal model of 'hydraulic societies'.

Equally consistent with a positivist method, Fritz Hommel published his *Geschichte Babyloniens und Assyriens* in 1885. The work follows a strict plan to study Babylonians and Assyrians separately. For Hommel, world history begins in Babylonia. To substantiate this statement, he enumerates some Mesopotamian original contributions to Western culture, as for example the division of an hour into 60 minutes, the naming of the days after the planets, or even some mythological motives. This influence was transmitted from Mesopotamia to Asia Minor, to the Greeks and Romans and from them, later on, to Romance and Germanic Europe. Immediately after, Hommel argues against a supposedly Egyptian stream of influence, which makes his line of reasoning quite apparent: Mesopotamian 'high culture' is synonymous with Sumerian culture, and, as such, it is non-Semitic.[6] Documents and chronology occupy a pre-eminent place in the book. Hommel classifies the sources into 'National', 'Western', and 'Biblical' and he explains the difficulties and advantages of each group. Unlike other Assyriologists, Hommel does not consider literary texts as historical sources in a strict sense.

5 In the author's words: 'The form of government is in every case a monarchy; the monarchy is always hereditary; and the hereditary monarch is a despot (...). Despotism is the simplest, coarsest, and rudest of all the forms of civil government. It was thus naturally the first which men, pressed by a sudden need, extemporized. And in Asia the wish has never arisen to improve upon this primitive and imperfect essay' (p. 36).

6 'Wir sehen die semitischen Babylonier, die noch als Nomaden ins Land kamen, hineinwachsen in die von ihnen angenommene und dann weiter ausgebildete sumerische Kultur, bis zuletzt als Ergebniß dieses Prozesses die so hoch entwickelte babylonische Gesamtkultur vor unsern Augen dasteht. (...) Als völlig gesichert wird sich dabei stets das ergeben daß, die Grundlagen dieser Kultur nichtsemitischen Ursprungs sin[d]' (Hommel 1885: 6).

Nevertheless, he still regards literature as a useful tool to study the past. As for chronology, he stresses the importance of king lists, and his chronological charts are devoid of any mythological allusion. Hommel's historical method is supplemented by a meticulous classification of archaeological and philological evidence, and when the sources allow him, political history becomes the central theme. When royal deeds cannot be traced, Hommel resorts to archaeological data to fill in the blanks, thus for instance in his chapter dealing with the second millennium.

The positivist methods of Rawlinson and Hommel include questioning the importance and meaning of history, the evaluation and systematization of evidence, and from them history emerges. In this sense, their work is less imaginative and more accurate than Smith's or Sayce's. These different approaches to Mesopotamian history are a matter or method, not just a matter of sources. In 1871 Rawlinson had at his disposal about the same number of documents that Smith had, but Rawlinson did not include the antediluvian period in his chronology. When compared with Rawlinson's study, Hommel's approach to the sources seems to be more exhaustive, for he tries to include every piece of information known to him. This, however, does not necessarily improve his conclusions, for 'history is not the accumulation of events of all kinds which occurred in the past' (Hobsbawm 1997: 75). It is precisely at this point where Hommel's method fails because excessive taxonomy suffocates his interpretations.

Methodological differences aside, Assyriologists in the nineteenth century shared some culture-based assumptions and thematic interest. The decipherment of cuneiform writing opened a wide range of topics that had been inaccessible until then. Native sources were initially read through the looking-glass of the Bible and Greek authors. Related to this, there was also a tendency to trace a unilinear development of Western history, which started in Mesopotamia, moved to Israel, ultimately to reach Europe. At the beginning of the twentieth century this explanation was common among members of the so-called Astral-mythological or Pan-Babylonian school which originated in Germany.[7] In addition, there was a firm attempt to classify peoples following racial criteria, which heavily influenced economic and social interpretation of societies.[8] This is the case with the approach

7 Albert Clay (1919: 9) interpreted the premises of the Pan-Babylonian school in these terms: [this theory] 'maintained that Babylonia had furnished the Hebrews with most of their religious ideas, including monotheism; in fact, the members of this school held that the civilization of Israel generally had its origins in Babylonia'.

8 Already in the early twentieth century some scholars questioned this theory. Thus, for example, Morris Jastrow (1980: 120 [1915]) wrote, 'There is no more foolish boast than that of purity of race. A pure race (...) if it exists at all, is also a sterile race'. However, Jastrow keeps the difference between the non-Semitic Sumerians and the Semitic Akkadians, and he further proceeds to describe the physiognomic features of each group. A similar approach appears in other works. Leonard King (1915: 138) states, 'The racial type presented by the heads appears to be purely

to nomadism and sedentarism, in which the former is regarded as a primitive stage in the chain of social evolution. There was, finally, a pronounced inclination to study political history and the deeds of great men. All those interpretations were the result of both availability of documents and contemporary theories. These historiographic tendencies and choices of topics in Assyriology originated in the second half of the nineteenth century and continued during the first half of the twentieth and beyond. The more imaginative histories gave way to more prosaic and factual approaches. Realism prevailed over imagination, facts and sources over narrative, and Mesopotamia was gradually regaining its lost history.

POLITICAL ECONOMY JOINS THE PICTURE

Studying the interaction of political and economic variables became possible as excavations shared new documents and philologists translated them. At the beginning of the twentieth century the interest in economic activities and their influence on society matched and supplemented the efforts of nineteenth-century scholars to establish political facts and chronology. This new approach to Mesopotamian history sought to establish the ways in which political behaviors were related to institutions of production, consumption, and distribution, and the ways in which social actors participated in this process (Yoffee 1995: 282). An interpretation based on those principles was the so-called *Tempelstadt* (city-temple) or *Tempelwirtschaft* (temple economy) theory formulated by Anna Schneider (1920) and Anton Deimel (1931). Schneider was not an Assyriologist but an economist who drew her conclusions from Deimel's work on economic texts of the 'temple' or 'household' of the goddess Ba'u in the region of Lagaš. This interpretation maintains that in pre-Sargonic Mesopotamia of the early twenty-fourth century BC all land belonged to the temple, and that temples controlled all economic activities.

Parallel to the temple economy arose the state economy theory. For the supporters of this model, during the Third Dynasty of Ur (c. 2100–2002 BC) the state together with the temple owned all the arable land while the entire population lived through the state. Certain authors even used terms such as 'Staatsozialismus' and 'Etatismus' to characterize the activities of the state.[9] Both, the temple and the state economy, gained wide acceptance among Assyriologists throughout the twentieth century (see, e.g., Frankfort 1948; Falkenstein 1954; Kraus 1954; Foster 1981; Steinkeller 1999). The significance of these explanations is that biblical and classical topics were relegated to a second place in favor of Mesopotamian sources,

Sumerian, and though one figure at least is bearded, the Sumerian practice of shaving the head was evidently in vogue.'

9 For the origins of the state economy see Gelb (1969: 146–48).

whereas economic and social themes joined political events. It is not by chance that Adam Falkenstein's (1954) article tracing the development of the temple and city economies, and Fritz R. Kraus's study (1954) focused on the role of the temple appeared in the *Cahiers d'histoire mondial* directed by Lucien Febvre, one of the co-founders of the *Annales* school.

The temple/state theory raised a prominent question related to agrarian societies, namely, land ownership. It seems safe to assume that the monopoly of land in the hands of the state was initially accepted at face value because that interpretation rested on political economy theories dealing with 'Asiatic' societies. In the eighteenth century reports on the East brought to Europe by officials and travelers influenced European scholars. The vast majority if not all of these political theories forged an image of the Orient as something essentially opposite to the Western world. The Orient was used as a mirror image to understand the West. Edward Said's ([1978] 1994) *Orientalism* and, since then, many other scholars, rendered a detailed account of the way in which Westerners fashioned Oriental otherness. Maybe one of the most picturesque examples is the display of an Egyptian street in the 1867 'Exposition Universelle' in Paris studied by Timothy Mitchell (1991). In the late seventeenth century, for instance, the French traveler François Bernier had emphasized the importance of state-owned land in the Orient. Adam Smith in his work *The Wealth of Nations* (1776) adopted Bernier's description and correlated it with the importance of state hydraulic works. The line of reasoning of thinkers such as Smith and Montesquieu continued in the nineteenth century, and were rather influential in Hegel's characterization of Indian despotism. Marx's studies of the Asiatic forms of property adopted and refashioned most of these concepts, especially as regards the antagonistic relationship between state and communities (Anderson 1974: 463–72). Finally, Max Weber's ideas, especially those concerning the patrimonial state, were also at the center of the debate. Notorious differences aside, the role of the state as the main landowner was a shared assumption.

The criticisms of Igor Diakonoff (1969) and Ignace Gelb (1969), however, undermined the consensus over the temple and state economy. Despite their specific differences in interpretation, both Diakonoff and Gelb rejected the state monopoly of arable land, and they further proved the existence of kin-groups holding and selling fields during the pre-Sargonic period. The essays by Diakonoff and Gelb represent a turning point in the analysis of social and political institutions, since they show that social and economic interactions were not as harmonious as they were depicted. Rather, both authors stressed conflicts among temples, states, and communities, and by means of those tensions it is possible to study historical changes. For his part, Gelb vehemently questioned the interpretation of sources by the supporters of the temple/state economy. He considered it fallacious that the economic model drawn from the single Ba'u archive was universally applied to the rest of ancient Mesopotamia during the third millennium. Gelb argued that those texts covered only some 25 years, and that sale documents were overlooked. Similarly, he warned about the limitations of those analyzes resting on the lack of evidence, or what he called *argumentum e silentio*. More recently Govert Van Driel (1998) came back to this argument to assess emphatically that the lack of documentation does not mean that what is not recorded does not exist.

The temple/state theory launched a discussion about interpretation of evidence, since relying on sources – albeit necessary – does not guarantee a successful understanding of social, economic, and political institutions and processes. Even in exclusively factual studies, previous assumptions, interpretations, and the making of hypotheses are still present. Miguel Civil (1980) has already argued against the alleged rigor of some 'recipes' applied to previously assorted information, as well as against the results of purely inductive methods used by certain Assyriologists. The temple/state model is an instructive example, for it shows that a meticulous study of sources was interpreted, overtly or not, in the light of premises originated from different branches of the social sciences as for instance political economy, and sociology. In mainstream Assyriological traditions the centrality of the state together with the institutional character of several archives seem to have left little room for posing the question about what was happening beyond the state, that is, in the midst of society.

REACTIONS AGAINST TRADITIONAL STUDIES

The tendency to dwell on political history was still firmly rooted in many historians at the beginning of the first half of the twentieth century. This was the result of the widespread acceptance of positivist history taught at Western universities since the second half of the nineteenth century, particularly in Germany, France, and the United States, while the creation of several journals helped propagate positivist methods (Iggers 1997: 27).[10] Ranke's most fervent opponent was Karl Lamprecht, whose *Deutsche Geschichte* published in 1891 initiated a controversy in Germany (Breisach 1994: 279–80). His criticism addressed two basic principles: the emphasis on political history and the deeds of great men, and the centrality of the state in historical analysis. He further proposed that psychological forces were the basic forces of history, and he insisted on the inclusion of economic, social, and cultural studies. At that time, however, Lamprecht's criticism and suggestions had little impact on professional historians, and his arguments were generally

10 Iggers mentions as examples the following newly founded journals: the *Historische Zeitschrift* (1859), the *Revue Historique* (1876), the *Rivista Storica Italiana* (1884), the *English Historical Review* (1886), and the *American Historical Review* (1895).

rejected. Early refutations also came from economists. Thus in 1903 François Simiand published a famous article 'against what he called the three "idols" of the tribe of historians, the idol of politics, the idol of the individual, and the idol of chronology' (Burke 1993: 11). New and influential challenges to positivism will come a few years later from the pen of historians gathered around the journal founded by Marc Bloch and Lucien Febvre in 1929. Their proposals stressed the study of economic and social history, the exploration of mentalities, as well as the multiplicity of historical times. In the first issue of the *Annales d'histoire économique et sociale*, Bloch and Febvre mentioned three main aims of their project. These were to provide a forum for historians and social scientists; to question the division of history into ancient, medieval, and modern and that of society into primitive and civilized; and to create a community of the human sciences (Hughes-Warrington 2003: 12).

Bloch's (1993) *Apologie pour l'histoire*, posthumously published in 1949, contains a refutation of the positivism of Auguste Comte's followers because he considered that these scholars were misled by a rigid image of science. Bloch also criticized Ranke's well-known dictum about reporting facts as they really happened, for the scope of history should be analytical instead of descriptive. For him, the historian's craft is not restricted solely to the compilation of data and artifacts – which belong to the domain of the antiquarian. Rather, the historian needs to render facts into historical problems, and go beyond the mere chronicle of leaders and their deeds. In ancient history, one of the earliest rebuttals to positivist methods came from the Australian archaeologist Vere Gordon Childe. His remarks share some of Bloch's concerns, and in *Man Makes Himself* Childe (1956 [1936]) objected to the political history that records the maneuvers of kings, statesmen, and those institutions – either religious or secular – related to them.

Historiography discussions tend to be absent or difficult to find in writings on the history of ancient Mesopotamia. Indeed, sometimes one gets the impression that, for the most part, the Assyriologist is skeptical about convoluted theoretical proposals and prefers to remain as loyal to the documented facts as possible.[11] Diakonoff (1995: 91) has gone so far as to express that certain Assyriologists overdo their rigorousness reminding him of a 'famous German scholar who is said to have announced that *denken ist unwissenschaftlich*'. Such a comment – albeit overstated – finds support in the number of works written under the strictest of the positivist methods. Articles organized list-fashion, which include some explanations to keep a narrative format, or history books on the ancient Near East that

11 Commenting on Claude Lévi-Strauss, Jean Bottéro affirms: 'Il n'est évidenment pas du tout de ma planète. Je crois subodorer chez lui trop de systèmes qui ne sont, que de mythologies modernes, fondées, non sur le vrai, mais sur le vraisemblable et pourtant, à notre façon, colorées d'un jargon pseudo-scientifique' (Bottéro and Monsacré 1994: 287).

resemble ancient chronicles and modern catalogues can be cited. When considering these examples, it is difficult to avoid certain similarities between the Assyriologist and the antiquarian. Arnaldo Momigliano (1990: 54) depicted the antiquarian as 'the type of man who is interested in historical facts without being interested in history', although he adds, 'the pure antiquarian is rarely met with'. Momigliano's antiquarian was a pre-historiography type of being and as such a rare specimen, but his characterization fits into Bloch's criticism of the positivist historian. In Assyriology, it was A. Leo Oppenheim who expressed one of the most vehement and systematic reactions against traditional methods (see Stolper 1992).

Oppenheim (1960) wrote his 'Assyriology – Why and How?' to point out some of the methodological flaws of the field.[12] One of his concerns was to reach a 'better understanding' of the institutional structure of Mesopotamia. He encouraged the co-operation of the Assyriologist and scholars in other fields such as economics, the social sciences, and, above all, cultural anthropology. Oppenheim privileged cultural anthropology because 'the Humanities have never been quite successful in treating alien civilizations with that care and respect that such understanding demands' (p. 419). Of course this statement is arguable, but this is not the place to do so. Let us consider, instead, Oppenheim's methodological observations. The treatment of written sources holds a central place in his arguments. He highlights the need to differentiate between those texts that belong to the 'stream of tradition' (mainly literary works) and those documents that record economic or legal transactions. This constitutes one of his landmarks for arguing against the use of literary texts as historical sources, especially because of the inclination to identify Mesopotamian literature with Greek or Western genres, and to trace back the origin of social and political institutions in literary compositions. As an alternative he stressed the potential richness of those cuneiform tablets pertaining to economic and legal activities. Oppenheim also criticized the arbitrary uses of sources by scholars who attempt to relate Assyriological data to the Old Testament, or to relate the same data to current fashions in any field of the humanities. Finally, he urges scholars to undertake historical studies that supersede the mere descriptive and unilinear development of facts.

Undoubtedly, some of Oppenheim's views reflect contemporary discussions in history and the social sciences, and his criticism encompasses Assyriological methods that go back to the beginnings of the discipline. His views encountered resistance, especially from those Assyriologists fond of tradition, who found Oppenheim's ideas too radical.[13] Therefore, his suggestions were criticized,

12 This article, slightly modified, appeared as the first chapter of Oppenheim's (1997) *Ancient Mesopotamia*, first published in 1964.

13 About some of the reactions to Oppenheim's article, Erle Leichty comments: 'His attempts to "reform" the field, expressed in *Assyriology – Why and How?* were considered as personal attacks by

rejected, and finally disregarded by some of his colleagues. One of the best examples of this reaction is the inaugural lecture delivered by Donald Wiseman (1962) at the School of Oriental and African Studies, University of London. As the new chair of the School, he sketched the history of the field as well as its prospective directions. The lecture was meant to acknowledge the merits of the fathers of Assyriology, to point out the progress that the discipline had experienced since the decipherment of cuneiform writing, and to express his disagreement with Oppenheim's views. Thus, for instance, Wiseman insists on the importance of comparing the 'epic of Gilgamesh' with Homeric literature, and of relating Assyriological research to the Old Testament. Wiseman's article attempts to 'show something of the impact Assyriology now has upon cognate learning' (p. 28). His enumeration of the ancient Mesopotamian's achievements, including the solution of the Pythagorean theorem before Pythagoras, points in that direction. His evaluation of the discipline is closer to the antiquarian than to the historian, and it is definitely uncritical. Wiseman's suggestions for the 'way ahead' offer few new perspectives, and it practically mirrors the 'way behind'. His advice is to continue in the same track because the accumulation of data naturally brings more knowledge.

Although contemporary historians may have thought that Oppenheim's claims were quite basic, Oppenheim was in the vanguard of his discipline. His discussions and Wiseman's responses clearly reflect that, in spite of philological achievements, while writing history some Assyriologists were still following those topics, methods, and traditions initiated in the nineteenth century. The descriptive instead of the analytical reading of the sources, the use of literary sources as historical documents, the importance of the Bible and classical authors in Mesopotamian history, and the centrality of the state and political history are some of the most recurrent examples.[14] Oppenheim's and Wiseman's disagreement on methodological grounds is unusual in Assyriology. Obviously, this does not mean that Assyriologists agree on everything. Their discussions, however, tend to be focused on very precise philological matters or specific interpretations of a text or a group of texts (Oppenheim [1964] 1997: 29). But generally, they do not address the issue of how they write Mesopotamian history, which seems also to be the case if to a lesser extent in classical studies (Morley 1999).

---

many of his contemporaries. His penchant for overstating everything to make his point often led his colleagues to feel personally abused and become angry with him' (Leichty 1975: 369).

14 Sasson (1981) has discussed the problems of using the Bible to interpret the history of the ancient Near East.

CURRENT PERSPECTIVES

Criticisms of positivism together with the efforts to install social and economic history at the center of historical debates in the first half of the twentieth century can be interpreted as a reaction against the use of nineteenth-century historical methods, which some intellectuals viewed as a regression from the eighteenth-century social theory. Advocates of economic and social history came from different backgrounds. They were mostly those historians subscribing to varied versions of Marxist theory, and the no less diverse group gathered around *Annales*. Despite their substantial interpretative differences, they shared certain common ideas. In the first place, there was the dislike of positivist history. Second, and specially since the 1950s, the great majority of these historians evidence a social science orientation concerned with culture and economic models. This is also present later in quantitative studies of both, the 'New Economic History' in the United States and the *histoire sérielle* in France. Finally, there was the well-established practice of macro-historical analysis used to explain processes of economic and social change. Such is the case, for instance, with works as dissimilar as Maurice Dobb's (1959) *Studies in the Development of Capitalism* published in 1947 in tune with orthodox Marxism, and Fernand Braudel's *La Mediterranée* (1949) in accord with certain views of *Annales*.

As the second half of the twentieth century progressed, history writing faced novel challenges. Lawrence Stone (1979), in his now classic article 'The Revival of Narrative', noted that since the 1970s there has been a change in the way of perceiving and writing history. The new tendency that Stone identifies involves questioning and rejecting the belief that it is possible to undertake a coherent scientific explanation of change in the past. As Stone has shown, the disappointment with previous historical models is related to contemporary political and economic developments. The responses to the new conditions took different paths. On the one hand, there is the emphasis on recovering the experiences of those individuals and people usually forgotten by history. This is evident in several studies including 'history from below', from E. P. Thompson's (1963) *The Making of the English Working Class* onwards. It is in this context that *microstoria* (English microhistory) arose in Italy as an attempt to rescue the life experiences of concrete human beings and to relate them to a macrosocial context (e.g. Ginzburg 1976). On the other hand, there is the 'linguistic turn', a criticism of previous ways of writing history originated in the theses of Roland Barthes (1967), Paul Veyne (1971), and Hayden White (1973), among others. For them, history is but another literary genre and, as such, it is unable to grasp an actual historical past. There is finally the prediction of 'the end of history' by Francis Fukuyama (1992), conveying the belief that 'there is no longer the possibility of a grand narrative that gives history coherence and meaning', as Georg Igger (1997: 141) has put it. Thus the premises laid for a 'total' history in the first half of the twentieth century paved the way for the fragmentation of the discipline into a multiplicity of areas with different methodological and theoretical claims: history from below, women's history, microhistory, history of the event, history of the body, and history of political thought, are only some of the examples (see Burke 1995).

Obviously, new orientations in Mesopotamian historiography cannot be measured with the same yardstick. Changes in ancient history writing are less influenced by contemporary political and economic changes, and they are also bound to the characteristics of the available evidence. The historian of ancient Mesopotamia, for instance, is unable to recover the life experience and world visions of a single individual as Carlo Ginzburg (1976) did with the miller Menocchio in northern Italy. Nor is it possible to trace the resistance and beliefs of an entire peasant community the way Emmanuel Le Roy Ladurie analyzed it in *Montaillou* (1978). In Assyriology, the limits and the fragmentary nature of textual information make the search for new historical problems even more difficult. In a broader perspective, however, certain Mesopotamianists are reconsidering the old visions of their craft, and studies in the field are becoming more diverse. There is, moreover, an increasing awareness of the importance of methodological problems. In the last three decades of Mesopotamian historiography, old traditions have coexisted with new and critical versions of the past. One of the remnants of former practices is the publication of general histories. With remarkable exceptions such as J. Nicholas Postgate's (1992) *Early Mesopotamia*, these books are chronologically arranged and present a partial assortment of facts. They cover Mesopotamian history from the third to the first millennium BC and usually, but not always, they also include Egypt, Israel, Syria, and Anatolia. Although these manuals have been criticized (e.g. Yoffee 1997), their persistence seems to rest on introductory classes on the ancient Near East taught at universities and, to a lesser extent, on the alleged interest of the general public.

Other general histories concentrate on particular themes, as for instance, the city. Two recent books on the subject are Marc Van De Mieroop's (1997) *The Ancient Mesopotamian City* and Gwendolyn Leick's (2002) *Mesopotamia: The Invention of the City*. Van De Mieroop studies Babylonian and Assyrian cities highlighting the fundamental role that they played in civilization, and including economic, social, and political aspects. He regards the ancient Mesopotamian city as a type that fits into Weber's and Moses Finley's models of the ancient city. Although Van De Mieroop characterizes his work as 'purely historical', his attempt to integrate the Mesopotamian city with Max Weber's ideal type brings the study closer to the sociological than to the historical tradition. Leick, for her part, sought to 'tell the story of ten Mesopotamian cities' from fifth-millennium Eridu to first-millennium

Babylon. Her approach combines ancient perceptions and modern interpretations to show that various narratives have produced different patterns for each city. A perspective aligned with Said's interpretation of Orientalism appears in an article by Mario Liverani (1997), who concludes that the ideologies and preconceptions of modern scholars have distorted our understanding of ancient Near Eastern cities. Alongside these approaches, there are works dealing with the urban spatial organization during a particular period (Keith 1999), and books on a single city, as for instance Rivkah Harris's (1975) 'demographic' study of Sippar, and Elizabeth Stone's (1987) *Nippur Neighborhoods*.

Studies of Mesopotamian political history experienced a significant change over the last decades. Former reconstructions of political events relayed heavily on royal inscriptions, chronicles, and literary sources that were, for the most part, read uncritically. The result was that the modern historian ended up reproducing the ancient Mesopotamian's perceptions of his own society. Naturally, these native views were biased, for the scribe's text without exception conveys royal ideology. Contributions from literary criticism furnished the historian with new tools to approach old sources. This led to a reconsideration of the way we use 'historiographic' or even literary compositions as historical sources (Liverani 1973). Revisionist proposals suggest that when newly interrogated, old and very well known documents can reveal more than is usually assumed (Liverani 1992: 13). In the case of Assyrian royal inscriptions, for instance, Liverani (e.g. 1979 and 1981) undertook alternative readings so as to unfold the royal ideology. He has also studied the 'Annals of Aššurnaṣirpal II' taking into account their morphology and topography to detect the differences among the king's campaigns (Liverani 1992). As for the Sargonic period, Piotr Michalowski (1993) has reevaluated documentary and archaeological evidence to assert the political expansion of the Akkad state. From a different though no less interesting perspective, Finkelstein's (1972) analysis of economic documents allowed him to discover a migration of priests from southern to northern Mesopotamia due to the turmoil of Samsu-iluna's reign (see also Charpin 1986).

Recent orientations in the interpretation of political history and the incorporation of a variety of methodological criteria promoted the study of how the ancient Mesopotamian wrote about the past. It has also stimulated an interest for the ways in which the modern scholar translates ancient documents into historical accounts. Studies on ancient 'historiography' had traditionally been focused on classical antiquity, ancient Israel, and the Persian world (see, e.g., Dentan 1955; Tadmor and Weinfeld 1984; and Momigliano 1990). Until recently, one of the few Assyriological articles devoted to the problem was Finkelstein's (1963) 'Mesopotamian Historiography', where he argues that omen texts are a historiographic genre. The concentration on areas other than Mesopotamia was recently expanded, and several essays on Mesopotamian ancient historiography have now appeared. This is the case with the papers read at the '45th Rencontre Assyriologique', and published under the title *Historiography in the Cuneiform World* (Abusch *et al.* 2001). Most of these studies include sections discussing the use of literary texts as sources for the writing of history. And in *Cuneiform Texts and the Writing of History*, Van De Mieroop (1999) revisited certain approaches to ancient Mesopotamia, while proposing new research avenues. From a different perspective, Michalowski's (1999) 'Commemoration, Writing, and Genre in Ancient Mesopotamia', addresses issues of historiography and genre as well as the challenges that the historian faces when writing about the past.

There is, moreover, an increasing interest in Mesopotamian women, especially apparent in the last three decades. Earlier historical and anthropological works usually neglected the role of women because gender studies were marginal not only in Assyriology but also in history and in other areas of the humanities and the social sciences. In recent years, however, certain scholars have strongly criticized traditional and orientalist views about Mesopotamian women (e.g. Van De Mieroop 1999: 138–60; Bahrani 2001). Contemporary literature on the subject focuses mainly on middle- and low-class women, but the historian of ancient Mesopotamia has limited possibilities of doing so. Generally, women recorded on cuneiform texts are elite: queens and princesses, priestesses and others related to the cult, or those engaged in economic transactions.[15] Their participation in politics, economy, and religion left a trace on the documentation and this makes it possible to study them. Slaves, servants, and female workers only appear in texts such as sale contracts or ration lists, and we have information about their names or their prices but not much more than that. Similarly, we know very little about the average women because, when they made it to written records, they appear in marriage, inheritance or other economic contracts, which are in themselves rather exceptional in nature. There are, nevertheless, a few articles on low-class women, as for instance Kazuya Maekawa's (1980) 'Female Weavers and their Children', and Norman Yoffee's (1998 and 2005: 123–30) study of the *kezertu*-women, who were hired for the performance of cultic ceremonies. Yoffee's is an original contribution, for he analyzes a small and laconic archive following some of the premises of microhistory, and the conclusions from a limited group of texts are then placed in a broader economic and social context.

15 On elite women see, for instance, Michalowski (1976b; 1978; and 1982) on the Ur III period; Harris (1964), Jeyes (1983), Diakonoff (1986), and Janssen (1991) on the Old Babylonian period; Dhorme (1914 and 1947), Albenda (1987), Beaulieu (1993) on the Neo-babylonian period. For women in a legal context see Roth (1998 and 1999). For articles on different periods and areas of the ancient Near East see the volume edited by Durand (1987).

It is certainly in the area of economic and social history where disagreements and the influence of economic and social models formulated outside Mesopotamian history are most evident. The approaches to economic history reflect the elaborate way in which the results of meticulous taxonomies of texts was exposed to different theories. Analytical categories to interpret ancient economy and society were originally taken from the writings of either Karl Marx or Max Weber, as it has been pointed out in recent studies (Snell 1997; Van De Mieroop 1999a). Over the course of time, however, both models had to be modified and adapted to match the findings from cuneiform sources. This was so because Marx's (1964) ideas about the Asiatic form of property were initially sketched around 1857 when cuneiform writing was just being deciphered, whereas Weber's model was composed when the understanding of those sources was just in its infancy. Adaptations are particularly clear in the case of Marxist scholars, who for the most part dropped the concept of 'Asiatic Mode of Production' while keeping other more general Marxist interpretations (see, e.g., Diakonoff 1963; 1969; 1975; Liverani 1975). One of the few contemporary supporters of the 'Asiatic Mode of Production' as a valid model for the ancient Near East is Carlo Zaccagnini (e.g. 1981).

The discussion of Mesopotamian economy experienced a new turn after the proposals of the anthropologist Karl Polanyi (1957; 1977) revived the debates between 'primitivists' and 'modernists' that had taken place in classical studies in the late nineteenth century (see Schneider 1990). For primitivists, ancient economies had their own laws and logic and they are fundamentally different from modern economy. On the contrary, modernists maintain that the functioning of ancient economies has many similarities with the modern ones, and therefore it is possible to study them with the same theoretical tools. Polanyi's theory concurs with those of the primitivists since he argued that societies without market, such as ancient Mesopotamia, could not be measured by the rules of neo-classical economic theory. For him, ancient economies were embedded within social relations, and they were not regulated by the rational principles of market economies. Since Polanyi emphasized the substance of exchange, the debate is now also known as '*substantivists* versus *formalists*'. His market-less economy was an easy target for criticism because cuneiform documents record evidence such as the existence of words for market place (Röllig 1976), sale transactions, as well as the profitable business of Assyrian merchants (see, e.g., Gledhill and Larsen 1982; Powell 1999). Rejections of the market-less economy generally concentrate on specific institutions or economic actors, but those criticisms are not articulated in broader explanations of Mesopotamian economy the way Johannes Renger (e.g. 1984), one of Polanyi's supporters, did.

Interpretations of the economy are narrowly connected to the ways we view social actors and evaluate their role in the process of production, consumption, and redistribution. Thus for instance advocates of the temple/state economy regard the state as the fundamental economic institution, while the rest of society only participated in state economic activities. Criticisms of the temple/state economy led to the formulation of a bipolar model that opposes the state to the communities. Despite many nuances, Marxist historians subscribe to this approach (e.g. Diakonoff 1963; 1969; 1975; Liverani 1975; Zaccagnini 1981; Klíma 1983). Also as a reaction to the all-encompassing role of the state in Mesopotamian economy, other scholars have proposed a tripartite interpretation of economy and society, which besides the state (or the institutions of temple and palace) and the communities, includes the private sector (e.g. Gelb 1969; Stol 1976; Yoffee 1977 and 1978; Charpin 1986; Postgate 1992; Van De Mieroop 1992; Renger 1995; and Van Driel 2001). These analyses, based mainly on the ownership of arable land, have been the starting point for the division of Mesopotamian society into groups defined according to their participation in those economic spheres. At present, most scholars seem to subscribe to the tripartite model, but there is no consensus as to the relative importance of each sector in the economy. Renger (1979), for instance, acknowledges the existence of private ownership of arable land during the Old Babylonian period, although he does not think that private property is the dominant feature. W. F. Leemans (1983), for his part, has seriously doubted the economic significance of communal property of arable land as well as the very existence of rural communities.[16] The objection to the economic role of the communities relies on the scanty amount of evidence that the communal sector has yielded; while others argue that lack of sources does not prove that poorly recorded institutions and activities did not exist. In the end, however, authors from different sides have privileged the study of the state.

The reasons why the state still occupies a central role in Mesopotamian history are complex and diverse. Those reasons seem to originate from both the legacy of a variety of historical traditions and the character of written records. Early nineteenth-century scholars followed the Bible and classical authors as a frame to interpret Mesopotamian sources. Their main concern was to identify familiar royal figures and events in order to fix a chronological sequence so as to include previously unknown kings and their deeds. At the same time, positivist historians concentrate on the role of the state because for them that is History. When theories of political economy were applied to the reconstruction of economic and political institutions, there was an interpretative shift and the economic role of the state supplemented the study of political history. More recently political and economic history as previously understood has been seriously questioned on

16 Leemans' (1983: 105) conclusion is categorical: 'En tout cas, vers la fin du 3e. millénaire, il n'existe pas de communautés rurales, et non plus dans la période vieux-babylonienne/assyrienne, à l'exception peut-être des tribus semi-nomades de la région du moyen Euphrate.'

several flanks. These new proposals have contributed enormously to our understanding of Mesopotamian history.

As I hope I have shown in this chapter, there are several Mesopotamian histories, more than are usually acknowledged. Or better, there are multiple ways in which Mesopotamian history has been written. But if we were to make an effort of synthesis and speak about Mesopotamian history in a generic sense, as one may do when talking about classical history, then, I think, we could say that Mesopotamian history is a history finding its own way through the entangled forest of theories that shape historical writing. It is in this broad picture that I place my study of local powers in the Old Babylonian period. My research on local authorities aims at showing that they acted as intermediaries between the state and the rest of society. It also tries to explore the ways in which social tensions and conflicts emerged and were negotiated. I think that such an approach contributes to our understanding of social history. My research relies heavily on the analysis of cuneiform sources. In that, I follow old traditions recently rescued by microhistorians, for I believe that historical study must be based on rigorous empirical analysis. In the next chapter, I will present an outline of the Old Babylonian period that will serve as a background to contextualize my research.

2

The Old Babylonian Period

BORDER AND CHRONOLOGY

Fernand Braudel (1949) chose a metaphor to depict the Mediterranean as 'the greatest document of its past experience'. Hardly any other characterization is so suitable for the geographical setting of ancient Mesopotamia, its soil a seemingly inexhaustible source of archaeological records. As a physical entity, Mesopotamia comprises roughly the political frontiers of today's Iraq and northern Syria. But the modern concept of political borders stipulated as clear and rigid lines sharply drawn on a map was alien to the ancient inhabitants of this region. In antiquity borders were flexible, malleable, and permeable. They were subject to ecological conditions, military campaigns, political endeavors, and ideological claims. The territory was shaped by royal incursions, but also by feelings of belonging. For the historian it becomes even more meaningful when inhabited. As a political unit, Mesopotamia was a shifting scenario, and it was an ancient ideal only rarely achieved. Cities and their hinterlands were the anchors of political aspirations, but they were also razed and abandoned. Thus Hammurabi's conquest of Larsa annexed a rich tributary area to the kingdom, but his devastation of Mari made him the master of a wasteland. Like the tides of the Mediterranean, Mesopotamian political geography was a changing reality.

The chronology of second millennium Mesopotamia is not yet definitely established, and there are competing versions as regards the dates of political events and the regnal years of certain kings. Different interpretations of available sources resulted in three chronological sequences: the High Chronology places the fall of Babylon in 1651 BC, the Middle Chronology in 1595, and the Low Chronology in 1531 (see, e.g., Campbell 1961; Rowton 1970; Huber *et al.* 1982; Åström 1987). Most recently, a reevaluation of written records such as king lists, chronicles, economic documents, as well as astronomical and archaeological data has challenged previous assumptions (Gasche *et al.* 1998). This new proposal maintains that the fall of Babylon occurred in 1499 BC, and that the dates of the widely accepted Middle Chronology should be reduced some 85 to 105 years. Difficulties in assigning absolute dates originate in the fragmentary character of the evidence of well-attested kings, while the dates and the order of succession of other monarchs such as those from Ešnunna and the Mananâ dynasty are not completely clear (see, e.g., Charpin 1978 and 1985; Wu and Dalley 1990). This is also the case with several other sovereigns of the early Old Babylonian period in southern and northern Mesopotamia. Their names may appear in royal inscriptions, dates, oaths, or seal impressions, but no year-name list for these kings has yet been recovered. A new discussion of Old Babylonian chronology can now be found in Dominique Charpin's political history of this period (Charpin 2004: 34–38). For the sake of convention, I follow the Middle Chronology wherein the Old Babylonian period spans from c. 2000 to 1595 BC (see Brinkman 1997).

Unlike chronology that seeks to identify the estimated date of past events and to assign them a correct order, periodization refers to the division of time in meaningful units related to political events, economic processes, cultural horizons, or the like. Of these two temporal parameters, Mesopotamian periodization has received less attention than chronology. It is common, therefore, to find a variety of classification of historical periods arranged according to the achievements of powerful kings, the success of kingdoms and empires, the preeminence of a given city, or to archaeological and linguistic criteria. The linguistic periodization of Mesopotamian history is easily one of the most frequently used. This taxonomy rests upon the language or language version attested in written documents. Such is the case with the Neo-Sumerian period, characterized by the number of administrative texts in Sumerian; and also with the Old Akkadian, the Old Assyrian, Old Babylonian, Neo-Assyrian, and the Neo-Babylonian periods, characterized by documents issued in one of these versions of the Akkadian language. Charpin (2004: 38) has recently argued against the denomination Old Babylonian on the basis that the Babylonian domination and hegemony in the region lasted only a few decades. Instead he proposes the expression 'Amorite period' because it emphasizes the importance of the Amorite population and the Amorite filiation of most dynasties of this period. But, besides being an ethnic term, Amorite was also a language, even if kings belonging to this group used Akkadian in their royal inscriptions and records. Because the linguistic periodization is relatively lax, it is usually calibrated by means of political events.

The Old Babylonian period is framed within two political and economic crises. It starts after the fall of the Third Dynasty of Ur around 2002 BC and ends with the collapse of the First Dynasty of Babylon in 1595 BC. Since the denomination Old Babylonian does not convey historical changes, it is usually split into different stages. The early Old Babylonian (c. 2000–1800) includes the antagonism among cities and small kingdoms competing for hegemony and for the absorption of rival states. The instability of this period led Dietz Otto Edzard (1957) to borrow the concept of *Zwischenzeit* or 'intermediate period' from the Egyptian periodization to describe the political fragmentation that followed strong governments. The middle Old Babylonian period (c. 1800–1750) pertains to the consolidation of territorial states, as was the case of Larsa under Rīm-Sîn in the south, the kingdom of Ešnunna in the north, and ultimately the all-encompassing realm that Hammurabi amalgamated towards the end of his reign. Finally, the late Old Babylonian period (c. 1750–1595) entails the dismemberment of Hammurabi's domain under the successive rulers of the First Dynasty of Babylon. This periodization obviously rests upon traditional and cyclical interpretations of historical times that focus on the rise, apogee, and collapse of states (see Yoffee 1988).

POLITICAL HISTORY

The political history of the Old Babylonian period has traditionally been based on the information from royal and votive inscriptions, literary texts, and lists of year names. Two main reasons account for the reliance on this kind of sources. On the one hand, early scholars were convinced that political history was History in capital letters. On the other hand, they had only a minimal number of economic and legal documents from which to draw conclusions regarding economic and social history. Royal inscriptions and literary texts offered readily available explanations of past events, while lists of year-names helped arrange the chronological sequence of rulers and their achievements. Modern approaches have questioned the uncritical reconstruction of political history that relies exclusively on those narratives stressing their propagandistic nature. Ancient narrative texts had limited purposes. The ancient Mesopotamian king commissioned self-laudatory literature for a highly selective audience: the gods. Certain texts also include a curse formula addressed to the hypothetical king or his appointee who might destroy the inscription or change the original name to his own (see Kupper 1990). Artifacts bearing these inscriptions were displayed in temple courtyards or buried in foundation deposits of temples and palaces. Some of these objects were hidden, whereas those on display had the power of the recondite because the common Mesopotamian was illiterate. Year-names enumerate the king's pious and righteous deeds of the previous year and had a practical purpose, for scribes needed them to date economic and legal documents.

The propagandistic bias of royal inscriptions is now frequently mentioned in historical analysis. These interpretations assert that not even the most powerful of the monarchs would have been able to rule by pure force, and that kings resort to royal inscriptions to keep a balance (e.g. Liverani 1995: 2365). Daniel Fleming (2004: 228), for instance, suggests that the 'Laws of Hammurabi' represent the king's effort to build consensus. This explanation, as I see it, carries an inherent contradiction. The equilibrium between consensus and coercion was undoubtedly important. Nevertheless, the number of potential readers of secretive texts was very small and, since readers were royal underlings, they were already familiar with the formulaic claims of these texts. The accessibility of this literature by less trained scribes is also doubtful. The stele with Hammurabi's laws, for instance, was purposely written in an archaizing script, and reading it required a specialized knowledge that was out of the reach of most people. But it also carries the representation of the king together with Šamaš, the sun-god of justice. Through iconography, the stele transmitted its message to the literate and illiterate alike (see Roth 2000: 10). For these reasons, it seems also possible to argue that a balance of power may have been achieved by means other than royal inscriptions, such as the performance of certain ceremonies. Public displays were propitious occasions where words and gestures could be effectively combined to generate consensus. Ironically, the propagandistic message of ancient texts seems to have had more influence on the modern scholar than on the ancient Mesopotamian.

The power of conviction that royal inscriptions exercised on the modern reader is apparent in certain history works that tend to convey the royal ideology. Maybe the most paradigmatic and extreme example is the depiction of Hammurabi as 'the' king of justice. This image was actually substantiated after 1902 when Scheil found the stele with the 'Code of Hammurabi' in Susa and translated it the same year. History books before 1902 quote some passages of Hammurabi's inscriptions related to building activities, and sometimes his victory over Rīm-Sîn of Larsa is also emphasized (e.g. Lenormant 1881: 101–102; Hommel 1885: 375). Towards the first decade of the twentieth century, the reading of the Code not only fashioned a new profile of Hammurabi as the king of justice, but also economy and society were now interpreted through this inscription (e.g. King 1915; Jastrow 1980 [1915]). Certain scholars have adopted this explanation and it still appears in recent works (e.g. Kuhrt 1995; Nemet-Nejat 1998; Launderville 2003). As Jack Sasson (1995: 901) has pointed out, 'Ḫammurabi and "Lawgiver" have come to be practically synonymous in most modern publications'. Approaches centered around famous kings usually omit social and political tensions, while the rich complexity of competing interests is overlooked.

The early stage of the Old Babylonian period is a remarkable example of political and economic struggles. The fall of the Third Dynasty of Ur (c. 2100–2002 BC) laid bare those internal and external conflicts that strong rule manage to suffocate and dissimulate by means of an organized apparatus. The final stroke to this highly centralized government came from a former subjugated territory in the eastern region of Elam. Ur had held Susa from the reign of Šulgi, one of the most powerful Ur III kings, until the reign of Ibbi-Sîn (c. 2028–2004), and probably earlier under Ur-Namma, the founder of the dynasty (Michalowski 1989: 3). But king Kindattu from Šimaški gained control of Susa and the rest of Khuzistan (Stolper 1982: 49). He finally took advantage of the debilitated internal conditions of the Ur III state to defeat king Ibbi-Sîn in his 24th year, and this formally brought to an end the Third Dynasty of Ur. Texts such as royal hymns mention some of these events (Van Dijk 1978), the 'Lamentation over the Destruction of Sumer and Ur' deals extensively with the demise of the city and its domains (Michalowski 1989), and economic documents also share information on the situation. From this moment, a number of kings will compete in order to fill the vacuum of power and to equal the territorial ambitions of the former kingdom. The earlier phases of these struggles in southern Mesopotamia are known as the Isin-Larsa period.

SOUTHERN MESOPOTAMIA FROM C. 2000 TO 1800 BC

The defeat of Ibbi-Sîn and the state of Ur III by the armies of Elam and Šimaški, paved the way for the royal aspirations of Išbi-Erra (c. 2019–1987 BC), a former official of the king of Ur and possibly an Amorite himself (Michalowski 1976: 120; Kamp and Yoffee 1980: 90). He established a new dynasty in the city of Isin and proclaimed himself the heir of the traditions of the state of Ur. In his 16th year-name he affirms having smitten the armies of Kimaš and Elam, and later in his 27th year he states that he expelled the Elamite garrison from the city of Ur. These two victories allowed him to be portrayed as the liberator of the land from foreign hands. Išbi-Erra and his successors seem to have managed certain administrative and governmental continuity with the state of Ur until around 1900 BC The efforts to keep cultic and ceremonial practices alive are apparent from the royal titles and hymns, and Išbi-Erra appointed his own daughter as *entum*-priestess at Ur after the death of Ibbi-Sîn's daughter. The effective control of former provinces, however, is difficult to evaluate due to the nature and provenance of the extant sources. Territories situated far away from the core area such as Aššur, Ešnunna, Dēr, and Susa broke from the control of the south relatively early.

A series of internal and external problems challenged the putative stability of southern Mesopotamia under the rulers of Isin. During this period Ilu-šumma, a king of Assyria, undertook the first interference in the south by a northern state. This might have happened during the reign of Iddin-Dagan (1976–1956 BC) or Išme-Dagan (1955–1937 BC) of Isin (see Larsen 1976: 71). Similarly, the rise of the rival dynasty at Larsa established by Gungunum around 1932 BC, seriously compromised the suzerainty of Isin. Lipit-Ištar (1936–1926 BC) was the last member of Išbi-Erra's dynasty and he struggled to secure the supply of water for Isin, challenged by the military actions of Larsa. This state of affairs encouraged the emergence of independent dynasties at cities such as Uruk in the south, and Kiš and Babylon in the north. The disputes over the control of irrigation canals and water supplies aggravated the political situation of Isin after kings such as Abī-sarē (1905–1895 BC) and Sūmû-el (1894–1866 BC) of Larsa cut off the water supply by diverting canals to the Larsa region (see Walters 1970). Although kings continued to rule in Isin, their power was significantly diminished. The conflicts between Isin and Larsa came finally to an end when Rīm-Sîn of Larsa (1822–1763 BC) defeated Damiq-ilīšu of Isin in 1794. This victory was of such importance for Rīm-Sîn that he named all of his remaining 31 years of reign after this conquest. This is, however, the history we are able to trace from royal texts. Earlier during his reign Rīm-Sîn had to face a large coalition of enemy forces formed by Uruk, Isin, and Babylon in his 13th year (Van De Mieroop 1993: 51), which clearly indicates that the situation was far from stable. But little is known about the leaders of those cities that powerful kings claimed to have had under their control.

The collapse of the Ur III state initiated a new period in Mesopotamian history characterized by the rule of Amorite kings in both northern and southern Mesopotamia. The atomization of power that followed the collapse of Ur seems to have prompted ideological strategies to justify the course of events. It is in this context that the inclusion of Isin kings in the 'Sumerian King List' (Jacobsen 1939) crowned the attempts to convey an ideal unification of Mesopotamia. This evidently supplemented the efforts at keeping control over the shrine of Nippur, and at maintaining religious rituals and royal traditions. In the case of the Larsa rulers, for instance, the appointment of the sister of Warad-Sîn and Rīm-Sîn as an *entum*-priestess, following an ancient practice initiated by Sargon of Akkad (Gadd 1951), had a similar purpose. Both brothers were successive kings of the usurper dynasty that had taken over the throne of Larsa, and were eager to preserve ancient royal customs as Išbi-Erra and others had done before them. Under the circumstance of purported continuity, the addition of Isin rulers to the 'Sumerian King List' was meant to show that Mesopotamia was still a political unit in which only one city ruled at a given time over all others since time immemorial, and that this tradition continued despite the fall of Ur. Thus for the ancient Mesopotamian, the rise and fall of cities and their dynasties was a natural continuum whose destiny the gods decided in the heavens.

NORTHERN MESOPOTAMIA FROM C. 2000 TO 1800 BC

Important changes also occurred in the northern region after the fall of the Third Dynasty of Ur, although the lack of documentation for certain areas makes the reconstruction of events rather difficult. The history of kingdoms such as Assyria and Ešnunna is drawn in part from indirect references that appear in texts from other places, Cappadocia and Mari for example. In Assyria, soon after the demise of Ur, the city of Aššur regained its independence and Puzur-Aššur I became the first king of the Old Assyrian dynasty possibly around 1980 BC. The last monarch of this dynastic line was removed by Samsī-Addu (c. 1833–1775 BC), an Amorite who took control of Ekallātum and of the rest of the Assyrian territories. Under his reign, the 'Assyrian King List' was composed to legitimate his usurpation of the throne (Larsen 1976: 34–40). Samsī-Addu's might was further consolidated when he established his capital at Šubat-Enlil and appointed his elder son Išme-Dagan to a post at Ekallātum, and his younger son Yasmaḫ-Addu at the city of Mari. Yaḫdun-Līm, the former ruler of Mari, had conquered territories on the Middle-Euphrates, and in one of his inscriptions he proclaimed himself king of Mari, Tuttul, and the land of Ḫana (Frayne 1990: 602–604). His ambitions were fulfilled after Zimrī-Līm (c. 1775–1766 BC) displaced the Assyrian Yasmaḫ-Addu and became the new ruler of Mari and one of the most active competitors in the Mesopotamian political arena (Charpin and Durand 1985).

Ešnunna, in the Diyala region, was yet another influential state after the fall of Ur. One of the earliest independent rulers, Šū-ilīya, bore the title *šarrum* 'king'. But after him, this title stopped being used and it was only resumed around 1850 BC. His successor, Nūr-aḫum, had received help from Išbi-Erra to access the throne, possibly around 2010 BC. The family ties among early kings of Ešnunna such as Nūr-aḫum and Bilalama and Amorite leaders are attested in documents from the early Old Babylonian period (Whiting 1987: 23–29). The succession of kings and events in early stages remains unclear. Some of the letters from Ešnunna record political affairs from the time of Ipiq-Adad I and Warassa that partially coincided with the reigns of Sūmû-abum (1894–1881 BC) and Sūmû-la-el (1880–1845 BC) of Babylon. The Diyala region is no exception to the fragmentation that characterizes the rest of Mesopotamia. A century later, Ešnunna appears as a great power that assisted the king of Mari to face the thread of Samsī-Addu of Assyria. The alliance of both kingdoms was later sealed by a treaty between Zimrī-Līm of Mari and Ibāl-pî-el of Ešnunna against their common enemy, Išme-Dagan of Ekallātum (see Charpin 1991). At this time, Ešnunna was consolidated as a powerful state. From an economic point of view, it was the tin route that brought Mari, Ešnunna, and Elam together (Charpin 1985: 61; Joannès 1991). From a political point of view, Assyria, Ešnunna and Elam had been in close contact, and Ešnunna was the joint that articulated them all. This seems to have been the case at least until the death of Samsī-Addu in Assyria, when Elam conquered Ešnunna.[1]

The kingdom of Elam in today's Iran became influential in Mesopotamian politics towards the 1800s BC. Išbi-Erra's year-name referring to the expulsion of the Elamite garrison from Ur was the only mention of the Elamites in year-formulae until some two centuries later. Most references to Elam during this period originate from the royal archives of Mari and illustrate commercial and diplomatic relations, including the exchange of presents during the reign of Zimrī-Līm (see

1 There is no certainty about the exact year in which Ešnunna was defeated. Although Charpin (1985: 52) argued that this event took place during Zimrī-Līm's seventh year, Durand (1986: 128) has suggested that the defeat of Ešnunna happened in Zimrī-Līm's ninth year.

Durand 1986). It is also known that the sukkal of Elam was the arbitrator who distributed the territories that had belonged to Samsī-Addu among Mari, Babylon, and Ešnunna around Zimrī-Līm's fourth year (Charpin and Durand 1991: 61). There are, moreover, at least two other examples in which the king of Elam refereed conflicts of Amorite kings. The first is a letter that documents a dispute between Rīm-Sîn of Larsa and Dāduša of Ešnunna (Rowton 1967: 269). The second is another letter in which Zimrī-Līm reminds Hammurabi that the sukkal has given him the territories of Ḫît, Ḫarbû and Yabliya (ARM 26 449). Some other Mari letters indicate that the Elamite ruler gave military instructions to Mesopotamian kings such as Rīm-Sîn of Larsa, Hammurabi of Babylon, and Zimrī-Līm of Mari (Charpin and Durand 1991: 63). These diplomatic ties resulted in a coalition among Mari, Babylon, and Elam that put an end to the supremacy of the kingdom of Ešnunna. But yet another alliance between Mari and Babylon defeated Elam in the battle of Ḫirītum to the south of Sippar, and therefore interrupted its influence on Mesopotamia. This victory is mentioned in Hammurabi's 30th year-formula, thus the event dates to one year earlier.

The history of the region that will later constitute the core area of the First Dynasty of Babylon also changed in the aftermaths of the fall of Ur. In this welter of shifting powers, Kiš, the first city to attain pre-eminence after the flood according to the 'Sumerian King List', appears as one of the independent realms (see Donbaz and Yoffee 1986). Early documents from Kiš reflect a complex political situation that alternates independent kings with local rulers acknowledging their subordination to other cities. During the reign of Sūmû-la-el (1880–1845 BC), the second king of the First Dynasty of Babylon, Kiš and many other cities of the area were incorporated into his domains. Cities like Sippar, however, remained under the control of local rulers during part of this period ultimately to be absorbed. It was from the territories assembled by Sūmû-la-el that Hammurabi, the sixth ruler of the dynasty created by Sūmû-abum of Babylon, entered the political arena willing to compete against a number of rival states. Indeed, when Hammurabi came to the throne in 1792 BC, he was but one of several rulers vying for position in the north.

MESOPOTAMIA FROM c. 1800 TO 1595 BC

A frequently quoted report from the chancellery of Mari illustrates the political scenario of Mesopotamia during the early eighteenth-century: 'there is no king who is powerful by himself: ten or fifteen kings follow Hammurabi of Babylon, as many follow Rīm-Sîn of Larsa, Ibāl-pî-el of Ešnunna, and Amūt-pî-el of Qatna, and twenty kings follow Yarīm-Līm of Yamḫad' (Dossin 1938: 117). This situation, however, took a new turn in successive years. After his defeat of Isin in 1794 BC,

Rīm-Sîn of Larsa had become the leading king in southern Mesopotamia. In the north, as already mentioned, Elam had conquered Ešnunna, while a coalition between Mari and Babylon later defeated Elam in 1763 BC. The following year, the same allies marched against Larsa finishing Rīm-Sîn's long reign of 60 years. This victory naturally resulted in the end of the collaboration between the kings of Mari and Babylon, and in 1761 BC Hammurabi's army invaded and razed the city of Mari, thus ending Zimrī-Līm's rule together with his political ambitions. It was only towards the end of his reign that Hammurabi was able to unify Mesopotamia. His successful campaigns on the battlefield were crowned with the issuing of his well-known 'Code' during his 43rd and last year (Roth 1997: 71).

Hammurabi's unification of Mesopotamia was short-lived. Samsu-iluna (1749–1712 BC) inherited from his father an immense territory that proved difficult to keep cohesive. Not surprisingly, the first problems originated in the region of Larsa, a province now subject to heavy tributes that flowed towards the authorities of Babylon. The revolt in the south occurred during the ninth year of Samsu-iluna. It was led by a certain Rīm-Sîn who seemed to have taken the throne-name of the previous king of Larsa and managed to retain some independence for about two or three years. There is evidence that Rīm-Sîn II briefly controlled Ur and also Nippur (Stone 1987). Samsu-iluna was able to overcome the insurrection temporarily, but the water supply for irrigation was seriously damaged. Archaeological records show that this crisis promoted the abandonment of southern cities already by Samsu-iluna's tenth year, while urban centers in central Babylonia such as Nippur and Isin were seriously affected (Stone 1977; Gibson 1980; Adams 1981: 165; Gasche 1989: 111; Armstrong and Brandt 1994). The process of deurbanization during this period also reached the Euphrates cities of Ur, Uruk, Larsa, as well as Girsu and Lagaš on the east side (Gasche *et al.* 1998: 8). During Samsu-iluna's 28th year, Iluma-ilu, the king of the Sealands, took over the city of Nippur and the rest of central Babylonia, and two years latter Isin and Nippur were also abandoned (Stone 1987).

The south was practically lost. Although Hammurabi's realm shrank considerably, his successors retained control of the northern territories for over a century. By the time of Ammī-ṣaduqa (1646–1626 BC), the penultimate king of the First Dynasty of Babylon, the kingdom was reduced almost to the original core area of the founders of the ruling house. From Ammī-ṣaduqa's reign comes the extant version of a list of Babylonian ancestors, dubbed in modern times 'the Genealogy of the Ḫammurabi Dynasty' (Finkelstein 1966a).[2] Its ultimate goal relates to the *kispum*-offering for the dynastic forefathers attested already in lists from the city

2 W. Lambert (1968: 1–2) criticized Finkelstein's interpretation arguing that 'the tablet is not a king list, dynastic ancestry, or any kind of historical or quasi-historical compilation, but it is a prayer to the shades of the dead for use in the rites called *kispum*'.

of Ebla. Despite their ritual character, these lists use past events to validate political actions (see Archi 2001). Ammī-ṣaduqa's text has also remarkable affinities with the 'Assyrian King List' of Samsī-Addu, which served similar purposes. Finkelstein has rightly noticed the use of the Sumerian term bala, the concept for 'age' or 'era', as the link that ties the genealogy of the Amorites to the canons of the Sumero-Akkadian tradition. Unlike Samsī-Addu, Ammī-ṣaduqa was not a usurper, but he was not a successful conqueror either. His legitimization strategy seems to have been no less ambitious, for he includes in a single text the entire Mesopotamian legacy. As was the case with the Sumerian and the Assyrian King Lists, the putative ancestry and lineage of the 'Genealogy of Hammurabi' relates the present to remote traditions, and the scribal ideal of a united Mesopotamia dissimulated the permanent flux. History shows, however, that the archetype of a pan-Mesopotamian unity recurrently conflicted with reality.

The collapse of the First Dynasty of Babylon finally occurred during the rule of Samsu-ditāna (1625–1595 BC), Hammurabi's fifth descendant. A similar pattern of deurbanization to that following the crises under Samsu-iluna seems to have happened towards the end of the Old Babylonian period. The last two kings, namely Ammī-ṣaduqa and Samsu-ditāna, began to lose hydraulic control over northwestern Babylonia, and some of the cities in this region were abandoned (Gasche *et al.* 1998). These are the archaeological indicators of a progressive decline that was already apparent under Samsu-iluna. But the germs of subsequent problems lay in the administrative policies that Hammurabi himself implemented. This is the case, for instance, with the changes in traditional systems of land tenure well recorded in epistolary complains, and also with tributary policies. The reasons for the fall of the First Dynasty of Babylon, therefore, ought to be sought in the structural weakness of highly centralized government (Yoffee 1988b: 54). The *coup de grâce* to the system in its death throes came from the raid of Muršili I, a Hittite king from Anatolia. This event is known to us from later Hittite and Babylonian sources. Certain kings exploited this event to claim for themselves the return of the statues of Marduk and Ṣarpānītum that the Hittites had looted. The recuperation of lost gods alluded to regained prosperity.

ECONOMIC AND SOCIAL HISTORY

The Old Babylonian is one of the best-documented periods not only of Mesopotamia but also of ancient history in general. Literary compositions, religious texts and royal inscriptions aside, several thousand clay tablets recording economic transactions, legal procedures, and letters are available (Stol 2004: 643). In some fortunate cases, professional and illegal excavations have unearthed complete archives covering the activities of Mesopotamian individuals and their families over several decades. The documents of Iddin-Lagamal in Dilbat, for instance, span some four generations, and they provide us with valuable information about economic pursuits and occasional legal disputes (Klengel 1976; Desrochers 1978; Yoffee 1988c). However, only a small number of houses with archives have been excavated and fully studied, among them are those in the cities of Ur, Nippur, and Sippar-Amnānum (see, e.g., Janssen 1992; Van De Mieroop 1999b: 255). Since the first archaeological missions conducted by Austen Henry Layard and Paolo E. Botta in the nineteenth century, Mesopotamian sites have been unevenly excavated. Certain locations are better explored than others. Big mounds are generally privileged over small ones, and within the same site some areas receive more attention than others do (Veenhof 1986: 3).

Earlier diggers, furthermore, did not take care, nor did they use techniques like those developed more recently. The urge to recover the past of those ancient kingdoms mentioned in the Bible and classical authors, together with the rivalries between the Louvre and the British Museum prioritized amount and size of objects over the ways these artifacts were dug. The lack of adequate methods also relates to the political and cultural context of that time. The first explorers were rather interesting men whose adventures in 'the Orient' had a romantic and risky touch. Mogens Larsen (1996: 52) has studied the early archaeological pursuits in Mesopotamia, and he compared A. H. Layard with the popular movie character Indiana Jones. But even in less picturesque and better conducted excavations, reports were incomplete and sometimes objects were mislaid and difficult to find in the magazines of museums.[3] In some other cases, documents from known sites were mixed with other lots of uncertain origin in the museum's process of cataloguing (Charpin 1980a). The modern scholar, therefore, faces the challenge of relating thousands of documents from disparate and sometimes unknown places. Archaeology and epigraphy occasionally help determining the provenance of some of these texts, and prosopography has proven useful to reconstruct some archives either natural or artificial (e.g. Yoffee 1977; Kalla 1999; Goddeeris 2002). Ancient Mesopotamians, furthermore, did not record all the transactions they made (Steinkeller 1989: 149), whereas many tablets were discarded in antiquity when considered useless. The problems pertaining to archaeological and textual data are relevant to analyzing and utilizing sources for the writing of history, and they are also critical to evaluating how representative of the economic and social reality texts are.

These records register institutional and private activities, and thanks to them Old Babylonian social and economic issues have been extensively explored. Yet

3 That was the case, for instance, with some of the hoard of the tools excavated by Loftus in Tell Sifr, which were found in the British Museum some 100 years after their discovery (Moorey *et al.* 1988).

there are competing theories to explain the functioning of economy and society and to characterize basic socio-economic institutions (Bobrova and Koshurnikov 1989: 53). The debate around the economic role and the institutional status of Balamunamḫe, a well-known inhabitant of the city of Larsa, could be quoted as an example.[4] The wide range of activities in which Balamunamḫe was engaged makes him a controversial figure, and scholars have different hypotheses to interpret his role in the history of Larsa. Elihu Grant (1917), for instance, considers Balamunamḫe a slave dealer. Denise Cocquerillat (1967: 168) regards him as a high official whose position was similar to the one held by Šamaš-ḫāzir, one of Hammurabi's administrators in Larsa. Leemans (1968: 64) sees Balamunamḫe as a manor-lord with close connections with merchants, but not necessarily a merchant himself. Renger (1979: 251) affirms that he was a merchant related to the state. For Van De Mieroop (1987b: 24), Balamunamḫe was a large landowner involved in agricultural activities and a slave dealer, whose connections with the palace are difficult to prove. Since Balamunamḫe also appears in contracts dealing with grain deliveries, Tina Breckwoldt (1995: 70) suggests that he was not necessarily a rich and influential private individual but a state official. Finally, Christian Dyckhoff (1998) regards him as a scribe and a priest representative of a major center of intellectual life. These interpretations of a very circumscribed case reflect, on a microscale, disagreements concerning major socio-economic problems of the Old Babylonian period.

Dissents about specific issues such as the role of certain individuals, the function of the state and ethnic groups, the existence of markets, and land ownership, obviously affect the ways of addressing macro socio-economic interpretations. Researches have consequently used the same data to test very dissimilar hypothesis and to substantiate no less dissimilar theories. This clearly shows the ways in which particular theoretical frameworks have influenced the evaluation of written and archaeological evidence. On a large scale, scholars usually contrast the social and economic characteristics of the Old Babylonian period (c. 2002–595 BC) with those of Ur III (c. 2100–2002 BC). While certain Assyriologists see a profound break between these two periods, others argue for continuity (see Powell 1999: 10). Most of these studies stress the geographic, political, and ethnic differences between northern and southern Mesopotamia. Sometimes this kind of comparison is not felicitous because there are different interpretations about the Ur III period itself. This is apparent from the discussion about the lack of sale documents of arable land, and the existence of private property of fields, orchards, and houses (see, e.g., Gelb 1969; Steinkeller 1989; Renger 1990). Postgate (1992: 183)

4 Balamunamḫe, the son of Sîn-nūr-mātim, is attested over a period of 38 years, from Warad-Sîn 6 (c. 1828 BC) until Rīm-Sîn 31 (c. 1791 BC). Later documents from his archive apparently belong to his grandson who bore the same name (Van De Mieroop 1987b: 2).

has already shown the difficulties of comparing the Ur III to the Old Babylonian period due to the nature of the extant sources.[5]

The differentiation between northern and southern Mesopotamia as regards private land ownership rests upon the discussion about the existence or nonexistence of sale documents (Kozyreva 1999: 354). Not surprisingly, the origins of these debates trace back to the disagreements pertaining to the temple-state economy. Due to the absence of sale contracts, those authors who adhere to some version of this model deny any possibility of private property of arable land in southern Mesopotamia during the Ur III and the early Old Babylonian periods. Others maintain that the lack of documentation is a feeble argument for disregarding private property. This topic received substantial attention after the formulation of the temple-state theory in the early 1920s. Vladimir Jakobson (1971), for instance, produced an evolutionary model based, according to him, on Diakonoff's theory. For Jakobson, private property in arable land during the Old Babylonian period was the result of a complex development. His reconstruction of ownership rights includes five hypothetical stages. Originally the community gods were the owners, and then land became the property of the community itself. Later, land passed to the hands of a clan or an extended family, and from this group the property was transferred to a patriarch. The final result was the rise of private property held by individuals.

Renger (1995), for his part, proposed a long-term model that sharply contrasts with Jakobson's. Incorporating Braudel's category of the *longue durée*, he analyzes political and economic changes and the relevance of private ownership from the end of the fourth to the end of the first millennium. Renger delineates a process that starts before writing, when rural or village communities were able to manage locally artificial irrigation. At some point, still before writing, the necessity to organize irrigation at a regional level gave rise to forms of an early state. During a second stage, from around 3200 to 2500 BC, communities became weak, and around 2400 BC institutional households gradually absorbed the remnants of communal systems. Renger considers sale documents of this period to be the result of a 'land consolidation' process, which was the consequence of the gradual disappearance of the communities. When dealing with the Sargonic period (c. 2334–2154), Renger remarks on a political and ideological change because of the arrival of a new dynasty of Semitic rulers. This explains, according to Renger, the first attestation of documents that record the transfer of ownership rights among individuals in the areas north of Isin and Nippur. The changes in northern Mesopotamian are thus related to the nomadic past of the new rulers, whereas

5 According to Postgate (1992: 183), 'in Ur III times the only substantial group of private documents is from Nippur, while from the Old Babylonian period we hardly have any public documentation relating to land outside Hammurapi's correspondence with his officials at Larsa'.

the south remains in the previous tradition. Renger infers that during the Ur III period (c. 2100–2000) the arable land that the rulers of Akkad had taken away from the temples was returned to them; as a result there was no private individual ownership of fields. Renger, nonetheless, acknowledges the existence of private property in orchards and houses. This explanation finally states that in the Old Babylonian period Amorite kings of 'nomadic origins' came to power, and that although a considerable number of private sale documents from the north are evident, the situation in the south was still similar to that of the Ur III period.

Piotr Steinkeller (1999) has similarly explained land-tenure conditions in the third millennium. He is particularly interested in the ecological, historical, cultural and religious factors that shaped the north-south dichotomy in ancient Mesopotamia. To account for the economic integration of ecological niches, Steinkeller resorts to John Murra's 'vertical control' model, initially formulated for the Peruvian Andes. As for the other factors, he coincides with Renger's 'ethnic' differentiation between 'the southern (Sumerian) and the northern (Akkadian) societies', which was the result of an evolutionary process. The identification of ethnic groups on linguistic grounds, however, does not enjoy full consensus (see, e.g., Kraus 1970; Cooper 1973; Kamp and Yoffee 1980). Steinkeller also stresses the importance of the city and temple economy as the essential feature of the organization of southern Mesopotamia. He proposes a critical approach to the concepts of 'private property' and 'individual ownership' because in ancient Mesopotamia different property rights overlapped, whereas the king was the ultimate owner of all land. He concludes then 'it is impossible to speak of private or individual ownership of land' (1999: 296). For Steinkeller, this remark does not hold for the ownership of orchards, houses and house-plots, because they could be freely alienated. The number of sale documents from the Ur III period substantiates this fact (Steinkeller 1989).

Other scholars, on the contrary, maintain that the absence or scarcity of sale documents is not conclusive evidence for the nonexistence of private property in arable land. Evidently these authors interpret the written evidence, as well as the lack of it, differently. Diakonoff (1985), for instance, analyzed a considerable number of field lease contracts from the city of Ur during the Ur III period. Diakonoff affirms that the lessors of these fields were male members of extended families who enjoyed full property rights. To explain the lack of land-sale contracts, Diakonoff poses the hypothesis of an embargo on land sale. But Gelb (1969: 47) has interpreted this absence rather as due to some legal restrictions that prohibited the sale of arable land. More recently Larisa Bobrova and Sergej Koshurnikov (1989: 54) adopted this interpretation to state that land sale 'was forbidden during the whole period of Ur III, as well as in the kingdom of Larsa'. For Postgate (1992: 183), however, the nonexistence of sale documents does not necessarily indicate the state's absolute ownership of arable land, or any sort of legal prohibition concerning land sale. As an alternative, he suggests that the sale of cereal fields was only a last resort, and that traditional restraints on these transactions may have existed because of family structure.

Judging from the comments scattered throughout different works, at present the existence of landed property in southern Mesopotamia seems to have considerable acceptance despite the scarcity of documents. None of these Assyriologists, however, has formulated and all-encompassing explanation such as the one that Renger proposed. Innumerable theoretical subtleties underlie these opposite interpretations. The understanding of Mesopotamian economy and society depends on the way the problem of cultivable land ownership is approached. The notion of Mesopotamian 'private property' as something different from the norm established in Roman law has been mentioned often. Nevertheless, this is not an entirely satisfactory explanation. As already said, there are documents that record real estate transactions in which orchards, gardens, house-plots, or even fields in northern Mesopotamia are exchanged for a specific amount of silver. These documents clearly show that private land was indeed sold (see Charpin 1986c), and speculations about the transferring of only certain rights over the object seem to complicate the issue unnecessarily.

The problem of land ownership is inevitably related to the discussion about the existence or nonexistence of market mechanisms during the Old Babylonian period. This controversy initially originated in the debates between Karl Bücher and Eduard Meyer in the late nineteenth century regarding Greek and Roman economy, and it gained new influence after Polanyi readdressed the discussion by opposing the *sustantivist* (or traditionalist) to the *formalist* (or modernist) interpretations (see Seri 2005). Renger (1984) has thoroughly reviewed different positions as regards trade and market in ancient Mesopotamia. He points out the decisive influence that Oppenheim's and Polanyi's ideas on markets have had on Assyriological studies. In fact Renger's article is mainly devoted to demonstrating that Polanyi's premises are wholly valid, and that criticisms to his market-less economy revolve around superficial semantic issues. Renger places the debate within the context of 'traditionalists' versus 'modernists;' that is, in terms of those who consider the *oikos* as the fundamental unit of production and consumption, and those who believe that the concepts of modern economics are suitable for the analysis of ancient societies. Renger (e.g. 1979; 1984; 1990) argues that reciprocity and redistribution were more important than any other form of local exchange. Thus the Old Babylonian period is characterized by the *oikos* economy, where 'the palace controlled most or all the arable land'. Renger (1990: 22) further adds, 'individual property of arable land (fields) did not exist to a measurable degree'. As for the 'modernist' theories, Hudson's (1996) introduction to a volume on privatization in the ancient Near East provides a good sample of some of the 'modernist' conceptions and premises. At some points it even makes one sympathize with some of the 'primitivist' overstatements. That is the case, for instance, when Hudson regards the Mesopotamian temple as 'civilization's first business corporation', and as a public entrepreneurial institution that gave way to the privatization of businesses in the third millennium.

The solution of those theoretical dilemmas prompted a pragmatic research of Old Babylonian economic and social history. Several articles aim at answering specific questions such as the ways in which property value was established. The study of real estate prices, unfortunately, has not yet cast any light on this problem. Jakobson (1971), for instance, attempted to determine the customary price for land. The parameter he set for the selection of his corpus only includes plots that were referred to as fields, were bordered by a canal, and were paid in silver. This criterion is highly selective, therefore only 11 documents dating to the First Dynasty of Babylon fit into the category. From these contracts, seven belong to the period from Sūmû-la-el to Samsu-iluna (barely one contract per king) and the rest are from kings outside Babylon but contemporary to the First Dynasty. The limited number of documents under consideration did not allow the author to draw any decisive pattern. Not surprisingly, he concludes that 'one shekel of silver may represent the price of a plot of any dimension, from 10 sar of field and up to 200 sar of field; that is, the rate of fluctuation is 2000 per cent!' (p. 36).

Howard Farber (1978) also discussed land prices in his study of price and wages for northern Mesopotamia. His sale-contract corpus is more inclusive than Jakobson's, for it comprises some 74 documents from Sippar, Dilbat, and Kiš. Like Jakobson, Farber also encounters difficulties in establishing a mean value for fields because of the enormous variation in price. According to him, the price fluctuation can vary from one-sixth shekel up to 40 shekels per iku-measure of field. He suggests that the differences in price per iku of land must have been related, among other things, to the location and productivity of the field, although documents do not mention these features. Farber ultimately concludes that there was a gradual decline in price of land in Sippar, and perhaps in other northern cities from the reign of Hammurabi onwards, possibly because of a drop in land productivity. Since the publication of his work, however, a considerable number of new documents has been published. A comparative study of all those texts might or might not change Farber's conclusions. But there is at least one recently published contract (VAS 29 15) that challenges the hypothesis of price decline. This tablet summarizes several sales of a same field over 80 years, from Abī-ešuḫ 2 to Ammī-ṣaduqa 21, and the price always remains 1 mina of silver (see Seri 2004).

The study of prices for urban dwellings shows similar difficulties because, as in the case of fields, the price fluctuation is also considerable. Koshurnikov (1996), for instance, has dealt with the price of houses in Dilbat taking into account the description of the property. The corpus consists of 23 contracts from Sūmû-la-el to Samsu-iluna.[6] Koshurnikov has noticed the difficulty of relating variables such as the good or bad shape or the location of the house with its price. He also considers exceptional circumstances that may have influenced the property value. These could be lower prices because of the removal of wooden parts, or higher because of special interest in buying the property. This would have been the case with a neighbor wishing to enlarge his or her own house. Similarly, Van De Mieroop (1999b) has studied the price of houses in Sippar, Nippur, and Ur in an attempt to identify price-setting mechanisms. Following Stone (1977), Van De Mieroop states that economic and political conditions, such as the economic upheaval in the south after 1739 BC, may also have affected the prices of real estate. He thinks that sales were usually to relatives or neighbors but not to people who had just moved into a neighborhood. On the contrary, in her analyzes of sellers and buyers of urban real state in southern Mesopotamia, Nelli Kozyreva (1999: 356) arrives at the opposite conclusion. She maintains 'that a considerable portion of urban real estate buyers were people who had moved into the cities rather recently, i.e., newcomers or their descendants'. Kozyreva further adds that because of this mobility, the sale of urban plots was not only an economic but also a social phenomenon. As for the existence of market mechanisms, Van De Mieroop (1999b: 274) affirms that there was not 'any real estate market in the modern sense of the word', because the prices seems to have depended on particular conditions, rather than on market mechanisms. It should be noticed, however, that these 'particular conditions' also affect price values in contemporary societies.

Other studies focused on movable goods challenge Renger's (1984) denial of the existence of domestic trade. Renger argues that even though some kind of barter and some sales may have existed, these cases should be considered as marginal because in traditional and non-institutionalized economies the 'social embeddedness' of the economy determines economic activities and behaviors. The results of Marsten Stol's (1982a) analyses of a group of documents from Larsa covering some 18 years (Ḫa 32 to Si 17) do not substantiate Renger's view. These texts relate to the collection of dates and other commodities of the region of Emutbalum, an area that included the cities of Larsa, Ur, Lagaš, Bad-Tibira and Kutalla. The goods mentioned in these tablets are dates, garlic, fish, barley, and wool. Dates and fish were collected from state officials who entrusted them to Šēp-Sîn, the Overseer of Five, of the *kārum* or quay of Larsa. The palace was

6 The sales include: nine é-dù-a (Ḫa to Si), one é-gi-(ni) (Sm), thirteen é-bur-bal (Sl to Sm), and one é-kislaḫ (Sm). The variation in price, according to Koshurnikov, is: 1 sar é-dù-a 10 to 30 shekels of silver; 1 sar bur-bal 2 to 4 shekels, and 1 sar é-kislaḫ about 1 shekel.

apparently not interested at all in the origin of the staples, it just valued them and expected Šēp-Sîn to pay the amount of silver stipulated at a point of time set by the palace (Charpin 1982). According to Stol's conclusions, the members of the *kārum* of Larsa sold the merchandise to private individuals. This indicates that a market for daily needs, categorically denied by Renger, existed in southern Mesopotamia. Markets, however, do not necessarily imply that ancient economies functioned according to the mechanisms of contemporary societies. Markets are well attested in other pre-capitalist areas. In modern times, they are only one of the several features that distinguish capitalism. Their functioning in today's economies cannot be isolated from specific relations of production, industrialization, wage-earning labor force, and world system, for example. The presence in antiquity of certain elements that may resemble modern institutions and their mechanisms does not make ancient societies modern.

This review of the Old Babylonian period provides a context to my study, but it was also intended to highlight some of the historical and methodological problems that I consider relevant in order to understand the ways in which Old Babylonian history has been written. The survey shows that most if not all of the discussions focus on a rather narrow range of topics including political history as well as the nature and economic power of the state. Today, some 150 years after the decipherment of cuneiform writing, our knowledge of Mesopotamian history has improved significantly. However, many scholars from different theoretical backgrounds concentrate on historical problems that place the state at the center of analyses. Even if documents and archaeological data impose certain limitations on the study of ancient history, it is possible to subject our sources to new questions. My study of local powers undertakes this challenge, shifting the emphasis from the state to other smaller institutions of power and individual authorities. Such an approach requires both research on the jurisdiction and activities of local powers beyond their judicial role, and a reevaluation of certain commonly accepted premises.

LOCAL POWER IN THE OLD BABYLONIAN PERIOD

Although it is common to find references to various structures of local authority in Assyriological literature, there has been no systematic investigation on local powers during the Old Babylonian period. Two decades ago, André Finet (1982) edited *Les pouvoirs locaux en Mésopotamie et dans les régions adjacentes*. This book originated from a colloquium presented at the Institut des Hautes Études de Belgique. Despite the suggestive title, the papers gathered in the volume deal with very restricted and disparate topics, and they do not present an integrated picture of Mesopotamian local authorities. Only two articles in the volume refer to the Old

Babylonian period. One of them analyzes the *kārum*, 'the port authority' (Kraus 1982), while the other studies local powers in the kingdom of Mari (Kupper 1982). Generally, most references to local institutions appear only tangentially in analyses not directly concerned with local authorities. Diakonoff (1969), for instance, explored the role of community institutions in his broader study of early Mesopotamian political systems. According to him, corporate bodies such as 'the council of elders' (*šībūtum*), 'the popular assemblages of the city' (*ālum, kārum, puḫrum*), and 'the city-ward' (*bābtum*) were the survivors of earlier organs of community self-government. Diakonoff maintains that although these institutions were still important in the times of king Hammurabi, by then they had become merely organs of the local administration. This new explanation challenged the temple-state model as originally formulated for the third millennium (see, e.g., Schneider 1920; Deimel 1931; Falkenstein 1954). Undoubtedly, Diakonoff's remarkable contribution is the identification of these authorities with community organs of self-government that coexisted with the state. In that work, local powers were not Diakonoff's main concern, and he did not analyze them thoroughly.

Other scholars have considered the role of corporate groups and community representatives when dealing with the Old Babylonian judicial system (e.g. Cuq 1910; Lautner 1922; Yoffee 2000; Dombradi 1996; Fortner 1996). Thus, while the participation of these authorities in the settlement of legal disputes is well known, their involvement in the city administration has been mentioned only briefly (see, e.g., Oppenheim 1967; 1969; Yokoyama 1994; Van De Mieroop 1997; Keith 1999). Although outdated, Arnold Walther's *Das altbabylonische Gerichtswesen* is still a valuable source, for the author included every attestation of those institutions and officials known to him in 1917. The studies by Eva Dombradi (1996) and John Fortner (1996) are important contributions to Walther's approach, especially because the authors produce an updated corpus of primary sources, while also providing new viewpoints. But Eva Dombradi and John Fortner do not dwell upon documents in which these authorities appear engaged in activities other than court disputes. The effect of these legal studies has not been to foreclose fuller research of local authorities (see Yoffee 1999). Harris (1975) has also listed various representatives of local powers under specific subheadings in her book dealing with Sippar. Currently, some of Harris's conclusions need revision in the light of the voluminous number of texts from that city recently published (e.g. Dekiere 1994a; 1994b; 1995a; 1995b; 1996; 1997; Klengel and Klengel-Brandt 2002).

One of the most extensive analyses of the *rabiānum* appears in Stol's *Studies in Old Babylonian History* (1976a), which includes two entire sections about this official. The author first undertakes a philological interpretation of the term *rabiānum*, translated alternately as 'chief', 'burgomaster', and 'sheikh'. According to Stol, the *rabiānum*-'burgomaster' headed a permanent settlement, while the *rabiānum*-'sheikh' was the leader of a nomadic group. He maintains that the office was initially a nomadic institution, and that it ultimately evolved to become an urban post that co-existed with its tribal forerunner. Stol studies some of the characteristics of the office, including its length, and the possibility that there was more than one *rabiānum* in a city at a time. He also analyzes the *rabiānum*'s role in harvest-labor contracts. His work is a valuable contribution towards the understanding of this official, but Stol does not solve several problems, as he himself pointed out. For instance, when he explains how the *rabiānum* acceded to the office, he affirms that the king appointed Tutub-māgir in Šaduppûm. This example, nevertheless, is arguable on textual grounds. Stol's proposal implies the possibility that the *rabiānum* was, at least in some cases, a royal official. A similar assumption seems to be present in Roth's translation of Hammurabi's laws, where she rendered *rabiānum* as 'governor' (Roth 1997: 85). The reasons why she opted for such a term are not explained and, interestingly enough, the *Chicago Assyrian Dictionary*, of which Roth is coeditor, does not provide that meaning. These interpretations seem to favor the *rabiānum*'s dependence upon the state. For other scholars, there is no consistent evidence to support this view (see, e.g., Yoffee 1978; Fortner 1996: 270). Yoffee (1977) has also pursued the role of the *rabiānum* as a community leader attested in documents pertaining to the hiring of harvesters, but he focused mostly on the economic role of the crown.

As for the elders (*šībūtum*), Horst Klengel (1960) analyzed this institution some 40 years ago, and, more recently, he supplemented his conclusions with examples from Ebla (Klengel 1989). His study of the elders during the Old Babylonian period is mainly a revision of the topic in the light of texts from the royal archives of Mari. For Klengel, the *šībūtum* were not only 'the elders of a city', but also kin-related officials of tribal groups. He further states that Mari evidence makes it possible to reconstruct the historical development of the institution of 'the elders'. Accordingly, Klengel traces the Sumerian and Akkadian words for 'elders' attested in the Ur III and Old Akkadian period. He implies that the *šībūt ālim* originated from tribal groups. This goes back to the time when the West Semitic inhabitants of Mesopotamia penetrated into the land between the Euphrates and the Tigris. Because the evidence for this migration is not directly found in written documents, Klengel resorts to analogies such as ethnographic studies of the Bedouins, and literary texts, for instance, Gilgameš and Akka, a classic for this subject matter. The author's identification of elders who advise the king/sheikh in nomadic groups is a valid one. But this fact does not necessarily mean that 'the elders of the city' are the result of a process of nomadic settlement, or that modern 'nomads' are appropriate analogies for 'nomads' of 4000 years ago. A new survey of the elders appears in a book dealing with collective decision-making groups in Mari (Fleming 2004). Although Fleming criticizes evolutionist approaches, he does not include elders from regions other than the Mari area.

Scholars today no longer adhere to the idea that nomadic groups are primitive peoples in an early stage of evolution towards a settled life (Kamp and Yoffee 1980). Rather, nomadism itself is a specialized adaptation that evolved in conjunction with urbanism. One may similarly critique Stol's interpretation suggesting that the *rabiānum* was originally a tribal sheikh, and that then, when the tribes had fully settled in cities, the *rabiānum* turned into a 'burgomaster'. Of course, Amorite dynasties became the hallmarks of the Old Babylonian period. Nevertheless, this fact does not allow us to conclude that all Amorites were nomads, or that their characteristic nomadic institutions came to pervade Mesopotamian social, economic, and political organization. This argument seems to be present, for instance, in Renger's (1979: 252) depiction of Hammurabi as a 'great sheikh, as the king called himself in his inscriptions'. Naturally, by the time Hammurabi acceded to the throne, the First Dynasty of Babylon had already been ruling northern Mesopotamia for a century. And one may very well be suspicious about arguments for a theory of government based on terms found in royal inscriptions.

The Old Babylonian assembly (*puḫrum*) and 'the city' (*ālum*) are usually studied together. References to these institutions appear in Geoffrey Evans' (1958) study on 'Ancient Mesopotamian Assemblies'. This article was conceived as a reaction to Thorkild Jacobsen's (1943) analysis of 'Primitive Democracy' in ancient Mesopotamia, and includes only a few documents. Evans employs examples from Uruk and *kārum* Kaneš, and he occasionally refers to Old Babylonian data and to comparisons with Roman and Greek assemblies. Evans's goal is to understand the constituency of the assemblies and its bodies, the elders and the guruš in 'Gilgameš and Akka', among others. He discusses at length the social rank and age groups of assembly members based on speculative grounds – as the author himself acknowledges. The conclusions of this approach are, on the one hand, that the assemblies of Uruk in the time of Gilgameš consisted of two bodies: the elders, representatives of powerful families and not necessarily biologically old; and the freemen of the city, regardless of their age. On the other, it is suggested that the assemblies at Kaneš, in the early second millennium, show a great decline in power, which had been transferred from the assembly to the 'great' men. In spite of his critical attempt, Evans never questions Jacobsen's idea that Mesopotamian 'autocratic kingship' was the result of an evolutionary process that started with an alleged 'primitive democracy'. In fact, Evans's second conclusion seems to substantiate this view. On his part, Emile Szlechter (1968 and 1970) undertook a chronological survey of assemblies from pre-Sargonic Mesopotamia to the Old Babylonian period, and most of his conclusions rest upon the works of Jacobsen and Walther.

There are, therefore, two kinds of approaches to local powers such as the *rabiānum*, the elders, the city, and the assembly. On the one hand, works concerned with legal procedures and the administration of justice include these authorities together with other officials and collegiate bodies as part of the Old Babylonian judicial system. Since the main goal of these analyses revolves around legal matters, the participation of local institutions in other activities is usually overlooked. In this group, I also include studies pertaining to city government, which usually cover two millennia or more. On the other hand, a number of articles deal with the *rabiānum*, the elders, and the assembly separately, but there has been no attempt at interconnecting their functions or at articulating the role of local authorities with state officials and the rest of society. These individual works are important contributions to our understanding of the Old Babylonian period, but most of them date from over 20 years ago. The reexamination of local authorities in the light of new documents, together with an approach that takes into account their vertical and horizontal connections, will allow us to explore mechanisms of power beyond the royal sphere. The analysis of these interactions is the subject of the following sections. I will first study the *rabiānum*, the elders, the city, and the assembly separately, and will progressively include their joint participation in city issues. The next chapter is devoted to the role, activities, and jurisdiction of the *rabiānum*, the chief of the city.

3

The Rabiānum

GENERAL REMARKS

The study of ancient institutions poses several challenges to the historian. Piecing together the fragments of what was recorded in antiquity and of what has survived into modern times implies the use of previous assumptions to analyze the evidence that has come down to us. The millennia that have passed from the Old Babylonian period to 'our' present continually bring the historian to the brink of anachronism. Bridging that gap is a rather difficult and not necessarily promising enterprise. When dealing with written sources, the transference of specific semantic connotations further complicates the understanding of ancient societies. In the seemingly simple process of translation, the philologist manipulates words and institutions alike. The choice of particular terms or categories drawn from modern societies bears the burden of historical connotations, and it also conveys particular visions and perceptions of the world. Imposing modern meanings, albeit necessary, inevitably compromises the ancient Mesopotamian's conceptual universe. Analyses of ancient Near Eastern institutions have been quite influenced by comparisons that are at best anachronistic (Yoffee 1978: 28). Linguistic rigor, as valuable as it is, plays a role in the maze of misconceptions about institutional issues. The more one tries to find a technical word for a translation, the more one risks being far removed from the connotation the word must have had in the society in which it was used. Concerns like this may seem excessive. Nevertheless, being aware of the difficulties inherent in the translation of resurrected languages helps to avoid the risk of enacting the well-known Italian pun *traduttore-traditore*.

The word *rabiānum*, usually rendered as 'burgomaster' or 'sheikh', illustrates certain problems pertaining to the translation of dead languages. Modern scholars tend to make ancient institutions resemble or fit into familiar categories. The meaning of *rabiānum* rests upon etymology, and the characteristics of the office are inferred from the context in which it appears. The first attestations of the noun *rabiānum* date from the Old Babylonian period and it is only written syllabically.[1] Stol (1976a: 73–76) has identified three different spellings, namely, *ra-bi-a-nu(-um)*,

1 Stol (1976a: 82–83) has argued that the logogram g̃ir-nita$_2$ could have been the equivalent of the title *rabiānum* in the Diyala region. I will address this issue under the subheading 'the *rabiānum* as an urban authority', later in this chapter.

ra-BI-*nu*(-*um*), and *ra-ba-nu*(-*um*) in Elam. He suggests that the second variant could have been a dialectal form from Mari and the Diyala region.[2] The 'plene' writing *ra-bi-a-nu*(-*um*), however, is also found in texts from that area. Similarly, texts from southern Mesopotamia also record the writing *ra-bi-nu*(-*um*).[3] This fact seems to indicate that rather than a regional characteristic, *ra-bi-nu*(-*um*) could be either a by-form or a misspelling. There is yet a fourth variant, that is, the use of the *bí*-sign instead of *bi*. The extant examples show that the *bí*-graph was exclusively used during the early Old Babylonian period.[4] Morphologically, the substantive *rabiānum* results from adding the nominal affix -*ān*(*um*) to the verbal adjective *rabû* or *rabiu*, 'great', 'important', 'powerful', etc. The morpheme -*ānum* works as a particularizing suffix (*GAG* § 56r), thus the basic meaning of *rabiānum* is, following Wolfram von Soden (*GAG*: 85), 'bestimmter Grosser', i.e., 'particular or specific great man'. Buccellati's (1976: 30) study of the affix -*ānum* shows that the exact nature of the particularizing effect is normally conditioned by the context or by the semantic value of the word taken as the basis for the derivation. Giorgio Buccellati's 'context-free occurrence' of -*ānum* provides a more precise nuance of this particle, therefore, *rabiānum* can also be interpreted as 'the one characterized by being powerful or great'. In a broad sense, it could be rendered simply as 'chief', or 'leader'. To avoid confusion with other titles similarly translated as 'mayor', I keep the word in Akkadian.

Morphology helped philologists to decipher the connotation of the word, while context allowed them to trace the characteristics of the office. Scholars initially encountered the term in economic and legal documents and noticed the presence of the *rabiānum* as the first witness to some of these transactions. Based on this

2 Following *GAG* § 16k, Stol (1976a: 74) explains that 'Only in texts from Mari and the Diyala region the reading *ra-bé-nu-um* could be certain, because the contraction *i* + *ā* = *ê* is often attested in those texts'.

3 In the case of Šamaš-ilī, the *rabiānum* of Ḫalḫalla, the title is written *ra-bi-nu-um* in CT 47 68: 16 (n.d. *ca.* AS-Sm) and MHET II/5 n° 618: 10 (n.d. *ca.* Sa-Sm); but it is also written *ra-bi-a-nu-um* in CT 47 19+ a: 20 (Sm, oath). The title of Ilī-ippalsam, from Kutalla, is always attested in 'plene' writing except in *TS* 81: 10 (Si 8/VIII/5), where we have *ra-bi-nu*; similarly, Dadi-išme-el's title is written *ra-bi-nu-um* in YOS 14 106: 19 but *ra-bi-a-nu-um* in UCP 10/3 6: 16 (envelope). Worth noticing is VAS 13 20 + 20a (Ḫa 30/X/Ø, Sippar), in line 19 the first witness is Ibni-Amurrum, *ra-bi-a-nu*, but the document also bears the notation kišib *ra-bi-nu*.

4 Thus for instance in D. Charpin (1985b: 191) and D. Parayre (1985: 233) (1. *Am-bu-na-a-ḫi* / 2. dumu *I-ša-nu-um* / 3. *ra-bí-a-nu-um*); AS 22: 119 pl. 27 (1. *I-túr-š*[*ar-ru-um*] / 2. *ra-bí-an* MAR.TU / 3. *ša Di-ni-i*[*k-tim*]…); RIM IV: 700 (1. *A-ri-im-li-im* / 2. dumu *I-ba-a-a* / 3. *ra-bí-an* MAR.TU); *RIM* IV: 702 (1. *A*-⸢*ia*⸣-*bu*-⸢*um*⸣ / 2. dumu *A*-[x x x x] / 3. *ra-bí-an* x x / 4. *ša Ba*-⸢*ti*⸣-*ir*^{ki}; RIM IV: 112 [= *Syria* 45: 243] (1. *Za-ba-a* / 2. *ra-bí-an* / 3. MAR.TU…); RIM IV: 121 [=UET 8 65] (22'. ⸢*A*⸣-*bí-sa-re-e* (…) / 27'. *ra-bí-a-nu-um* MAR.TU me-en); RIM IV: 152 [=*MDOG* 15:13] (1. *I-túr*-^{d}Utu / 2. *ra-bí-an* / 3. *Ra-ba-bi-ma*); and BIN 9 199 (8. ki *Bir*$_5$-*bi-ru-ma* / 9. *ra-bí-a-nu-um-ma*), from the time of Išbi-Erra.

fact, Bruno Meissner (1893: 129) translates *rabiānum* as 'Präsident' or, more specifically, 'president of the court', as King (1900: 39) renders it. The discovery of the 'Laws of Hammurabi' in 1901 affected interpretations of the *rabiānum*'s role.[5] Édouard Cuq (1910: 84–85) discusses the office and, following LH §§ 23-24, he states that the *rabiānum* was 'le magistrat chargé de maintenir l'ordre dans la ville, celui que nous appelons aujourd'hui le maire'. Cuq mentions that, along with his duty as an authority in charge of local justice, the *rabiānum* was also the president of an assembly, which encompassed the notables and the city elders. After Cuq, the translation 'mayor' or 'burgomaster' became common.[6]

Early in the twentieth century Walther (1917) undertook the first thorough study of those Old Babylonian officials and institutions engaged in the administration of justice. He compiled all the available *rabiānum* sources, including legal and economic documents, letters, as well as royal inscriptions. After some general remarks, Walther proceeds with a geographic approach. He considers first southern and then northern cities. In the south, his evidence is limited to a small number of documents mainly from Larsa and Kutalla. References are to the *rabiānum* of Medûm (*LIH* I 19), the *rabiānums* Ali-tillati (*LIH* I 6), Amurrum-mālik (Holma *ZATH* n° 1), and Ubbalum (VAS 13 100) from Larsa, and those from the city of Kutalla.[7] As for northern Mesopotamia, Walther refers to the *rabiānums* Imgur-Sîn (VAS 7 149, 7, and 14), Aḫum-ṭābum (VAS 7 8, 49, and 60) and Ibni-Marduk (VAS 7 100) from Dilbat. He finally studies some 20 documents mentioning the *rabiānums* of Sippar and vicinity, especially the city of Ḫalḫalla. Walther

5 In LH, the *rabiānum* is mentioned only twice (§§23 and 24). In both paragraphs, the *rabiānum* and the city are made responsible for any robbery committed within their jurisdiction. In §23 one of the variants has unken, 'assembly', instead of uru, 'city'. Finkelstein (1967: 45) – the editor of this tablet written by Ina-é-ulmaš-zēru, a 'junior scribe' (dub-sar tur) – dates the copy to the time of Ammī-ditāna or Ammī-ṣaduqa. Following Walther (1917: 50, 64), Finkelstein explains the variant unken (uru x bar) vs *ālum* (uru) because 'uru is used to denote "the city" as a judicial body, equally with unken "assembly"...'(p. 47). Due to the similarity between the two signs, Finkelstein also considers the possibility of the variant being a scribal mistake.

6 See, e.g., Driver and Miles (1952/5: 21), *AHw* ('der Große', 'Bürgermeister'), and *CAD* ('mayor', 'headman'). Besides 'mayor' there are also other renderings. Schorr ([1913] 1971: 364) translates *rabiānum* as 'Präfekt', as does Finet (1973a: 51, 'préfet'). Pinches (1915: 130) has 'presiding scribe', whereas Roth (1997: 85) has 'governor'. And Stol (1976a: 73) further suggests 'tribal sheikh' as one of its meanings, followed by Oppenheim who translates 'chief magistrate of a town or tribe', in the index to YOS 12 (p. 67).

7 Walther specifies that the *rabiānum* Abī-lūmur was not from Kutalla – as originally thought – but from Ašašir. Thus he is left with only three *rabiānums* of Kutalla, namely, Qīšti-Erra, Ilī-ippalsam, and Sîn-imguranni. However, Walther (1917: 115) already suspected that Sîn-imguranni might have been the *rabiānum* of another town. More recently, Charpin (1980a: 144–45) has argued that Sîn-imguranni was not *rabiānum* of Kutalla, but from some other place, possibly Ašduba. As regards the *rabiānum* Qīšti-Erra, Walther notices – as did B. Meissner (1893: 122) before him – that Qīšti-Erra is also recorded bearing the title *rabi sikkatim*.

affirms that in several cases the *rabiānum* was the foremost judge of the city and the president of the court. The *rabiānum* was, moreover, the head of the city elders. Then the *rabiānum*'s direct involvement with local affairs made him an important witness to many contracts because, for Walther, the *rabiānum* is always an urban official.[8]

Six decades after the publication of Walther's *Das altbabylonische Gerichtswesen*, Stol (1976a: 73–89) revisited the *rabiānum* office. Stol maintains that *rabiānum* was not only the title for a city authority, 'burgomaster', but it also designated a tribal chief or sheikh (see also Stol 2004: 650). For him, the office originated as a tribal institution and it later evolved into an urban post. To substantiate his interpretation, Stol provides various instances in which the term *rabiānum* appears in the bound form with nouns other than city names. The examples include *rabiān bābtīšu* (Langdon 1924: 40), *rabiān nārim* (*LIH* I 66), *rabiān Rababî* (*MDOG* 15: 13), *rabiān Amnān-Šadlaš* (CT 48 83), and *rabiān Amurrim* (e.g. RIM IV: 810). Since most of these titles refer to ethnic groups, Stol concludes that the translation of *rabiānum* depends on the context. 'Burgomaster' would apply to the *rabiānum* who is in charge of a permanent settlement, whereas 'sheikh' would refer to the leader of a tribal group. Stol specifically quotes three inscriptions (OIP 43: 145, RIM IV: 810 and AS 22 n° 3) as examples of *rabiān Amurrim*, apparently unrelated to royal bearers. Although critical of the gradual sedentarization theory, Van De Mieroop (1999c: 153) accepts Stol's distinction between a sedentary and a nomadic *rabiānum* throughout the Old Babylonian period. More recently, Steinkeller (2004a: 35 n. 41) comments that 'while *rabiān Amurrim* is a generic term for 'sheikh', specific sheikhs are designated by the construction *rabiān* Tribal Name'. He finally compares the titles *abu Amurrim* and *rabiān Amurrim* and further suggests that the first may have been a higher rank whose bearer controlled several *rabiānum*s. The publication of new evidence, nonetheless, seems to suggest that *rabiānum* plus a gentilic was always used as a royal title. In this chapter, I examine previous documents and include new ones to show that the evolution of the *rabiānum* office from an alleged tribal origin to an urban institution is not apparent. It is my contention that the term *rabiānum* represents two different concepts. On the one hand it was a royal title borne by early Old Babylonian rulers, on the other it designates a city authority. I will also explore the characteristics and activities of the urban office.

8 He states: 'Der *rabiānu* ist immer der *rabiānu* einer bestimmten Stadt, mag der Name der Stadt hinzugesetzt sein oder nicht' (p. 107).

RABIĀNUM AS A ROYAL TITLE

Mesopotamian royal titulary is a rather complicated subject, because a number of titles and epithets coexisted and changed according to temporal, regional, and individual uses (see Hallo 1957). A survey of royal inscriptions clearly shows that scribes carefully selected and employed royal titles. Particular choices served specific purposes, and they usually illustrate changes in the political arena (see, e.g., Charpin 2004: 233–34). Depending on the aim of a given inscription, titles portrayed the king as a mighty man, as a pious observer of rituals and the restoration of shrines, as a successful conqueror, as a just ruler, or as the leader and protector of the land and its inhabitants. Traditional titles provided a putative continuity with the ancestral kingship as depicted in the 'Sumerian King List', while innovative variants usually included current events. In some cases the connotation of these inscriptions is quite obvious, but subtleties are occasionally difficult to grasp. Thus the degree of suzerainty that certain titles may have conveyed is often difficult to evaluate. Similarly, the existence of other titles as for instance *rubûm* in Ešnunna has only been noticed recently (Charpin 1985a: 62–66). *Rabiānum* was one of the many royal titles attested in the early Old Babylonian period (e.g. Kraus 1974; Michalowski 1983).

I. *RABIĀN AMURRIM*

Two well known kings of Larsa used the title *rabiān Amurrim*, 'chief of the Amorites'. They were Zabāya (*Syria* 45: 243; RIM IV: 112; Steinkeller 2004b: 146) and Abī-sarē (UET 8 65) during the early Old Babylonian period. A seal impression on an expenditure of oil rations dated to Abī-sarē also mentions the king's title (YOS 14 207 + seal n° 93). The inscription reads, 'Dannīya, the overseer of the barbers, servant of Abī-sarē, the *rabiān Amurrim*.'[9] Simmons (1978: 14), the editor of this tablet, thought that *rabiān Amurrim* qualified Dannīya, the *wakil gallābī*, 'overseer of the barbers', instead of Abī-sarē. But Charpin (1979: 196) has shown that the title refers to the king, as already attested elsewhere. Charpin's explanation is convincing, for it seems unlikely that a person would be at the same time 'overseer of the barbers' and *rabiān Amurrim*, that is, a royal official and a 'sheikh' of the Amorites. Similarly, two kings from Diniktum in northern Mesopotamia bore the title *rabiān Amurrim*. The first was Itūr-šarrum, and the second Sîn-gāmil.

The *rabiān Amurrim* Itūr-šarrum appears in a seal impression on a tablet envelope from the Diyala region (AS 22: 119, RIM IV: 683). The fact that this tablet was found in association with seals from servants of Ipiq-Adad I of Ešnunna indicates

9 *Dan-ni-ia* / ugula šu-i / arad *A-bi-sa-re-e* / *ra-bí-an* MAR.TU (YOS 14 207 + seal n° 93, Abī-sarē 10/VII/∅).

that Itūr-šarrum reigned in Diniktum about a century before Sîn-gāmil became the ruler of that city. Itūr-šarrum's seal legend exactly parallels an inscription of Sîn-gāmil.[10] Robert Whiting (1987: 119) suggests that the similar structure of both texts implies that the title *rabiān Amurrim* had a long tradition in Diniktum. Because Sîn-gāmil's inscription was written on baked-cistern bricks, Stol (1976a: 88) concludes that the brick is 'a link with the life of nomads ("Amorites") and offers a context in which Sîn-gāmil's nomadic title is meaningful: did he built cisterns for herdsmen?' Unfortunately, the excavation context is lost because non-professional diggers produced both of Sîn-gāmil's extant bricks. One of them was given to Sidney Smith in 1931 (*Sumer* 2: 20), and the other was brought to the Iraq Museum in 1960 together with six Ur III/Larsa cylinder seals (Adams 1965: 165). Based on his archaeological surveys in the Diyala region, Robert McC. Adams considers that the site of ancient Diniktum represents a zone of continuous settlement. The fact that Sîn-gāmil's inscription was written on a well brick does not guarantee, therefore, that the cistern was exclusively used by herdsmen nor does it suggest that Sîn-gāmil was himself a nomad.

These two bricks are, at present, the only inscriptions of Sîn-gāmil. Nevertheless, a letter from the archives of Mari mentions him as lugal *Di-ni-ik-tim*[ki], 'king of Diniktum' (Dossin 1956).[11] Yarīm-Līm, the ruler of Aleppo, sent this letter to Yašūb-Yadad, king of Dēr, as a complaint about the way Yašūb-Yadad behaved towards him and the god Adad, who had saved Dēr from destruction. Yarīm-Līm further threatens Yašūb-Yadad with a siege of his city. Charpin and Durand (1985: 308) have already pointed out the historical importance of this document in which Yarīm-Līm claims to have also protected Babylon and Diniktum. It is precisely in this context that the king of Aleppo negatively compares Yašūb-Yadad with Sîn-gāmil. Apparently, Yarīm-Līm had sent five hundred boats to Diniktum and had helped Sîn-gāmil to protect his territory, but his protégé seems not to have shown any sign of gratitude (see Durand 1997: 395).

Charpin and Durand (1985: 310) maintain that the initial support to Diniktum must have taken place towards the end of Samsī-Addu's reign (c. 1776 BC), which would explain the presence of such a large fleet from Aleppo in the quay of Diniktum. Then the letter must have been written around the year Zimrī-Līm 9' (c. Ḫa 12/13, i.e, 1780 or 1779 BC), the most probable time for Yarīm-Līm's threat.[12]

10 Itūr-šarrum's seal reads: Itūr-šarrum / the *rabiān Amurrim* / of Diniktum / son of Ilī-[ ] (AS 22: 119, pl. 27), while Sîn-gāmil's inscription has: Sîn-gāmil / *rabiān Amurrim* of Diniktum / son of Sîn-šeme (*Sumer* 2: 20; Adams 1965: 165).

11 Dossin (1956: 64) explains that the reason why a letter addressed to the king of Dēr was found in the royal archives of Mari is because Mari officials must have intercepted it. For Charpin and Durand (1985: 308), however, the letter was one of the copies that the king of Aleppo sent to his allies.

12 J. Sasson (1985: 252–53), however, has questioned some of the assumptions and synchronisms made by Charpin and Durand.

It is therefore possible to date the reign of Sîn-gāmil to the early years of Hammurabi in Babylon. The intervention of the king of Aleppo in Mesopotamian political affairs took place before the consolidation of Hammurabi's kingdom. This is a clear example of the degree of political fragmentation, and of the changing alliances in Mesopotamia. The fact that the king of Aleppo calls Sîn-gāmil lugal, 'king', reflects the royal status of the title *rabiān Amurrim*, which is, of course, unrelated to the degree of effective power this ruler held.

Another lesser-known king from the Diyala region also appears in relation to the title *rabiān Amurrim* (RIM IV: 700). In this text, Arīm-Līm, son of Ibāya, the *rabiān Amurrim*, claimed to have built the wall of Mê-Turān. The inscription of Arīm-Līm appears on a stone foundation tablet reused as a door socket. Although it was found out of context near Neo-Assyrian buildings at the site of Tell Haddad in the Hamrin basin, it originates from the early Old Babylonian period (see Al-Rawi 1994: 35). Douglas Frayne (1990: 700) suggests that Arīm-Līm could be the same person as the Yarīm-Līm mentioned in the year name of a treaty between Šadlaš and Nērebtum.[13] If that is the case, then Arīm-Līm was contemporary with king Sūmû-la-el of Babylon (1880–1845 BC), and he could have ruled Mê-Turān before Ipiq-Adad II of Ešnunna conquered the city. In this inscription *rabiān Amurrim* seems to qualify Ibāya rather than Arīm-Līm, for the title closely follows the name of Arīm-Līm's father. Similar attestations show the pattern king name + *rabiān Amurrim* + paternal filiation, as for instance the inscriptions of Zabāya of Larsa (RIM IV: 112), and Itūr-šarrum (RIM IV: 683) and Sîn-gāmil (RIM IV: 685) of Diniktum.

The title *rabiān Amurrim* is also recorded on a votive inscription written on an onyx vase (RIM IV: 810). The provenance of this object is unknown, but it is said to have come from Nippur. The passage that interests us reads: 4. [*Am-mi*]-*iš-ta-mar*, 5. [x*D*]*i-da-ni-um*, 6. [*ra-b*]*í-an* MAR.TU (Frayne 1990: 810). The restoration of line 6 is not completely certain. Stol (1976a: 87) reads lines 5 and 6 slightly differently, that is: 5. [(x) x]-x-*da-ni-um*, 6. [*ra-bi*]-*a*(?)-*an* MAR.TU. However, Frayne comments that 'the traces before the –*an* sign in the photo favor a reading [*b*]*í* rather than ⌜*a*⌝'. The use of the *bí* sign fits well into the pattern of the writing *rabiān Amurrim* during the early Old Babylonia period.[14] Frayne thinks that the *rabiān Amurrim* is Ammī-Ištamar, whose territorial sphere of influence is unknown; whereas Stol suggests that line 5 might contain the gentilic *didānum*. As I

13 This year name reads: mu ús-sa *Ia-ri-im-L*[*i-i*]*m* ba-ug$_x$, 'The year after Yarīm-Līm died' (Greengus 1979: 75, ln. 55).

14 As far as I am aware, there is no attestation of *rabiān Amurrim* written **ra-bi-a-an* (see footnote n° 4). Although this writing is attested in a similar context, i.e., *ra-bi-a-an* / *Am-na-an Ša-ad-la-aš* (seal impression on CT 48 83), this seal is, however, later. The year of CT 48 83 is lost, but on a prosopographic basis the document can be safely dated to the time of Hammurabi.

understand this inscription, *rabiān Amurrim* is actually *[D]idānum.[15] This interpretation is based on the comparison with other inscriptions in which *rabiān Amurrim* qualifies the name of the person who is mentioned immediately before the title, as already mentioned. Then this inscription could be understood as follows: 4. Ammī-Ištamar, 5. [the son/servant(?) of] Didānum, the *rabiān Amurrim*.

A brick excavated at Tell al-Suleimah, possibly the ancient city of Batir, bears a building inscription of Ayābum: 1. Ayābum, 2. son of A-[ ], 2. *rabiān* x x (RIM IV: 702). Ayābum was apparently an independent ruler of Batir, near or on the Diyala River (Frayne 1990: 702). Unfortunately, the text is, as usual, broken in the key passages, and the personal name and the gentilic that goes with the title are missing. Taking into account the inscriptions of Sîn-gāmil and Itūr-šarrum from Diniktum, and Arīm-Līm of Mê-Turān, all of them from the Diyala region, it might be possible to restore *rabiān* [MAR.TU] in line 3 of Ayābum's brick. If Frayne's transliteration is accurate, and there are indeed two signs after *rabiān*, such restoration would be justified. There is still another *rabiān Amurrim* in an early letter from Ešnunna (AS 22 n° 3). The name of the sender is not written down, and the recipient is *be-*[*lí-ia*], 'my lord'. Whiting (1987: x) dates the text to the early Old Babylonian period, more precisely to the time of Bilalama (c. 1995 BC), who was contemporaneous with the kings of the Isin-Larsa period. The letter is very damaged and there is a lacuna from line six of the obverse to the beginning of the reverse. The sender informs us that an unspecified city is safe and asks for news. Whiting restores lines 5' to 7': *ki ša ra-bi-*[*a-an*(?)] / *A-mu-ri-im* ⌜x⌝-[ ] / *ti-šu* (...), 'You have [...] just like the *rabiān Amurrim*'. This restoration, however, is problematic. Granting that the linking of the extant and the restoration of the missing signs is correct, the word is written with the *bi* graph instead of *bí*. This was not the usual writing during the early Old Babylonian period. The presence of the word *Amurrum*, furthermore, does not guarantee the reading *rabiānum* in the previous line. In any event, this letter is unfortunately too fragmentary to shed any light on the interpretation of the *rabiān Amurrim*.

Finally, a seal impression from Ešnunna (RIM IV: 486) mentions a certain Abda-el with the title *rabiān Amurrim*.[16] The text was written in two columns and

15 Of course, there is no certainty that Didānum is, in this broken context, a personal name. However, such an interpretation is not impossible. According to *CAD* D: 165a, *sv. ditānu*, 'The word *di-ta-nu* explained as 'Sutean' in Malku I 235 (...), explained as 'Amorite' probably refers to the gentilic Tidanum and Tidnum(...), which occurs in WSem. personal names as *Ditana* (see Landsberger Fauna 94), *Didnum* (in *Su-mu-di-id-nu-um,* see Chiera, PBS 11/2 p. 119 n° 36).' During the Old Babylonian period, this noun appears as one of the constitutive elements of two royal names from the First Dynasty of Babylon, namely, Ammī-ditāna and Samsu-ditāna. Therefore, the *Didānum of our text could be interpreted either as a partial – or complete – personal name preceded by a dumu-sign (e.g. RIM IV: 683 and 485), or by an arad sign (e.g. *LIH* I 66).

16 This seal impression was first published in OIP 43: 145 seal legend n° 10. For photographs, hand

is a composite of three impressions on a letter envelope fragment (Whiting 1987: 26). It informs us that king Nūr-aḫum gave this seal as a gift to Ušašum, his son-in-law, and the son of Abda-el, the *rabiān Amurrim*. The presentation of seals by rulers to high officials and relatives is attested from southern Mesopotamia and Ešnunna.[17] Nūr-aḫum was a ruler of Ešnunna during the early Old Babylonian period (Edzard 1957: 67, 71), contemporary with Ibbi-Sîn of Ur and Išbi-Erra of Isin. It was possibly Išbi-Erra who appointed Nūr-aḫum to the throne after his predecessor had been defeated and Ešnunna was in danger of falling into the hands of Subartu (Whiting 1987: 24). Eight year names (OIP 43: 170, 172, 175, 176, and 184) and some inscriptions are known for the reign of Nūr-aḫum (RIM IV: 485–88). Ušašum and his father Abda-el also appear in other documents from Ešnunna (AS 22 ns. 11, 12, and 24), and in one text from Isin (BIN 9 316).[18]

Whiting's (1987) study of these sources is an important contribution to the history of Ešnunna during the early Old Babylonian period, and it reveals the family ties between Nūr-aḫum and Abda-el. Our inscription mentions that Ušašum married a daughter of Nūr-aḫum. We also know that still another of Abda-el's children, his daughter, married king Bilalama, the son of Kirikiri and possibly nephew to Nūr-aḫum. These weddings are undoubtedly diplomatic marriages, and they ought to be read in terms of the alliances that Old Babylonian rulers were continually interweaving.[19] After the fall of Ur, the political situation of Mesopotamia was unstable, and it nourished the hopes of those ambitious monarchs who tried to extend their domains. The rulers of a number of former subject kingdoms, therefore, sought to detach themselves from the southern capitals by strengthening diplomatic ties with neighboring states. Although Nūr-aḫum's degree of independence from Isin is difficult to ascertain, as a ruler of Ešnunna, he might have had or claimed certain royal prerogatives during this period. Whiting (1987: 27) has characterized Abda-el as an Amorite of high status, and he also implies that Abda-el

---

copy and a discussion of the iconography, see Franke (1977: 63, and microfiche C-8). It was later collated by Whiting (1987: 29).

17 In the case of Ešnunna, the extant examples include the seals presented by Kirikiri to Bilalama, his son; by Bilalama to Wusum-bēlī, a singer; by Ur-Ningišzida to Erra-bāni, his son; by Ibāl-pî-el to Nir-[ ], his wife, and by [ ] to Bēletī, (?). For a catalogue of these seals see Sollberger (1965: 29).

18 BIN 9 316 contains a list of Amorites who receive gifts, Abda-el and his son Ušašum are mentioned in lines 13-14. The document is dated to the 15th year of Išbi-Erra, it is part of the so-called Isin craft archive, and belongs to step 5 'disbursement of finished products', according to Van De Mieroop's (1987a: 10) typology. It is worth noticing that Fitzgerald (2002: 27) has recently suggested that Iemṣium, the person listed in ii: 17, is probably the homonymous king of Larsa.

19 Alliances were sealed by means of treaties, gift exchange, and marriages. Political marriages are best documented in the archives of Mari. But evidence from other kingdoms is also available. For instance, a daughter of Hammurabi of Babylon was married to Ṣillī-Sîn of Ešnunna (Durand 1992: 108). A marriage alliance was also established by Sîn-kāšid of Uruk, who married a daughter of Sūmû-la-el of Babylon (Falkenstein 1963: 6-7).

could have been an Amorite chief because Bilalama waited until Abda-el's death to fight the Amorites, as mentioned in one of Bilalama's year names. But the fact that Abda-el called himself *rabiān Amurrim* does not necessarily indicate that he was the leader of those Amorites whom Bilalama fought. Evidently, the term Amorite had many nuances and was used for different purposes in antiquity. There were hostile Amorites, but there were also kings who called themselves 'chief of the Amorites', as for instance Abī-sarē of Larsa.

Marriage was not the only strategy that related Abda-el to the rulers of Ešnunna. A gift exchange also took place between Abda-el and king Bilalama. A letter presumably issued by Ušašum, asks Bilalama to send him the gifts promised to Abda-el, and to dispatch presents for Abda-el's funeral separately (AS 22 n° 11). The sender of this letter refers to king Bilalama as 'brother'. In diplomatic parlance of that time, this could mean either a kinship relationship or that sender and addressee had the same rank.[20] That Abda-el's funeral was an important event is clear from the letter itself, for it states, 'all the envoys of the land are coming to the funeral of Abda-el, and all of the Amorites are gathering' (ll. 20-26). The apparent magnitude of Abda-el's burial may indicate that he was something more than a simple Amorite of high status. In addition, the diplomatic marriages that he established with the kings of Ešnunna together with the presents that he was expecting from Bilalama before he died, suggest that Abda-el could very well be considered an Amorite king. Those instances in which *rabiān Amurrim* is clearly a royal title in the Diyala region seem to substantiate Abda-el's kingship.

II. *RABIĀN RABABÎ*

Unlike *rabiān Amurrim,* the title *rabiān Rababî* is attested only once. It was bore by Itūr-Šamaš, the son of Iddin-ilum, ensi$_2$ of Kisurra (*MDOG* 15: 13). The inscription appears on bricks reported to have come from modern Abū-Ḥaṭab, ancient Kisurra. Scholars have interpreted the word *Rababî* in different ways. Thureau-Dangin (VAB I: 153) does not translate this term. Walther (1917: 109) interprets Itūr-Šamaš as being the *rabiānum* of Kisurra, and he objects to Meyer's opinion that Itūr-Šamaš was himself the ensi$_2$ of Kisurra. Edzard (1957: 136) thinks that Itūr-Šamaš was a 'mayor', for he comments '[*MDOG* 15: 13] ist die Bauinschrift eines Bürgermeisters von Rababûm'. More recently, Stol (1976a: 86) and Frayne (1990: 651) maintain that Itūr-Šamaš was the chief of the Rababeans, an ethnic group. Although the interpretation suggested by Walther and Edzard finds support in the fact that Rababî is attested with the city (uru) and place (ki) determinative,

20 The beginning of the letter reads as follows: 1. [*a-n*]*a Bi-la-la-ma* / 2. [*qí*]*-bí-ma* / 3. *a-*⌈*na*⌉*-ku a-ḫu-kà* / 4. *ši-ir-kà ù da-mu-kà* 'Speak to Bilalama, I am your brother, your flesh and blood' (AS 22 n° 11).

it is also possible to consider Rababî as a gentilic, as Stol did.[21] A collation of this text, seems to confirm Stol's point of view, for *Rababî* is not followed by the city determinative.[22] His hypothesis also finds support in the fact that during the Isin-Larsa period, several kings bore the title *rabiān* plus gentilic. Based on the 'Schriftduktus', Edzard (1957: 136) dates this brick to the early Old Babylonian period, around the time of Sūmû-el, Nūr-Adad, and Sîn-iddinam. Like many other Old Babylonian cities, Kisurra was independent from time to time, to be finally conquered and annexed to Larsa, according to Rīm-Sîn's 20th year formula. Itūr-Šamaš was possibly a prince by the time of this inscription, since the text mentions his father, Iddin-ilum, as the $ensi_2$ of Kisurra. Later in his life, Itūr-Šamaš must have succeeded his father as a ruler, because several tablets excavated at Kisurra record a number of Itūr-Šamaš's year names (e.g. Kienast 1978). No other inscription of this ruler is known, but there is a seal impression of one of his servants on a British Museum tablet.[23]

III. *RABIĀN AMNĀNIM*

A tablet from Sippar has the seal impression with the otherwise unrecorded title *rabiān Amnān-Šadlaš* (CT 48 83). This is a message releasing a man and a family from the *dikûtu* agricultural duty of the men of Šadlaš. The text states, 'Erīb-Sîn, son of Puzur-Akšak, and the household of Irra-gāmil are exempt in the recruitment of the men of Šadlaš for the harvest.' The document is sealed by Sūmû-Šamaš, the son of Apil-Sîn, the *rabiān Amnān Šadlaš*. Erīb-Sîn, the son of Puzur-Akšak, is known from several other documents.[24] He was active during the reigns of Sîn-muballiṭ and Hammurabi, and his sister Lamassī was a *nadītum*-woman of Šamaš

21 For the city of Rababî see, for instance, BIN 2 77: 33, YOS 12 434: 4, BIN 7 182: 3 and YOS 12 126: 5 (RGTC III: 192).

22 Different readings were suggested for the last sign of the word *Rababî-ma,* thus, *Ra-ba-bí-***x** (Walther 1917: 109), *Ra-ba-bí-**ma*** (Thureau-Dangin 1972: 52), and *Ra-ba-bí-*$\mathbf{ke_4}$ (Stol 1976a: 86). More recently, Frayne (1990: 651) has given fuller details about the history of these bricks and the reading of the last sign of *Rababî*. According to him, 'None of the Itūr-Šamaš bricks could be located in Istanbul or Berlin. The inscription was collated from Babylon photo 1145, which shows the brick which was published in *MDOG* 15: 13. The last sign in line 3 was read as $\mathbf{ke_4}$ by Hommel, Stol, and Heltzer. Collation of the excavation photo reveals a clear *–**ma***'.

23 The tablet dates to the first year of Manna-balti-el, king of the Mananâ dynasty (see RIM IV: 652).

24 He is mentioned, for instance, in CT 2 22: 2 (Sm) and CT 2 46: 6 (Sm 14) concerning a litigation for the division of the profits between Erīb-Sîn and the heirs of his deceased partner, Irra-gāmil (see Veenker 1974: 14 note 47). In CT 2 26: 2 (Sm 19) Erīb-Sîn inherits his father's house. CT 2 28: 1 (Ḫa) is about *tappûtu*-partnership with Nūr-Šamaš. CT 4 6a: 7, CT 6 34b: 5 both are litigation documents. CT 8 43a: 3, 8, 18 (Ḫa) is litigation between Erīb-Sîn and the heirs of Irra-gāmil over a slave girl. In VAS 9 18: 3 (Ḫa 22) and 46: 11 he delivers barley to the temple of Sîn. In VAS 9 48: 11 (Ḫa 32) he is a witness.

in Sippar.[25] Stol (1976a: 86–87) cites Sūmû-Šamaš's seal as evidence for *rabiānum* followed by a tribal name. He compares Amnān-Šadlaš to Sippar-Amnānum, with Amnānum referring to Amorite nomads who had settled in a section of Sippar. Stol also adduces the cases of Baḫlukulim (lugal *Tu-tu-ub*^{ki} *ù ma-at Am-na-nim*), and Sîn-kāšid and Ilum-gāmil (both lugal *Am-na-nu-um*), who are 'kings of the Amnānum'. In a letter to Sîn-muballiṭ (Falkenstein 1963: 56) there is a mention of the Amnān-Yaḫrur which, according to Stol, parallels the Amnān-Šadlaš. From this set of comparisons, Stol arrives at the conclusion that Sūmû-Šamaš was the sheikh of a tribal group, the Amnānum who lived in or near the city of Šadlaš. Stol himself sees the difficulty in this interpretation, because a tribal name followed by a city name is unusual. Despite this, he states, 'CT 48 83 bearing the seal impression of the sheikh of the Amnān-Šadlaš seems to suggest that part of the population of Šadlaš led a nomadic life' (p. 86).

However we may consider the 'tribal', 'nomadic', or 'ethnic' components of the town of Šadlaš, there is no implication that the *rabiānum* of the place is anything other than an urban authority. Although this is not the place to discuss the city of Šadlaš, we do know that parts of Sippar were named Amnānum and Yaḫrurum, and the same situation might have also applied to Šadlaš. The question is not who gave the name to these places, but whether the population of cities consisted of 'nomads' who were led by 'sheikhs'. There is unfortunately no archaeological evidence from Šadlaš, which was situated in the Diyala region (Harris 1976: 148), and its exact location remains unknown (Charpin 2004: 97 n. 365). Nonetheless, in Sippar-Amnānum, also named after a 'tribal group', the names of wide streets where houses were located as well as the existence of a city wall and gates are known (Harris 1975: 15). In her article on foreigners in Old Babylonian Sippar, Harris (1976: 150) refers to CT 48 83. According to her, Sūmû-Šamaš was the *rabiānum* of Amnān-Šadlaš. From this study we learn that Puzur-Akšak, the father of Erīb-Sîn, and Irra-gāmil were originally not from Sippar but from Šadlaš. In Sippar, Erīb-Sîn was engaged in overland and city trade, and in the time of Sîn-muballiṭ (1812–1793 BC) he had a partnership with Irra-gāmil. A number of lawsuits in which Erīb-Sîn and the descendants of Irra-gāmil are involved show that the dealings among these persons continued after Irra-gāmil's death (e.g. CT 2 22, 46 [Sm 14], CT 8 43a [Ḫa]). In CT 48 83 Irra-gāmil's household is mentioned after the head of the family even though he had already died.[26] As natives of Šadlaš, Erīb-Sîn and the members of Irra-gāmil's household were responsible for performing the *dikûtum*-service in the harvesting of that city, but

25 Lamassī was one of the *nadītums* of considerable wealth (see Harris 1962: 9 and 1970: 317).

26 According to Harris (1976: 148–50), Irra-gāmil died at some point during the reign of Sîn-muballiṭ. Judging from the lawsuits, his family included two sons, two daughters (at least one of them, Iltani, was a *nadītum* of Šamaš), two wives, and Irra-gāmil's brother.

CT 48 83 granted them an exemption from the duty. It is difficult to believe, therefore, that Sūmû-Šamaš, who rolled his seal on the tablet, was a tribal sheikh because harvesting is usually not a nomad's affair. Under these circumstances, Harris's suggestion that Sūmû-Šamaš was the *rabiānum* of the city of Amnān-Šadlaš seems more plausible.

This interpretation, however, does not solve the problem of why the city of Šadlaš is mentioned as Amnān-Šadlaš on the seal, whereas the service is characterized as the *dikûtum* of the men of the city of Šadlaš. It is also remarkable that there seems to be no other attestation of a city Amnān-Šadlaš (see RGTC III: 215). Things are further complicated by the fact that the seal impression of Sūmû-Šamaš does not correspond to the legend of extant seals of other *rabiānums* who were city authorities. There is, nonetheless, one possible exception to this: the seal of Ambuna-aḫi, to which I will refer later. The typical seal of a *rabiānum* acting as a city authority or 'mayor' always follows the pattern PN (i.e. *rabiānum*'s name), dumu PN (father's name), arad DN (servant of the god[s]'s name[s]). Thus the title *rabiānum* is not included as part of the seal legend in any of the existing instances.[27] Rather, Sūmû-Šamaš's seal resembles Itūr-šarrum's,

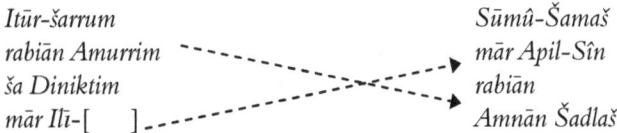

Itūr-šarrum	*Sūmû-Šamaš*
rabiān Amurrim	*mār Apil-Sîn*
ša Diniktim	*rabiān*
mār Ilī-[ ]	*Amnān Šadlaš*

The intersecting arrows indicate that the *rabiān* Amnān-Šadlaš could actually have been Apil-Sîn. From the parallel between these two seal impressions, still another comparison of the titles suggests itself,

rabiān Amurrim ša Diniktim	= *rabiān Amurrim* of Diniktum
rabiān Amnān Šadlaš	= *rabiān Amnānim* of Šadlaš

The gentilic Amnānum is clearly a bound form. Therefore, the construct chain *rabiān Amnān Šadlaš* substitutes for the genitival construction *rabiān Amnānim ša Šadlaš*, with the determinative pronoun *ša*, 'the one of'. Itūr-šarrum and Sîn-gāmil, both kings of Diniktum, use a similar title, namely, *rabiān Amurrim ša Diniktim*. It is then likely that *rabiān Amnān Šadlaš* was the title borne by the ruler of the city

27 Thus, for example, ^{d}Utu-dingir / dumu *Wa-tar-I-ku-nu-um* / arad AN.AN.MAR.TU (CT 47 19 + 19a); *Ra-ab-bu-ḫa-du-ú* / dumu *Ta-ri-du-um* / arad ^{d}EN.ZU (CT 47 58); *Im-gur-rum* / dumu *Ig-mil-*^{d}EN.ZU / arad ^{d}Nin-šubur; and *Sa-*⌈*ar*⌉*-ri-ia* / dumu *I-zi-ga-bu*(?) / arad *ša* ^{d}EN.ZU (both in CT 48 44); *Nu-úr-*^{d}Utu / dumu *Zi-ia-tum* / arad AN.AN.MAR.TU (CT 48 70); *Na-bi-ì-lí-šu* / dumu *E-te-el-li-ia* / arad AN.AN.MAR.TU / *ù* ^{d}Nin-⌈si$_4$⌉-an-na (TIM 4 5/6), etc. I will refer to the *rabiānums*' sealings, in more detail, later.

Šadlaš. The lack of other inscriptions of this ruler can be attributed to the fact that Šadlaš has not been excavated.[28] If Harris (1976: 150) is right dating CT 48 83 to the early Hammurabi period, more precisely Hammurabi's fifth year, then it is possible that kings who ruled over independent cities were still using the title *rabiān* plus gentilic. Sîn-gāmil of Diniktum, for instance, bore the title *rabiān Amurrim* at about the same time.

IV. *RABIĀN BĀBTĪŠU*

An inscription on four stamped bricks found at modern Isān-Dhadāk, ancient Mutalû, 18 miles north-east of Kiš, has the title *rabiān bābtīšu*. Of the four bricks that Stephen Langdon (1924: 40) reported, only two could be found in the Ashmolean Museum (Frayne 1990: 659). The text mentions that GA/BI-NI/IR-*ma-bi-de-e*, son of Masalum, the *rabiān bābtīšu*, built the wall of Mutalû. The reading of the first personal name is uncertain, and there seems to be no other attestation of it. The unique title *rabiān bābtīšu* is difficult to interpret because the meaning of the word *bābtum* itself is controversial, and it apparently conveys different nuances. The Akkadian dictionaries render *bābtum* as 'quarter of a city, neighborhood, or ward' (*CAD* B: 9b, *AHw* B: 94b). But Gelb (1968: 43) suggests that in certain cases *bābtum* could have denoted 'small encampments, each probably restricted to individuals belonging to a certain tribal grouping'. Similarly, Donbaz and Yoffee (1986) speculate that *bābtum* could have been a lineage group. Following Gelb's interpretation, Stol (1976a: 80) infers that there were *rabiānum*-sheikhs heading small encampments, and that 'particular "sections", consolidated as "wards" of a settlement, could have their own *rabiānum*, now "alderman"'. This would explain, according to Stol, the existence of more than one *rabiānum* in a city. This interpretation, however, seems to reverse Gelb's proposal, because Gelb states that in his list of Amorites *bābtum* cannot denote so large a section as a

28 Yet two inscriptions of another king of Šadlaš, Sūmû-Amnānim, are known. The first appears on two stamped bricks found at Iščhali; the second, on an object that was possibly a bench for offerings. In both cases Sūmû-Amnānim is characterized as lugal *Ša-ad-la* [*aš*^{ki}] (see RIM IV: 694-9). Still a third king from Šadlaš, Sūmû-numḫim, is known from a treaty that he concluded with Ammī-dušur, the king of Nērebtum (see Greengus 1979: 74). A king Sūmû-numḫim ruled over Marad (Edzard 1957: 127) and has been associated with the one that signed the treaty with Ammī-dušur. Based on tablets found in Marad from the time of Sūmû-la-el of Babylon, Jacobsen (1940: 124) established the synchronism between Sūmû-numḫim of Šadlaš and Sūmû-la-el of Babylon (see also Greengus 1979: 20 n. 97). However, this is problematic because the only reason why Sūmû-numḫim is considered king of Šadlaš is because most scholars have taken Ammī-dušur as king of Nerēbtum and have assigned Šadlaš to Sūmû-numḫim (Greengus 1979: 22). If Sūmû-numḫim was king of Šadlaš, the chronological sequence is, then, Sūmû-numḫim contemporary of Sūmû-la-el, and Sūmû-Šamaš, contemporary of Hammurabi. The place of king Sūmû-Amnānim in the chronology of Šadlaš remains to be determined.

quarter of the city. In other words, for Gelb the Amorite *bābtums* were smaller than city wards. In contrast, the hypothesis of a consolidation process would imply that Mesopotamian cities were mostly the result of nomadic sedentarization. It seems unlikely, furthermore, that a 'sheikh' or even an 'alderman' should claim to have built the city wall of Mutalû. Frayne's (1990: 658) remark that this inscription belongs to the local city ruler is pertinent. Then Donbaz and Yoffee's suggestion to regard *bābtum* as a lineage group fits nicely into the pattern *rabiānum* + gentilic, in this particular case, 'chief of his lineage group'.

V. *RABIĀNUM* WITHOUT A GENTILIC OR A CITY NAME

A seal legend that includes the title *rabiānum* was published in transliteration by Charpin (1985b: 191), while Parayre (1985: 233–35) provided a photograph, hand copy, and an iconographic description. Both studies agree on dating this cylinder seal to the early Old Babylonian period, Isin-Larsa, according to Charpin, or pre-Hammurabi according to Parayre. The three-lines inscription reads: 'Ambuna-aḫi, son of Išānūm, *rabiānum*'. For Charpin the name Išānūm means 'powerful', and he comments on the etymology of Ambuna-aḫi. Apparently, none of these names are attested elsewhere. Charpin compares this seal with that of CT 48 83 and concludes 'Ici, toutefois, le nom de la tribu ou de la ville dont le propriétaire du sceau était "cheikh" ou "maire" (…) n'est pas indiqué'. Similarly, Parayre suggests that 'L'amorite Ambuna-aḫi fut alors maire ou cheikh, fonction légitimée par ce cylindre de présentation au roi' (p. 234). Ambuna-aḫi's cylinder is certainly more difficult to interpret than the seal on CT 48 83 because it is of unknown provenance and it lacks any contextual reference. As already mentioned, none of the seal impressions of *rabiānum* who acted as city 'mayors' bears the official's title. If our line of reasoning as regards the *rabiān Amnān Šadlaš* is correct, and in view of the fact that only the seals of rulers include the title *rabiānum* in their inscriptions, it seems reasonable to conclude that the cylinder seal under consideration belonged to a king or his son.

Rabiānum with no other specification further appears in the earliest dated document mentioning this title (BIN 9 199). The tablet was issued on the 24th day of the first month of king Išbi-Erra's 32nd year. This text deals with leather products from the so-called Isin craft archive of the early Old Babylonian period. It presumably originated from a workshop located at the city of Isin. In this case, Birbirrū, the *rabiānum*, and a certain Iddin-Amurrum received two goat skin water-bags.[29] As is the case with other tablets from this archive, the interpretation of this document is problematic because there is no verb. It is difficult, therefore, to

29 The obverse of BIN 9 199 reads: 7. 2 ^{kuš}ummu máš gal / 8. ki *Bir$_5$-bi-ru-ma* / 9. *ra-bí-a-nu-um-ma* / 10. *ù I-din-*^{d}MAR.TU / 11. *Šu-*^{d}Nin-mug maškim / 12. šà é-gal / 13-14. date

ascertain whether the text records a receipt or a disbursement (see Van De Mieroop 1987a: 9). But the presence of a maškim-official seems to indicate that Birbirrū, the *rabiānum*, and Iddin-Amurrum received the products.[30] Van De Mieroop (1987a: 98) points out that a maškim was often present 'when goods are issued to foreigners, mostly Amorites'. This characterization of the Amorites as foreigners is surprising, especially because the tablet bears an Išbi-Erra date, and this king, the founder of the Isin dynasty, was possibly an Amorite himself. For his part, Buccellati (1966: 309) seems to consider the possibility that Birbirrū was an urban official, for he translates *rabiānum* as 'mayor (?)', and comments 'we also find for the first time the title *rabiānum* attested, possibly at least, in connection with the Amorites'. On the contrary, Stol (1976a: 85) affirms 'the word means here probably "sheikh"', and he takes the text as the basis for his evolutionary theory and henceforth to substantiate the tribal origin of the *rabiānum* office.

A comparison with the *rabiān Amurrim* Abda-el in the Diyala region may help elucidate the role of Birbirrū. As we have seen, Abda-el had family ties and exchanged gifts with kings of Ešnunna who were contemporary with Išbi-Erra of Isin. Abda-el and his son Ušašum are also mentioned in a document from the Isin craft archive dated to Išbi-Erra 15th year (BIN 9 316). This text is a list of Amorites who received official gifts (níg-šu-tag$_4$-a) such as containers with oil and leather bags. Madeleine Fitzgerald (2002: 26–28) has noticed that Iemṣium, mentioned as a ruler in the 'Larsa King List', appears in the same tablet with Abda-el, and in another document from the same archive, Iemṣium gets a leather bag (BIN 9 217, Išbi-Erra 32). King Iemṣium of Larsa, Abda-el, the *rabiān Amurrim*, and Birbirrū, the *rabiānum*, are then Amorite leaders or Amorite kings to whom Išbi-Erra gave presents. This is meaningful from a historical perspective. In a letter of Ibbi-Sîn, the last king of Ur, to Puzur-Numušda, Ibbi-Sîn expects that the Amorites will help him against Išbi-Erra. But the Amorites joined Išbi-Erra instead (Whiting 1987: 25). These documents from the Isin craft archives show the diplomatic ties that Išbi-Erra was interweaving to fulfill his political goals, and they also show the no less-ambitious leaders who were willing to co-operate to accomplish their own political aspirations. The 'Larsa King List' corroborates Iemṣium's royal status, but Amorite rulers who did not make it to such an official record may escape our notice. This could very well have been the case of the *rabiānum* Birbirrū.

30 The exact role of the maškim is not completely understood. B. R. Foster (1982: 79) suggests that in the Sargonic period, the maškim was 'supervisor of a transaction'. S. Kang (1972: 255) thinks that in texts from Drehem maškim could be translated as 'the requisitioner', because it 'denotes the fact that specific authority had been given to an official to expend government property'.

VI. THE ALLEGED *RABIĀN NĀRIM*

The title *rabiān nārim*, 'chief of the river district', appears in a two-columned votive inscription written in Sumerian (*LIH* I 66), possibly from Sippar. The slab was dedicated to the goddess Ašratum by Itūr-ašdum, the *rabiān* íd ⌈x⌉ [ ], son of Šubān-ilān, for the well being of Hammurabi. Walther (1917: 109) was unable to decide whether the signs after *rabiānum*, of which only íd is visible, referred to a river district, or whether it was part of a place name. Stol (1976a: 83) has restored the line *rabiān* ^{íd}*S*[*í-lá-ku*(?)], a reading most Assyriologist now follow (e.g. RGTC III: 307, RIM IV: 359). In this inscription, Hammurabi is characterized as lugal MAR.TU, 'king of the Amorites'. Stol suggests that Hammurabi adopted this title after the destruction of the city walls of Mari and Malgium, which took place in his 34th year (c. 1758 BC). The date is important because the latest reference to the title *rabiān Amurrim* available to us, the inscription of Sîn-gāmil of Diniktum, is contemporaneous with the first years of Hammurabi, that is, before the consolidation of his all-encompassing kingdom. If that is the case, then it is possible to assume that Hammurabi adopted the title *šar Amurrim*, 'king of the Amorites', because it subsumed and replaced the title *rabiān Amurrim* earlier held simultaneously by kings of different cities.[31] This titulary change could have been intended to denote that Hammurabi had conquered and subjugated those independent rules who bore each the title *rabiānum* + gentilic. If Itūr-ašdum's inscription dates indeed from the late part of Hammurabi's reign, it seems unlikely that Itūr-ašdum was one of the Amorite leaders competing for power. The personal name Itūr-ašdum is well attested in Sippar documents, and there is even an Itūr-ašdum, *rabiānum* of Ḫalḫalla, recorded in a lawsuit dated to the 27th year of Hammurabi (CT 48 19). This Itūr-ašdum is, however, the son of Sîn-rēmēni. The patronymics of other homonymous names from Sippar do not coincide with that of the Itūr-ašdum of the votive inscription.

The title *rabiānum* in connection with watercourses also appears in two Old Babylonian letters. Thus in an official communication about transportation of grain to the city of Larsa dated to the first year of Rīm-Sîn, every *rabiānum* of the river bank (*rabiān rabiān ša kišādim*) is requested to send an escort city by city so that the grain arrive safely (AbB 10 67). In his edition of this letter, Kraus (1985: 73) wonders whether *kišādum* is used here in a generic sense or whether it designates a specific area of a river or canal.[32] As I understand this text, the connection

31 Judging from the published royal inscriptions, no other king bears the title lugal MAR.TU. It is interesting to notice, however, that Kudur-Mabuk is called ad-da kur MAR.TU, 'father of the Amorite land', in certain inscriptions of his son, Warad-Sîn (see RIM IV: 206, 208).

32 He comments, 'Der Transport erfolgte wahrscheinlich auf einer Haupt-Wasserstraße. Oder bezeichnet *kišādum* hier etwa eine bestimmte Gegend an einem bestimmten Flusse/Kanale, ist also Art *nomen proprium*?'

between *rabiānum* and the river/canal bank is only circumstantial. In this letter, an official who is most probably in Larsa gives instructions to another official to get ready for the transportation of grain. The recipient of this message is then supposed to perform two tasks. He has first to inform every *rabiānum* of those cities on the river bank that the cereal is coming, and second he has to send an escort to every city in order to protect the cargo. These protective measures were important in the water transportation of goods because, as Charpin (1983–84: 105) has shown, the closing of watercourses was one of the strategies employed to block the circulation of merchandise.[33] This is particularly relevant in times of political instability, but prevention might have also been necessary in case of robbery. *Rabiānum* in this context could refer either to rulers of cities that were under the domain of Rīm-Sîn of Larsa, or to local authorities of cities belonging to Rīm-Sîn's kingdom.

The second letter in which *rabiānum* is related to a river bank is a tablet of unknown provenance (AbB 13 109) possibly from Larsa (see Van Soldt 1994: iv). Here, a certain Nabium-mālik states that the man of the Kittum temple who will come to collect the silver should not do it himself. Instead the *rabiānum* of gú ^íd^Idigna has to gather the silver and give it to the temple envoy. Even though gú ^íd^Idigna, or *kišād Idiglat*, literally means 'the Tigris bank', the context of the letter seems to refer to a city located in the area. Mentions of a wall in or nearby gú ^íd^Idigna appear in two year formulae, Apil-Sîn 12a and Hammurabi 42. Most important is that the letter clearly states that the *rabiānum* has to collect the silver of the city (kù-babbar *ālim*), instead of the temple official. The explicit reference to the city seems to leave little room for doubting that we are dealing with the headman of a city. The lack of background information limits our understanding of the circumstances under which the events described took place. It is clear, nonetheless, that the sender of this letter considers it more convenient that a city authority, the *rabiānum*, undertakes the task instead of a city outsider. The fact that such a request is made points to the unusual character of the situation, one should expect that under normal conditions, the temple representative would have collected the silver himself.

The question that arises from these examples is then whether or not **rabiān nārim*, 'chief of the river district', was a title, as Stol (1976a: 83–85) seems to imply when he refers to the 'unique title *rabiān* íd G[N]'. Stol approaches this problem from two different angles. In the first place, he compares *rabiān nārim* and the also rare *abi nārim* ('official in charge of the canal') of the Diyala region with the title *šāpir nārim* ('governor of the river system') as attested in the 'Laws of Ešnunna'.[34]

33 Charpin (1983–84: 105) refers specifically to goods going from Ešnunna to Larsa, which had been withheld by the *šakkanakkum* Ipqu-Ištar in Diniktum.

34 For these translations see *CAD* N/1: 370 and Š/1: 454.

What follows as a result is the hypothesis that the *šāpir nārim* is a representative of a centralized and well-organized government, whereas the *rabiān nārim* could have held only local jurisdiction in irrigation activities. The title *šāpir nārim*, however, is well attested in Old Babylonian documents, while *rabiān nārim* GN appears only in a broken line of a votive inscription. In the second place, Stol considers the possibility that Itūr-ašdum, the *rabiān nārim*, could have supervised or controlled the Amorites in the river Silakku area because in this inscription Hammurabi is called 'king of the Amorites'. If Itūr-ašdum was indeed an Amorite leader who acknowledged Hammurabi's kingship by means of a votive inscription, then it seems unlikely that he would have been in charge of local irrigation. Although the material at our disposal unfortunately does not allow us to comment further on the *rabiānum* Itūr-ašdum, it is worth emphasizing that there is no conclusive evidence to support the existence of a *rabiān nārim* office.

RABIĀNUM AS A ROYAL TITLE DURING THE EARLY OLD BABYLONIAN PERIOD

The analysis of the extant data shows that during the early Old Babylonian period several kings used the title *rabiānum* often followed by a gentilic. This is the case with well-known rulers such as Zabāya and Abī-sarē of Larsa, Itūr-šarrum and Sîn-gāmil of Diniktum, and with other rulers of cities like Mutalû, Kisurra, and Šadlaš, from whom only a small number of royal inscriptions are available to us. Other bearers of the *rabiānum* title seem to have been either kings of unknown cities or ethnic leaders, but since we do not have enough information about them, it is difficult to ascertain their exact status. Table I maps the chronological and geographical distribution of *rabiānum* as a royal title. When studying political history, we are often limited to tracing only those kings whose cities were excavated or whose inscriptions were recovered. As Van Driel (1969: 79) pointed out some years ago, we know very little about small independent local rulers. This lack of knowledge, however, should not prevent us from granting them royal status. Kraus (1974: 236) has already argued against the idea that a 'proper' king should bear the title 'lugal'.[35] And Charpin (1999: 106) has recently criticized what he considers 'une définition beaucoup trop restreinte de "roi" par les Assyriologues'.

The welter of shifting powers that followed the fall of Ur left an imprint on the Mesopotamian political arena. Political atomization was the rule, although the idea of a unified Mesopotamia was fondly kept and further promoted in the literary

35 In Kraus' (1974: 236) words, 'Wäre König nur derjenige, welcher sich sumerisch lugal, akkadisch *šarrum* nennt bzw. so genannt wird, so hätte es zu Beginn der altbabylonischen Zeit nach dem Sturze der III. Dynastie von Ur in Mesopotamien nur einen König gegeben, den König von Isin.'

tradition. In the early Old Babylonian period, other terms were also used alongside *šarrum*. Such is the case with ensi$_2$ (*iššiakkum*) mainly in Aššur and Ešnunna, gìr-nita$_2$ (*šakkanakkum*) in Dēr, *rubûm* in Ešnunna, and *rabiānum* in both northern and southern Mesopotamia.[36] Some of these titles are listed together in the curse formula of one of Yaḫdun-Līm's inscription from Mari (Dossin 1955: 1–17),

> '[2-5](he who) erases my name, or has it erased, (and) writes his own name which was not there (before), or has it written (for him), [6-7]or because of the curses he instructs somebody else to do so, [8]that man, whether he is a *šarrum* (=king), [9]a *šakkanakkum* (=king), [10]a *rabiānum* (=king), [11]or anybody else, [12-15]may Enlil, the judge of the gods, diminish his kingship among all of the kings'.

Other translators have rendered the titles listed in lines 8-10 as if they were arranged in a hierarchical order, that is, *šarrum*, 'king', *šakkanakkum*, 'governor', and *rabiānum*, 'mayor' (e.g. Dossin 1955: 16; Frayne 1990: 607; Van De Mieroop 1999c: 153).[37] It should be noticed, however, that the abstract substantive *šarrūssu*, 'his kingship', in line 14 clearly qualifies each and every bearer of the previous titles. Interpreting *šarrum*, *šakkanakkum*, and *rabiānum* hierarchically is, therefore, anachronistic, because the inscription of Yaḫdun-Līm is pre-Hammurabi, that is, from the time when all these titles still meant 'king'. It is only later when the titles *iššiakkum* and *rabiānum* lost any traces of royal connotation. The first later designated an agricultural official, and the second, the 'mayor' of a city.

The earliest attestations of the word *rabiānum* relate to rulers of cities and ethnic groups. The title was used in both northern and southern Mesopotamia from the Isin-Larsa period presumably until the first years of Hammurabi's reign. None of these early texts allows us to track the origins of the *rabiānum* in his role as one of the city officials to an 'alleged' nomadic institution in which 'sheikhs' presided over tribal groups settled in urban centers. Nor do they record the coexistence within the same city of *rabiānums* who were 'sheikh of the nomads' and *rabiānums* who were 'burgomasters'. What written records show is that during the

36 In earlier studies of the Ešnunna documents it was unclear whether *rubûm* was a royal name or a royal title (for a summary of these views see Greengus 1979: 13, n. 15). More recently, however, Charpin (1985a: 62–64) has shown that *rubûm* was not only a title used by the kings of Ešnunna, but it was even adopted by Yaḫdun-Līm of Mari. According to Charpin, 'La solution consiste peut-être à admettre que Yaḫdun-Līm imita l'usage d'Ešnunna en adoptant le titre *rubûm*, alors qu'avant lui les souverains de Mari portaient celui de *šakkanakkum*' (p. 64). For a discussion of the titles gìr-nita$_2$ and lugal in Mari see Gelb (1992: 161).

37 Another inscription of Yaḫdun-Līm has a similar, though more simplified, curse: 55. *ša te-em-me-ni-ia* / 56. *ú-na-ak-ka-ru-ma* / 57. *te-em-me-ni-šu* / 58. *i-ša-ak-ka-nu* / 59. *a-wi-lum šu-ú* / 60. *lu* lugal *lu* ensi$_2$ / 61. *Anum ù* ^{d}En-líl / 62. *er-re-tam le-mu-ut-tam* / 63. *li-ru-ru-šu*. [55-58]'The one who removes my foundation deposits and puts his own foundation deposits (in their places), [59-63]that man, whether he is a lugal or an ensi$_2$ – may the gods Anum and Enlil inflict a terrible curse on him' (RIM IV: 603).

Old Babylonian period the word *rabiānum* designated two different authorities. On the one hand it was a royal title used by several kings. On the other, it was a post held only temporarily by certain representatives of local authorities. These two institutions were per se completely unrelated, except for the fact that in both cases the title denotes leadership.

THE *RABIĀNUM* AS A CITY AUTHORITY

The uneven and fragmentary character of the extant evidence makes it difficult to trace certain characteristics of the *rabiānum* office such as the length of time the post was held, or the way it was designated. The issuing of cuneiform documents pertained to record-keeping practices in temple and palace institutions. Individuals, on their part, resorted to written contracts in case a potential legal claim might arise from any of the parties to the transaction. Most Mesopotamian economic and legal documents share these features. Thus we know about those people engaged in specific activities under the exceptional circumstances that required them to be recorded. Letters provide us with the kind of information that is absent from other laconic sources, but our lack of background knowledge about the issues discussed in these messages is often problematic. The interaction of individuals beyond these tablets remains usually unknown.

Rabiānum sources have their own particular problems. In several instances, the title appears on the envelope but not on the tablet itself. If the envelope is not preserved, the *rabiānum* without a title might pass unnoticed.[38] Sometimes it is also difficult to identify the city where a *rabiānum* was in charge, for the city name does not always follow the title. This is also apparent when dealing with neighboring towns. Prosopography alone may not help distinguish the sites because residents from nearby places frequently interacted. The dealings among the inhabitants of Sippar and Ḫalḫalla are examples.[39] Homonyms are often misleading, especially when the provenance of the tablet cannot be determined

38 Thus for instance, Šamaš-ilī is the first witness on the tablet, but only the envelope mentions the title (CT 47 19: 20, Sm). It is because of the case that we know that the *nadītum* Ruttum was the daughter of the *rabiānum* Ḫayaum (MHET II/2 n° 323, Ḫa). A person may appear as the first witness with or without the title in documents issued around the same time. In those cases where the title is missing, it is possible that the man was acting as *rabiānum* (e.g. MHET II/1 n° 81: 16 igi Išme-Eraḫ *rabiānum* [Sm], and MHET II/1 n° 82: 11 igi Išme-Eraḫ [Sm]; YOS 14 106: 19 igi Dadi-išme-el *rabiānum*, UCP 10/3 6: 16 igi Dadi-išme-el *rabiānum* <title only on the envelope>, and YOS 14 107: 17 igi Dadi-išme-el, all of them dated to Abdi-Eraḫ I 'xx'/VI/Ø). But, of course, this assumption could be misleading.

39 See, for instance, the list of *rabiānums* from Sippar and Ḫalḫalla produced by Harris (1975: 61–62) and the corrections by Stol (1976a: 148). Stol (1998: 435–37) has recently studied the *rabiānums* of Ḫalḫalla and suggested that some documents attributed to Sippar are from Ḫalḫalla.

Table 1. Chronology of *rabiānum* as a royal title

				Diyala Region				
	LARSA	KISURRA	MUTALÛ	BATIR	DINIKTUM	MÊ-TURĀN	ŠADLAŠ	UNKNOWN
2000 1950/1800								**Abda-el** ***rabiān Amurrim*** Ešnunna region (Nūr –aḫum) *AS* 22: 26
1700/1800	**Zabāya** (1941–1933) ***rabiān Amurrim*** *Syria* 45:243 RIM 4:112 Steinkeller 2004a: 146 **Abī-sarē** (1905-1895) ***rabiān Amurrim*** UET 8 65 YOS 14 seal 93	**Itūr-Šamaš** ***rabiān Rababî*** *MDOG* 15: 13			**Itūr-šarrum** ***rabiān Amurrim*** AS 22: 119			
Sūmû-la-el 1880–1845						**Arīm-Līm** dumu **Ibāya** ***rabiān Amurrim*** RIM 4: 700		

				Diyala Region				
	LARSA	KISURRA	MUTALÛ	BATIR	DINIKTUM	MÊ-TURĀN	ŠADLAŠ	UNKNOWN
Hammurabi (1792–1750)					**Sîn-gāmil** ***rabiān Amurrim*** *Sumer* 2:20		**Sūmû-Šamaš** dumu **Apil-Sîn** ***rabiān Amnānim*** CT 48 83	
No date			**GA/BA-NI/IR-ma-bi-de-e** dumu **Masalum** ***rabiān bābtīšu*** Langdon *Kiš*: 40	**Ayābum** dumu **A-[ ]** ***rabiān* x x** RIM 4: 702				**Ambuna-aḫi** ***rabiānum*** *RA* 79: 191 **Ammī-Ištamar** ***rabiān Amurrim*** [D]idānum RIM IV: 810

with precision and there is no paternal tie or geographical name in relation to the bearer of the title. The case of the *rabiānum* Aḫum-ṭābum is worth mentioning. He is well attested in documents from Dilbat during the reigns of Ammī-ditāna and Ammī-ṣaduqa. The extant texts mentioning Aḫum-ṭābum date from Ammī-ditāna 2 to Ammī-ṣaduqa 2 (c. 1681 –1644 BC), a period of around 35 years that could be within the lifetime of the same person. It is thanks to seal impressions, however, that we can identify two different *rabiānums* called Aḫum-ṭābum. The first occurs during the early reign of Ammī-ditāna and was the son of Sa-gi(?)-[ ]. The second was active from Ammī-ditāna 34 to Ammī-ṣaduqa 2 (1649–1644 BC), and his father was Šamaš-nāṣir (see Desrochers 1978: 368). There is still another Aḫum-ṭābum, *rabiānum*, the son of Awīl-arši, presumably from northern Mesopotamia. His name appears in contracts from Samsu-iluna 19 and 24 (c. 1730–1725 BC). Unfortunately, in other instances all these clues are missing. Therefore, in documents of unknown provenance, without seal impressions, or paternal filiation, it is difficult to decide whether two homonymous names bearing the title *rabiānum* refer to the same person.

LENGTH OF THE APPOINTMENT TO THE *RABIĀNUM* POSITION

There are different opinions about the length of time this office was held. In his analysis of the archive of the soldier Ubarrum from Ṣupur-Šubula, Benno Landsberger (1955: 127) inferred, based on the list of witnesses, that the *rabiānum* office rotated year by year among the city elders (*šībūt ālim*). Two decades later, Harris (1975: 60), in partial confirmation of Landsberger's suggestion, postulated that in Sippar the office could be 'held for only one year, but might be held several times'. Szlechter (1958: 109), however, questioned the assumption of a yearly rotation, because he found that Aḫum-ṭābum from Dilbat was *rabiānum* during three consecutive years. Taking into account former evidence, new documents from Dilbat, as well as examples from Kutalla, Stol (1976a: 80) maintains that the yearly rotation of the office was not a general custom. Charpin (1980a: 191, and 1982: 64) argues similarly against the annual alternation of the office as proposed by Landsberger and Harris. Despite the many temporal lacunae in the available sources, the examples from Sippar, Dilbat, and Kutalla are still the most representative, because short sequences can be established for certain *rabiānums*. Nevertheless, it is not possible at present to reconstruct a complete list of *rabiānums* in most cities for long periods because records are discontinuous. In the case of Kutalla, for instance, the names of only two *rabiānums* have been recovered. The extant evidence substantiates Stol's and Charpin's remarks. It further implies that there was neither regularity nor rule concerning the number of years nor how many times the post could be held.

DESIGNATION TO THE *RABIĀNUM* OFFICE

Related to the characteristics of the *rabiānum* office are also the questions of who were the bearers of the title, what were the qualifications that a person should have for the position, and who appointed him to office. Although written sources give no explicit information about these matters, the study of a variety of texts from a range of spatial and temporal settings allows us to recognize certain general patterns. The co-occurrence of the *rabiānum*, the city (*ālum*), and the city elders (*šībūt ālim*) suggests a close association among them, particularly in legal documents, but also in other cases. Klengel (1960) has already pointed out the relative independence of the elders from the king. The same observation applies to the *rabiānum*. Fortner's (1996: 270) study of adjudicating entities during the Old Babylonian period includes the elders, the city, and the *rabiānum* among the 'non-estate/local functional adjudicating entities' whose office is not appointed or supervised by the crown. Documents recording those local authorities show their interactions, and they also seem to imply that the office originated from the elders and the city. The *rabiānum* was apparently appointed to act as the representative of other local powers. The members of these institutions were undoubtedly city notables who acted on behalf of city inhabitants, especially of other elites. Judging from dispute and inheritance documents, the parties involved were not poor city dwellers or peasants living in the countryside. But this fact is not conclusive, for it relates to the kind of transactions that were recorded. The activities of certain *rabiānums* substantiate their influential economic and social position in society, and daughters of some of these men were *nadītum*-women of Šamaš in Sippar.[40]

Landsberger (1955: 127) noticed that in Ṣupur-Šubula the *rabiānum* came from the ranks of the elders. But he did not elaborate on this idea, and he just mentioned it briefly in a footnote. Only four *rabiānums* appear in the archive of Ubarrum: Luḫād-Marduk, Ana-Šamaš-līṣi, Ibni-Sîn, and Šallūrum.[41] These men are frequently present together in the same document. Thus Ana-Šamaš-līṣi is the second witness after the *rabiānum* Luḫād-Marduk (*JCS* 5: 86). Luḫād-Marduk is the second witness after Ana-Šamaš-līṣi (*JCS* 5: 80), and he also appears as second

40 *Nadītums* of Šamaš known to be the children of certain *rabiānums* are, for instance, Amat-Māmu, daughter of Nannatum, and Iltani, daughter of Tappûm (see Renger 1967: 151 note 282); add now Ruttum, daughter of the *rabiānum* Hayaum (MHET II/2 n° 323, Ḫa [ ], field lease).

41 Luḫād-Marduk is mentioned in *JCS* 5: 78 = MAH 15.916 (Ae 'a'/III/25); *JCS* 5: 79 = MAH 15.885 (Ae 'a'/XII/12); and as the first witness without title in *JCS* 5: 86 = MAH 16.505 + 16.215 (Ae 'a'/diri-ga/5). Ana-Šamaš-līṣi occurs in *JCS* 5: 81 = MAH 15.993 (Ae 'ga'/IV/10); *JCS* 5: 80 = MAH 15.970 (same date). For Ibni-Sîn, see *JCS* 5: 88 = MAH 15.985 (Ae 's'/IV/5), add now also BIN II 90 (Ae 'k'/VIII/5), and possibly *ASJ* 12 n° 19 (Ad 1/V/5, first witness without title). And Šallūrum appears in *JCS* 5: 84 = MAH 15.982 (Ae 'r'/III/16); *JCS* 5: 82 = MAH 16.143 (Ae 'r'/III/20).

witness after the *rabiānum* Šallūrum (*JCS* 5: 84). There is no indication, however, that these people were indeed city elders at a given time. But documents from the area of Sippar partially confirm Landsberger's hypothesis. This is the case with a sale contract in which Sîn-tayyār buys a plot of land from the *rabiānum* Rabût-Šamaš and the city elders (MHET II/2 n° 164, Ḫa 11/XI/8). This tablet is one of the few that mentions the elders by name, and explicitly characterizes them as such. Of the six elders listed in this text, two of them at least are attested as *rabiānum* in other transactions, namely, Apil-ilīšu and Etel-pîša.[42]

Other tablets show that apart from the city elders, the *rabiānum* also originated from the members of the city. Thus, for instance, Iltani, the *nadītum* daughter of Šamaš-nāṣir, buys a plot of land from the *rabiānum* Etel-pîša and the city (MHET II/ 5 n° 617, date lost, Ḫa). As was the case with the previous sale, there are here some eight city-members mentioned by name and paternal filiation. One of them is Sîn-iddinam, a man who is known to have been the *rabiānum* of Sippar during the reign of Hammurabi.[43] Similarly, Bēlessunu, the daughter of Mutum-el, buys a piece of property from the *rabiānum* Warad-Sîn, the city, and the elders (MHET II/5 n° 706, date lost, pre-Ḫa?). Here Sîn-iddinam appears again among the members of the city, while the elders are mentioned collectively. A fragmentary tablet from Dilbat may also record a similar case (YOS 13 352, Ad 34/VII/22). In this transfer of real estate, the list of people who give the property to Uṣrīya includes the *rabiānum* Aḫum-ṭābum and other important leaders of the community (see Yoffee 1977: 107). Among these men there are at least two future *rabiānums* of Dilbat, Sîn-nādin-šumi and Ibni-Marduk.[44] Unfortunately, documents of this kind are uncommon and they come from a limited number of cities. But examples in which men listed as city members or elders are *rabiānums* in other tablets substantiate the hypothesis that the *rabiānum* was appointed by these bodies to act as their representative.

Other scholars, however, have considered the possibility that the king could have designated the *rabiānum* (e.g. Stol 1976a: 83; Desrochers 1978: 377). Stol, for instance, affirms that in the case of Tutub-māgir it is clear that the king had installed him in the position. Nevertheless, this case is unique and arguable (see Gallery 1979: 75). Albrecht Goetze (1958) published this document in transliteration, translation, and autographed copy (see IM 51.237). In the text, the term

42 Apil-ilīšu appears in VAS 9 202 (Ḫa 'd'/V/Ø), and possibly also in VAS 8 101 as the first witness without title (Ḫa 3/Ø/Ø); and Etel-pîša in MHET II/5 617 (lost Ḫa).

43 See, for instance, VAS 8 102 (Ḫa 4/VIII/[ ]), CT 48 3 (Ḫa 6/VIII/[ ]), CT 47 31 (Ḫa 11/V/10), and MHET II/2 162 (Ḫa 11/V/Ø).

44 Sîn-nādin-šumi was *rabiānum* in Aṣ 10/I/18 (*TJA* H 79: 94, harvest labor contract), Aṣ 13/XII/3 (YOS 13 482, harvest labor contract), Aṣ 13/XII/4 (YOS 13 357, harvest labor contract); and Ibni-Marduk was *rabiānum* in Aṣ 14/X/3 (VAS 7 100, rental of an orchard).

rabiānum is the result of a doubtful restoration. Goetze reads lines 6 and 7 as follows: *i-nu-ma a-na ra-bé-[nu-tim(?)] / šarrum ú-wa-e-ru-[ka]*, 'When the king appointed you to the position of *rabiānum*'. He further comments that the restoration of the word *rabiānūtim* is only conjectural.[45] This abstract noun seems to be unrecorded in any other legal and economic document or letter. What is more, aside from this example, Tutub-māgir is not mentioned as *rabiānum* anywhere else. Thus far he is only known as *šakkanakku Šaduppêm*.[46] The grammar and lexical difficulties related to this interpretation seem to indicate that instead of the king, it was Goetze who appointed Tutub-māgir as a *rabiānum* of Šaduppûm.

The extant seal impressions of different *rabiānums* strengthen the relative independence of the post, because *rabiānum* sealings do not mention either the title or the king. This clearly contrasts with the seals of royal officials who call themselves servants of the ruler, and in certain cases they even have their titles engraved on their cylinder seals. Unlike the *rabiānum*, another urban official, the *ḫazannum*, whose title is also translated as 'mayor, burgomaster, or headman', was a royal official (see Walther 1917: 123; *AHw* Ḫ: 338b; *CAD* Ḫ: 163). This seems to be confirmed by the only *ḫazannum* seal impression known to me.[47] Usually, *rabiānum* seal legends have the name of the owner, his patronymic (dumu PN), and the name of the deity or deities whom the *rabiānum* reveres.[48] There is, nonetheless, at least one exception to this regular pattern, the seal of the *rabiānum* Ibni-Eraḫ from Šaduppûm. It reads '*Ib-ni-[E-ra-aḫ]* / dumu *Su-mu*(?)-[ ] / arad *Da-du-ša*' (YOS 14 42, seal on envelope). The document is undated, but the oath lets us know that it was issued during the reign of Ibāl-pî-el II, the successor of Dāduša, the king mentioned in Ibni-Eraḫ's seal. Evidently, Ibni-Eraḫ kept using this seal although the former ruler was dead, but this fact does not necessarily imply that he held the title *rabiānum* under Dāduša.[49]

45 Goetze (1958: 41) states, 'The restoration *a-na ra-bé-[nu-tim]* for *rabiānūtim* is conjectural. No passage has been found where *wu'urum* is constructed with *ana* and an abstract...'

46 On pages 5–6 Goetze assumes the restoration as correct and explains, 'a tablet in which his death is mentioned calls him [i.e. Tutub-māgir] *Šakkanakku Ša-du-up-pé-em* "governor of Šaduppûm". At an earlier time he had apparently been – likewise under royal appointment – *rabiānum* (IM 51.237 = n° 17).'

47 The seal impression of the *ḫazannum* Sîn-išmeanni in TCL 1 157 (post Ad 24, Kiš) reads: ᵈEN.ZU-*iš-me-a-ni* / dumu *Ib-ni*-ᵈ[ ]/ [ara]d *Am-mi-di-ta-na*. Although the *ḫazannum* is attested from Ur III on, there are only a few references from the Old Babylonian period. Oppenheim (1967: 7) has already pointed out the royal character of the *ḫazannum* office in Sippar, see also Stol (1976a: 73 note 38). Note that Diakonoff (1985: 50) also states that both the *ḫazannum* and the *rabiānum* were royal appointees.

48 In some cases, the seal owner seems to be tied to two deities, thus for instance in TIM 4 5/6 (Si 10/X/15, environs of Nippur): *Na-bi-ì-lí-šu* / dumu *E-te-el-li-ia* / arad AN.AN.MAR.TU / *ù* ᵈNin-⌈si$_4$⌉-an-na; VAS 7 48 (Ad 2/XI/1, Dilbat) ⌈*A*⌉-*ḫu-um-*[*ṭābum*] / dumu [ ] / arad ᵈ[ ] *ù* ᵈ[ ]

49 The use of seals with the name of a deceased king was not unusual in other areas. In Larsa, for

The exceptional legend of Ibni-Eraḫ's seal is related, furthermore, to Stol's (1976a: 82) hypothesis that in the Diyala region the title g̃ìr-nita$_2$ could have been an artificial Sumerogram for *rabiānum*.[50] Stol produces two examples to support this theory. First, the case of Tutub-māgir, but this piece of evidence should be left aside because of the reasons adduced above. Second, he mentions Igeḫluma, who is the *rabiānum* of Zaralulu in a document from Šaduppûm (YOS 14 40: 8), and g̃ìr-nita$_2$ of the same city in another (*JCS* 26: 142). Other scholars, however, do not share this interpretation (see, e.g., Gallery 1979: 75; Charpin 1999: 103). Maureen Gallery argues against the alleged logographic use of g̃ìr-nita$_2$ for *rabiānum*. She explains that, since neither text has a date, Igeḫluma's situation could be the result of a promotion from his post of *rabiānum* to the position of 'governor'.[51] Nevertheless, although the documents are technically undated, they belong to the reign of different kings. Thus the oath formula of one of them is by Dādušа (*JCS* 26: 142), while the other (YOS 14 40) was assigned to the time of Ibāl-pî-el II (see Simmons 1959: 74; Westbrook and Wilcke 1974–77: 116). If this chronological sequence is correct, then Igeḫluma would have been demoted instead of promoted. Of course, one could still argue that since Dāduša was the predecessor of Ibāl-pî-el, YOS 14 40 could have been issued under Dāduša.

Regarding a 'governor' as more important than a 'mayor' is a modern idea, because the *rabiānum* was not necessarily a 'burgomaster' in the sense we understand the office today. The standard translation of *rabiānum* as 'mayor' is misleading because it inevitably recalls a modern western office in which a person sits everyday in a city hall, works for the numbers of hours for which s/he is paid, and returns home. This was probably not the case in ancient Mesopotamia. In the Old Babylonian period, being in charge of local resources could have been, in several respects, more prestigious, or even a more powerful rank, than holding a royal appointment. What is at issue here is the source wherein the power of these titles originated: the g̃ìr-nita$_2$ was a royal official, whereas the *rabiānum* derived his authority from local elites. The solution to this problem might benefit from a comparison between Igiḫluma and Ibni-Eraḫ, since both of them were royal officials under Daduša and *rabiānums* under Ibāl-pî-el. This might have been the result of some sort of political change or even political instability. Historical changes are

instance, the sealing of Iballuṭ, the servant of Hammurabi, appears in a document issued in Si 3 (*RA* 69: 120 n° 8).

50 Steinkeller (2004: 176–77) has recently shown that g̃ìr-nita$_2$ should be read kiš-nita$_2$ = šagina. Unfortunately, this article came to my notice after submission of the manuscript, and too late to change all occurrences of the term. I wish to thank Piotr Steinkeller for the reference.

51 Gallery (1979: 75) affirms: 'Granted that Igeḫluma is known once as *r.* of GN and as g̃ìr-nita$_2$ of GN, it could be more simply explained as the result of promotion (both texts are undated)'. D. Charpin (1999: 103 note 31) also disagrees with Stol's equation of *rabiānum* with g̃ìr-nita$_2$ in similar terms 'mais s'agit-il d'un simple maire ou d'un gouverneur?'

undoubtedly more flexible than historical accounts, simply because writing is a linear device in which complexities can only be rendered successively. Ethnological and anthropological research regarding another community leader, the Andean *curaca*, during and before the Spanish conquest is telling (see Murra 1975). We learn from Spanish records that dealings between local leaders and government officials were multifarious, and that the *curaca* could act either on behalf of his community, on behalf of the Spanish or Inca government, or in his own interest seeking personal rewards. In terms of negotiation strategies, the analogy could apply to the Old Babylonian *rabiānum* – without implying that the *curaca* and the *rabiānum* are, in other ways, analogous.

The equation gìr-nita$_2$ / *rabiānum* is not the only isolated attempt to relate other titles to the *rabiānum* office. When dealing with the documents from Kutalla, Charpin (1980a: 192) suggested that *rabiānum* might have functioned as an abbreviation for *rabi sikkatim*. This hypothesis is based on the alternation between the two titles as used by Qīšti-Erra on the one hand, and on the etymology of *rabiānum*, on the other. Since Qīšti-Erra is also known as nu-banda$_3$, *laputtûm*, Charpin further proposes that this is an occupation independent from the 'rôle au sein de la municipalité'.[52] Stol (1998: 435) includes some of these suggestions in his analysis of Ḫalḫalla, and concludes that *awīlum, laputtûm*, and *rabi sikkatim* are some kind of substitute words for the term *rabiānum*.[53] This interpretation is problematic for various reasons. Legal and economic documents are not literary texts where the scribe has the poetic license to choose the synonym that he considers more suitable for the occasion. This is especially evident when these titles appear in the same document. That a same person bore different titles could also be explained by the fact that *rabiānum* was not a lifelong position. In the case of Qīšti-Erra, for instance, his post as a *rabiānum* does not overlap with the use of the title nu-banda$_3$.[54] Little is known about the characteristics of this office, and systematic research is needed before equating it with *rabiānum* on the basis of the *CAD*'s rendering of *laputtû* as 'mayor of the city'. A similar remark applies to the title *rabi sikkatim* (see Ellis 1968: 46; Charpin 1980a: 192; Van De Mieroop 1999b: 268).

52 Charpin will argue similarly to explain that, besides his role as a *rabiānum*, Ilī-ippalsam is also recorded as PA.PA. During the Old Babylonian period, both titles PA.PA and *laputtûm* were military posts (see Charpin 2004: 282).

53 'Das normale Wort für Bürgermeister ist *rabiānum*. Man kann aber beweisen, daß auch "der Mann von Ḫalḫalla" auf einen Bürgermeister hinweisen kann, s. unten unter Imgur-Sin. Auffällig ist weiter "der *laputtûm* (nu-banda$_3$) von Ḫalḫalla", s. unten unter Warad-Sin. Man fühlt sich erinnert an Kutalla, wo die Titel eines Bürgermeisters wechseln können: *rabiānum, rabi sikkatim*, nu-banda$_3$ PA' (Stol 1998: 435). For the use of nu-banda$_3$ in Ḫalḫalla see also Stol (2004: 676).

54 He is attested as nu-banda$_3$ in Ḫa 36 and 37, and there is no document of him acting as *rabiānum* in those two years.

NUMBER OF *RABIĀNUMS* SIMULTANEOUSLY ACTIVE IN A PARTICULAR CITY

Related to the characteristics of the *rabiānum* office is the possible existence of more than one *rabiānum* in a city at a given time, as Stol (1976a: 80) suggests (see also Van De Mieroop 1997: 130). Stol thinks it conceivable that 'a town had several aldermen (*rabiānum*), headed by *the* burgomaster (*rabiānum*) of the town'. Based on the expression *rabiān bābtīšu* of a royal inscription (Frayne 1990: 659), Stol interprets the term *bābtum* as 'small encampments', each headed by a *rabiānum*-sheikh. At some point, presumably during the early Old Babylonian period, these encampments were consolidated as 'wards' and the 'sheikhs' became alderman. But as already shown in the previous section of this chapter, *rabiānum* plus a gentilic referring to an ethnic group appears only in royal titles, and it is never found in connection with city 'mayors'. Stol's evolutionary approach further rests upon certain documents mentioning more than one *rabiānum*. He distinguishes between those tablets with two or even three *rabiānums* who clearly come from different cities, and those in which two *rabiānums* are 'mayors' of the same place simultaneously. The evidence used to substantiate the existence of two *rabiānum* in a city includes the pairs Sîn-išmeanni and Gimil-Marduk in Kiš (VAS 16 119), Ilī-awīlim and Nabium-mālik of unknown origin (TLB 1 207), and Šēlebu and Kurû in Mārū-Uqnî (VAS 18 18). A close look at these and new documents seem to indicate that there was only one *rabiānum* per city.[55]

The letter referring to Sîn-išmeanni and Gimil-Marduk as *rabiānums* of Kiš pertains to a field rental (VAS 16 119 = AbB 6 119). According to Frankena's (1974: 74) rendering, Sîn-išmeanni, the *rabiānum* of Kiš, will cultivate as an additional field the property that Gimil-Marduk, the *rabiānum* of Kiš, had rented from the ensi$_2$. This statement, however, does not necessarily indicate that both men held the post at the same time. Rather, it is possible that the new *rabiānum* took over a field from the previous bearer of the office. Although Frankena's translation of the passage: 4. a-šà-*am ša* ^{d}EN.ZU-*iš-m*[*e*]-*an-ni* / 5. *ra-bi-an* Kiš^{ki} *i-p*[*e-šu*] / 6. ^{I}*Gi-mil-*^{d}AMAR.UTU / 7. *ra-bi-an* Kiš^{ki} (…) / 11. *ú-še-ṣi* is plausible, the lines could also be analyzed differently. He considers lines 5 and 7 to be a relative clause, for he restores the verb *epēšum* with a *–šu* ending because he understands the *ša* in line 4 as a relative pronoun. But if the *ša* is taken as introducing a genitive, and the verb *epēšum* is restored *i-p*[*e-eš*], not only does the sense of the text change, but also one of the *rabiānum* vanishes. The text will then be rendered as follows: 'the *rabiānum* of Kiš will cultivate the field of Sîn-išmeanni. Gimil-Marduk,

55 Note that Van De Mieroop (1992: 233) seems to disagree with the existence of several *rabiānums* in a city at a given time. For the case of Ur he comments: 'The entire town was headed by an official called *rabiānum* in Akkadian, a word sometimes translated as "burgomaster".'

the *rabiānum* of Kiš rented (it) as an additional field for tenancy from the *iššiakkum*'. Gimil-Marduk, the *rabiānum* of Kiš, appears in another letter (AbB 13 180), whereas there seems to be no attestation of Sîn-išmeanni as a *rabiānum* of Kiš.[56]

The pair Ilī-awīlim and Nabium-mālik, both *rabiānums* without city name, are the first and second witnesses respectively in a field lease contract (TLB I 207, Si 26/III/20). They also appear together as the first and second witnesses without title in a house lease contract (*TJDB* MAH 15.958, Si 28/IV/1). Nabium-mālik is the first witness in other documents, such as a field rental (*TJDB* MAH 15.934, Si 27/II/1) and a harvest labor contract (YOS 13 480, Ae 'o'/X/23). Even though there is no sealing or paternal filiation, in both tablets the presence of Lipit-Ištar, the dumu é-dub-ba-a, indicates that the name Nabium-mālik refers to the same person in each. The *rabiānum* Ilī-awīlim is the first witness, followed by a Gimillum in a field lease (Riftin 41, Si 27/XII/27), whereas Nabium-mālik is the second witness after the *rabiānum* Ibbi-ilum in yet another field lease contract (YOS 12 496, Si 27/VIII/18). The presence of Ibbi-ilum together with Nabium-mālik, both *rabiānums*, shows that Nabium-mālik and Ilī-awīlim were not necessarily an inseparable pair of *rabiānums* in charge of the same city. The fact that they appear together in two sources is, therefore, a feeble argument to conclude that they were *rabiānums* of the same place simultaneously, especially when the geographical name is lacking. The parties engaged in these transactions were possibly inhabitants of two different neighboring cities, which would explain the presence of the two *rabiānums*.

The case of the *rabiānums* Šēlebu and Kurû as being active in the same town is also questionable.[57] They are recorded together as witnesses in a document presumably from Kiš (VAS 18 18, Ae 28/IX/15).[58] Only Šēlebu has the title *rabiān* Mārū-Uqnî, and Kurû is *rabiānum* without a city name. In this document, Bēlētum, an *ugbabtum*-priestess of Marduk in Babylon, sells a field located in the district of Mārū-Uqnî to another *ugbabtum*, Amat-Asalluḫi. The contract is rather exceptional because it gives a detailed account of land and people alike, and it mentions previous owners and professional and paternal ties of most persons.[59] In

56 The other Sîn-išmeanni's with the title *rabiānum* known to me are from other cities. One is possibly from Larsa (VAS 13 77, RS 37/III/10), and the other one is from Sippar (CT 47 63, Si 14/IX/20).

57 To my knowledge, there is no other reference to a *rabiānum* Kurû. As for Šēlebu, a *rabiānum* with that name appears in *LFBD* n°9 (= AbB 10 9), from the archive of Gimil-Marduk, possibly from Kiš; but this Šēlebu was, judging from the context, the *rabiānum* of Ḫabbuz. Thus 11. *ša ta-aš-pu-ram* / 12. *a-na Ḫa-ab-bu-uz*^{ki} *aš-pur* / 13. ^{I}*Še-le-bu-um ra-bi-a-nam* / 14. *it-ru-nim-ma*, 'with reference to what you wrote, I wrote to Ḫabbuz, and they fetched Šēlebum, the *rabiānum*'. A *rabiānum* Šēlebu is also mentioned in TLB 1 151, possibly from Lagaba.

58 Sommerfeld (1982: 88) proposed Kiš as the provenance of VAS 18 18, see also Pientka (1998: 306 note 125).

59 Thus, the first owner of the field was Bēltani, *ugbabtum* of Marduk of Babylon and daughter of

order to prevent future conflicts with the family of Bēlētum, the seller, her brothers are included in the clause of no further claim and listed as the last witnesses before the scribe. Worth mentioning is the variety of geographical references: the field is located in Mārū-Uqnî; the owners are Babylonian priestesses; one of the neighbors, Sîn-bēl-aplim, is from Pada, and his field had been given to the *ṣābū* of Šadlaš. The list of witnesses enumerates 21 persons, and it also reflects the complexity of the transaction.

The witnesses from line 30 to 36 are listed by name, profession, and paternal filiation; but the one in line 37 is followed only by the father's name. In line 38 we encounter Šēlebum, the *rabiānum* of Mārū-Uqnî and, after him, there are six persons, the second of which is Kurû, *rabiānum* (no GN), son of Ibni-Marduk. Indented between lines 46 and 47, is the description 6 lú-igi dumu^{meš}-za-gìn-na^{ki}, 'six witnesses of Mārū-Uqnî'. This notation is problematic because if Šēlebum is included, there are seven men; and if Kurû is considered an inhabitant of Mārū-Uqnî, it is hard to explain why he was not listed right after Šēlebum with a city name. Evidently, Šēlebum, the *rabiānum* of Mārū-Uqnî, was deliberately identified among a group of witnesses who did not belong to his own city, namely those persons listed above him up to line 45. Kurû was, presumably, the *rabiānum* of another place, and he might have been well enough known not to be individualized with a city name. The variety of geographical places cited in the tablet favors this interpretation.

The number of documents mentioning two or more *rabiānums* is relatively small when compared with tablets with only one *rabiānum*. Aside from the cases already discussed, other examples including two or more *rabiānums* encompass contracts from northern and southern Mesopotamia. A pair of *rabiānums* witnessed the sale of an orchard during the reign of Rīm-Sîn of Larsa (*RA* 12 201, RS 36). In the north, Imgur-Sîn the *rabiānum* of Ḫalḫalla is the first, and Apil-Ištar the *rabiānum* of Šubula is the ninth witness on a tablet concerning the sale of a field from Sippar dated to king Apil-Sîn (CT 45 9). Two documents from the time of Hammurabi have each a pair of *rabiānums*. The first is a litigation in which the *rabiānum* of Sippar Sîn-iddinam together with other officials rendered a verdict, and years later Sîn-erībam also *rabiānum* of Sippar has the plaintiff issue a document of no further claim (CT 47 31, Ḫa 11/V/10). The second is an unpublished receipt of straw that mentions the *rabiānums* of Ḫullanu(?) and Damrum (YBC 8591, Ḫa 41). Three documents from the environs of Sippar during the reign of Samsu-iluna have two or more *rabiānum* belonging to different cities. Thus Ana-

---

Etel-pî-Marduk; the second was Bēlētum, *ugbabtum* of Marduk of Babylon and daughter of Mannīya, who sells it to Amat-Asalluḫi, *ugbabtum* of Marduk of Babylon and daughter of Ipiq-Annunīya. One of the neighboring fields is characterized as 'the field of Sîn-bēl-aplim, the man of Pada, which was given to the *ṣābū* of Šadlaš' (ll. 7-8).

Šamaš-līṣi, *rabiānum* of Tegila(?), is differentiated by means of the city name from his colleague Mār-erṣetim (Stol 1998: 444, Si 1). In a court case, Zimrī-Eraḫ, the *rabiānum* of Sippar, and the port authority of Sippar certified the property of Bēlessunu and rendered a verdict against the claimants. But after the death of Bēlessunu that tablet disappeared and the *rabiānum* of Sippar Sîn-išmeanni and the port authority issued a new document (CT 47 63, Si 14/IX/20, Si 14). Yet another tablet from the Sippar area has the *rabiānum* Awīl-ilī and the elders selling a house, while a certain Apil-Adad, *rabiānum*, is the fifth witness. Since the place Yamutbal is mentioned, it seems safe to assume that an inhabitant of Sippar or a nearby site bought a house in a city other than his own (MHET II/6 n° 871, Si 22/IV/10). In a document from unknown provenance, the *rabiānum* Ilī-puṭram and three other men certify that Rīmat-Sîn is an *ugbatum*, and the *rabiānums* Imgurrum and Sarīya are witnesses (CT 48 44, Si 2/IX/20). As Stol (1976a: 79) mentions, the presence of *rabiānums* of different places was necessary in this kind of procedure. Finally, two *rabiānums* are the first and second witnesses in a joint tenancy field lease from the reign of Abī-ešuḫ, which also indicates that people from different cities were involved (YOS 13 417, Ae 'ba'/II/27).

The available examples demonstrate that when two *rabiānums* of the same city appear in a document they do not hold the office simultaneously (e.g. CT 47 31 and 63). A possible exception to this could be the case of the *rabiānums* Aḫum-ṭābum, son of Šamaš-nāṣir, and the *rabiānum* Sîn-nāṣir in Dilbat. Although they do not occur in the same tablet, Sîn-nāṣir's only attestation as *rabiānum* (YOS 13 231, Aṣ 1/X/6) overlaps with Aḫum-ṭābum's term.[60] Because of this, Desrochers (1978: 383) thinks that Sîn-nāṣir could have been the *rabiānum* from a smaller nearby town. Since there is at present no contract with Aḫum-ṭābum from the tenth month of Ammī-ṣaduqa's first year, it could be also possible that Sîn-nāṣir was acting as the temporary substitute for Aḫum-ṭābum. This is an option that Desrochers himself considers in the case of Sîn-nādin-šumi and Baši-el during Ammī-ṣaduqa's tenth year. In those instances in which a geographical name is attached to the title, it is clear that each *rabiānum* belongs to a particular city, probably because the parties are from different places. Thus every *rabiānum* must have represented the inhabitant(s) of his own city who were involved in the transaction. This seems to find support in the fact that, systematically, most tablets with two *rabiānums* have them as witnesses.[61] In the rest of the examples, one *rabiānum*

60 Aḫum-ṭābum is also *rabiānum* in Ammī-ṣaduqa's first year, thus, e.g., in YOS 13 26 (Aṣ 1/I/3), *TJDB* 16.381 (Aṣ 1/IX/1), *TJDB* 16.508 (Aṣ 1/XI/29).

61 See, e.g., CT 45 9: Imgur-Sîn *rabiān* [Ḫalḫalla] (1st witness) and Apil-Ištar (9th witness) *rabiān* Šubula; *RA* 12: 201 x x x x (xth witness) and x x x (xxth witness); Stol 1998: 444 Mār-erṣetim *rabiānum* (1st witness) and Ana-Šamaš-līṣi *rabiān* Tegila ? (4th witness); TLB 1 207: Ilī-awīlim (1st witness) and Nabium-mālik (2nd witness); VAS 18 18: Šēlebu (9th witness) and Kurû (11th

appears in the body of the document and the other as a witness.[62] Remarkably, none of the extant documents have two *rabiānums* of a same city acting together. When a *rabiānum* makes decisions or sells properties, for instance, he acts in concert with the city elders, the city, the judges, the *kārum*, or other individuals, but he is never paired with another *rabiānum*. Thus, the evidence at our disposal seems to stand against the existence of several *rabiānums* in charge of the same city at a given time.

THE ACTIVITIES AND FUNCTIONS OF THE *RABIĀNUM*

The activities of the *rabiānum* during the Old Babylonian period are well attested from both northern and southern Mesopotamia. In the Diyala region, the *rabiānum*'s role as an urban authority dates from the time of kings Dāduša and his successor Ibāl-pî-el II, the latter was contemporaneous with Hammurabi of Babylon. Certain *rabiānum* documents dated to Abdi-Eraḫ also come from this area. Most of the references at our disposal originate from the First Dynasty of Babylon, and one of the earliest tablets is from the reign of Sūmû-la-el, the second king of the Hammurabi dynasty (c. 1880–1845 BC). This text records the sale of a person and has the *rabiānum* Rīš-ilī as the first witness (*RA* 54 n° 38, Sl 23/V). *Rabiānum* documents become more numerous from the time of Sîn-muballiṭ onwards (1812–1793 BC). In southern Mesopotamia before Hammurabi conquered Larsa, *rabiānum* tablets were mostly issued during Rīm-Sîn. But new evidence from earlier kings might come to light in the future. As already said in the previous section, the first attestation of the word *rabiānum* in a document dated to Išbi-Erra of Isin may refer to an Amorite king or an ethnic leader rather than to the *rabiānum* as an urban official. In southern as well as in northern areas, the *rabiānum* played a role in both urban and agricultural activities.

I. THE *RABIĀNUM*'S ROLE IN URBAN AFFAIRS

The *rabiānum*'s leading role in Mesopotamian cities is apparent from a variety of documents. As an urban authority, the *rabiānum* had the responsibility to protect certain properties and their owners. In a letter that Samsu-iluna sent to the *rabiānum* and the elders of an unknown city, the king asked that nobody should

witness); YOS 12 496: Ibbi-ilum (1st witness) and Nabium-mālik (2nd witness); YOS 13 417: Ina-Esagil-balāṭu (1st witness) and [ ]-Marduk (2nd witness).

62 CT 48 44 the *rabiānum* Ilī-puṭram testifies, and Imgurrum and Sarīya are the first and second witnesses respectively; MHET II/6 n° 871: the *rabiānum* Awīl-ilī sells a house and Apil-Adad is the fifth witness; YBC 10973 Sîn-imguranni, *rabiān* Damrum, supervises a transaction and Batūlum, *rabiān* Ḫullanu(?) is the first witness.

approach or touch the bricks of a house that he bought from Ummi-waqrat, the dream interpreter (ABIM 3). Similarly, another message states that the *rabiānum* of Meḫrum should not protect the house of a certain Nūr-ilīšu, who seems to have been involved in a case of robbery (CT 43 110). The *rabiānum* must also have supervised the works undertaken in urban properties. A certain Aḫūšina, for instance, recommends that Kalūmum bribe the *rabiānum* with a sheep if he obstructs the digging of earth for the terrace of a house (AbB 13 111).[63] The *rabiānum*'s intervention in real estate dealings also included exchange of property, as becomes clear from a document from Kiš (*TJA* H 57, Si 23/IX/15). In this case, Zababa-mušallim, the *rabiānum* of Kiš, together with the *šakkanakku*, the *nāgiru*, and the elders of Kiš, give Dān-erēssa, an *entum* of Zababa, a house at the behest of the king (*ina qabê šarrim*). In exchange, they transferred another house to the Ebursag, the temple of Zababa. The ordering of this list of officials and the fact that the city name appears only after the *rabiānum* and the city elders could indicate that the other men were royal officials not necessarily from Kiš (see Szlechter 1963: 55).

The *rabiānum*'s jurisdiction over urban property naturally included his authority over the city inhabitants. Occasionally he collaborates with royal authorities regarding the activities of residents. Thus king Ammī-ṣaduqa sent a letter to Sîn-aḫam-iddinam, the *rabiānum* of Sippar, Ipqu-Nabium, and Ibni-Šamaš concerning Ipqum-Nabium's participation in certain rites (AbB 12 61). The king instructs that after Ipqu-Nabium performs the *taqribtum*-rites in Sippar-Yaḫrurum, he should return to his duties. Remarkably, Ammī-ṣaduqa was relying on the *rabiānum* to control Ipqu-Nabium's deeds. In some other cases, royal officials requested the *rabiānum* to fetch certain persons. For instance, Sîn-iddinam, Hammurabi's administrator in Larsa, asks the *rabiānum* of Kutalla to send him the litigant of Nawwirtum (*LIH* I 47). In another tablet from the time of Samsu-iluna, Awīl-ilī, the *rabiānum*, is held responsible for producing a man by the name of Aplum within five days. The texts further states that in case the *rabiānum* fails to hand the man over, he himself will have to perform Aplum's duty (YOS 12 60, Si 3/I/10). As an urban leader familiar with city affairs and its inhabitants, the *rabiānum* eventually gives testimony about the activities of certain people (e.g. *LFBD* 9).

The *rabiānum*'s jurisdiction also included crimes committed within the city's domain (see Stol 1982b: 365). Paragraph 22 of the 'Laws of Hammurabi' mentions that if a man, *awīlum*, commits a robbery and is seized he shall be killed; and § 23 specifies that if a thief is not seized, the city and the *rabiānum* have to restore the stolen property. The next paragraph states that if a murder takes place, these

63 11'. *šum-ma ra-bi-a-nu ú-da-ab-ba-ab-ka* / 12'. 1 udu-nita$_2$ *Ḫa-bil-da-du li-ša-am-ma* / 13. *li-ṭe$_4$-eḫ-ḫi-šum*, 'If the *rabiānum* harasses you, let Ḫabil-dadu buy one sheep and bring (it) to him'. Transliteration and translation after W. Van Soldt (1994: 101).

authorities will have to pay 60 shekels of silver to the relatives of the deceased (Roth 1997: 85). Almost certainly the fine did not come from the authorities' personal funds, and most likely they disposed of the city 'treasury'. Certain documents are thought to corroborate the provisions of LH, but that correlation tends to be only partial and mostly incongruous (Leemans 1957: 666). In Šaduppûm, for instance, a certain Sîn-iddinam was arrested in possession of stolen property belonging to an Ilšu-nāṣir (YOS 14 40).[64] The judges punished the delinquent with a fine of 1/3 mina and 4 shekels of silver. Presumably, Sîn-erībam could not afford that amount, because it was Igeḫluma, the *rabiānum* of Zaralulu, who paid the fine with 10 gur of barley. This seems to indicate that the thief was an inhabitant of Zaralulu. Since the stolen property is not specified, there is no way to say whether the fine represented the total value of the stolen objects. This case is interesting because the authorities of Šaduppûm made Igeḫluma responsible for a robbery committed outside his own town, which could mean that Šaduppûm controlled Zaralulu. How, if at all, Sîn-erībam is to pay back the *rabiānum* is not mentioned. However, there must have existed such a duty, for it is difficult to believe that the city authorities were doing charity.[65]

Apparently if the theft occurred within the domain of his own city, the *rabiānum* made sure that the thief himself returned the stolen property, thus preventing the city from spending silver. This is the case in an undated document from Larsa that belongs to the archive of Balamunamḫe (YOS 8 1). According to this tablet, eight sheep from the sheepfold of Balamunamḫe and Sîn-imguranni turned up in the possession of Awīl-Adad, the shepherd. The city elders and the *rabiānum* convened and they had the sheep returned to the owners. The document ends with what Van De Mieroop (1987b: 23) interpreted as an ironic sentence by Balamunamḫe to the defendant. It is not directly stated that the animals have to be given back to the owners, although that seems to have been the case.[66]

The *rabiānum*'s commitment in tracking down stolen property is also evident in a letter from the *rabiānum* and the city elders to other officials (YOS 2 109 =

64 In their study on buyers of stolen goods, R. Westbrook and C. Wilcke (1974–77) include YOS 14 40 as well as other documents from the Old Babylonian and Ur III periods. According to them, Sîn-erībam is the 'innocent partner' (p. 117). But this judgement should be nuanced, because it only arises from the deposition of Sîn-erībam himself: 1. [^{d}Sîn]-*e-ri-ba-am* dumu *Ì-lí-ma-a-ki* / 2. [*i*]-*na šu-ur-qi-im ša Ìl-šu-na-ṣi-ir* / 3. *iṣ-ba-tu-ú-ma um-ma šu-ú-ma* / 4. *ša id-di-nam tap-pí-e i-ba-aš-ši* / 5. *a-na* Ká-dingir-ra *it-ta-bi-it*, '1-3. Sîn-erībam, the son of Ilīma-aki, was arrested in possession of stolen property belonging to Ilšu-nāṣir. 3-5. He (said) as follows: "There is someone, my partner, who gave it to me, (but) he has fled to Babylon".'

65 For robbery and its punishment, see Leemans (1957), Renger (1977), and Wilcke (1992).

66 According to Van de Mieroop (1987b: 23), 'll. 31-38 seem to be an ironic exclamation by Balamunamḫe to the defendant "For god's sake, learn how to keep track of all two of your sheep!" I owe the reading and interpretation of this passage, which is given here with all due reserve, to B. Foster.'

AbB 9 109). The city authorities report that the 'royal barber', šu-i lugal, came to the city with his assistant, Muḫuški the Kassite, to collect the *nēmettum*-tax. After their departure, a goat belonging to Yattinu turned up apparently in the hands of Muḫuški, together with a bag full with onions. The city, however, released him and he got away. Although the broader context is missing, it is remarkable that the city, after finding the goods in the possession of the royal barber's assistant, decided to set him free and to write to other officials to settle the matter.[67] This may be explained because of the thief's royal connections. The *rabiānum*'s responsibility regarding robbery seems also to have included abduction, as becomes apparent from another letter (VAS 16 181 = AbB 6 181). The sender, whose name is lost, reports that four years previously, Ibbi-Ilabrat abducted Ana-Marduk-liddinam, his servant from Girlum. Ibbi-Ilabrat kept the man in the city of Suqûm. Finally, the servant's owner arrived at Suqûm with two soldiers and, even though they were not allowed to enter the house of Ibbi-Ilabrat, the *rabiānum* and the elders declared that the servant had been living in the house of Ibbi-Ilabrat for three years.

There are reasons to believe that the *rabiānum*, the city, and the elders were the administrators of certain city properties and that they may have disposed of those possessions and, possibly, of the revenues originating from them. Several tablets from Sippar and vicinity and also from other cities record urban real estate sold by the *rabiānum*, the elders, and the city in their role of city authorities. That is, the transactions were not private but institutional. In a document from Sippar, the *rabiānum* Warad-Sîn, six men who were probably city members, and the elders sold an é-ki-gal-plot described as *bīt ālim*, 'the house of the city'. The buyer was Bēlessunu, daughter of Mutum-el, and she paid five shekels of silver (MHET II/5 n° 706, date lost, pre-Ḫa). In the 11th year of Hammurabi, Sîn-tayyār purchased an é-kislaḫ-plot for 3 shekels from the *rabiānum* Rabût-Šamaš and the city elders. In this document also from the Sippar area, no reference is made to the owner of the house (MHET II/2 n° 164, Ḫa 11). Another tablet from the time of Hammurabi and of unknown provenance, has the *rabiānum* and the city as sellers of a kislaḫ-plot. The buyer is Sîn-adallal, and he paid two-and-a-half shekels of silver (YBC 4207, Ḫa 18). From Hammurabi's reign and from the city of Sippar also comes the sale of an é-kislaḫ-plot sold by the *rabiānum* Etel-pîša and city members to Iltani, the *nadītum* daughter of Šamaš-nāṣir (MHET II/5 n° 617, Ḫa, lost)

67 We do not know how the authorities handled this case, but, judging from the context, it seems unlikely that they follow LH §8. According to this paragraph, if a man steals an ox, a sheep, an ass, a pig or a boat from the state, he shall give it back thirty-fold. And, if the property belongs to a commoner (*muškēnum*) he shall restore (it) ten-fold. Finally, if the thief has not the means to pay, he shall be put to death.

Similar transactions took place during Samsu-iluna. The *rabiānum* and the city sold a ki-šub-ba-plot characterized as *ša bēlam lā īšu*, 'without owner', to Amurrum-muballiṭ, son of Nūr-ilīya. The line with the amount he paid is unfortunately broken (YOS 12 194, Si 6). In the area of Sippar, Sîn-erībam, the son of Sîn-iddinam, purchased an é-kislaḫ-plot from the *rabiānum* Awīl-ilī and the elders. The property is described as *bīt ālim u rabiānim*, 'the house of the city and the *rabiānum*', and it cost seven shekels (MHET II/6 n° 871, Si 22). In Kār-Šamaš, Šattum, the son of Ipqatum, bought an é kislaḫ-plot characterized as *bīt ālim*, 'the house of the city', from the *rabiānum* Ilšu-ibni, ten men, and the elders of Kār-Šamaš. He paid two-and-a-half shekels of silver (VAS 18 17, Si 26). There is also a document from Dilbat dated to king Ammī-ditāna in which Sîn-iddinam, the son of Adad-rabi purchased a ki-šub-ba-plot for one shekel. The seller is Nidittum, who acted at the behest (*ina qabê*) of the *rabiānum* Ibbi-Ilabrat, six other men, and the elders of Tabnuk (*MAOG* IV: 290, Ad 22). Yet another tablet from Sippar records a similar transaction during the reign of Ammī-ṣaduqa. In this case, the sellers are the *rabiānum* and the elders of Kullizum. The property is described as *bīt rabiān Kullizum u šībūt ālim, bēlū bītim*, 'the house of the *rabiānum* of Kullizum and the city elders, the owners of the house'. The buyer was Sîn-rēmēni, son of Abu-waqar, who paid 11 ¼ shekels of silver (MHET II/6 n° 903, Aṣ 12(?)/IX/2).

Although it is clear that several of these properties belong to the city, the documents do not mention why these local authorities owned or got to manage real estate and why they decided to sell it. Equally unknown is the use they made of the silver obtained from those transactions. Only one document states that the house does not have an owner, but there is no explanation as to why the local authorities got hold of this property (YOS 12 194). One could speculate that the proprietor died without heirs, that s/he was an absentee, or that the house had been previously expropriated to pay off a debt. A legal case from the time of Samsu-iluna is interesting because it lets us suspect that the circumstances under which the city sold a house might not have been transparent (YOS 12 321, Si 10/XI/1). According to this document of unknown provenance, the city had sold an é-dù-a, the house of Šamaš-rabi, to Mār-erṣetim, the son of Pala-Erra. Later, Ibni-Amurrum, the son of Šamaš-rabi, seemed to have approached the *rabiānum* and the city elders to raise a claim concerning his father's house. The document is broken in this passage, but when it resumes, we learn that *rabiānum* and the elders made Mār-erṣetim and Ibni-Amurrum reach an agreement. As a result, one of the parties had to pay for the house and its improvements. It is unfortunately impossible to reconstruct the exact context of all these dealings, but it is evident that the elders and the *rabiānum* considered Ibni-Amurrum's objections legitimate. Otherwise, they would have punished him for raising a claim without ground. This document reflects that these local authorities revoked a sale that the city had previously made.

A limited number of texts show that the *rabiānum* had some participation in the collection of taxes. At present, however, his exact role in this activity cannot be fully ascertained, and in small locations it might have been different from big cities. These references usually allude to exceptional circumstances. In one case, a letter explains that a *rabiānum* instead of the temple envoy has to collect the silver for the Kittum temple (AbB 13 109). As already mentioned, this seems to have not been customary. An example of the *rabiānum*'s fraudulent performance in the collection of taxes comes from the city of Ḫarādum (Joannès 1992: 33). This unpublished document dates to king Abī-ešuḫ, and it is a legal case in which Ḫabāsanum, the *rabiānum*, is accused by the city of having diverted to his own benefit silver and sheep from the *igisûm*-tax.[68] Similarly, a tablet from the reign of Ammī-ditāna from Sippar also seems to refer to an irregular situation involving the *rabiānum* (AS 16: 211). In this text, various *rabiānums* and elders swear that they had not concealed any tavern keeper or cook, and that they had not had any tavern keeper or cook liable to pay the *nēmettum*-taxes inscribed on the list of tax-exempt people. After the oath, the document states that if those irregularities should occur, the local authorities will be responsible to the palace.[69] A document from Iščhali, seems also to imply that the *rabiānum* was the recipient of certain revenues from the selling of sheep (*OBTIV* n° 108). This is a laconic list of amounts of silver and persons, in which the last line states: kù-babbar udu-nita$_2$ *a-na ra-bi-nim*, 'silver (of) the male sheep for the *rabiānum*'.

The responsibilities of the *rabiānum* also include his presence as a witness in economic and legal activities, a role perfectly justified by his position as the head of certain city authorities. Indeed in the vast majority of documents mentioning the *rabiānum*, he is the first witness, though there are instances in which he is the second, third, fourth, or, even in one case, the eleventh. These records encompass a variety of transactions comprising family issues such as marriage, adoption, and nursing contracts, bequests and donations, as well as inheritance. Similarly, the *rabiānum* is usually found at the head of the list of witnesses in loans and receipts pertaining to silver, grain, and other products. He occasionally witnesses sales and hiring of slaves, and labor contracts. But his participation as witness is most apparent in tablets relating to lease and sale of houses, fields, and orchards. These real estate transactions originate from both northern and southern Mesopotamia. In certain instances, litigations regarding inheritance, dowries, land, houses,

68 As far as I know, this document has not yet been published. One cannot but eagerly await the publication of the Ḫarādum texts since some of them have been found in the house of the *rabiānum*; some of the Ḫarādum documents also mention the city elders (Joànnes 1992: 33).

69 This rather exceptional and difficult text has been edited and studied by Goetze (1965). See also the comments in Yoffee (1977: 28) and Roth (1999).

and other goods also required the *rabiānum* to be present.[70] His role as a witness can be explained because the action of issuing a document implied in itself the possibility of future conflict, in which case the *rabiānum* himself might settle the matter. In fact, the *rabiānum* acted on many occasions as mediator in disputes that took place within the city and its hinterland. In legal matters, however, the *rabiānum* rarely decided alone. Since in lawsuits he usually acted in concert with other urban authorities, his role in those documents will be discussed in the next chapters.

II. THE *RABIĀNUM*'S ROLE IN AGRICULTURAL AFFAIRS

Tablets that have the *rabiānum* as one of the witnesses usually deal with loans of grain for seeding, silver to purchase agricultural products, the hiring of harvest labor forces, as well as the sale of cows and oxen. These products, animals, and people must have been often the objects of disputes. A letter sent to the *rabiānum*

70 Examples of *rabiānum* as a witness in different documents include: **1- Marriage contracts** (YOS 12 371, YOS 12 457, UET V 87); **2- Adoption contracts** (OECT 13 202, Waterman 54, YOS 12 363); **3- Nursing contracts** (CT 48 70); **4- Bequests** (MHET II/1 81, II/5 618, *TS* 35, BE 6/2 85, VAS 7 48 and 49); **5-Inheritance contracts** (YOS 14 145, CT 47 19, CT 8 1a, CT 45 23, MHET II/2 257, CT 47 58 and 64, Peek 14 24); **6- Loans** (silver: YOS 12 344 and 71, YBC 6720, YOS 13 34, Richardson BM 80421, YOS 13 22; oil: YOS 13 515 and 525; grain: BIN II 90, *TJDB* 16536, Richardson BM 97641, 97494, 97642, 97592, 97830, and 97826, YOS 13 358, 467, 464, 392, 398, 394, and 463, MLC 800); **7- Receipts** (YBC 19.973, YOS 12 27 and 3, *TS* 78, *Nippur Neigh.* 25, *OBAT* 66, *OBAT* II 52, YOS 13 479 and 308, Richardson BM 97.379); **8- Debts** (OECT 13 172 and 146); **9- Transactions pertaining cattle** (*TJDB* 16.194 and 16.414, TIM V 56 and 52, YOS 13 243, *RA* 14: 153, YOS 13 322, Richardson BM 104.804, YBC 6723); **10- Real estate documents** (houses, rent: VAS 13 22; houses, sales from the south : *TS* 53, 55, 62, 64, 65, 66, *Warka* 74, *TS* 72, 73, 74, 76, *Nippur Neigh.* 54, *TS* 79, 82, 81, 83, 75, 85; sales from the north: CT 47 16, MHET II/3 388, YOS 12 102, 153, MHET II/3 418 and II/6 869, YOS 12 390, 536 and 537, VAS 22 11, OECT 13 289, Riftin 34; fields, rentals from the south: YBC 4326, from the north: VAS 9 62, CT 47 75, VAS 9 202, YOS 12 135, 258, 375, 286, TLB I 207, *TJDB* 15.934, YOS 12 496, Riftin 41, TIM IV 43, YOS 13 417, MHET II/4 469, *JCS* 5: 84, 5: 82, and 5: 88, *ASJ* n°19, YOS 13 496, 9, 414, *TJDB* 16.146, TCL I 155, *TJA* H 13: 74ff. *TJDB* 16.510, MHET II/4 551, BIN 7 211; sales from the south: VAS 13 77, *TS* 49 and 51, from the north: UCP 10/1 109, 10/3 6, YOS 14 106 and 107, MHET II/6 843, CT 45 9, YOS 14 152, 157, 160, TCL I 73, OECT 13 156, MHET II/2 329, CT 47 56, YOS 12 277, MHET II/3 426, VAS 18 24, MHET I/1 2, orchards, rentals from the north: *OBAT* II/123, VAS 7 100; sales from the south: *RA* 12: 201, YOS 8 134, Holma *ZATH* 1, *DCS* 94); **11- Slaves** (hire: Richardson BM 97.324, sales: *RA* 54 n° 38, Richardson BM 92.606); **12- End of partnership** (*JCS* 5: 78, 79, 81, and 80); **13- Harvest labor contracts** (YOS 13 480, 223, VAS 7 60, *TJDB* 16. 448, YOS 13 222, 50, *TJDB* 16.305, 16.381, YOS 13 231, *TJDB* 16.148, 16.508, *TJA* H 79: 94, YOS 13 226, *TJA* H 34: 94, YOS 13 218, 482, 357, *TJDB* 16.426, YOS 13 389, 466, 465, *TJDB* 16. 147); **14- Legal documents** (from the north: YOS 14 42, 161, MHET II/1 82, VAS 8 101, *BAP* 80, CT 4 22b, VAS 7 149, TLB I 141, CT 48 43, YOS 13 532, MHET II/5 692, *AuOr* 15 n ° 15; from the south: VAS 13 100, *TS* 58, *Nippur Neigh.* 22, Riftin 47, TIM IV 5/6). Documents are arranged chronologically within categories.

and the elders of Laliya tells us of an Ilī-iddinam approaching the authorities to complain about grain for seeding (*JCS* 23: 29). This man affirms that he had given barley to his son to sow a field, but apparently the son did not follow his father's instructions, employed the grain for other purposes, and he further gave the field to a tenant farmer. This letter is interesting because it shows that these kinds of conflict also arose in transactions between relatives that probably did not involve the issuing of written obligations. In addition, the *rabiānum* and the elders also participated in the settlement of disputes concerning water supplies (e.g. AbB 10 171).

The *rabiānum*'s participation in agricultural affairs, however, was not solely restricted to his role as a witness or as the mediator in legal disputes. In a letter referring to irrigation, a certain Alī-talīmī is said to have reported that Gimil-Marduk, the *rabiānum* of Kiš and another man prevented him from closing a branch of a canal (AbB 13 180). Furthermore, brief references in other documents seem to indicate that the *rabiānum* must have had certain authority over local granaries, but his exact participation in their management is not apparent (see, e.g., CT 52 54, UCP 9/4 5). Other contracts show that in places such as Aḫut, the right to collect barley from the *miksûm*-tax was transferred to the *rabiānum* and the elders, and the same was the case with grain and dates that these local authorities had first to collect and then pay back the palace (MLC 202, 203, Si 18; and MLC 256 and 443, date lost). The *rabiānum* and the elders, moreover, occasionally distributed grain among hired workers. Certain letters mention that these rations come from other authorities such as the *šāpiru* (AbB 13 44), and from the palace. On one occasion, the *rabiānum* and the elders confirm that they received 60 gur of barley for food rations and instruct Mār-erṣetim to send a sheep worth of two-thirds of a shekel of silver to the palace gate, possibly to be understood as a token of acknowledgement (OECT 13 193).

The *rabiānum*'s ability to recruit workers is also apparent from other sources. In harvest labor contracts dating to the late Old Babylonian period, for instance, the *rabiānum* acted as a middleman between the state and local communities (see Stol 1976a: 90–96; Yoffee 1977: 94–109). From his study of the Uṣrīya archive, Yoffee concludes that those workers were free community members hired to perform work on state lands. He argues that the *rabiānum* provided harvesters, while the *mu'errum*-official was the agent acting on behalf of the state. Yoffee maintains that there were two mechanisms for the recruitment. Thus crown officials could either hire harvesters directly from the *rabiānum*, or from a third party with the approval of the community leader who witnessed the transaction. The latter is evident from the number of harvest labor contracts in which the *rabiānum* is usually the first witness. Yoffee also mentions that the *mu'errum* office and his activities regarding workers were expanded during the late Old Babylonian period because by then the state was unable to remunerate a large number of permanent workers.

Several documents also show that the *rabiānum* played a role in the distribution, assignment, and sale of arable land and orchards. This can be seen from the many real estate contracts that have the *rabiānum* as one of the witnesses, but also from those tablets in which he has an active participation in these transactions. The *rabiānum* seems to have also mediated between community members and the state in certain agricultural affairs. Such is the case, for instance, with a field lease contract dated to king Ammī-ṣaduqa (BIN VII 211).[71] In this document, Nanna-mansum, at the behest of Erībam-Nanāya, the *iššiakkum*-official, rents a field for one year from three individuals who are acting on behalf of Sîn-nādin-šumi, the *rabiānum*. This field, however, does not belong to the *rabiānum* himself but to Asqūdum, the son of Ilūni.[72] One of the interesting features of this contract is the different mediations that took place, thus

From the lessor side:

1. Asqūdum, son of Ilūni, owner of the field

⇩

2. Sîn-nādin-šumi, *rabiānum* (1st mediation)

⇩

3. Ubarrum, the son of Tarībatum ⟺ 2. Nanna-mansum, the *mu'errum*
Ibbi-Ilabrat, the son of Anun-pî-^{d}Nanāya
Bēlšunu, the son of Ilī-sukkallum
(2nd mediation)

From the lessee side:

1. Erībam-Nanāya, the *iššiakkum*

⇩

2. Nanna-mansum, the *mu'errum*

The document does not mention the reasons why Ubarrum, Ibbi-Ilabrat, and Bēlšunu are acting at the behest of the *rabiānum*, but it is almost certain that they were close collaborators. It is also worth highlighting that in this contract the *rabiānum* is the intermediary between the owner of the field and the royal officials who are renting it as a *biltum*-field for one year. It seems possible that the state

71 The provenance of this document is not certain. Renger (1969: 112) included the sanga of Urkītum mentioned in line 3 among the sanga-priests of Sippar; but Charpin (1986a: 405) has questioned Renger's view and instead he proposed the region of Kiš-Dilbat. C. Wilcke (1976: 275) suggests Kiš, and for Pientka (1998: 641) the text might come from Dilbat.

72 While I am following the reading Asqūdum son of Ilūni, as proposed in the onomastic section of BIN 7 211, M. Stol (1976a: 96) has interpreted line 4 differently. He reads a-šà *gìr-ma-di-i I-lu-ni* and refers to *MSL* 9. In the copy, the third sign in line 4 actually looks more like a 'gìr' than like an 'as' sign. However, the word *girmadû* means, according to *CAD* G: 89a, 'part of a ship', and there seems to be no attestation of this word in the Old Babylonian period.

would assign the field to somebody who will have to cultivate the field for the crown.[73]

Similarly, a fragmentary document from Dilbat dating to the reign of Ammī-ditāna, records the transfer of 20 sar of real estate from the *rabiānum* and 12 other persons to Uṣrīya, the son of Warassa (YOS 13 352, Ad 34/VII/22). Uṣrīya was an *iššiakkum*-official who managed fields from Ilī-iqīšam, and he was also in charge of the collection of the *biltum*-tax as part of his royal agricultural duties (Yoffee 1977: 102). Stol (1976a: 92) suggests that the 12 men mentioned after the *rabiānum* could have represented the city. And Yoffee (1977: 107) characterizes them as important leaders of the community. That some of these 12 men were either city members or city elders is substantiated by the fact that at least two of them, Sîn-nādin-šumi and Ibni-Marduk, are *rabiānums* in other documents from Dilbat.[74] The *rabiānum*'s involvement with *biltum*-fields, is also mentioned in a letter from the Sippar area (CT 52 110 = AbB 7 110). Here Nidnat-Sîn informs a sanga-priest of Šamaš that the *rabiānum* of Kār-Šamaš had assigned 2 iku of a *biltum*-field to the corvée workers. And in a very fragmentary contract from unknown provenance, the *rabiānum* Ibni-Amurrum together with several other men assign a *biltum*-field to a person whose name is not preserved (YBC 4496, Ḫa 41/VII/15?).[75]

The intervention of the *rabiānum* in certain agricultural issues was not always appreciated by some of the city inhabitants. Thus, for instance, in a letter to his superior, Sîn-išmeanni complains because Išum-abī, the *rabiānum*, has been pestering Warad-Kūbi concerning the *ilku*-duty (*JCS* 30: 249 = AbB 10 151). Sîn-išmeanni further tells his addressee that he must get angry at Išum-abī because the *rabiānum* should not bother a man who performs his obligation profitably. Although the tablet is of unknown provenance, it is possible to infer that Išum-abī was the *rabiānum* of Ḫabbuz, because Sîn-išmeanni says that Warad-Kūbi lives in that city. The *rabiānum*'s exceeding of authority and his interference with royal jurisdiction is already apparent under the reign of Hammurabi. An example of such overstepping of authority comes from a message that the king himself sent to Sîn-iddinam, one of his administrators in Larsa (*LIH* I 6). According to Hammurabi,

73 1. 5 iku a-šà ab-sín / 2. a-gàr *na-gú-u* / 3. *i-ta* sanga ^{d}*Úr-ki-tum* / 4. a-šà *As-qú-di* dumu *I-lu-ni* / 5. *a-na qá-bi-e* ^{d}EN-ZU-*na-di-in-šu-mi ra-bi-a-nu-um* / 6. *U-bar-rum* dumu *Ta-ri-ba-tum* / 7. ^{I}*I-bi-*^{d}Nin-šubur dumu *Anum-pi*$_{4}$-^{d}*Na-na-a* / 8. *ù Be-el-*⌜*šu*⌝*-nu* dumu *Ì-lí*-sukkal / 9 .*a-na qá-bi-e Eri*$_{4}$*-ba-am-*^{d}*Na-na* ensi$_{2}$/ 10. ^{d}Šeš-ki-ma-an-sum gal-unken-na eren$_{2}$ ká é-gal / 11. *a-na er-re-šu-tim* / 12. ⌜*a-na*⌝ gú-un *a-na* mu 1-kam / 13. íb-ta-an-è, etc.

74 Sîn-nādin-šumi was *rabiānum* in Aṣ 10/I/18 (*TJA* H 79), Aṣ 13/XII/3 (YOS 13 482), Aṣ 13/XII/4 (YOS 13 357), and possibly also in Aṣ 17+a/I/10 (BIN 7 211). Ibni-Marduk was *rabiānum* in Aṣ 14/X/13 (VAS 7 100).

75 An Ibni-Amurrum, the *rabiānum*, is known from a Sippar document issued in the tenth month of Hammurabi's 30th year (VAS 13 20).

Lalum the miller reported that the *rabiānum* Ali-tillati claimed a field that Lalum had held for many years, and that the *rabiānum* even took the barley of the field. Hammurabi also tells Sîn-iddinam that there is a tablet in the palace that ascribes a 36 iku field to Lalum. Sîn-iddinam is instructed to investigate the matter and to punish the *rabiānum* if he had committed a wrong. This letter clearly shows that not even the bureaucratic machinery of Hammurabi was exempt from tensions between local powers and royal policies. The challenge of power by local authorities, however, seems to have increased during the final stages of the First Dynasty of Babylon (see Yoffee 1977).

CONCLUSIONS

The word *rabiānum* and the office it designates are unattested before the Old Babylonian period. The earliest extant reference comes from a document belonging to the Isin craft archive dated to the 32nd year of Išbi-Erra of Isin (BIN 9 199). Since the title originates from the period when Amorite dynasties dominated Mesopotamia and because the Amorites are frequently attested in the Isin craft archive, certain scholars have proposed that the *rabiānum* as an urban office can be traced to a nomadic past. This interpretation further maintains that the institution evolved throughout the Old Babylonian period when the Amorite tribes fully settled. Consequently, from being a sheikh of the nomads the *rabiānum* became an urban leader, namely, a 'burgomaster'. The study of the former and new evidence has shown, however, that the alleged nomadic origin of the office is not immediately apparent. Rather, the *rabiānum* title represented two unrelated institutions. On the one hand, it was a royal title borne by several kings during the early Old Babylonian period. On the other, it was an urban office. The use of the same word to name different authorities does not imply any connection between the two of them. A similar change of word usage occurs with the word $ensi_2$, *iššiakkum*, a term that was once a royal title and during the Old Babylonian period came to designate an agricultural post.

When used as a royal title, the noun *rabiānum* is usually combined with a gentilic. Evidence comes from royal inscriptions and seals from both northern and southern Mesopotamia. Examples include *rabiān Amurrim, rabiān Rababî, rabiān Amnānim,* and *rabiān bābtīšu*. Of these titles, *rabiān Amurrim* is at present the best documented. The earliest attestation refers to Abda-el, who was contemporaneous with Nūr-aḫum and also had family ties with him. Interestingly, Abda-el and his son Ušašum are also recorded as recipients of official gifts in a list from the Isin craft archive dated to the 32nd year of Išbi-Erra of Isin (BIN 9 316). In this case, however, Abda-el's title is omitted. This text also mentions Iemṣium, a king of Larsa, who also receives a leather bag gift in another document from the same archive (BIN 9 217, Išbi-Erra 32). This seems to indicate that the *rabiānum* Birbirrū, who also received a leather bag in the first dated document with the earliest *rabiānum* reference, was himself an ethnic leader or an Amorite king thus far unattested. Aside from Abda-el, other kings from the Diyala region bearing the title *rabiān Amurrim* were Itūr-šarrum and Sîn-gāmil, both rulers of Diniktum, and Arīm-Līm of Mê-Turān. As for the south, at least two kings of Larsa used the title, as becomes apparent from inscriptions of Zabāya and Abī-sarē. Instances of *rabiānum* plus gentilic other than *Amurrum* are rather poorly attested. Such is the case with the *rabiān Rababî* Itūr-Šamaš from Kisurra, the *rabiān Amnānim* of Šadlaš, and the *rabiān bābtīšu* from Mutalû. Apparently, as a royal title *rabiānum* seems to have fallen into disuse early during the reign of Hammurabi, for the latest example comes from a text possibly issued during Hammurabi's fifth year. Finally, it is worth mentioning that, judging from the extant evidence, no king of the First Dynasty of Babylon bore the title *rabiān Amurrim*, 'chief of the Amorites'.

Documents recording the *rabiānum* as a city authority do not seem to support any association between the bearer of the title and the nomads. On the contrary, the chief of the city always deals with urban and agricultural affairs pertaining to the city and its surrounding countryside. The *rabiānum* office is well attested in cities from both northern and southern Mesopotamia. One of the earliest examples from the north comes from a contract dated to king Sūmû-la-el, whereas in the south I could not find *rabiānum* documents previous to the reign of Rīm-Sîn of Larsa, with the sole exception of BIN 9 199. This lack, however, might be attributed to the chance of discovery. Due to the fragmentary character of the evidence, the characteristics of the office are difficult to trace. Unfortunately, the available texts do not allow us to establish a complete sequence of *rabiānums* in any city, but it seems possible that the length of the office varied. There are cases in which the same person held the position during successive years, while certain *rabiānums* are documented only once, and yet other men were *rabiānum* several times discontinuously. Contracts listing the elders and the city members clearly show that the office originated from the midst of these corporate bodies. Apparently, the elders and the city appointed the *rabiānum* to act as their representative, especially in those transactions where it was necessary to identify the person who acted on behalf of the local authorities. The procedures for such a selection are unknown, but it is certain that the *rabiānum* as well as the elders and the city were urban elites. The periodic renewal of the office further substantiates the existence of only one *rabiānum* in each city at a given time. That the *rabiānum* was not a royal appointee becomes clear from *rabiānum* seals, which do not mention the name of the king, as was the case with the seals of royal officials. The only exception to this is the case of Ibni-Eraḫ in Šaduppûm, which could have been the result of negotiation strategies between the state and certain local powers.

The responsibilities of the *rabiānum* encompass a wide range of activities. Many tablets have the *rabiānum* as a witness, usually the first one, but there are also instances in which he is the second, the third, or even the eleventh witness. These records include sale, rental, and lease of real estate, loans, adoption and inheritance documents, and harvest labor contracts. This variety reflects the diversity of economic and social issues that urban authorities closely supervised. Documents from northern cities also show that the *rabiānum*, together with the elders and the 'city', participated in the sale of urban properties described as the house of the city or the house of the *rabiānum*. Apart from these sales, the *rabiānum* also played an important role in the distribution, assignment, and sale of arable land, orchards, and houses. In some of these instances, he interacts with royal officials. This is evident in the recruitment of the labor force but also in certain real estate dealings. Furthermore, sometimes the *rabiānum* seems to have cooperated with the state in the collection of taxes. As a local authority, the *rabiānum* was also responsible for cases of robbery committed within the jurisdiction of his city. Finally, in several documents, the chief of the city acts as a mediator in legal disputes. His participation in these cases will be discussed in the following chapters.

4

*The City Elders (*šībūt ālim*)*

GENERAL REMARKS

The institution of the city elders, unlike the office of *rabiānum*, has a long tradition in ancient Mesopotamia. It appears in economic and legal documents as well as in literary texts. But while administrative or epistolary records are laconic and offer very little information unless a considerable number of them is brought together, myths and 'epics' offer at face value a more coherent picture. In the extant Babylonian story of the flood, for instance, the god Enki instructs Atra-ḫasīs twice to save humankind from those natural catastrophes planned by Enlil. Each time, Atra-ḫasīs convenes the elders and tells them what to do to avoid disaster.[1] Facing the flood, however, salvation is individual and Atra-ḫasīs informs the elders that he will depart to dwell in Enki's abode. The flood is, then, anticipated by means of a euphemism because Enki lives in a watery milieu, the Apsû. Instead of lying or hiding the truth, Atra-ḫasīs, the exceedingly wise, resorts to a pun. Lambert and Millard ([1969] 1999: 10) have pointed out that to understand the narrative it is important to know that Atra-ḫasīs is a king who mediates between the god Enki and the city elders, and that from the elders decisions are passed on to the people. The elders seem to be in this context intermediaries between the king and the people. Parts of the flood narrative were interwoven later into another well-known literary composition, the 'Epic' of Gilgameš.

Certain stories about Gilgameš indirectly refer to the role of the city elders in government affairs. In these cases, however, they act as advisors rather than intermediaries. Thus, in 'Surpassing all other kings', the Old Babylonian version of the 'Epic' of Gilgameš, the king of Uruk tries to obtain the elders' consent before his expedition to the Forest of Cedar where he aims to kill Humbaba, the protective spirit of the forest.[2] Similarly, the Sumerian composition 'Gilgameš and

1 The extant lines of these passages are verbatim repetitions, thus, in tablet I: 385–88 and in tablet III: 38-41. ^{I}*At-ra-am-ḫa-si-is il-qí-a te-er-tam / ši-bu-ti ú-pa-aḫ-ḫi-ir a-na ba-bi-šu /* ^{I}*At-ra-am-ḫa-si-is pí-a-šu i-pu-ša-am-ma / is-sà-qar a-na ši-bu-ti* 'Atra-ḫasīs received the command, and gathered the elders to his gate, Atra-ḫasīs opened his mouth, and addressed the elders' (Lambert and Millard [1969] 1999: 69 and 91).

2 This episode is preserved in only one of the extant Old Babylonian versions, the 'Yale tablet' III: 178–221 (see George 1999: 107–113).

Akka', known in antiquity by its incipit 'The envoys of Akka', depicts king Gilgameš addressing the elders of Uruk and seeking support for going to war against Kiš.[3] In both instances, the elders reject Gilgameš's proposal; and in the Humbaba issue, they further assume a paternalistic attitude: 'You are young, Gilgameš, borne along by emotion, /all that you do, you don't understand' (George 1999: 112). These literary texts have been repeatedly quoted to prove many different things about Mesopotamian government. For our present discussion, suffice it to say that the image of the city elders as the king's advisors seems to have influenced certain scholarly approaches to the Old Babylonian institution.[4] Nevertheless, it is important to remember that the Gilgameš who has come down to us through literature is not a historical figure but a literary character who fights against fantastic creatures and talks with the flood hero, another immortal literary being.

The institution of the city elders is, moreover, relatively well-attested in economic and legal records and it can be traced back to the pre-Sargonic period, that is, before the twenty-fourth century. A survey of these documents is important for the study of the city elders and their role in earthly matters as opposed to the perception we gain through literary texts. In cuneiform sources, we find the expression 'city elders' written either syllabically, *šībūt ālim*, or logographically, usually ab-ba (uru^{ki}).[5] Besides this writing, seemingly common in Ur III and Old Babylonian texts (see *PSD* A/II: 131 for earlier references), the use of other synonyms is also recorded in various periods, regions, or both.[6] In Mari documents, for instance, the Sumerian word šu–gi$_{(4)}$ and its variant forms of spelling – such as $^{lú\text{-}meš}$šu-gi(-a) and ^{lú}šu-gi^{meš} (+ GN or gentilic) – seem to have been used instead of ab-ba, at least in certain cases, as will be discussed later in this chapter. In addition, the logogram abba$_2$ (= AB + ÁŠ) is attested earlier, from the pre-Sargonic to the Ur III period, ranging geographically from Susa to Ebla (Gelb 1984: 264–74).[7]

3 Thus in lines 3-4, ^{d}Gilgameš igi ab-ba uru^{ki}-na-šè / inim ba-an-gar inim ì-kin-kin-e (see the composite text in Vanstiphout 1987: 138). The 'Envoys of Akka', lú-kin-gi$_4$-a ak-kà, is known from nine manuscripts all dating to the Old Babylonian period. The interpretation of the text remains controversial. For a summary of the different approaches, see D. Katz (1993).

4 That is the case, for instance, with Kupper's (1957: 62) and Klengel's (1960: 361) approach to the elders as recorded in the Royal Archives of Mari.

5 Variants of these writings include ab-ba / *šībūt* + city name. D. Owen (1981: 67) mentions that 'The occurrence of the term ab-ba in association with specific city names as opposed to the more commonly attested ab-ba uru is quite rare for the Ur III period'.

6 During the Old Babylonian period ab-ba uru seems to have been more commonly used in literature than in economic and legal documents. In our corpus of texts from Babylonia, the word is written logographically only once (MHET II/2 n° 164, Ḫa, Sippar).

7 For the logogram abba$_2$ (uru) = 'city elders', Gelb ([1957] 1973: 256–58) had already provided a number of examples dating to the Old Akkadian period. This earlier list, however, does not include a discussion of the term and its nuances, as does one of his later articles. The geographical distribution of these documents encompasses Ebla, Susa, al Gasur, the Diyala region, Ešnunna,

There is, finally, still another Sumerian writing for 'city elders', ad-da uru, less common than ab-ba uru (see *NSGU* 1 p. 36 n. 3 and 3 p. 90).[8] As a syntactic category, the Akkadian word *šību* can function either as an adjective or as a substantive when treated as a nominal form. The adjective *šību* (šu-$gi_{(4)}$) means unequivocally 'old', but the noun carries a wider semantic range including 'old man', 'witness', and 'elder' (see *CAD* Š/II: 390a, *AHw* Š: 1228).

The term *šību* may present some ambiguity for the interpretation of those texts wherein either '(city) elder' or 'witness' could have been meant. The distinction is clearer in the plural because while the inflection for 'witnesses' is *-ū*, 'elders' takes the morpheme *-ūtum* (see Schorr [1913] 1971: 366 n. 4, *GAG* § 61k). Nevertheless, for periods earlier than the Old Babylonian, the logogram $abba_2$ is attested in the plural with the phonetic indicator *–bu-ut* (i.e. $abba_2^{bu\text{-}ut}$) with both meanings (see Gelb 1984: 264 and 270).[9] Generally, in Old Babylonian economic and legal documents ambiguous interpretations seem to have been avoided by using the Sumerian logograms ^{lú}igi$^{(meš)}$ or ^{lú}inim-ma$^{(meš)}$ for 'witness(es)' and the Akkadian syllabic writing *šībūtum* for 'elder(s)'. There are, however, a few exceptions.[10] Walther (1917: 52) pointed out that although in most cases the plural ending makes it possible to distinguish between 'elders' and 'witnesses', such a distinction is less apparent in other instances, especially when the two roles overlapped. His examples include *ši-bu-ut šarrim*, 'Zeugen des Königs' (CT 29 43: 35 = *BB* 218), and *ši-bu-sú-nu šá* ^{d}A-ba_4, 'ihre Zeugen vom Gotte A' (CT 23 41: 39-40). Walther affirms that despite the numerous connections between the elders and the temple, in CT 23 41 the *šībūtum* are 'witnesses' and not 'elders'.[11]

---

and Nippur. In addition, $abba_2$, meaning 'witness', also comes from Kiš and Sippar (see Gelb 1984: 264–74). See also *PSD* A/II: 131.

8 ad-da uru is not attested in our corpus of economic and legal documents.

9 $abba_2$ meaning 'witness' was taken as one of the Akkadian extra-linguistic features to determine the linguistic filiation of 'ancient Kudurrus' and related sale documents, because this logogram was used instead of the Sumerian lú-ki-inim-ma (see Gelb *et al.* 1991: 11). According to Gelb *et al.*, besides $abba_2$ there are still two other terms for 'witnesses' in ancient kudurrus and sale documents: lú-ki-inim-ma (the standard Sumerian word from the Fara to the Sargonic periods in texts written in Sumerian, but attested also in Ur III) and lú-inim-ma (the standard term during Ur III and Old Babylonian times), p. 233.

10 In OECT 3 40: 25 (= AbB 4 118), an Old Babylonian letter from Awīl-Ninurta to Šamaš-ḫāzir, the bound form *šīb ālim* is used instead of the plural *šībūt*: 25. *ši-ib* uru^{ki} *ù a-wi-lu-ú la-bi-ru-tum*, 'the city elders and the old men', (see also *GAG* § 64 m: 103). Similarly, in PBS I/2 pl. 53 n° 10 (= AbB 11 159), the singular is used in a context that clearly means 'elders', thus: 4. *ra-bi-a-nu-um ù ši-bu* [Ì]-[si-i]n^{ki}*-ma*. Notice that in ḪAR-ra = *ḫubullu*, the word 'elder' in line 25 is in the singular; it is replaced in the following lines by 'ditto' but in line 29 one of the variants has *šībūt ālim* and another has 'ditto' *ālim*. The plural in one of the manuscripts may imply that the plural form might have also applied to line 26, 'elders of the city' (see Walther 1917: 52 and note 1).

11 'Hier also wieder der adjektivische Plural; aber trotz mehrfacher Verbindung der Ältesten mit dem

Earlier studies of the Old Babylonian 'elders' referred almost exclusively to their role as a city authority, and the urban character of the institution was unquestionable. This view prevailed until well into the 1950s. Most references to the city elders related them mainly, if not exclusively, to the Mesopotamian judicial system. É. Cuq (1910: 84–85), for instance, briefly mentioned the close cooperation between the *rabiānum* and the city elders in certain cases pertaining to the administration of local justice.[12] For Cuq, the *rabiānum* presided over the 'assemblée de justice' constituted by city elders or city notables. For his part, Walther (1917: 52–63) attempted to reconstruct the characteristics of the institution, particularly its constituency and functions. But some of his conclusions remain hypothetical because of the laconic nature of the sources. Walther suggested that the city elders might have consisted of a closed circle whose members were selected by age or vote. This analysis includes, furthermore, the elders' participation in legal matters and local issues, as well as a discussion of those documents where they act in concert with other local powers. Until the late 1950s, most Assyriologists adopted and supplemented Walther's conclusions. The institution of the elders was then considered a full-fledged urban office, and it never seems to have entered the debate on the nomadic features pervading Old Babylonian institutions, especially after the advent of the First Dynasty of Babylon.

The documents that became known after the discovery of the royal archives of Mari encouraged new interpretations concerning the role of the elders in Mesopotamian society. The institution of the elders was now tinged with nomadic strokes. Indeed, many Mari letters and administrative documents mention the elders of small kingdoms and nomadic groups. Based on these sources, Jean-Robert Kupper (1957: 46) described the Ḫaneans as a semi-nomadic people in the process of sedentarization under the auspices of the kings of Mari.[13] Although Kupper acknowledged that the social and political organization of the Ḫaneans was poorly known, he maintained that they were headed by the *sugāgu* and the elders (p. 16).[14] Kupper resorted to a similar explanation to account for the political

---

Tempel sind hier natürlich nur Zeugen (wenn auch zur Gerichtsstätte gehörende) gemeint' (Walther 1917: 52).

12 See also Schorr ([1913] 1971: 366 fn. 4), Jean (1929: 37), and Driver and Miles (1952: 492).

13 Several different interpretations regarding the Ḫaneans have appeared since the publication of Kupper's book. See, e.g., Gelb (1961: 27), Charpin and Durand (1986: 153), Anbar (1991), Durand (1992: 113; 1998: 417), and Fleming (2004: 85–92).

14 For Kupper (1957) the *sugāgum* was a municipal official with functions similar to those of the *šāpirum, ḫazannum* or *rabiānum* (p. 18), and he later equates *sugāgum* with sheikh (p. 60). Finet (1982: 9) argued similarly when dealing with local authorities in Mari. For Sasson (1969: 13), the *sugāgum* was a community leader, a role similar to the *moqtar*. Durand (1997: 206–208) has criticized previous interpretations of the *sugāgum* and remarked on his role as an intermediary between the palace and private individuals. Durand (1998: 494–96) also distinguished the *sugāgum* of sedentary regions from that of the Bedouins.

institutions of the Benjaminites, a system comparable to that of the modern Bedouins, where each tribe was in the hands of a hereditary sheikh counseled by the elders (p. 62). It was Klengel (1960: 357), however, who directly stated that the elders in the Mari documents were not only city elders but also blood-related officials of tribal groups. In this manner, the evidence from these archives opened the possibility of tracing the historical development of the institution.[15] The Bedouin origins of the population of certain oases in Arabia are, according to Klengel, a suitable analogy to explain the transition from the nomadic to the sedentary character of the elders in ancient Mesopotamia.[16]

A few years after the discovery of the royal archives of Mari, the texts excavated at Ebla since the mid-1960s allowed Klengel (1989: 61) to extend the nomadic origin of the elders half a millennium further back in time. Giovanni Pettinato (1986: 147), the first epigraphist of the Italian archaeological mission at Ebla, had already remarked on the connection between the elders and the king. He interpreted Ebla as a tribal society led by elders, whose ruler was elected from the midst of wealthy families to perform the role of *primus inter pares* for a limited period. According to Pettinato, 'il potere a Ebla era nelle mani degli anziani' (p. 151), but he adds that the specific functions of the institution remain unknown. Klengel's (1989) comparative analysis of the elders at Ebla and Mari agrees on the close relationship between the ruler and the elders. From documents such as ration lists and a letter, Klengel infers that the elders at Ebla played the role of advisors, confidants, and experts. In this interpretation, then, their power seems to be more restricted than in Pettinato's approach. Finally, Klengel maintains that the geographical distribution of the elders in the region of Mari already in the pre-Sargonic period suggests a certain continuity in the social development of the area, namely, the inclusion of a pre-state institution in a state administration.

The alleged nomadic origin of the elders is controversial. Instead of an evolutionary pattern towards sedentarization, the scanty information that can be drawn from cuneiform sources suggests the co-existence of two different, and probably

15 According to Klengel (1960: 357): 'Hierbei verdienen insbesondere die Texte aus dem königlichen Archiv von Māri Interesse, da sie die *šībūtum* nicht nur als Älteste einer Stadt bzw. Siedlung (*šībūt ālim*) kennen, sondern sie auch als Funktionäre einer blutsverwandten Stammeseinheit bezeugen und damit eine Aussage hinsichtlich der geschichtlichen Entwicklung dieser Institution ermöglichen'. More recently Klengel (1989: 61) argued that the rendering 'city elders' for the logogram $abba_2$ is safe only when followed by uru. In this respect, he disagrees with Gelb (1984: 267–74) whose list of 'elders (of the city)', that is AB + ÁŠ without uru, is longer than his list with the expression 'city elders' written out fully.

16 Klengel's hypothesis, however, has not been fully accepted. Van De Mieroop (1997: 124), for instance, argues that: '[t]his interpretation relies entirely upon the unproven model of gradual sedentarization of the nomads in Mesopotamian history, and does not explain the common appearance of "elders" in texts pre-dating the second millennium'.

unrelated, institutions of elders. The evidence for the political influence of elders in nomadic societies does not necessarily imply a particular stage in the ladder of social evolution towards a settled life. Rather, nomadism itself is a specialized adaptation that evolved in conjunction with village life and urbanism. It is worth recalling that, aside from those texts mentioning the elders of 'nomadic' societies in early times, there is also at least one pre-Sargonic administrative document from Ebla recording the expression AB+ÁŠ.AB+ÁŠ *Ma-ri*^{ki} 'the elders of Mari' (see Pettinato 1979: 156, n° 1663 = TM.75.G.2225, and Gelb 1984: 267). The text is a delivery of metal by Mari officials. In this instance, the reference to the city leaves little room for doubting the 'sedentary' character of the elders of Mari, attested as early as the pre-Sargonic period. This attestation is unique, because although references to the elders appear frequently in Mari documents, these elders belong to places or groups other than Mari itself (see Table II). The absence of examples pertaining to the elders of Mari is due, perhaps, to the royal character of the available texts.[17] A recent study of Mari (Fleming 2004: 199), does not necessarily relate the elders to a nomadic origin but regards them as survivors of premonarchic collective authorities. In the following sections of this chapter, I discuss first the elders at Mari and then those from Babylonia.

THE ELDERS ATTESTED IN MARI DOCUMENTS

The documents from the royal archives of Mari record the word 'elders' in various writings. The term is written syllabically *ši-bu-ut a-lim*, 'city elders', and in certain cases it further appears with the Sumerian determinative for 'men', $^{\text{lú-meš}}$*ši-bu-ut a-lim*. Variants include the city name, and the expression $^{\text{lú-meš}}$*ši-bu-ut ma-tim*, 'elders of the land'.[18] Besides the syllabic writing, the scribes of the Mari region and northern areas used the logogram ^{lú}šu-gi^{meš} with the nominal meaning of 'elders', although the word šu-gi in Babylonia regularly functions as an adjective (i.e. *šību*, 'old').[19] That ^{lú}šu-gi^{meš} is the logographic equivalent of *šībūtum* becomes apparent from examples in which elders of a single place are attested with both writings.[20]

17 This situation might change after the publication of the *Documents judiciaires de Mari*, announced in Durand (2000: 152).

18 Thus for instance, ***šībūt ālim*** (e.g. ARM 3 73: 10; ARM 14 121: 29; *RA* 52: 166, n° 312: 23); $^{\text{lú-meš}}$***šībūt ālim*** (e.g. ARM 26 411: 73); $^{\text{lú-meš}}$***šībūt* GN** (e.g. ARM 26 404: 36, ARM 26 503: 5-6; ARM 28 50: 25'); $^{\text{lú-meš}}$***šībūt mātim*** (e.g. ARM 26 438: 8).

19 This logogram is also attested in documents from Tell al Rimah, e.g., *OBTTR* 201: 5. 3 udu $nita_2$ ^{lú}šu-⌜gi⌝ [^{uru}]*Ia-ši-ba-tim*^{ki}, '3 rams from the elders of Yašibatum;' and 267: 11. ⌜1⌝ (bán) *a-na* ^{lú}šu-gi lú *Šu*!-*šar-ra-iú,* '1 bán [of fine beer] for the elder, the man of Šušarā (= Šemšara)'.

20 Thus for instance ^{lú}šu-gi^{meš} *Ur-gi-iš*^{ki} (ARM 23 504: 5; 28 45: 12'; *MARI* 7: 182, n° 7:5), but *ši-bu-ut Ur-gi-iš*^{ki} in *MARI* 7: 178 n° 5: 16.

This fact also finds confirmation in a letter wherein a scribe from Ašnakkum wrote the logogram with a gloss for the Akkadian reading, i.e., ^{lú}šu-gi$^{\text{meš-}ti}$-*ia*, 'my elders' (ARM 28 103: 24). Worth mentioning is the mistake of the scribe of Ašlakkā who started writing the word logographically and unwittingly slipped into Akkadian, as a result writing $^{\text{lú-meš}}$šu-*bu-ti* (ARM 28 64: 5). The variants ^{lú}šu-gi$_{(4)}^{\text{meš}}$ and $^{\text{lú-meš}}$šu-gi$_{(4)}$-(a) are easily explained due to the diverse provenance of the Mari letters, since many of them originated in peripheral areas.[21]

That in Mari texts the words *šībūtum* and ^{lú}šu-gi^{meš} refer to an institution similar to – though in certain cases more 'nomadic' than – the 'city elders' in Babylonia seems to have been taken for granted. Bottéro (1957: 241 §55), for instance, included the elders from Mari documents under the category 'community representatives'. He characterized them as officials and administrators constituting 'une sorte de "Conseil des Anciens", de "Sénat" en réduction' (see also Kupper 1973: 170). Bottéro based his comparison on studies of the city elders written before 1933, when the city of Mari had not yet been discovered. Similarly, Jean-Marie Durand (1983: 518) characterized the elders attested in ARM 21 388 as a group of notables composed of the chiefs of important families that constituted the municipal assembly. The elders, according to Durand, were civil dignitaries with priority over the military because in this administrative text they – together with the *mārū damqūtim* – precede a list of military officials.[22] More recently, Moshe Anbar (1991: 154) maintained that 'the elders' is both an urban and a tribal institution. In his interpretation, the body represents its own community and it is in addition a decision-making group (see also Luke 1965: 88-90; Fleming 2004: 190–200). Although Finet (1982: 13) has briefly mentioned that the term 'elders' may apply to military veterans as well as to local representatives of the 'citizens', the military aspect has not been further investigated.[23]

ACTIVITIES AND FUNCTIONS OF THE MARI ELDERS

The majority of Mari documents mentioning the elders are letters dealing with political affairs and disputes involving kings, princes, kinglets, and royal officials from northern Syria. In most instances these elders seem to be more closely related to military than to civil matters. In a letter from Yaqqim-Addu, the governor of

21 The different writings are transcribed in the list of documents at the end of this section.

22 Durand (1988a: 259 and 2000: 159) further described the elders mentioned in ARM 26 249: 7, 12 as 'autorités civiles indigènes'.

23 According to Finet (1982: 13), 'Le terme [*šībūtum*] est ambigu: il désigne tantôt des vétérans de l'armée (III, 19; XIV 48), tantôt des délégués locaux représentant leurs concitoyens et agissant souvent de conserve avec le *sugāgūm*'. See also Finet (1973b: 23-24).

Saggarātum, to the king of Mari, it is clearly mentioned that a group of elders is guarding (*ana maṣṣartim*) Saggarātum while another is guarding Dūr-Yaḫdun-Līm (ARM 14 48: 30-35).[24] Similarly, Yapḫur-Līm, a king from one of the cities of Ida-Maraṣ, informs Zimrī-Līm that the seven 'reserve elders' ($^{\text{lú-meš}}$šu-gi dirig-ga) appointed to guard the city gate are hungry; and that the same urge affects 15 reserve men recruited for the guard (*ana maṣṣartim*). In order to keep control over them, Yapḫur-Līm asks for the king's intervention (ARM 28 114).[25] Kupper (1998: 169) suggested that Zimrī-Līm himself posted those men, as part of a Mari garrison, in one of his vassal cities. The protection of settlements does not fit into the functions of city elders as traditionally described. The defensive role explicit in these texts may have influenced Birot's (1974: 91) rendering of ^{lú}šu-gi^{meš} as 'vétérans' instead of elders.

Another letter from Yaqqim-Addu, written probably during the year ZL 2' (Durand 1998: 442), refers to the ^{lú}šu-gi of Dūr-Yaḫdun-Līm (ARM 14 70). In this case, the official of Saggarātum asks the ruler whether he should put aside a group of people who cannot campaign and assign them to protect (*ana maṣṣartim*) the fortress. This group was formed by the ^{lú}šu-gi and the ^{lú}tur^{meš}. Both terms were previously interpreted as an age category 'vétérans' and 'jeunes' (Birot 1974: 125), and 'vieux' and 'enfants' (Durand 1998: 441). Since the reasons why they are unable to campaign (*ša ḫarrānam lā ile'ū*) are not stated, one could argue that being too old or too young is the obstacle.[26] It seems unlikely, however, that a fortress wherein troops are posted (ll. 7-8) is going to be left in the hands of such a powerless party.[27] Maybe in this context ^{lú}tur^{meš} should be interpreted as 'petit gens' (Durand 1998: 584d, see also ARM 26 38 n. b), or it could even be read ^{lú}dumu^{meš}, 'inhabitants', since the word with this connotation also appears together with ^{lú}šu-gi^{meš} in another document (ARM 13 148: 3).[28] An exemption from military duty similar to the one reported in ARM 14 70 is found in a letter from Kibrī-Dagan, the governor of Terqa (ARM 3 19). Here the governor informs that a group of soldiers is now resting at home while those who replaced them were sent to Babylon. Kibrī-Dagan further explains that the 'gentry' (*mārū awīlim*) and those who were ill (see Durand 1998: 182) were not recruited, and that the elders

24 Yaqqim-Addu may not yet have been appointed governor of Saggarātum when this letter was issued (see Durand 1998: 423).

25 The name of the city over which Yaḫpur-Līm ruled is unknown.

26 The logogram šu-gi with the meaning 'old' is attested at least in one case referring to an old lady who is unable to work: 1 munus šu-gi *ši-ip-ra-am e-pé-ša-am, ú-ul il-le-i* (ARM 27 38, 12'-13').

27 Kupper (1985: 465) seems to have interpreted ARM 14 48 and 14 70 similarly, for he briefly comments, 'les *muškēnū* sont convoqués pour une brève campagne, tandis que les Anciens sont affectés à la garde des remparts'.

28 Similarly, in ARM 28 31: 5-6, (...) *ma-*[*a*]*-tam* [*ù* ^{lú}šu]-gi^{meš} (...) 'the population and the elders...'

who were unable to go also remained at home.[29] Again, the reasons why these $^{\text{lú-meš}}$šu-gi-a cannot campaign are not given. It is worth mentioning, however, that, in this case, there is no reference to the youths. It is most likely then that these elders were officials related to the military instead of old people.

The close connection of the elders with military affairs is also apparent from several other documents. A letter (ARM 2 75), for instance, states that Yamruṣ-el together with the elders of Qâ and Isqâ have assembled a troop of 200 men to assist Hammurabi – most possibly the king of Kurdā rather than his namesake from Babylon – thus betraying their loyalty to Zimrī-Līm. The elders' authority in disposing of soldiers for a king also appears in a missive from Yaqqim-Addu to Zimrī-Līm (ARM 14 64). In this case, the governor of Saggarātum prompted the *sugāgū*, the *laputtû*, and the *šībūt ḫalṣim* to provide substitute soldiers for Babylon.[30] The mustering of troops is also the subject of another letter (ARM 28 59). In this case, Ibāl-Addu answers Zimrī-Līm's request for soldiers by saying that in a couple of days royal officials (arad^{meš} *bēlīya*) will be meeting with the elders of Ida-Maraṣ, presumably to deal with the king's demand. The elders concern for the army, moreover, transcends the terrestrial sphere, for it also encompasses prayers on behalf of the king and the troops, as recorded in two letters from Terqa (ARM 3 17 and ARM 13 117).[31]

Aside from their management of troops, the elders seem to have had an active military role in political and inter-city/state affairs. Thus, Sibkuna-Addu, the king of Šudā, writes to Ḫālī-ḫadun, a *Ḫanean* leader, about the gathering of the elders and the troops, and he promises to dispatch some 120 of his elders as requested (ARM 28 31). These elders probably belong or are closely attached to the army, since it is hard to believe that the chief of the 'nomads' is asking for such a large number of advisors from the king of a city with whom he is not always on good terms.[32] The demand for elders in certain cases seems to be related to defensive activities. Thus, for instance, Buqāqum informs Zimrī-Līm that the enemy has fortified Yabliya and Ḫarbû, and that Yassi-Dagan asked him to send the elders (^{lú}šu-gi^{meš}) back to the king (ARM 26 479).[33] The context of this letter lets us suspect that these elders were engaged in the defense of the city, for after referring to

29 29. *ù* [^{lú}]$^{\text{-meš}}$šu-gi-a *ša a-n*[*a ge-er-ri-im*] / 30. *a-la-*[*ka*]*m la i-le-*[*ú qa-tam-ma*] / 31. *a-na ra-ma-ni-šu ša-*[*ap-ru*]. For the restoration of lines 29 and 30, see Durand 1998: 181 n. 377.

30 Yaqqim-Addu further comments on the subject in ARM 14 65.

31 In these letters, Kibrī-Dagan informs Zimrī-Līm that he and the 'elders of the city' ($^{\text{lú-meš}}$š u-gi *a-lim*^{ki}) keep praying to Dagan for the king and the army.

32 Note that Sibkuna-Addu reminds Ḫālī-ḫadun about his desire for establishing peace (ll. 15-17) and about the importance of taking an oath by the gods.

33 The exact position of Buqāqum is unknown. Yabliya was on the left and Ḫarbû on the right bank of the Euphrates, to the north of Ḫît (see Lackenbacher 1988b: 401 and 409).

sending them back to Mari, Buqāqum demands reinforcements because Šallūrum has threatened an attack within five days.[34]

The degree of mobility of the elders attested in Mari documents is worth emphasizing because it relates them to inter-city/state relationships, as well as to the interaction of urban rulers with non-urban chiefs. The elders' mobilization had different purposes, in certain cases the main reason being the delivery of messages or additional information.[35] In a message to the ruler of Mari, Ibāl-Addu, the king of Ašlakkā, writes about his dealings with other leaders, and he complains about some of Mari's tributary villages that had become allies with Tawakûm (ARM 28 50).[36] Ibāl-Addu finally states that he is sending the elders of Ašlakkā together with a messenger of Zimrī-Līm to provide the king with a complete account. Diplomatic responsibilities were also within the elders' domain, and, on certain occasions, they had to travel to accomplish this duty. We know that messengers and elders of Yarkib-Addu, the king of Ḫanzat, went to Talḫayûm to obtain Yāwi-Ilā's support in their dispute with Būnūma-Addu, the ruler of Niḫriyā (ARM 13 145). Yāwi-Ilā, however, makes it clear that he is an ally of Zimrī-Līm and writes to the king of Mari for instructions on how to proceed. Although the reasons why Yarkib-Addu sent not only messengers but also elders are not indicated, it is possible to infer that the importance of the mission required persuasive delegates. Another document mentions that Yāwi-Ilā sends the elders with instructions so that they will be able to answer all of Zimrī-Līm's questions (ARM 13 148). This letter was probably issued as one of the preliminary steps to concluding a vassalage treaty with Mari. The elders played, furthermore, the role of peace mediators representing their king. A letter written in the year ZL 9' records the siege of the city of Razamā by an army of Elam and Ešnunna under the command of Atamrum, the king of Allaḫad in Andarig (ARM 14 104^{+}). After ten days, the elders of Razamā left their city to negotiate with Atamrum on behalf of their king, Šarrīya.[37]

A seemingly large movement of elders is reported on several occasions. In one instance, Išme-Addu of Ašnakkum, the elders of Ida-Maraṣ, Urgiš, Šinaḫ, Ḫurrā, and Yapṭur led by Yatar-mālik of Šuduḫum and Apil-Sîn of Ašnakkum went to Mal(a)ḫatum requesting the sacrifice of a goat so that they could conclude an alliance (*MARI* 7: 182–84, n° 7).[38] In a partially published letter mentioning the peace

34 According to Lackenbacher (1988a: 401), Buqāqum was probably the governor of a city or region to the south of Mari. As for Šallurum, he was possibly a king of Ešnunna and, according to Durand (1988a: 145–46), he campaigned in the area and conquered Ḫanat in ZL 3.

35 There is also one instance (ARM 28 52) where Ibāl-Addu arrested and interrogated a man called Tašbir and two elders – if Kupper's (1998: 77) restoration of line 9' is correct.

36 The location of this place is unknown (Kupper 1998: 76).

37 For a detailed analysis of this letter, see Charpin (1993b: 197–203).

38 Unfortunately, part of this passage is broken and the restoration [*za-ka-r*]*i-im* is not completely sure (Charpin 1993a: 185).

with the Benjaminites, the writer instructs the addressee of a previous letter that, in case certain conditions are met, a man called Atamri-el should lead 10 or 20 elders to the writer's presence to explain their proposal (ARM 26: 181 M.6874).[39] Yet another party of 10 elders of the 'tent-dwellers' (*ḫanû*) headed by a certain Irida(n)num is on its way to approach Zimrī-Līm, according to a brief message from Yaqqim-Addu to Kibrī-Dagan (ARM 3 65). In one case, Niqmān and the elders of Qâ went to express their proposal to Asqūdum and Ḫālī-ḫadūn, but they sent this official delegation to the king (ARM 26 48).[40] Yumraṣ-el, the king of Abī-ilī, proceeded similarly when the elders of Qirdaḫat approached him, and he wrote a letter to Zimrī-Līm announcing his decision to send these men to the king (ARM 28 140). Apparently, elders of other places or groups often visited other kings or city authorities on diplomatic missions, although it is not always possible to infer the exact reasons for this. Thus, when the *sugāgum* of Ḫurrā was planning a rebellion, he sent five elders to Elaḫut; unfortunately, his purposes for doing so are unknown (ARM 28 67). Another instance is when Zimrī-Līm required Baḫdī-Līm to bring six elders (no place or gentilic filiation mentioned) to his presence. Nevertheless, due to irrigation work Baḫdī-Līm had to delay his coming and the gathering of the people that the king requested (ARM 6 12).

The elders received, in certain cases, food rations from the king of Mari, a fact that stresses the submission of this institution to the royal authority. As already mentioned, on one occasion the reserve elders assigned to the defense of a city complain because they are hungry (ARM 28 114). Yapḫur-Līm then asks Zimrī-Līm to give instructions to Yaqqim-Addu, so that these men can eat their rations (še-ba *līkulū*). Judging from Yapḫur-Līm's concluding remarks, feeding these elders will keep them quiet. Another letter describes a similar situation, although it is possible that it refers to a banquet rather than to rations (*MARI* 7: 178 n° 5). In this case, the instigator of hostilities against Zimrī-Līm gave food and drinks to the elders of Urgiš, apparently to obtain their political support.[41] The elders seem also to have owned and disposed of animals, and at least some of them were borrowed by or transferred to the palace. For instance, 20 oxen belonging to the elders in service at Saggarātum and 30 oxen of the elders guarding Dūr-Yaḫdun-Līm had to perform some work for the palace (ARM 14 48). In this letter, Yaqqim-Addu reported to Zimrī-Līm that instead of using the 'commoners" (*muškēnū*) oxen for

39 Apart from being partially published, this letter is also partially broken. Unfortunately, the names of the parties are unknown to me.

40 Durand (1997: 415) suggests that Niqmān could have been the predecessor of Yumraṣ-el, king of Abī-ilī, the capital of the kingdoms of Qâ and Isqâ (see also Guichard 1994: 243).

41 This letter is fragmentary and it also has certain linguistic peculiarities. For an interpretation that differs from Charpin's (1993a: 182–91), see Durand (1997: 635).

threshing the grain of the palace, he resorted to the elders' animals. According to certain administrative documents, furthermore, the elders had to deliver some of their animals as well as other products to the palace. An administrative document dated to the year ZL 11' records the delivery of one ox and six sheep by the elders of Šunā, two oxen by the elders of Urgiš, and one ox by the elders of Šinaḫ (ARM 23 504). A text registers the delivery of one sheep by the elders of Tizraḫ (ARM 7 130), and yet another administrative document shows that the elders of Zabalum sent two pots of honey to the palace at Mari (ARM 9 241). Moreover, in a letter from Išme-Dagan to Yasmaḫ-Addu (ARM 2 16), the elders of Zalluḫān seem to have obtained a reduction in an amount of sheep and goats after Išme-Dagan defeated the city.[42] These deliveries of cattle and products indicate a certain dependence that could assume the form of either an alliance or a total or partial submission (see Bardet *et al.* 1984: 504).

The dependence of the elders upon leading figures, mainly kings and kinglets, becomes apparent from a number of documents where they are mentioned as 'elders of PN', or elders plus a possessive pronoun, referring to a figure of authority. Thus, a group described as 'the elders of Yarkib-Addu', the king of Ḫanzat, delivered a message to Yāwi-Ilā, king of Talḫayûm (ARM 13 145). In several instances, kings refer to the elders as 'my elders'. That is the case with the promise of Zibkuna-Addu, king of Šudā, to send a number of elders ([^{lú}š]u-gi^{meš}-*ia*, i.e. 'my elders') to another leader (ARM 28 31). Similarly, in a letter from Šūb-rām of Šušā to Ibāl-Addu, king of Ašlakkā, Šūb-rām reminds his colleague that he has sent his elders (^{lú}šu-gi^{meš}-*ia*) to Zimrī-Līm (ARM 28 96, see also ARM 28 91). In a letter to the king of Mari, Šadûm-labua, the monarch of Ašnakkum, also speaks about 'my elders' (^{lú}šu-gi$^{\text{meš-}ti}$-*ia*, ARM 28 103). The use of the second and third person possessive pronouns is also attested. Išme-Addu, king of Ašnakkum, refers to Ibāl-Addu's elders as 'your elders' (^{lú}šu-gi^{meš}-[*k*]*a*, *MARI* 7: 175 n° 2). On his part, Šūb-rām mentions Ilī-Ištar, the king of Šunā, and 'his elders' and Ilī-Addu, the king of Kiduḫḫum, and 'his elders' (^{lú}šu-gi^{meš}–*šu* in both cases, ARM 28 95). Moreover, in a letter to Zimrī-Līm, Ḫabdu-mālik also uses the third person pronoun for the elders of Hammurabi of Kurdā (ARM 26 391). Documents wherein the elders are characterized as 'the servants' of a king further illustrate the elders' dependence upon certain rulers. For instance, Abī-mekin characterizes the notables and the elders of Numḫā as the servants (arad-*du*) of Simaḫ-ilānē, the king of Kurdā (ARM 26 463). Similarly, in a letter from Ḫammān, the governor of Dēr-upon-Baliḫ, he describes the elders of that city as 'servants of my lord', i.e., Zimrī-Līm (*MARI* 6: 75).

42 For the restoration of this line and the interpretation of the passage see Durand (1997: 93).

'ELDERS' FOLLOWED BY GEOGRAPHIC OR GENTILIC NAMES

Aside from their close association with leading figures, the elders from Mari texts are also related on the one hand to specific geographic entities, as for instance the city (*ālum*), the district (*ḫalṣum*), the land (*mātum*), and specific geographic names (see Table II). On the other, the noun can be qualified by a gentilic, as for instance, the elders of the Benjaminites. It is important then to see whether it is possible to establish a functional difference among all these variants. In the case of the city elders, most of the examples show their involvement in military, political, and diplomatic affairs. There seems to be no document, however, that unambiguously depicts them as a council of elders functioning as the ruler's advisors or as community representatives. In problems concerning their own city, the elders seem to have pursued their own agenda, presumably to accommodate themselves within the framework of an unstable equilibrium of powers. Thus, for instance, after the city of Kawalḫûm (i.e. Kalḫû) passed from Išme-Dagan into the hands of Asqur-Addu, the king of Karanā, the city elders approached the new lord, who granted them presents before they returned to their city (ARM 26 411). This reminds us of the episode wherein a rival of Zimrī-Līm gave food and drinks to the elders of Urgiš, most probably to obtain their support against the king of Mari (*MARI* 7: 178 n° 5). There is evidence, moreover, that certain kings negotiated with the elders of other cities. Zimrī-Līm, for example, tells Šibtu, the queen, that he has established an alliance with the elders of Šenaḫ and that he has further installed a *ḫazannum* in the city (ARM 10 121).[43] This case is interesting because the elders are in fact accepting the imposition of an external authority, and although Zimrī-Līm receives the *biltum*-tax, usually paid by vassals, there is no mention of a local ruler. The fact that the king of Mari established an allegiance with the elders may also indicate their military status because it seems unlikely that Zimrī-Līm would have cared about the city council of a vassal city. Gaining the elders' support was a way of securing a potential military force. As showed earlier, on several occasions the elders were directly engaged in the recruitment of soldiers.

The city elders' concern about both the internal and external affairs of their city is well illustrated in a letter that the elders of Talḫayûm sent to Zimrī-Līm immediately after the ruler of their city was murdered (*RA* 82: 98). Apparently, the envoys of a rival city put an end to the life of the unnamed king of Talḫayûm,

43 Durand (1997: 471) suggests the reading *ḫaṣṣannum/ḫaṣṣiânum* instead of *ḫazannum*. In his analysis, the word derives from the base **ḫalṣi'*- plus the suffix -*ānum* (-*annum*), with an assimilation of /l/ to /ṣ/, that is, /lṣ/ becomes /ṣṣ/. In Durand's view, the *ḫaṣṣannum* is a direct representative of the king.

whom Durand (1988b: 111) identifies with Yāwi-ilā.[44] As a reaction against the regicide, the elders ask for Zimrī-Līm's intervention, suggesting that troops should enter Talḫayûm to prevent the spread of panic among the city inhabitants. The elders further suggest that Zimrī-Līm should write to the people of Luḫā reaffirming his authority over the city of Talḫayûm. The way Zimrī-Līm handled this case is unknown, but his decision must have depended on the importance the issue had for Mari foreign policy. If the matter was not serious enough, a powerful ruler could have neglected the request. There is at least one example of such an indifferent attitude towards the elders of dependent regions. Thus, because the country of Ḫiwilat and Talmuš revolted, the notables ($^{lú-meš}$*we-d*[*u-tu*]*m*) and the elders ($^{lú-meš}$šu-gi) of that land approached Išme-Dagan with gifts, but the king of Ekallātum reports to his brother in Mari that he has rejected their presents. Undoubtedly, this is a clear sign that Išme-Dagan was not willing to intervene in this matter (ARM 4 68). In other cases, influential kings adopted an intermediate position, especially when they were not interested in privileging one petty king over another. Under circumstances like this, instead of sending troops to mediate in a conflict between Šūb-rām and Hāya-Sūmû, Zimrī-Līm recommended a river ordeal, which spared the king of Mari the mobilization of his soldiers.[45]

The expression 'elders of the district' is less frequently attested than the expression 'city elders'. There are two examples that clearly relate the elders of the district to the recruitment of troops. In the first case, Yaqqim-Addu informs Zimrī-Līm that the elders, together with other officials, will provide soldiers for Babylon; these elders presumably belonged to the area of Saggāratum (ARM 14 64). In the second, Yaqqim-Addu approached the same group of officials – i.e. the *sugāgū*, the *laputtû*, and the *šībūt ḫalṣim* – to tell them that they should recruit soldiers and that the elders of different districts had gathered (ARM 14 65). Because Yaqqim-Addu mentioned that people from Yamḫad and Qatna had already marched to Babylon, it is possible that this and the previous letter refer to the same recruitment. The reference to several districts (*ḫalṣānū*) in ARM 14 65 and the mention of the elders of the upper district ($^{lú-meš}$šu-gi-a *ḫa-al-ṣí-im* [*e-l*]*i-im*) in ARM 26 447 may imply that the term was mainly an administrative category. Mari officials used the word *ḫalṣum* for organizational purposes. *Šībūt ḫalṣim* seems to have been, therefore, a broad category encompassing the elders of those unnamed specific places

44 The murder of Yāwi-ilā is also mentioned in a letter from Ibāl-el to Zimrī-Līm (*MARI* 7: 182–84, n°7: 12'–16' ff.). From the last sentences of *RA* 82: 98–101, it is possible to infer that the murder was committed by people from Luḫā.

45 There are two letters referring to this river ordeal. The first (ARM 26 249) is a report narrating the results of the test; the river god favored Šūb-rām. The second (ARM 28 91) is a letter from Šūb-rām to Zimrī-Līm, wherein the ruler of Šušā describes the episode, and he further asks the king of Mari for military support to deal with the district of Yapṭur.

that formed a particular district controlled by Mari. When an official thought it was important to make the expression *šībūt ḫalṣim* less indefinite, he provided a list of names, probably to facilitate the identification of these persons with a king or a place (e.g. ARM 26 447, and ARM 27 67).[46] In the second document, Zakira-ḫammû, the governor of Qaṭṭunān, reports having received a letter from Bīna-Ištar, the king of Kurdā, who complained about the confiscation of the *ḫûratum*-plants that some people from Numḫā had pulled out.[47] Then the governor informs Zimrī-Līm that he had read the tablet in the presence of the elders of the district, apparently seven in total, in the presence of 100 witnesses of the city and of the main servants of the king. Zimrī-Līm, who had to decide on the issue as requested, would have had no problem in recognizing his servants, while the elders of the district were listed by name to make the identification of these men easier.[48]

The land, *mātum*, is the third and last territorial category related to the elders. As is the case with the elders of the district, the *šībūt mātim*, 'the elders of the land', are rather poorly documented when compared with the city elders. Unlike the district (*ḫalṣum*), the land (*mātum*) does not necessarily refer to an administrative area. Rather, *mātum* designates a political territory similar to the concept of 'country' with the proviso that, in antiquity, borders were not conceived as rigid lines. The term could apply both to the land proper as well as to its inhabitants. Our corpus of Mari documents records the existence of the elders of the lands of Andarig (ARM 26 438), Apûm (ARM 28 95), Dumātum (ARM 4 29), Ḫiwilat and Talmuš (ARM 4 68), Ida-Maraṣ (ARM 28 59, *MARI* 7: 182 n° 7, Durand 1999–2000: 192),

46 ARM 26 447 is a letter from Yanṣib-Addu to the king regarding the district of Qaṭṭunān. Unfortunately, the document is fragmentary but there seems to be a list of at least eight persons who are the elders of the district. ARM 27 67 is also partially broken, but the elders are probably seven. The listing of elders by their names is unusual in Mari documents, but there are individuals qualified as elders in administrative documents (e.g. ARM 22 12 rev i: 22'; ARM 22 14 ii: 18, iii: 16; ARM 24 6 iii: 31'-32'; ARM 24 247: 8').

47 Birot (1993: 133), the editor of this letter, argues that the restoration of the name of the king of Kurdā is safe, especially because Kurdā was the capital city of the land of Numḫā.

48 Birot (1993: 133) had already pointed out that two of these elders, Šubiša and Nabû-nāṣir, are possibly the same persons attested in two other documents. One of them, Šubiša, appears in ARM 27 62: 14, where Zakira-ḫammû tells the king that he is sending Šubiša, Dādum, and his brothers as requested. The other man is recorded in a letter from the same governor to Šunuḫra-ḫālū (ARM 27 36: 24). Zakira-ḫammû mentions that a problem he previously had with Nabû-nāṣir reached the king's ears. Since the day he arrived at Qaṭṭunān, the governor continues, Nabû-nāṣir has been talking badly about him in the district. Zakira-ḫammû ends the letter asking Šunuḫra-ḫālū to remove Nabû-nāṣir from the district and to assign him to some other place. If this Nabû-nāṣir is indeed one of the elders listed in ARM 27 67, the fact that Šunuḫra-ḫālū, the 'secrétaire privé du roi' (Kupper 1998: 68), can remove him shows that the king posted these elders. The influence of Mari authorities over the permanence in office of these *šībūtum* shows, furthermore, that they were royal officials and did not fulfill the role of a council of elders.

and Numḫā (ARM 26 393 and 463, *FM* 2: 210). The elders of Andarig are mentioned in a letter sent to the king of Mari in the context of plotting political alliances (ARM 26 438). Zimrī-Līm's informant reports the dealings of Atamrum, the king of Allaḫad, with other kings and the envoys of Babylon. The sender of the letter complains because Atamrum excluded Zimrī-Līm's delegates from all the meetings and from a banquet where even the palace attendants (*gerseqqû*) and the elders of Andarig were invited.[49] Apparently, in the event that Atamrum does not submit to Zimrī-Līm, the army of Mari posted in Atamrum's domains should leave.

The elders of the land of Apûm appear in a letter from Šūb-rām to the king of Mari (ARM 28 95). Zimrī-Līm had previously suggested that Šūb-rām and the chief elders of Apûm, as well as elders and ruler of Šunā and Kiduḫḫum, should accept the verdict of Ḫāya-Sūmû, the king of Ilān-ṣūrā, concerning a dispute over the city of Šunḫum (ARM 28 95).[50] Ḫāya-Sūmû declared that a river ordeal should take place and that two men and two women of Šunā and the same number from Apûm should throw themselves into the river. Ilī-Ištar, the man of Šunā, did not accept Ḫāya-Sūmû's solution and kept sacking Apûm. For that reason Šūb-rām writes to the king of Mari. At the end of his message, Šūb-rām blames Atamrum, the king of Andarig, for supporting Šunā's actions. This text is a good illustration of how convoluted these territorial disputes could get. As I interpret the document, Šūb-rām, the king of Šušā, at the request of Zimrī-Līm, is representing the interests of the people of Apûm. Kiduḫḫum was possibly one of the cities of the land of Apûm, while the city of Šunā belonged to the land of Ida-Maraṣ. The following chart illustrates the complexity of the situation:

49 The document refers to the $^{\text{lú-meš}}$*ši-bu-ut ma-ti-šu*, with the possessive pronoun referring to Atamrum king of Allaḫad, the capital city of Andarig (ARM 26 438: 8').

50 Note that although Ilī-Ištar was known to be the king of Šunā (Durand 2000: 257), in this letter he is mentioned as lú Šunā, the man of Šunā, possibly to highlight his vassal condition. This interpretation is, however, not certain because in Ešnunna and Karanā, for instance, lú meant king (Dalley *et al.* 1976: 32-33).

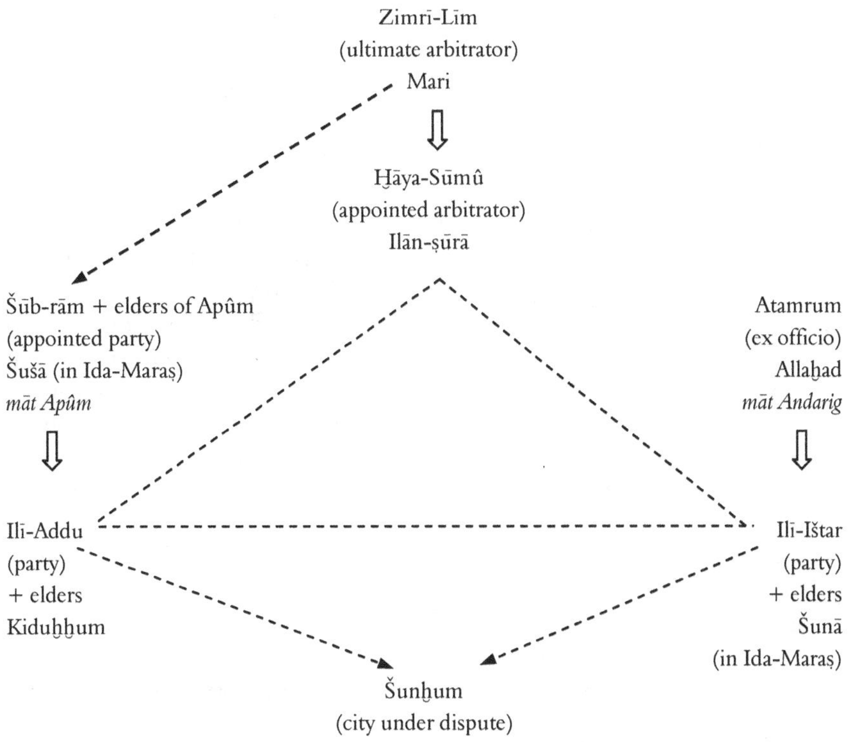

The elders of the land of Dumātum (ARM 4 29) and the elders of Ḫiwilat and Talmuš (ARM 4 68) are recorded in two letters that Išme-Dagan sent to Yasmaḫ-Addu. In the first case, Išme-Dagan reports that, while he was away, the elders of Dumātum went to Šubat-Enlil the same night that relief troops from Dumātum arrived at the city. Apparently, the elders' visit had the purpose of making it clear that they did not approve of the deeds of Ribīya, who seems to have been the man in charge of the troops of Dumātum (see Durand 1998: 105 e). It is possible that Ribīya had had hostile intentions toward Šubat-Enlil, because the elders' statement made Išme-Dagan rejoice. In the second letter, Išme-Dagan tells his brother that he rejected the presents that the elders of the land of Ḫiwilat and Talmuš brought to him after the land revolted. As already mentioned, the elders may have attempted to secure Išme-Dagan's support, but apparently they did not succeed.

The elders of the land of Numḫā are attested during the reigns of two kings of Kurdā, Simaḫ-ilānē and Hammurabi. In a letter to Zimrī-Līm, Abī-mekin reports a meeting of the notables and the elders of Numḫā, as well as an inspection that took place in the land of Numḫā (ARM 26 463).[51] During his early years on the throne of Mari, Zimrī-Līm was already concerned about the challenge Hammurabi of Babylon represented in the area, and he persistently tried to impose his authority over other kings. On one occasion, he complained because Simaḫ-ilānē did not address him as 'my father', as he addressed Hammurabi, but as 'my brother'. As a result, and to keep on good terms with the king of Mari, a person by the name of Išḫī-madar had to write a letter to Zimrī-Līm justifying Simaḫ-ilānē's politically incorrect greeting formula (*FM* 2: 210 n°117). Išḫī-madar blamed the *sugāgū* and the elders of Numḫā because they had told Simaḫ-ilānē that Aštamar-Addu, a former king of Numḫā, addressed Yaḫdun-Līm as 'brother' and that he should do the same. In his interpretation of this document, Bertrand Lafont (1994: 219) remarked on the role of the elders as a counter-weight that balanced the royal authority. He further understood that the elders recommended remaining independent because they were the 'gardiens des usages et traditions politiques du royaume'. It is also possible to maintain, however, that the elders, aware of the unstable and changing political scenario, had some other ally in mind, or that they considered Simaḫ-ilānē's kingdom strong enough to oppose Mari if necessary. Similarly, Hammurabi of Kurdā also seems to have been doubtful about submitting to Zimrī-Līm, and in order to put pressure on Hammurabi, Ḫabdu-mālik suggested that the elders of the country had perhaps influenced him (ARM 26 393). The case of the land of Numḫā is interesting because besides a territory, it also implies the Numḫā people, and this brings us to the elders of gentilic groups.

The elders of gentilic groups are poorly documented, as is the case with the elders of the district and the elders of the land. Aside from the Numḫeans, the examples from our corpus include references to the elders of the Benjaminites. In a letter to Asqūdum, Ašmad reports on the occupation of Aḫunā and Tuttul by the Benjaminites, while in the temple of Sîn in Ḫarrān, the *sugāgum* and the elders of the Benjaminites established an alliance with Asdi-takim, the king of Zalmaqqum (ARM 26 24). Among those who entered Tuttul is Atamri-el, probably the same man who was asked to lead a group of 10 or 20 elders of the Benjaminites to negotiate a peace agreement (ARM 26: 181 M.6874, only partially quoted). In another letter written early during Zimrī-Līm's reign, Mari officials try to persuade the *sugāgū* and a group of elders related to the Benjaminites to join a campaign aimed at looting Samsī-Addu's treasures still in Šubat-Enlil after the king's death (*FM* 2: 204 n°116).[52] Finally, the elders of *ḫanû*, 'the tent dwellers', possibly a generic name for an unspecified gentilic group, appear in ARM 3 65.

51 According to Lackenbacher (1988a: 387) this letter was written at the end of ZL 2' or at the beginning of ZL 3'.

52 These were the *sugāgū* and the elders of Mutê-bal. For Mutê-bal as a Benjaminite group see Durand (1988a: 175 n. 20) and Eidem (1994: 208 d).

ON THE ELDERS OF THE MARI REGION

Although there are fewer references to the 'elders of the district', the 'elders of the land', and the 'elders of gentilic groups' than to the 'city elders', all of them were engaged in the same kind of military and diplomatic activities. The characterization of the elders in Mari documents as a municipal authority presided over by a mayor – or a 'sheikh' (*sugāgum*) – originated in a comparison with the alleged role that the elders played in Babylonia. Similarly, the *rabiānum* seems to have been the model after which the interpretation of the *sugāgum* was shaped. As was the case with the *rabiānum*, certain scholars have defined the *sugāgum* as a 'mayor' when presiding over sedentary people, and as a 'sheikh' when leading nomads (e.g. Kupper 1957: 18 and 60; Finet 1982: 9, etc). J. Sasson (1969: 13), however, included the *sugāgum* in his study of the military establishment at Mari. Accordingly, he remarked on the military role of this office. Sasson considered the *sugāgum* as a mediator that the king appointed to negotiate with local communities. As I understand it, this interpretation implies a reversal of previous approaches, because instead of a community representative, the *sugāgum* is a royal appointee who represents the community. On his part, Ichiro Nakata (1989) has argued that the *sugāgum* was appointed 'for the purpose of holding the reins of the locality or area' (p. 117), and that the institution was unrelated to nomadic or sedentary factors. Durand (1997: 206 and 1998: 494) has pointed out that even though the state had to approve of the *sugāgum*, this does not mean that he was a royal official; rather, the *sugāgum* had an administrative role comparable to the *rabiānum* in Mesopotamia.[53] More recently, Fleming (2004: 63–75) has discussed the *sugāgum* institution and its tribal origin; he thinks that 'the *sugāgum* should not be viewed as a royal appointee in the usual sense of the word' (p. 75).

Even if this is not the place to study the office of *sugāgum*, the occurrence of this official together with the elders in several documents cannot be ignored, and I shall refer only to these texts. In our corpus, the *sugāgum* appears in the same document with the elders in eight cases, and in none of these instances does the *sugāgum* perform any of the activities of the *rabiānum*. His functions seem to be closer to the military role that Sasson ascribed to him.[54] Thus, in two documents

[53] Durand (1998: 494) affirms, 'l'étymologie qui a été proposée pour le terme permet de considérer le *sugâgum* comme l'équivalent du *rabiânum* des textes mésopotamiens. Une traduction par "maire", au moins en ce qui concerne les scheichs dont dépendent des villes, respecterait globalement la réalité de leur pouvoir et l'étymologie de leur appellation. Celui que l'on avait, jusqu'ici, et bien à tort, tenue pour le "maire" d'une ville, c'est-à-dire le *ḫazannum*, n'a en fait que des fonctions de représentant politique.'

[54] These documents are ARM 14 64 and 65; ARM 26 24; ARM 28 67; ARM 28 120; ARM 28 147; *FM* 2: 204 n° 217; and *FM* 2: 210 n° 117. The elders in connection with the *sugāgūtum* appear in *RA* 52: 164 n° 311).

(ARM 14 64 and 65), the *sugāgū* are listed before the *laputtû* and the elders, all of them clearly engaged in the recruitment of troops. In one of the texts, moreover, the *sugāgum* and the elders of the Benjaminites are celebrating an alliance with the king of Zalmaqqum (ARM 26 24). None of these functions are attested for the *rabiānum*. A letter from Ilī-Ištar, king of Šunā, to Zimrī-Līm, clearly illustrates the loyalty of the *sugāgum* towards the king, another aspect that differentiates the *sugāgum* from the *rabiānum* (ARM 28 147). In this case, Ilī-Ištar resorts to a comparison with the *sugāgum* to express his loyalty to Zimrī-Līm. He wrote: *emūq abīya ul akaššad, anāku kīma wardīka abašši ū lū kīma sugāgu*, 'I do not equal the strength of my father. I am actually like your servant, or like a *sugāgu*', and he further added *māru ša kīnātim ša mātim anummīm anāku*, ' I am a loyal inhabitant of this country'. Of course, not every *sugāgum* was so ideally trustworthy, because we know from a letter of Ibāl-Addu that the *sugāgum* of Ḫurrā seems to have had rebellious intentions against Zimrī-Līm (ARM 28 67).

There is no evidence from Mari documents that unambiguously depicts these elders as a body of notables representing the interests of community members. Rather than a municipal authority, the elders from Mari sources were royal officials engaged in military and diplomatic issues. The textual information does not allow us to trace the origin or social position of the men who constituted this institution. Nevertheless, the nature of their activities seems to relate them to local elites. In certain cases, they were in charge of guarding fortresses or cities, as for instance Dūr-Yaḫdun-Līm and Saggarātum. In other examples, they had to assemble and provide troops to assist the king of Mari in his own campaigns or in his collaboration with other kings, as for instance Hammurabi of Babylon. Zimrī-Līm even invited a group of elders to share in the booty of the treasuries that were left in Šubat-Enlil after Samsī-Addu's death. Some elders were dependents of the king of Mari, to the extent that they received food rations when in service, and, occasionally, they were even called 'servants' of the king. There are, moreover, examples where they send animals and other products to the palace at Mari, another indicator of their close ties or dependence upon the king. Not all of the elders, however, were loyal to the monarch of Mari.

Mari letters depict a complex political situation where rulers with varying degrees of power and independence were trying to keep or extend their dominion over their neighbors. In this respect, the degree of mobility of the elders mentioned in Mari documents is important because their movements were related not only to military enterprises but also to diplomacy, for they had a role in negotiating peace treaties and alliances. Under ideal circumstances, the elders answered to their king's command. This assumption finds confirmation in those examples referring to the elders 'of' a particular ruler and in those instances where the king calls the elders 'my elders'. Every city big or small, vassal or free, seems to have had a group of elders loyal, at least in theory, to the local ruler. As frequently happens to be the case, however, loyalty is not everlasting, and allegiance changes. Thus for example, Ḫammi-kūn's confidence in the elders to recover his father's throne as the king of Šuduḫum might imply that they have to betray somebody else (ARM 28 111). Terru, the king of Urgiš, is even more explicit when in a letter to Zimrī-Līm, he warns the king of Mari that the elders of Urgiš should not know about their dealings (ARM 28 45). The elders' activities and the political context of Mari documents indicate that, in these texts, the use of the term ^{lú}šu-gi^{meš} (= *šībūtum*) instead of ab-ba (= *šībūtum*) seems to reflect reasons other than local lexical preferences. These were clearly two different institutions. Besides the functional differences, the nature of the textual evidence is also telling. In Mari, the sources recording the elders are royal letters and a few administrative texts from the palace whereas in Babylonia, tablets attesting the elders are mainly legal records and economic contracts mostly dealing with private transactions. This does not mean, however, that in Mari and in those cities from northern Syria mentioned in the Mari archives, an institution similar to the city elders in Babylonia did not exist. It simply means that, because of the nature and provenance of the extant documents, the council of elders is not attested in the sources currently available. A better understanding of the elders from Mari will benefit from a comparison with the role of the elders in Babylonia, the subject of the next section of this chapter.

Table 2. **^{lú}šu-gi^{meš} = *šībūtum* of specific geographic places**

Place name	**Attestation**	
Andarig (*mātum*)	The connection between the elders and this place arises from the context.	ARM 26 438: 8'
Apûm (*mātum*)[55]	šu-gi^{meš} *ma-a-at A-pí-im*^{ki}	ARM 28 95: 11
Ašlakkā[56]	$^{\text{lú-meš}}$*ši-bu-ut Áš-la-ka-a*^{ki}	ARM 28 50: 25'
	The connection between the elders and this place arises from the context.	*MARI* 7: 175, n° 2: 19
Ašnakkum[57]	The connection between the elders and this place arises from the context.	ARM 28 103: 24

55 See Charpin 1987: 129–40.

56 Ašlakkā was the capital of Ida-Maraṣ; it was situated on the upper Ḫabur (Kupper 1998: 65).

57 The location of Ašnakkum is uncertain, it laid on the upper Ḫabur and was part of Ida-Maraṣ (Charpin 1993: 165).

Place name	Attestation	
Dabiš	^{lú}šu-gi^{meš} *ša Da-bi-iš*^{ki}	Durand 1992: 117
Dēr	^{lú}šu-gi *De-e-er*^{ki}	*MARI* 6: 77
Dumātum (*mātum*)[58]	The connection between the elders and this place arises from the context.	ARM 4 29: 21–25
Dūr-Yaḫdun-Līm	^{lú}šu-gi^{meš} *ša a-na ma-ṣa-ar-ti* bàd^{ki} *ka-lu-ú, e-si-iq-ma*[59]	ARM 14 48: 34–35
Emār	^{lú}[š]u-gi^{meš} *ša I-ma-ar*^{ki}	*MARI* 6: 52, A 885: 15
Gaššum[60]	^{lú}šu-gi^{meš} *Ga-aš-ši-im*^{ki}	ARM 27 32: 8
Ḫanzat	The connection between the elders and this place arises from the context.	ARM 13 145: 5–6
Ḫiwilat (*mātum*)[61]	The connection between the elders and this place arises from the context.	ARM 4 68: 5–8
Ḫurrā	The connection between the elders and this place arises from the context.	ARM 28 67: 23–26
	^{lú}šu-gi^{meš} (…) *ša Ḫu-ur-ra-a*^{ki}	*MARI* 7: 182, n° 7: 5–6
Yapṭur	^{lú}šu-gi^{meš} *Ia-ap-ṭú-ur*^{ki}	ARM 28 113: 9, *MARI* 7: 182, n° 7: 6
Yašibatum	^{lú}šu-⌈gi⌉[^{uru}] *Ia-ši-ba-tim*^{ki}	*OBTTR* 201: 5
Yasûm[62]	^{lú}šu-gi^{meš} *I-ia-si-im*	ARM 28 103: 23
Ida-Maraṣ (*mātum*)	[^{lú}]$^{\text{-meš}}$šu-gi$_4$, [*ša I-d*]*a-ma-ra-aṣ*	ARM 28 59: 10–11
	^{lú}šu-gi^{meš} *ma-at I-da-ma-ra-aṣ*^{ki}	*MARI* 7: 182, n° 7: 4, Durand (1999–2000: 192)
Ilūna-aḫī	^{lú}šu-gi^{meš} *I-lu-na-a-ḫi*^{ki}	*FM* II: 237 n° 122
Isqâ[63]	^{lú}šu-gi^{meš} *Is-qa-a*^{ki}	ARM 2 75: 7

58 This country was located southeast of Apûm (Durand 1997: 122).

59 Durand (1998: 361 j and 442 c) argued that in this context, *Dūrum* is to be interpreted as Dūr-Yaḫdun-Līm. Cf. Birot's (1974: 91) translation 'rempart'.

60 This city might have been located in the western Ida-Maraṣ (Birot 1993: 90 n. b).

61 Ḫiwilat and Talmuš were probably located north of Nineveh, see Durand (1998: 119).

62 Yasûm was part of Ida-Maraṣ (see Kupper 1998: 151).

63 Isqâ and Qâ were situated on the Ḫirmaš, i.e. Djaghdjagh (Durand 1998: 173 a).

Place name	Attestation	
Kalḫû[64]	The connection between the elders and this place arises from the context.	ARM 26 411: 72–73.
Kiduḫḫum	The connection between the elders and this place arises from the context.	ARM 28 95: 10
Kulḫītum[65]	The connection between the elders and this place arises from the context.	ARM 3 83: 2'–4'.
Kurdā[66]	The connection between the elders and this place arises from the context.	ARM 26 391: 7, 11, and ARM 26 393: 8[67]
Kurgiš[68]	^{lú}šu-gi^{meš} lú *Kur-gi-iš*$_{7}^{\text{ki}}$	ARM 14 114: 8–9
Numḫā	$^{\text{lú-meš}}$*ši-bu-ut Nu-um-ḫa-a*^{ki}	ARM 26 404: 36–37
	The connection between the elders and this place arises from the context.	ARM 26 463: 6
	^{lú}šu-gi^{meš} *ša Nu-ma-ḫa-a*	*FM* 2: 210 n° 117
Qâ[69]	^{lú}šu-gi^{meš} *Is-qa-a*^{ki}, *ù Qa-e-em…*	ARM 2 75: 7–8
	^{lú}šu-gi^{meš} *Qa-a*	ARM 26 48: 6 (= ARM 2 95: 6)
Qirdaḫat	^{lú}šu-gi^{meš} *Qí-ir-da-ḫ*[*a*]-*a*[*t*]^{ki}	ARM 28 140: 5
Razamā[70]	The connection between the elders and this place arises from the context.	ARM 14 104^{+}: 11–12
Saggarātum	^{lú}šu-gi^{meš} *ša a-na ma-ṣa-ar-ti Sa-ga-ra-tim*^{ki} *ka-lu-ú e-si-iq-ma*	ARM 14 48: 30
	[^{lú}šu-gi *S*]*a-ga-r*[*a-tim*^{k}]^{i}	ARM 26 100: 5

64 This city name in ARM 26 411 is written Kawalḫûm which, according to Durand (1988: 253), is the Amorite form of the name Kalḫû.

65 Kulḫītum was a city dependent on Terqa (Durand 1997: 308).

66 Kurdā was the capital of Numḫā (Lackenbacher 1988a: 387 n. a).

67 This example could also fit under Numḫā, because the elders are described as the elders of Ḫammurabi's (of Kurdā) country.

68 For the possible alternation Kurgiš/Urk(/g)iš see Durand (1997: 424).

69 See note on Isqâ.

70 According to Charpin (1993b: 197), there were several cities of Razamâ; the one attested in ARM 14 104^{+} was the capital of the country Yussân, situated north to the Djebel Sindjar.

Place name	Attestation	
	The connection between the elders and this place arises from the context.	ARM 26 206
	^{lú}šu-gi^{meš} *Sa-ga-ra-tim*^{ki}	*RA* 52: 164, n° 311: 15
Samānum[71]	The connection between the elders and this place arises from the context.	ARM 3 73: 9–10
Šinaḫ	The connection between the elders and this place arises from the context.	ARM 10 121
	^{lú}šu-gi^{meš} *Ši-na-aḫ*^{ki}	ARM 23 504: 8–9
	^{lú}šu-gi^{meš} (…) *ša Ši-na-aḫ*^{ki}	*MARI* 7: 182, n° 7: 5
Šudā[72]	The connection between the elders and this place arises from the context.	ARM 28 31: 6, 13, 19
Šunā	^{lú}šu-g[i^{meš} *Šu-n*]*a*^{ki}	ARM 23 504: 4
	The connection between the elders and this place arises from the context.	ARM 28 95: 10
Šušā	The connection between the elders and this place arises from the context.	ARM 28 91: 11; ARM 28 96: 6; see also ARM 26 249
Talḫayûm[73]	The connection between the elders and this place arises from the context.	ARM 13 148: 3
	^{lú}šu-gi^{meš} *ša Ta-al-ḫa-wi-im*^{ki}	*RA* 82: 98: 3–4
Talmuš	The connection between the elders and this place arises from the context.	ARM 4 68: 5–8.
Terqa	The connection between the elders and this place arises from the context.	ARM 3 17: 14–20, ARM 13 117: 6'
Tizraḫ	^{lú}šu-gi^{meš} *Ti-iz-ra-aḫ*^{ki}	ARM 7 130: 2

71 Samānum was a Benjaminite city in the district of Terqa, possibly to be identified with Meyyadîn (Durand 1990: 44).

72 Šudā was one of the four cities of Zalmaqum (Durand 1997: 407); ARM 28 31 refers to Sibkuna-Addu, who was the king of Šudā.

73 Talḫayûm was the capital city of Yapṭurum, which encompassed the area situated on the right bank of the upper Ḫabur (Durand 1988b: 112).

Place name	**Attestation**	
Tuttul	^{lú}šu-gi^{meš} *Tu-tu-ul*^{ki}	ARM 25 749: 2-3
	The connection between the elders and this place arises from the context.	ARM 14 55: 22
Urgiš[74]	^{lú}šu-gi^{meš} *Ur-gi-iš*^{ki}	ARM 23 504: 5, ARM 28 45: 12', *MARI* 7: 182, n° 7: 5
	$^{\text{lú-meš}}$šu-gi *Ur-gi-iš*^{ki}	*FM* 2: 254 n° 125
	ši-bu-ut Ur-gi-[*iš*^{ki}]	*MARI* 7: 178, n° 5: 16
Urubān[75]	^{lú}*ši-bu-ut Ú-ru-ba-an*[^{ki}]	ARM 26 503: 5
Zabalum	$^{\text{lú-meš}}$šu-gi *Za-ba-lim*^{ki}	ARM 9 241: 8
Zalluḫān	The connection between the elders and this place arises from the context.	ARM 2 16: 9-14.

THE ELDERS IN BABYLONIA

CHARACTERISTICS OF THE INSTITUTION

The characteristics of the institution of the city elders are difficult to trace from the extant sources, and many questions regarding the composition of this corporate body remain uncertain. The word *šībūtum* undoubtedly carries an age connotation, but it is impossible to find out whether there was a strict age criterion, or whether other factors such as wealth or family ties also influenced the designation of the members of this institution. The few documents bearing a list of persons characterized as city elders are, unfortunately, not sufficient to establish a possible hereditary pattern. There is, furthermore, no way of knowing the duration of tenure in the position, whether it was a life-long office or whether it was periodically renewed. Equally unknown is the number of men who constituted the city elders, because nothing proves that those individuals mentioned as elders in some contracts represented the totality of the body. In addition, it is also probable that the number of members varied from one city to another, depending on the size of the settlement. For instance, a certain Munawwirum had previously reported to

74 Urgiš was located in modern Tell Mozan (Buccellati 1998: 11–18).
75 This city was situated on the lower middle Euphrates on the left riverbank (Durand 2000: 17).

Tišanātum, the sender of this letter, that he had assembled 20 city elders to deal with the case of an adopted youth who had run away (YOS 2 50). This reference to 20 city elders is the largest number of elders mentioned in any single document of our corpus; other contracts have only 6 (*MAOG* IV: 290), 7 (MHET II/2 n° 164), and 8 (YOS 13 499).

Unfortunately, the three documents listing the elders by their names are problematic because there are few references to the places where these elders were active, for instance, Mārū-Uqnî and Tabnuk. Furthermore, texts may come from a well-known city as Sippar, but the paternal filiation of the elders is not provided. Therefore, such texts give little information about these men and their personal activities. The elders of Tabnuk appear in a document from Dilbat dated to Ammīditāna 22/XII/10 (*MAOG* 4: 290). These men are,

1. Išme-Sîn, son of Ēṭirum,
2. Ubarrum, son of Ilī-a[ ],
3. Ibni-Marduk, son of [ ],
4. Nabi-ilīšu, son of Ilšu-abūšu,
5. Ibbi-Ilabrat, son of Marduk-nīšu,
6. Buladatum, son of Ilī-[ ],
   the elders of Tabnuk.

A Sippar contract dated to Hammurabi 11/XI/8 (MHET II/2 n° 164), records the following elders:

1. Puzur-Šamaš,
2. Aḫam-arši,
3. x-x-x-x-num,
4. Apil-ilīšu,
5. Etel-pîša,
6. Maḫnub-el,
7. Šamaš-nīšu,
   the city elders.

Finally, the elders of the city Mārū-Uqnî named in YOS 13 499 (Kiš?, date lost) are,

1. Sîn-išmeanni, son of Etel-pî-Gula,
2. Sîn-iddinam, son of Elmēšum,
3. Warad-Ištar, son of Ilīyatum,
4. Ibni-^{d}[ ],
5. Mār-ešrê, son of Warad-Šamaš,
6. Ib-[ ], son of [ ]-iqīšam,
7. Ibni-Šērum, [ ],

8. Warad-Sîn,
   the elders of Mārū-Uqnî.[76]

All these three documents have the city elders listed directly after the name of the *rabiānum*. Two of them are land sales. In the first case, Nidittum, at the behest of the *rabiānum* and the elders of Tabnuk, sells a property to Sîn-iddinam, the son of Adad-rabi (*MAOG* 4: 290). Sîn-iddinam seems to have been an inhabitant of Dilbat because in another document from that city (YOS 13 243), he buys a two-year-old cow from Nūr-ilīšu; this transaction has Mār-ešrê, the *rabiānum*, as the first witness. In the second land sale, Sîn-tayyār buys a plot of land from the *rabiānum* Rabût-Šamaš and the elders of Sippar (MHET II/2 n° 164). Two of these elders, Apil-ilīšu and Etel-pîša, are *rabiānums* in other documents.[77] The third example is a legal tablet in which Šalli-lūmur, the *rabiānum* of Mārū-Uqnî, and the city elders mediate a dispute, and their verdict favors Nanāya-ibnīšu, the smith (YOS 13 499). Unfortunately, the available information about the elders listed in these documents is minimal.

Unlike in Mari, where the elders are related to such different entities as the district (*ḫalṣum*), the land (*mātum*), or gentilic groups, in Babylonia the elders are always city elders. The only exception appears in a letter that Samsu-iluna sent to Etel-pî-Marduk announcing the death of Hammurabi, Samsu-iluna's ascension to the throne of his father, and the issuing of a *mīšarum*-edict (TCL 17 76: 21, see Kraus 1958: 225). Franz H. Th. de Liagre Böhl (1951: 51–52) transliterated line 21 as follows: *at-ta ù ši-bu-ut ma-ti*, and he translates 'du dich mit den Aeltesten (…)', without rendering *mātum* (see also *CAD* E: 116a). In George Dossin's (1933) autograph copy, however, the *ma-* sign is partially broken, and the extant traces do not resemble the same sign as copied, for example, in lines 19 or 20. Piotr Michalowski has kindly collated this tablet for me from a Louvre photograph because the tablet was not available when he visited Paris. His collation confirms a *ma-*[*ti*] reading. While in Mari the examples mentioning the elders of the land usually deal with foreign affairs, in TCL 17 76 the new king is informing one of his officials about internal issues, that is, his coming to power and the cancellation of debts of specific groups (Charpin 2000: 89).[78] In this text, then, *šībūt mātim* is used as a general expression to denote the elders of every city under the authority of Etel-pî-Marduk (see Charpin 2004: 269).

76 Line 11 reads: *ù* Arad - Sîn *ši-bu-ut* ZAG.NÁ.KI. For the identification of this place with Mārū-Uqnî (i.e. Dumu^{meš}-z a-gìn-na^{ki}), see Wilcke (1976: 270 n. 25).

77 Apil-ilīšu (VAS 9 202, Ḫa 'd'/V/Ø; and possibly also in VAS 8 101, Ḫa 3/Ø/Ø, first witness without title), and Etel-pîša (MHET II/5 617, lost Ḫa).

78 Thus, 13. [*ku-nu-uk*] *ḫu-bu-ul-li* / 14. *ša* aga-uš šu-ḫa *ù mu-uš-ke-ni* / 15. *e-eḫ-te-pi mi-ša-ra-am i-na ma-ti aš-ta-ka-an*, 'I have canceled the debt-documents of the *rēdûm*-soldier, the *bā'irum*-soldier, and the "commoner". I have established a *mīšarum*-edict in the land'.

Elders from both northern and southern cities are well represented in economic and legal texts as well as letters. The documents in our corpus record the elders of the following urban centers:

Table 3. **Elders from specific cities**

City	Attestation
Aḫut	MLC 202; MLC 203; MLC 443; MLC 610
Akšak	CT 48 2
Ašduba	*TS* 58
Atašum	*JCS* 26: 142 text D; AbB 13 44
Būlum	VAS 16 142
BUR.ZI.BI.ŠUR^{ki}[79]	VAS 22 28
Damrum	YOS 2 52
Dilbat	VAS 7 7 + 152; VAS 18 23; YOS 13 256; YOS 13 519; VAS 7 131; VAS 7 187
Eblaḫ[80]	VAS 13 32
Ḫalḫalla	CT 8 6b; CT 48 19
Ḫarbānu	Waterman *BDHP* 27
Ḫarḫarrû	*JEOL* 25: 46
Ḫašur	YBC 4355
Ḫirītum	AbB 13 107
Ḫuda[81]	CT 2 9
Isin	PBS I/2 n° 10
Kār-Šamaš	VAS 18 17; VAS 29 19; YOS 13 491
Karisu(?)	Holma *ZATH* n° 9

79 The reading of this geographical name is uncertain. For the reading BUR.ZI.BI.ŠUR^{ki} see Klengel (1983: 14) and Charpin (1985c: 276). Von Soden (1986: 246) reads Bur-zi-EDEN^{ki}, while Wilcke 1990: 298 reads BUR.ZI.BÁḪAR^{ki}. For further comments on this city see Pientka (1998: 295).

80 According to Groneberg (1980: 66), this Eblaḫ is identical to Yabliya, and she comments: 'Das Eblaḫ des Itinerars liegt zwei Stationen vor Razamā'.

81 For this reading see RGTC III: 100 (*ḫu-da*^{ki}, coll. Walker), against Ḫudadi (Harris 1975: 132).

City	Attestation
Kikalla	*LFBD* n° 19
Kiš	*TJA* H 57: 53; VAS 7 56, *Kich* 2 D: 16
Kullizum	MHET II/6 n° 903
Kutalla	*TS* 71
Lagaš	TCL 1 232
Laliya	*JCS* 23: 29
Larsa	*RA* 69: 120 n° 8; Riftin 47; TCL 11 155; YOS 8 1
Mārū-Uqnî	YOS 13 499; CT 43 52
Meḫrum	Boyer, *CHJ* HE 123
Nabrarâ	YBC 11014
Namgata	Riftin n° 89
Nērebtum	UCP 10/I 107
Pada	TIM 4 5/6
Sardai	CT 48 2
Sippar	*BAP* 80; Dalley, *Edinburgh* n° 24; MHET II/2 n° 164; MHET II/2 n° 706; MHET II/2 n° 871; VAS 13 20.
Suqûm	VAS 16 181
Šaduppûm	YOS 14 72
Šī-šarrātum	AbB 10 37
Tabnuk	*MAOG* 4: 290
Zaralulu	*JCS* 26 text D
Zibbatum	YBC 9934

This list is of course incomplete and it is limited by the chance of discovery. Yet, it seems to account for a fair distribution of the elders in different regions. The fact that the elders from Babylonia are only related to the city is not the sole feature that differentiates them from the elders attested in Mari documents. In Babylonia, the elders are never so directly associated with a king as to be characterized as the elders of PN, or the servants of a royal name. Worth mentioning is a division of property from Šaduppûm dated to king Dāduša (*JCS* 26 D). The transaction is witnessed by Igeḫluma, the gìr-nita$_2$ of Zaralulu, and the elders of his city (*ālīšu*), and by Gudasum, the gìr-nita$_2$ of Atašum, and the elders of his city. In this instance, the use of the pronoun *–šu* attached to the city instead of the elders, as was the case in certain Mari documents, makes it clear that the elders are connected with the city and not with the official in charge of it. There seems to be little doubt, therefore, about the relative independence of these elders with respect to other authorities.

THE ACTIVITIES OF THE CITY ELDERS

The city elders have direct participation in certain real estate dealings, such as the sale of city property, and the rental and exchange of fields and houses. In those sales, a *rabiānum* usually heads the transaction, occasionally including also the members of the city. The extant documents originate from the northern cities of Sippar, Dilbat, and Kār-Šamaš; the earliest attestation of these sales is from Sîn-muballiṭ 18 and latest dates from Ammī-ṣaduqa 12. In a Sippar document, the elders of Ḫarbānu and Sîn-erībam, the son of Ilšu-bāni, are the sellers of a house (é-kislaḫ) described as the house of Sîn-erībam (Waterman *BDHP* 27, Sm 18/Ø/Ø). This Sîn-erībam is attested in another tablet (PBS 8/2 251: 11), and he is possibly the *rabiānum* of Sippar recorded in the 11th year of Hammurabi (CT 47 31), although his paternal filiation is not mentioned in the latter document. The city elders together with the *rabiānum* are the sellers of houses in five other contracts from Sippar, and in one of them the sellers are the *rabiānum* and the elders of Kullizum (MHET II/6 n° 903).[82] In one of the tablets from the environs of Sippar, Nakarum, the nu-banda$_3$-official, several men and the elders of Kār-Šamaš sell a house described as 'the house of the city' (é uru^{ki}) to Mār-erṣetim, the son of Šamaš-rabi (VAS 29 19, Si 25/XII/17). Almost one year later, the elders of Kār-Šamaš, the *rabiānum*, ten men, and the city elders sell another 'house of the city' to a certain Šattum, the son of Ipqatum; at least four of the men listed between the elders and the *rabiānum* Ilšu-ibni appear in the previous transaction (VAS 18 17, Si 26/IX/25). The sale document from Dilbat lists the name of six elders (*MAOG* 4: 290). Aside from sales, the elders had also a role in the rental of fields and in the exchange of houses. Thus, in a contract from Kār-Šamaš, Sippar-liwwir, the son of Tarībatum, rents a field for cultivation from a number of men and the elders of Kār-Šamaš (YOS 13 491, Ae 'u'/V/12). And another tablet records an exchange of houses where Zababa-muballiṭ, the *rabiānum* of Kiš, Munawwirum, the *šakkanakku*-official, Munawwirum, the *nāgirum*, 'herald', and the elders of Kiš

82 These documents are MHET II/5 n° 706 (lost, pre-Ḫa), MHET II/2 n° 164 (Ḫa 11/XI/08), VAS 13 20 (Ḫa 30/X/[ ]), MHET II/6 n° 871 (Si 22/IV/10), and MHET II/6 n° 903 (Aṣ 12(?)/IX/02).

at the behest of the king gave a field in exchange to Dan-erēssa, an *entum*-priestess of Zababa (*TJA* H 57: 53, Si 23/IX/15).

The city elders' activities also involved the management of agricultural affairs concerning the distribution of holdings, irrigation, and produce. In a partially broken letter, the *rabiānum* and the elders of Šī-šarratum write to the *šāpiru* about the estimated yield of a garden which had apparently been neglected, and they further claim no responsibility for the matter (AbB 10 37). Another letter shows that a man approached the elders of Damrum with a complaint regarding the size of his flock (YOS 2 52). This shepherd used to take care of 500 sheep, but that number had tripled and he could not handle such a large number. The elders then investigated the case and decreased the number of sheep under his responsibility to 1000 head. It is unclear who were the owners of the sheep, but the context of this letter lets us suspect that the animals might have belonged to the temple of Sîn. Concerning irrigation problems, in a letter from Larsa, king Hammurabi instructs Šamaš-ḫāzir that the city elders and the members of the irrigation district (dumu^{meš} *ugārim*) must be present during work on the canal Gabûm (BIN 7 7).[83] The presence of the elders was probably related to their potential role as arbitrators in case a claim might arise in the future. A letter indirectly substantiates this assumption (AbB 10 171). According to this text, Marduk-mušallim and Šērum-namer had a dispute over the control of the ditch irrigating their fields. Things went so far that Marduk-mušallim broke the jaw of Šērum-namer's son, at which point the parties approached the *rabiānum* and the city elders. Consequently, these local authorities handled the case and sent a letter to the *šāpirum*-official reporting on the affair.

Several documents record the elders' authority over certain agricultural holdings, including not only the assignment but also the confiscation of land. Thus for example, a person called Uqnûm and the city elders intended to seize the field of Nanna-intuḫ, who owed them silver and barley. On that occasion, however, Nanna-intuḫ promised to be responsible for his debt, and later Uqnûm sent a letter to the debtor prompting him to pay what he owed (CT 33 20).[84] Similarly, the unnamed writer of another letter complains because while he was in service (*ina ḫarrān bēlīya*) and dwelling in Sippar, the city elders took away half of his field

83 According to Stol (1982b: 354), Hammurabi undertook a reorganization of local administration, and the *ugārums* became administrative units. The dumu^{meš} *ugārim* then, 'had their fields in one and the same *ugārum* and stood up for their common interests'. See also Driver and Miles (1952: 152).

84 9. *um-ma ni-nu-ú-ma* / 10. *a-na ṣe-ri-ka a-na* a-šà-*im ṣa-*[*b*]*a-tim* / 11. *ni-la-ka ki-a-am ta-pu-la-na-a-ti* / 12. *um-ma at-ta-ma* / 13. *a-na aḫ-ḫi-ia* / 14. *ša* 2 gín kù-babbar in-nu-da / 15. *a-ma-ra-ku-nu-ši-im* / 16. *ù a-na* še-*im a-na ḫi-še-eḫ-ti-ku-nu* / 17. *a-za-az-za-ku-nu-ši-im*, 'Thus we said: "we came to you to seize the field". (And) you answered us as follows: "For my brothers I will find you 2 shekels of silver worth of the straw, and concerning the barley, I will stand responsible for your requirement"' (CT 33 20).

and gave it to another man. It becomes clear from the context that the claimant was a soldier (CT 6 27b).[85] The elders seem to have transgressed their jurisdiction, for they re-assigned a plot that the crown had granted to a soldier. Similarly, in a document from Ḫalḫalla dated to Samsu-iluna, the *rabiānum* and the city elders re-assigned the house of a transferred soldier (Stol 1998: 444). To prevent future problems, the text includes a clause stating that if the soldier returns and raises a claim, the *rabiānum* and the elders will respond.[86] In a letter from Larsa, however, a royal official, Awīl-Ninurta, instructs Šamaš-ḫāzir to resort to the city elders and to the old men (*awīlû labirūtum*), who know the parties, in order to determine the tenancy of a field (OECT 3 40). Moreover, the elders together with another person, whose name is lost, assigned (*esēḫu*) a field to Ilī-ḫari and Igmil-Sîn in a legal document dated to Rīm-Sîn 12 (*JCS* 31: 33). Likewise, a text from Larsa (TCL 11 155, Ḫa) records a number of fields that a man without a title and the city elders assigned (*šaṭāru*) at the behest of another person to several individuals (see *CAD* Š/2: 238). The elders' role in the assignment (*kânu*) of land is further illustrated by three documents from Dilbat, two of them (VAS 18 23 and YOS 13 256) dated to Abī-ešuḫ; the third (YOS 13 519) is from the reign of Ammī-ditāna (see Desrochers 1978: 127–33).

The city elders from Babylonia participated, furthermore, in the settlement of a number of legal issues, for instance robbery, division of property, inheritance contracts, and litigations, among others. In case of robbery, the elders usually acted in concert with the *rabiānum* or other authorities. Thus, Āmur-rabût-Šamaš sent a letter to the *rabiānum* and the city elders concerning lost property (*ḫulqum*) from Nabrīya's house (ABIM 33). Because the local authorities had seized Amur-rabūt-Šamaš's dependents (*suḫārū*) and suspected them of the crime, their master instructs the *rabiānum* and the city elders that in case his servants were guilty, the authorities should proceed in accordance with the regulation which is in their hands.[87] Veenhof (1997–2000: 74) has already pointed out the risks of relating this *ṣimdatum* to the rules about lost property found in LH (§§9–13), particularly because the provenance and date of ABIM 33 are unknown.[88] Another letter records a similar case (Holma *ZATH* n° 9). In this example, Ibni-Marduk and Alī-talīmī write to Ibni-Marduk, Nabium-[ ], and the city elders about the missing

85 Thus in lines 14-15 the writer refers to the a-šà *ṣi-bi-it* aga-uš / 1 *a-lik i-di-ia*, '[a] field, the holding of a *rēdûm*-soldier, one of my colleagues'.

86 11. u$_4$-*u*[*m* aga]-uš *na-si-ḫu-um* / 12. *it-*<*ta*>*-*⌈*al*⌉*-kam-ma a-na* é*-šu* / 13. *a-na I-ku-un-pi*$_4$*-Sîn* dumu *Sîn-ta-ia-ar* / 14. *i-ra-gu-mu* / 15. *ra-bi-a-nu-um ù ši-bu-ut* uru^{ki} / 16. *i-pa-lu*. 'If the day when the transferred soldier returns to his house he raises a claim against Ikūn-pî-Sîn, the *rabiānum* and the city elders will respond'.

87 12. *šu-um-ma i-na qa-ti ṣú-ḫ*[*a-ri-i*]*a* / 13. *i-ba-aš-ši ki-ma ṣi-i*[*m-da-ti*]*m* / 14. *ša i-na qá-ti-ku-nu.*

88 There are no references to the city elders in any of the Ur III (Ur-Namma) and Old Babylonian Laws (Lipit-Ištar, Ešnunna, and Hammurabi).

goods of Ibbi-Ilabrat. The *rabiānum* and the city elders also deal with robbery in a case concerning the sheep of Balamunamḫe (YOS 8 1), and in a letter compromising the tax-collector's assistants (YOS 2 109). There is, in addition, a court record from Nērebtum where the city and the elders imposed a punishment upon Tarībum who was caught when he broke into the house of Ilšu-nāṣir and, afterwards, pleaded guilty in front of the authorities (UCP 10/1 107). Finally, the *rabiānum* and the elders of Kikalla also seem to have had responsibility, presumably as witnesses, in a case of murder that happened in their city and was further investigated in the palace (*LFBD* 19).

Other legal transactions concerning the elders are documents dealing with family affairs. A contract from Šaduppûm, issued under the reign of Dāduša, records the division of the property belonging to Zibbatum, a *nadītum* of Šamaš; the elders of Zaralulu and Atašum are listed among the witnesses (*JCS* 26: 142-3, text D). Although the text does not mention the paternal identity of the heirs, who were brothers, or their relationship with the *nadītum*, it is possible to argue that they were either blood-related members of the *nadītum*'s family or her adopted children.[89] The division of inherited property is also the subject of a letter that the city elders sent to the *šāpiru*-official describing the way in which the children of Sîn-ma-ilum divided their shares (CT 43 25). There is, in addition, another rather peculiar document from Larsa dealing with a couple (*RA* 69: 120–25, n° 8. Si 3/VI/25); Anbar (1975: 120) dubbed this text an 'acte de séparation de corps'. In this contract Šāt-Marduk takes an oath by the life of Samsu-iluna, the king, declaring that she will not have sex with Aḫūni, and that if he approaches her, she will tell the *rabiānum* and the city elders. On his part, Aḫūni also takes an oath, stating that he will not approach Šāt-Marduk. The first witness of the document is Tarībum, the *šakkanakkum*-official of Larsa. The third witness is Sîn-šeme, the son of Sîn-imguranni. This Sîn-šeme could be the same person as the *rabiānum* of Larsa attested in Samsu-iluna first year, especially because of the reference to the *rabiānum* in line 12 (YOS 12 3, 1 b/I/30).[90]

The elders played, moreover, an important role as mediators in the settlement of conflicts and legal disputes. Lawsuits and the formal aspects and procedures related to them have been one of the Assyriologist's favorite topics for many years and I shall address this subject in the last chapter. For now, I shall present those documents where the city elders managed those complaints brought to them by individuals seeking a solution to their problems. The texts under consideration

89 For the analysis of the peculiarities of this text and the identity of the parties, see M. de Jong Ellis (1974: 148).

90 Note that in his seal Tarībum, the *šakkanakkum*, is the servant of Samsu-iluna. Whereas the seal of Sîn-šeme has the legend, servant of a (broken) divinity name, as was the case with the *rabiānums*' seals; this also shows that Sîn-šeme was not a royal official.

include not only court records but also letters reporting on conflicts. In the examples from our corpus, the elders handled these cases by themselves or in concert with other authorities. The following combinations are attested: 1) city elders + *rabiānum*, 2) city elders + *rabiānum* + judges, 3) city elders + *rabiānum* + city, 4) city elders + city, 5) city elders + *bābtum*, 'city ward'. The elders by themselves dealt with complaints in cases involving family disputes and the division of properties. For instance, a certain Munawwirum, the son of a *nadītum*, approached the city elders to disinherit his young adopted brother who had run away and, apparently, his demand was granted (YOS 2 50). Another family litigation that the elders decided appears in a legal case dated to Ḫa 30 (CT 48 2). Here, Tarībatum and Bananum, the cousins, and Rīš-Šamaš and Iqqududum, the brothers of Mārat-erṣetim, raised a claim against her concerning a female slave and her daughter, whom Mārat-erṣetim received from her parents when she was installed as a *qadištum*. The elders of two cities, Akšak and Sardai, sat, heard the old document of her installation, and decided in favor of Mārat-erṣetim. Finally, in a legal record from Sippar dated to Ḫa 17, the elders of Ḫuda were the mediators in a case where Pala-Šamaš raised a claim against Apil-ilīšu concerning a house, a boat, slaves, and other possessions (CT 2 9).

The collaboration of the *rabiānum* and the elders in handling disputes is attested in court records dealing with litigations about real estate, and also with other rather disparate examples. In a document from Sippar, Nawwirtum, a *nadītum* of Šamaš, and Sîn-iddinam, the children of Ikūnīya, brought forward a claim against Niḫuššim for a field that she had previously bought from them (CT 48 19, Ḫa 27). Since Niḫuššim's witnesses confirmed her payment, Itūr-ašdum, the *rabiānum* of Ḫalḫalla, and the city elders declared that the land was hers, and they had the plaintiffs issued a tablet of no further claim. Similarly, in a document from Dilbat dated to Hammurabi, Marduk-nāṣir, resorting to a royal edict (*ṣimdat šarrim*), sued Aḫam-utta, the buyer of a field that Marduk-nāṣir had inherited (VAS 7 7+152). Imgur-Sîn, the *rabiānum*, and the elders of Dilbat rendered a verdict and gave 1 iku to Aḫam-utta and the remainder to the claimant; unfortunately, the original amount of land is unknown. In YOS 13 499 (date lost, Kiš?), although broken, it is clear that Šalli-lūmur, the *rabiānum* of Mārū-Uqnî, and the city elders rendered a verdict that favored Nanāya-ibnīšu. Consequently, this man received an amount of silver as compensation. There is finally an interesting document from Larsa dealing with the theft of the vestments and the headdress of (the statue of) the goddess Nin-MAR.KI (TCL 11 245, n.d.).[91] In order to deal with this case, the *pašīšum*-priests, the *rabiānum*, and the city elders assembled in the courtyard of

91 The reading of this divinity name is problematic. For a summary of different interpretations of the meaning of this name, see Whiting (1985: 1–3).

Nin-MAR.KI and they listened to the depositions of four persons. Since all the evidence pointed towards Iddin-Ištar, he was convicted.

There are also documents recording interaction among the city elders, the *rabiānum*, and the judges in the resolution of disputes. For example, after an estate was apportioned, Pala-Šamaš returned and raised a claim against Apil-ilīšu, and they took the case to the judges and the elders (*BAP* 80, Sippar, Ḫa 24).[92] The judges and the elders divided the house and the *ilkum*-duty equally and the *rabiānum* Nannatum was the first witness. Further south, in Kutalla, Ḫammu-rābi-lū-dāri and Awīl-ilī raised a claim against Iddin-Enlil regarding a garden (*TS* 71, Si 5). Iddin-Enlil approached the judges of Larsa, and in the presence of the *rabiānum* of Kutalla and the city elders he went around the garden with the weapon of the god Lugal-Kiduna and confirmed his rights over the property.[93] There seem to have been cases where one of the parties was not satisfied with a verdict and appealed to another authority. Thus, in a family dispute, Ilī-iddinam brought the matter to the *rabiānum* and the city elders. It is probable, however, that, not pleased with their arbitration, Ilī-iddinam addressed the judges, for in a letter to the *rabiānum* and the elders of Laliya, the judges make it clear that they will take over the case (*JCS* 23: 29). A similar transfer of jurisdiction, though in this case voluntary, appears in a letter from Nippur (PBS I/2 n° 10). The *rabiānum* and the elders of Isin handed over a case to the judges of Nippur because they were unable to cope with a dispute involving the silver of a partnership.

Those documents where the elders, the *rabiānum*, and the city are the arbitrators of conflicts will be discussed in the next chapter, after analyzing the role of the city as an urban institution of authority. I shall refer now to those rather exceptional examples in which the elders interact with authorities other than the *rabiānum*, the city, and the judges. As regards the collaboration between the elders and the *bābtum*, 'the city ward', a text from Kiš that records a litigation over a house has these authorities as mediators (VAS 7 56, Ad 24). This was, apparently, another instance of transferring jurisdiction over a real estate dispute. In this case, Ilīyatum and Ibbi-Ilabrat, the children of Kunnīya, approached Elmēšum, the *šandabakkum*-official, and Ilī-iqīšam, the *mu'errum*-official, and raised a claim against Riš-Edub concerning his house.[94] Instead of arbitrating, the royal officials had the elders of Kiš and the residents of the ward convene and clarify the

92 Pala-Šamaš had already raised a claim against Apil-ilīšu for certain properties seven years earlier, in Ḫa 17 (CT 2 9). On that occasion, the elders of Ḫuda rendered a verdict.

93 For the use of the divine symbol in this text and the interpretation of this ceremony see Harris (1965: 218). Harris holds that what was at issue were the boundaries of the orchard. See also Walther (1917: 203).

94 For the role of Ilī-iqīšam and Elmēšum in the crown's affairs, see Yoffee (1977: 93).

matter.[95] There is finally a case from Šaduppûm where the city elders, three men, and two military officials, adjudicated a case (YOS 14 72, Ibāl-pî-el II). The fact that two men who bore military titles (ugula šu-ḫ a^{meš} and gal-ku$_5$^{meš}) participated in the decision lets us suspect that at least one of the parties was engaged in military activities (see Dombradi 1996: 251 §330, and Fortner 1996: 293).

Although legal records have been thoroughly studied (see Yoffee 2000: 47–48), little has been said about the reasons why different officials and institutions acting alone or in concert mediate in disputes. For obvious reasons, this problem cannot be fully addressed here. I would like to point out, however, that certain characteristics can be inferred from those documents considered in this section. In the first place, it seems that the participation of any of the authorities (e.g. the *rabiānum,* the elders, or the judges) depended on the persons involved in the conflict, rather than on the object of the dispute itself. In the second, the circumstances under which a specific litigation took place seem to have influenced the appointment of the arbitrators. Indeed, the elders were adjudicating entities by themselves or in cooperation with other powers in cases dealing with similar claims, that is, the ownership of land and slaves, and inheritance disagreements, among others. The *rabiānum*'s association with the elders is not exceptional because, as has already been seen, the office of *rabiānum* rotated periodically among the members of the city elders and 'the city' (*ālum*). These local authorities seem to have been the first instance which city inhabitants who were not office holders resorted to when they had a conflict. These people had no strong institutional ties (as was the case with palace officials, soldiers, or merchants, for example) and no means of approaching a high royal official. The tablet recording the theft of Balamunamḫe's sheep, could be quoted as an exception (YOS 8 1). However, it is possible to argue that this case was not serious enough as to require the intervention of higher authorities, or that robbery was under the jurisdiction of the *rabiānum* and the elders.

There are several reasons to explain why other authorities entered the picture and acted together with the *rabiānum* and the elders. In the document where the elders and military officials decided a case, it is possible that one of the parties belonged to the army, whereas the other party had the city authorities as his representatives (YOS 14 72). Similarly, in the trial over the vestments and headdress of the goddess Nin-MAR.KI, which took place in the temple courtyard, the local authorities handled the case with temple representatives, the *pašīšum*-priests. In two lawsuits Pala-Šamaš raised a claim against Apil-ilīšu (CT 2 29 and *BAP* 80). In one of them the elders arbitrated by themselves (CT 2 29), and in the other the mediators were the judges and the elders (*BAP* 80). Although the objects under dispute were similar (i.e. real estate, as well as other goods), the fact that *BAP* 80

95 Thus, in lines 12-13, (…) *ši-bu-ut* Kiš^{ki}, *ù* dumu^{meš} dag-⌈gi-a⌉ *li-iz-zu-zu*.

also includes the *ilkum* (a grant from the crown with attendant responsibilities) may account for the presence of the judges in this text.[96] In a tablet from Kutalla (*TS* 71), because a claim was brought against him, Iddin-Enlil approached the judges of Larsa, then in front of the *rabiānum* and the elders, he took the divine weapon and went around the garden to confirm his right over it. In his study of this document, Charpin (1980a: 188) comments that the role of the judge(s) is unclear, and that the scribe may have omitted the phrase *dīnam ušāḫissunūti*. It is also possible, however, that the judge sent Iddin-Enlil to the *rabiānum* and the elders of Kutalla so that the authorities could decide whether the man was the owner. This interpretation finds support in a similar procedure from Larsa (OECT 3 40). In this letter, to determine the tenancy of a field, Šamaš-ḫāzir has to resort to the city elders and to the old men who know the parties.

The elders were community members familiar with the city's problems and the city inhabitants. That is why certain royal officials and judges rely on their judgment and testimony to clarify disputes. Thus for instance, the judges of Borsippa and Babylon interrogated the elders of Eblaḫ to handle the litigation between Qurrudum and Sîn-māgir (VAS 13 32, Ḫa 13, Sippar). Similarly, the *rabiānum* of Ḫalḫalla and the city elders gave their testimony in a case that the judges of Babylon and the judges of Sippar investigated (CT 8 6b, Si, Sippar). The knowledge that the elders had of the city and its people may also account for the reasons why, in some cases, palace officials delegated the solution of certain disputes to the elders, even though the parties had directly approached a royal representative (VAS 22 28). The elders' role as a hinge between the state and urban communities is not only evident from disputes, but also from other documents. Thus, the *rabiānum* of Atašum and the city elders were engaged in the recruitment of workers (AbB 13 44). In this case, the *šāpirum* had given barley to the *rabiānum* and the elders, and they redistributed it among the hired laborers.[97] Similarly, in a letter from Kiš (OECT 13 193), the *rabiānum* and the city elders are involved to the distribution of 60 gur of barley (c. 18,000 litres) for food rations (*nebrītum*). In addition, a letter from Šaduppûm seems to imply that the elders assigned rations to harvesters.[98] The evidence from these documents may explain the attestation of

96 The office of 'judge' is still poorly understood, but different judges are attested, for instance, 'the royal judges' (di-$ku_5^{meš}$ lugal), the 'judges of the city' (di-$ku_5^{meš}$ (*ša*) GN), the 'judges of the temple' (di-$ku_5^{meš}$ *ša* Temple Name). See Dombradi (1996: 29 §35).

97 7. *aš-šum* še-*e-im ša ša-pí-ir-ni* / 8. *id-di-na-an-né-ši-im-ma* / 9. *a-na* ^{lú}ḫun-$gá^{meš}$ *ni-id-di-nu*, 'Concerning the barley which our *šāpiru* had given to us and (which) we had given to the hired laborers (…)'.

98 This evidence is only indirect, but the reference to the 'help for the harvest', can be interpreted as an allusion to recruitment of a labor force. Goetze's (1958: 65) translation of this passage goes: 'The elders of the town spoke as follows: "Your honored father used to give barley t[o us]. One *kur* of the required (?) barley to which all of us are entitled and the oil, our balance, we would like

the city elders in two ration lists from Dilbat, both dated to the reign of Ammī-ṣaduqa (VAS 7 131 and VAS 7 187). From these lists, Walther (1917: 53) thought that the elders received rations as regular or occasional payments.[99] Nevertheless, it is also possible to argue, in view of the documents mentioned above, that those products assigned to the elders were meant to be redistributed.[100] Finally, the crown seems to have resorted to the *rabiānum* and the city elders to facilitate the collection of taxes.[101] Collaboration, however, does not mean total dependence and submission because, in several cases, it is possible to discern tensions and conflicts between the state and the community representatives. This problem, however, will be addressed in the last chapter.

A REAPPRAISAL OF THE ROLE OF THE (CITY) ELDERS DURING THE OLD BABYLONIAN PERIOD

This chapter started with an overview of previous interpretations about the role of the elders during the Old Babylonian period. Most of these studies considered the epic of Gilgameš as an example that helps portray the functioning of the institution in earlier times and the way it evolved in later periods. Until the discovery of Mari in 1933 the elders were considered a full-fledged urban institution and this view prevailed until well into the 1950s. Certainly, before then there was no allusion to a 'nomadic origin' for this institution. The publication of the texts found at Mari revealed the existence of elders related to ethnic groups, and this evidence – together with the documents found at Ebla since the mid-1960s – led some to the conclusion that it was possible to trace the origin of the elders back to a nomadic past. According to this interpretation, the Amorites who entered the valley of the Tigris-Euphrates brought the institution of the elders to Mesopotamia. In this line of reasoning, the texts from Mari and Ebla are an invaluable source for reconstructing the evolutionary stages of the institution. My skepticism about using evolutionary models to explain the development of society and political institutions led me to review previous interpretations. In order to do that, I decided to study Mari documents and contrast them to those sources that originated in Babylonia.

In Mari documents, the word for elders is written syllabically and logographically, ^{lú}šu-gi^{meš}. This logogram, meaning 'elders', is not attested in letters

---

to have stored. This town is under your control and like every town we would like to help our father with the harvest"'.

99 He comments: 'Daß die Ältesten als solche regelmäßige oder gelegentliche Bezahlung erhielten, möchte man aus 2 Dilbater Rechnungen schließen'.

100 See also Riftin 89, an account of unknown provenance dated to Si 22/IX/28, which mentions 12 4/5 gur 12 sila$_3$ of barley under the responsibility of the *rabiānum* and the elders of Namgata.

101 See AS 16: 211; Joànnes 1992: 33; MLC 202; MLC 203; MLC 256 and MLC 443.

and economic and legal records from Babylonia. In the case of Mari, I found no functional difference between the activities of those elders written syllabically and those written logographically. The use of one form of writing or the other seems to rest on scribal preferences rather than institutional differences, perhaps because most Mari letters originated in places other than Mari itself. Furthermore, in Mari documents, aside from the 'city elders', there are also references to the 'elders of the district', the 'elders of the land', and the elders of ethnic groups; all these variants are unattested in Babylonia.

The elders in Mari documents were mostly engaged in political, diplomatic, and military affairs and disputes involving a number of kings, kinglets, and royal officials from the Mari region and northern Syria. Concerning military activities, they were in charge of protecting fortresses, recruiting soldiers, and joining royal campaigns; in certain cases, they also received rations and delivered products to the palace. The elders were further engaged in diplomatic affairs including the dispatch of messages and mediation of peace agreements. Besides their role in external affairs, the elders in Mari documents also participated in internal political issues concerning their own cities. Furthermore, it becomes apparent from a number of examples that these elders always depended on a figure of authority. Nevertheless, whether they were loyal to the ruler of their own city, or to a king with expansionist intentions depended on particular circumstances. It is difficult, and maybe useless, to trace a clear delimitation among all these different activities. As I interpret these elders, they constituted an elite group acting in close connection with rulers. Birot's (1974: 91) translation of ^{lú}šu-gi^{meš} as 'vétérans' is felicitous, for it conveys the idea of expertise and it carries a military nuance, while also maintaining the age connotation of the word.

The documents from Babylonian cities give a completely different vision of the institution of the elders. In the letters and economic and legal documents from this area, the word 'elders' is mostly written syllabically, but the logographic writing ab-ba uru^{ki} is also attested. The elders from Babylonia are always the elders of a city. Although the documents record the variants *šībūt ālim* or *šībūt* + geographic name, there is no attestation of the elders of other geographic or ethnic categories. Unlike the elders from Mari documents, the elders from Babylonia very seldom leave their city on an official mission, and when they do so, it is to appear before a higher authority. This shows a sharp contrast with the degree of mobility of the elders in Mari letters. Unfortunately, because of the laconic character of most of Babylonian sources, the information that can be inferred from them does not cast much light on the characteristics of the institution. We can find out what these elders did, but since the sources do not dwell upon the elders themselves, the way they reached their position and retained it is unknown. It is clear, however, that another city authority, the *rabiānum*, came from the ranks of the elders and the city. It is not surprising, therefore, that many documents record them acting in concert.

In Babylonian cities, the elders together with the *rabiānum* had a certain authority over local real estate transactions. In some cases they sell houses, usually described as the 'house of the city', or the 'house of the *rabiānum*'. It is completely unknown, however, how they attained such ownership and what they did with the silver they received from those transactions. Other activities concerning the management of real estate include the elders' participation in the rental and exchange of properties, as well as the distribution of agricultural holdings. Related to this is also the elders' mediation in conflicts dealing with control of water for the irrigation of arable land. The elders from Babylonia also participated in the settlement of legal issues relating to the local community. These cases include robbery, division of property, inheritance disputes, and lawsuits, among others. In the mediation of social conflicts, the elders usually interact with the *rabiānum* or with other institutions such as the judges, the *bābtum*, or other authorities. Finally, because the city elders were community representatives who knew the city's problems and its inhabitants, on certain occasions, the state relied on them to solve disputes and to facilitate the collection of taxes.

The sources studied in this chapter clearly show the existence of two distinct institutions of the elders in Mesopotamia during the Old Babylonian period, that is, the 'elders' from the Mari area, and those from Babylonia. The results of this study, furthermore, allow us to challenge two widely held assumptions regarding the role of the elders in ancient Mesopotamia. In the first place, it is possible to argue against a nomadic origin of the institution of the elders as it was interpreted from the documents found in the royal archives of Mari. In Mari sources, those elders related to ethnic groups seem to have answered to the authority of certain city rulers. There is no evidence that their role was any different from the activities performed by their sedentary colleagues. Evidently, the ancient Mesopotamians were less concerned about the nomadic or sedentary character of the people with whom they interacted than modern scholars are. In the second place, it is also apparent that the Old Babylonian institution of the elders as depicted in economic and legal documents and letters does not coincide with the image of the elders portrayed in Mesopotamian literary compositions. Indeed, none of the texts discussed here depicts any king seeking advice from a group of elders, or discussing state affairs in the midst of a council of elders. If such an institution existed, it cannot be equated with those elders recorded in letters and economic and legal documents from Babylonia. For many years, the stories about Gilgameš, as well as other literary texts, have been the starting-point for explaining the role of the city elders in Mesopotamia. Based on mundane economic and legal documents and letters, however, this study has shown that the institution of the elders during the Old Babylonian period had little – if anything – in common with the body of the elders of those literary texts. It seems time to quit searching for the origin of political institutions in those texts that the ancient literati passed on to us, and to start enjoying them for what they are – stories about fictitious characters.

5

The City (ālum)

GENERAL REMARKS

The city was the center that articulated different spheres of the ancient Mesopotamian's social and individual life. It was a place of intense economic activity, it housed temples and cultic areas, and it was the seat of the authorities. For the ancient Mesopotamian, however, the city contained more secrets than those unveiled by the historian. Because gods inhabited the city, it was a safe space as opposed to the wilderness and its creatures. Nevertheless, the gods' presence did not neutralize all harmful forces; for intangible beings haunted the city streets, as certain incantations let us know. The ancient scribe was himself an elite city dweller, and his texts usually connect the city's welfare with the relationship between gods and rulers. It is not surprising, then, that the city occupies an important place in Mesopotamian imagery. Throughout the three millennia of cuneiform literature, hymns and laments were composed for the city, and the compilation of a late omen series, *šumma ālu*, has the city as its leitmotif. One of the compositions that best depicts the city as a place of ruling power is the 'Sumerian King List' (see Jacobsen 1939). To portray the ideal of Mesopotamian unity, the 'Sumerian King List' emphasizes the hegemonic role of various cities since time immemorial, and it relegates to the background those kings so dutifully praised in their royal inscriptions. Aside from royal officials, several local powers acted in the city. In this chapter, I will discuss an aspect of the city completely ignored in literary texts and usually neglected in contemporary studies, that is, the role of the city as an institution of authority.

As was the case with the word *šībūtum*, 'elders', the Akkadian term *ālum* and the Sumerian uru$^{(ki)}$, meaning 'city', are attested well before the second millennium.[1] In Mesopotamia during the Old Babylonian period, the word 'city' denotes at least two realities. On the one hand, it refers to a geographical entity;

1 The Sumerian word uru is already recorded in the city of Šuruppak between the end of the Early Dynastic II and the beginning of the Early Dynastic III period. For the <é>-uru, 'the city house(hold)', as an administrative center during this time, see Visicato (1995: 1 and 113, 2001: 115). Obviously, this does not mean that this institution bears any relationship with the Old Babylonian 'city'. For the city (uru) as a spatial category in Early Dynastic IIIa texts mentioning land and garden located in the city see, e.g., Pomponio and Visicato (1994: 299 n° 112). *CAD* A/1: 379 provides attestations of the word 'city' in lexical lists, as well as several instances from various

on the other, the term alludes to a corporate body similar to, and connected with, the city elders. Several works deal with the city as a physical and political organization. Archaeological publications about cities are numerous, although not every attested city was excavated and many of them were poorly and rudimentarily dug. Kathryn Keith (1999) has recently studied Old Babylonian cities known from textual records and material evidence. Her analysis focuses on the relationship between the spatial and social organization, and it provides a summary of previous approaches and an extensive bibliography. As a corporate body, however, the Old Babylonian city is one of the least documented and least understood local institutions of authority.

There is no article dealing exclusively with the city, although one frequently finds references to its role as an adjudicating entity in works concerned with Mesopotamian legislation (e.g. Dombradi 1996: 244 §317; Fortner 1996: 284–93). In one of the earliest treatments of the Old Babylonian city (Walther 1917: 64), the analysis barely covers one page due to the limited amount of documents available at that time. Walther relates the city to other urban authorities such as the *rabiānum*, the elders, the assembly, and the *kārum* ('port authority');[2] but he does not seem to interpret the city as a collegiate institution in itself. Rather, Walther's approach gives the impression that 'the city' was a means of referring to the sum of local authorities, or an abbreviated reference to some of them. Thus, after mentioning the close association of the *rabiānum* with the city elders, he concluded that in certain documents 'city' is the short form for 'city elders', an inference that he also applies to the assembly and the *kārum*.[3]

The Old Assyrian tablets excavated at Kaneš have strengthened the hypothesis of an identification of the city with several other local authorities grouped in smaller institutional units. In Anatolia and northern Syria, there existed several *kārums*, 'business quarters', where Assyrian traders worked and lived. The most important of these 'colonies' was the *kārum* Kaneš, the administrative center of the commercial settlements in Anatolia (see Veenhof 1995a: 867). Because the *kārum* Kaneš dealt with political, economic, legal, and administrative issues, some scholars have compared it with the city of Aššur as a political body, meaning 'the City

documents and periods. For Old Akkadian examples in both languages, see Gelb ([1957] 1973: 3). For the Sumerian uru in Ur III legal documents see, e.g., *NSGU*: 173.

2 For the role of the *kārum* in Babylonia during the Old Babylonian period see Kraus (1982). For the *kārum* in the Assyrian colonies in Anatolia during the Old Assyrian period see, e.g., Larsen (1976: 230) and Veenhof (1995a).

3 According to Walther (1917: 64), 'In CT VI 27b wechseln die Ältesten der Stadt mit dem kürzeren Ausdruck: die Stadt. Auch für die Versammlung von Dilbat wird einmal (VS VII 149, S. 49) kurz gesagt: Dilbat. Die Stadt für die Ältesten der Stadt vielleicht auch noch Str 45_7 = M 45 (S 13). Ähnlich, "die Stadt Sippar" wohl einmal für das *kāru* von Sippar, in der Geschäftsurkunde CT VIII $27b_{23}$'.

Assembly'. Landsberger (1924: 223), for instance, has briefly pointed out that as a political organization the *kārum* parallels the city (*ālum*).[4] Based on the same comparison, Klaas Veenhof (1995a: 867–68) explained that the *kārum* in Anatolia was a bicameral structure comprising 'big' and 'small' members, similar to the political organization of Aššur where the city elders acted alongside the city assembly.[5] In a similar vein, Larsen (1976: 161) considered *ālum* as a synonym of *puḫrum*, 'assembly', although he stressed that 'the City' is a complex concept encompassing geographical, religious, and social aspects. Van De Mieroop (1997: 128) argued similarly about the use of 'the city' and 'the assembly' in the Old Assyrian letters, concluding that this interchangeability of terms suggests that the assembly was a powerful institution similar to the Classical Greek assembly. Veenhof (1995b: 1719–36) also equated both terms and added that the City Assembly (*ālum*) was the highest judicial authority of Aššur, and that it consisted of representatives belonging to different elite groups, among them the merchants. This institution then acted in conjunction with the ruler and passed many verdicts, known as the 'rule' or 'word of the city' (*awāt ālim*), which had 'general validity and hence can be defined as rules' (p. 1736).

Veenhof further compared the Old Assyrian decrees from the city with the *ṣimdat šarrim* and the *awāt šarrim*, 'royal decree', during the Old Babylonian period. He exemplified the resemblance with a case where similar expressions – that is, 'the order of the king' (*qabûm*) and 'the decree of the city' (*awātum*) – appear together in an early document from Sippar dated to king Immerum (Veenhof 1999: 610). The conclusions drawn from this example are that the role of the city in early Sippar is similar to that of the city of Aššur, and that in both cities there were three powers related to the restoration of equity: the city-god, the ruler, and the city assembly. The king presided over the assembly, and the jurisdiction of this college included the passing of verdicts, the issuing of decrees, and the drafting of laws. Veenhof notes, furthermore, that this 'cooperation' between the city ruler and the city assembly is attested in 'real city-states', as was the case of Sippar before its integration into the territorial state created by Sūmû-la-el of Babylon. The fact that the collaboration between the king and the city is an early case unattested in the 'classical' Old Babylonian period led Veenhof to conclude that there had been an institutional change. Consequently, the powerful kings of territorial states such as Larsa or Babylon took all responsibility over certain actions (e.g. the redemption of

4 He affirms: 'Als politische Organisation steht *kārum* genau parallel *alum*. So *kārum dīnam idīn, kāram imḫur* || *alum dīnam idīn, alam imḫur* (…)'.

5 The fragmentary tablets known as 'Statutes of the *kārum*' distinguish between 'big' and 'small' members, and they also provide some information about the way the *kārum* assembly met and reached decisions (see, e.g., Larsen 1976: 183 and Veenhof 1995a: 868). It is worth mentioning that this assembly dealt with conflicts mostly related to commerce. Unfortunately, we do not have similar 'statutes' for the Old Babylonian Period.

houses) that were previously shared with the 'city assembly and its elders' (p. 613). The function of the elders and the assembly in later times was reduced then to the local administration of justice. According to this interpretation, *ālum* means not merely 'city' but also 'City Assembly', and, in that sense, the city implies the sum of other local powers, as was the case with Walther's analysis. Following Jacobsen (1943), Fortner (1996: 295) considers that the city (*ālum*) was a highly comprehensive term and that it was interchangeable with the assembly (*puḫrum*), an institution '[o]pen to the citizenry at large'.

R. Harris (1975: 59), however, seems to disagree with the equation of 'the city' (*ālum*) with 'the assembly' (*puḫrum*), for in her study on Sippar she considered them as two distinct institutions. Harris' interpretation, nevertheless, has been questioned because of the lack of convincing evidence.[6] The current understanding of the Old Babylonian city as a collegiate body relies heavily on our knowledge of the Old Assyrian case, including both Aššur and the colonies in Anatolia, and on scattered and fragmentary examples from Babylonia. Clearly, an examination of the constitution and role of the city during the Old Babylonian period is needed. The study of the documents from Babylonia may contribute to the appreciation of the city and its interaction with other powers. For years, several Assyriologists under the influence of Jacobsen regarded the evolution of political institutions as a linear development. In this view, Mesopotamian government evolved from a kind of democratic pluralism ruled by a general assembly to a monarchic and rather authoritarian system. This interpretation maintains, furthermore, that the centralized and territorial state relegated the role of the 'democratic' organs of government to a secondary position. In the previous chapter, however, we have seen that the 'city elders' were rather active well after the unification of Mesopotamia at the hands of Hammurabi, and that their function was not solely related to the administration of local justice. In addition, it is important to examine whether the 'city' during the Old Babylonian period was a designation encompassing the elders and other institutions, or whether it was an independent collegium, as Harris has suggested for Sippar.

CHARACTERISTICS OF 'THE CITY'

Disagreements on the nature and functions of 'the city' derive in part from the different nuances the word seems to have had in Old Babylonian documents. In certain cases, it might simply designate the inhabitants of an urban center gathered on specific occasions (see, e.g., TCL 17 30, ARM 8 85 and 14 123). In other

6 Thus for instance Larsen (1976: 162 note 5) comments: '[a] kind of distinction between *ālum*, 'the City', and *puḫrum*, 'the Assembly', seems to be made, but there are no good arguments for that'.

examples, the term apparently refers to a local institution of authority. But, according to current interpretations, the characteristics and composition of such an institution are ambiguous because 'city' could denote both the totality of the urban powers and a particular collegiate body that interacts with other organizations concerning local affairs. There seems to be a vague use of 'city' in certain tablets where specification about city membership was not needed. In those cases, the sole allusion to the city in general was enough to convey the idea that the local authorities handled the issue. This is most apparent in those documents mentioning the city assembly, *puḫur ālim* (e.g. CT 52 87: 10'), or the gathering of the city, *ālum ipḫur*, (e.g. CT 47 68a: 9–10, *TS* 42: 7). It is possible, although not completely certain, that in those instances the city assembly encompasses different local authorities. Nevertheless, despite the skepticism of certain scholars, there seems to be no definite argument against the existence of the 'city' as an independent collegium and no certain evidence favoring the all-encompassing character of the city as the sum of multiple local authorities during the Old Babylonian period. In this section, I shall investigate the possibility that in the Old Babylonian period the city represented a relatively independent body similar to the elders. As such, the city did not necessarily represent the city assembly as an all-encompassing category including other local institutions of authority.

A legal document from the environs of Nippur shows that the city does not include the elders, because they are listed side-by-side as separate bodies (TIM 4 5/6, Si 10). In this dispute involving two brothers, Ṣillī-Ištar and Ninurta-gāmil, the local authorities act in two steps. First, the city of Pada assembled (*ālum* ^{uru}*Pada*^{ki} *ipḫur*), investigated the case, and rendered a verdict. Second, before the city and the elders, Ninurta-gāmil gave what he owed to his brother, literally, 'Ninurta-gāmil satisfied the heart of Ṣillī-Ištar, his brother'. The elders, together with the city, witnessed the settlement of the dispute but the elders did not participate in the legal procedure that decided the matter. In addition, the document has Nabi-ilīšu, the *rabiānum*, as the first witness. From this case, it becomes apparent that the expression *ālum ipḫur*, 'the city assembled', does not necessarily imply the gathering of several institutions; otherwise there would have been no need to specify the elders' participation together with the city. From lawsuits we also learn that at least in certain cases the city and the elders could act with relative independence, that is, without debating in a general assembly. This assumption finds confirmation in a legal contract from the time of Samsu-iluna, in which the *rabiānum* and the elders mediate in a dispute concerning a house sold by the city (YOS 12 321). There are still several other attestations wherein the city and the elders are recorded as distinct entities in the same document.[7] Similarly, the

7 See, for instance, TCL 1 232 (RS 28), NBC 6757 (RS), VAS 13 20 (Ḫa 30), *JEOL* 25 46 (Ḫa 31), *TS* 58 (Ḫa 41), TCL 7 40 (Ḫa), Riftin 47 (Ḫa [ ]), OECT 3 47 (n.d), and UCP 10/1 107 (n.d.).

judges were apparently not members of the city institution, because they are specifically mentioned in the same text together with the city and other authorities.[8]

Other tablets from the time of Sîn-muballiṭ and Samsu-iluna illustrate the city's relative independence in rendering a verdict (YOS 14 161, Kiš, Sm 16), or assigning barley for irrigation works (TCL 1 125, Sippar, Si 8). Additionally, in an undated letter, the *rabiānum* and the elders state that the city set free a thief who was the tax collector's assistant (YOS 2 109). Evidently, the *rabiānum* and the elders did not agree with the city's procedure, and it is clear that they considered 'the city' as a distinct authority. In yet another letter, Ibbi-Sîn writes to the *rabiānum* and the elders of Būlum about a claim that the city brought against Watar-Šamaš concerning a garden (VAS 16 142). Ibbi-Sîn further instructs the *rabiānum* and the elders to investigate the case and to render a verdict according to the royal edict (*kīma ṣimdatim*). The elders and the *rabiānum* are here the appointed mediators of a claim that the city raised. Dealings among royal officials, the city, and the elders are also attested in Larsa during the reign of Hammurabi. A letter mentions that Šamaš-ḫāzir, the royal governor of Larsa, handled a legal case together with the city and the elders, and, because of a new claim on the property in question, the king himself instructs his governor on how to proceed (TCL 7 40). Once again, in this case the elders and the city are mentioned separately. This example is important for it shows that the collaboration of the city with the king – or his local representative – was not limited to the city-states of the early Old Babylonian period.

Thus, instead of comparing the role of the city in early Sippar with Aššur and the colonies in Cappadocia, which is a different problem, I analyze the situation in Babylonia starting from Old Babylonian documents. Veenhof's (1999: 610–13) interpretation regarding the collaboration of the city with the king in city-states of the early second millennium is based on the translation of *awāt ālim* as 'the decree of the city'; and on the equation of this expression with *ṣimdat/awāt šarrim*, 'the royal decree'. *Awātum*, however, may also be rendered simply as 'word' or 'report'. As I understand the passage, it means that Adad-rabi bought the field after Immerum had ordered the redemption of fields and houses, and after the city had made the redemption public.[9] It is in this sense that the city 'plays a role in the promulgation, or rather in the execution, of Immerum's decree', as Anne Goddeeris (2002: 330) has put it. If this interpretation is accepted, then the city during the reign of

8 E.g. MHET II/5 n° 837 (Sippar, date lost, *ca.* A-S-Sm), and *TS* 58 (Ašduba, Ḫa 41).

9 Literally, 'after the word of the city', *warki awāt ālim*. Note that Simmons (1960: 27) translates *awāt ālim* as 'the affair (i.e. the duty) of the town'. Aside from Veenhof AOAT 267: 610, the expression *awāt ālim* is also attested in *ED* II 27 (Ed-Dēr, Ammī-sura x), and in YOS 14 35 (Šaduppûm, n.d.). In neither of these two instances is there a clear connection between the city and the king, although the documents are also early Old Babylonian.

Immerum is not a royal institution presided over by the king but the representative of the urban community acting as a link between the state and the city inhabitants, a role still attested during the reign of Hammurabi. As a collegiate body, the city has to be aware and has to inform inhabitants about royal decisions. This case brings to mind Samsu-iluna's letter issued right after the death of his father by which the new king convenes certain elders of the country after he has proclaimed his first *mīšarum*-edict canceling the debts of soldiers and commoners (TCL 17 76). Documents from the time when territorial states were consolidated show that the interaction among king, city, and elders was not restricted to 'real city-states'.

The precise ways in which Old Babylonian local authorities deliberated and reached their decisions are unknown to us, but it is possible to assume that their meetings took place in a specific space, either a building or an open area. An undated document from Sippar (*An. St.* 30: 17–22), probably issued around the reign of Hammurabi, mentions the house of the city (*bīt ālim*), an expression previously known from Old and Middle Assyrian texts.[10] When editing this document, Christopher Walker (1980: 16–17) pointed out that, although the tablet is written in Babylonian script, two of the 14 loans recorded (H and M) probably took place in Aššur because of the mention of the weight-stone of the 'city-house' (na_4 é *a-lim*) and the *līmu*-dating attested in transaction H. For Walker, the contract is relevant to illustrate the central position of Sippar in trading relations between Babylonia and the northern kingdoms, especially Aššur. In his study of Assyrian commercial activities in Sippar, Veenhof (1991: 297–303) has analyzed the activities of Warad-Sîn, who issued the first loan of the contract edited by Walker. In Veenhof's view, Warad-Sîn was an Assyrian merchant who married a Sippar woman. Once settled in Sippar, he continued his commercial activities, and he must have traveled to Aššur regularly. Accordingly, the document was issued in Aššur, possibly by a Babylonian scribe, and brought to Sippar by Warad-Sîn together with other documents belonging to him. Judging from these conclusions, the house of the city attested in the Sippar document is not a Babylonian organization. In this example, the expression refers to the well-known Assyrian institution clearly connected with trade (see Dercksen 2000: 137).

10 Thus, in *BIN* 4 220:20; 6 56:14; CCT 3 23b; TCL 4 21:19; 4 29:44; 14 43: 23 (Old Assyrian); and *KAJ* 12:3 and *KAV* 78:30 (Middle Assyrian). See *CAD* A/I: 389a. For 'the house of the city' or the house of the eponym (*bīt līmim*) in Aššur, see Larsen (1976: 193), and more recently Dercksen (2000: 136–37).

COMPOSITION OF THE CITY

That the members of the city had a leading role in urban affairs is apparent from a tablet from Ur dated to the reign of Rīm-Sîn (UET 5 246). According to this legal record, Ipquša, an inhabitant of Zibnātum approached the influential persons (*kabtūtum*) of that place and obtained a sealed document of the city (*kunuk ālim*); he then brought it to Ur as evidence. This suggests that city dwellers were aware of the importance of getting a city tablet to argue their cases elsewhere. Here the city is clearly the institution issuing the document. It is less evident, however, whether these *kabtūtum* themselves belonged to the collegium or whether they interceded with the city on behalf of Ipquša. The use of a generic term such as 'the important persons' is ambiguous, but there is certainly a connection between these men and the city as a corporate body. Like the elders, the city is usually mentioned as a collective group without further specification concerning membership, which reinforces its corporate character. As we have seen in the previous chapter, however, there are a few instances wherein a list of men is followed by the annotation 'city elders'.

Likewise, certain documents pertaining to city affairs enumerate a number of men presumably belonging to the city, although in these cases there is no additional annotation. These contracts deal with real estate transactions, and they generally include the *rabiānum* or other authority, a list of persons, and the elders. Since in the documents that are well preserved the city is the owner or seller of the property, it seems safe to assume that the men listed between the *rabiānum* and the elders are members of the city. Two of these tablets originate from Sippar. In the first example (MHET II/5 n° 706, pre-Ḫa?), Warad-Sîn, the *rabiānum*, six men, and the city elders sell a house belonging to the city (*bīt ālim*, 'the house of the city'). Although their paternal filiation is not provided, Goddeeris (2002: 422) traced five of the six sellers listed after the *rabiānum*. Most of them are attested in other documents from Ḫalḫalla. One of them, Sîn-šadûni, was the well-known sanga–priest of Ikūnum, and it is likely that Itūr-ašdum is the *rabiānum* of Ḫalḫalla attested elsewhere during the reign of Hammurabi (CT 48 19). In the second case (MHET II/5 n° 617, lost Ḫa), the *rabiānum* Etel-pîša and some nine men sell a house. The inclusion of patronymics facilitates the identification of these people. This text further substantiates the hypothesis that these persons are city members because Iltani, the *nadītum* of Šamaš, bought the house from 'the city' and [Etel-pîša].[11] Similarly, a fragmentary certification of ownership of fields from Dilbat

11 The restoration of the name of the *rabiānum* in this line (i.e. line 3") is mine. MHET II/ 5 n° 617 only has ^{I}x x x x, the number of xs seems to allow the restoration ^{I}[*E-tel-pi*$_4$*-ša*], the *rabiānum* who appears as one of the sellers in line 5'.

(YOS 13 256, Ae 'bb') has a list of four men and the city elders. Although the city is not mentioned, comparison with other texts makes it possible to assume that these men were presumably city members, which is, of course, entirely hypothetical. These individuals are the son of Uraš-iddinam, Ibni-Uraš, the son of Awīl-Šamaš, Ibbīya, the son of Iddin-Lagamal, and Ibni-Marduk, the son of Ilī-iddinam, all of them well-known Dilbatians.

Three documents from Kār-Šamaš, dealing with the sale of houses and the rental of a field, provide additional information regarding the composition of the city. In the first tablet dated to the 25th year of Samsu-iluna, Nakarum, the nu-banda$_3$-official, more than 18 men (some of the lines are missing), and the elders of Kār-Šamaš sell a property described as 'the house of the city' (VAS 29 19). The second contract comes from the 26th year of the same king, and it records the sale of a 'house of the city' by Ilšu-ibnīšu, the *rabiānum*, ten men, and the city elders (VAS 18 17). As was the case with the documents from Sippar, it is possible to assume that the persons listed between the first authority and the city elders are city members, because the property belongs to the city. The third document was issued during Samsu-iluna's successor, most precisely, the year 'u' of king Abī-ešuḫ, but unfortunately the exact location of this year in the list of Abī-ešuḫ's year names is unknown (YOS 13 491). As can be seen from the following list, the name of some of these men appear in the three tablets,[12]

VAS 29 19, Si 25 A house of the city sold by the *laputtû*-official, several men, and the elders	VAS 18 17, Si 26 A house of the city sold by the *rabiānum*, ten men, and the elders	YOS 13 491, Ae 'u' Field rented from four men and the elders
6. from Nakarum, the nu-banda$_3$	13. Nakarum, the son of Warad-Amurrum	7. Nakarum, the son of Warad-Amurrum
7. Marduk-nāṣir, son of Apil-ilīšu		9. Marduk-nāṣir
8. [ ]-dum, son of [Aḫu-wa]qar	9. [ ]-dum, the son of Aḫu-waqar,	
11. Paluḫ-rigimšu and Bayaum, the sons of Ibni-Šamaš	11. Paluḫ-rigimšu, 12. Bayaum, the sons of Ibni-Šamaš,	
13. Ilšu-ibnīšu, son of Bēlšunu	8. from Ilšu-ibnīšu, the *rabiānum* of Kār-Šamaš	6. Ilšu-ibnīšu, the son of Bēlšunu,

12 I have kept the line numbering omitting certain names and changing the order of others.

14. [Id]din-Sîn, son of Anun-pîša and ⌜Mār-erṣetim, son of ^{d}Utu-maš-zu⌝	14. Iddin-Sîn, the son of Anum-pîša, 16. Mār-erṣetim, the son of ^{d}Utu-maš-zu	
20. Ipiq-Ištar, son of [ ]	17. Ipiq-Ištar, son of Ballal-[ ]	
27'. and the elders of Kār-Šamaš	19. and the elders of Kār-Šamaš	10. and the elders of Kār-Šamaš.

These documents are rather unusual for several reasons: they come from the same city, they record similar transactions, they have the elders at the end of a list of men, they were issued during a relatively brief period, and finally they have come down to us despite the accidents of discovery. Nakarum, the son of Warad-Amurrum, is attested in two of the contracts (i.e. VAS 18 17 and YOS 13 491). This fact is relevant because Samsu-iluna reigned for 38 years; thus, if Abī-ešuḫ 'u' is the king's second year, there is at least a span of 14 years between the two documents. Similar is the case with Ilšu-ibnīšu, the son of Bēlšunu, who also appears in two of these three tablets over a period of some 15 years or more (VAS 29 19 and YOS 13 491). An Ilšu-ibnīšu, the *rabiānum* of Kār-Šamaš, is also present in the second sale contract (VAS 18 17). But he might have no connection with his namesake from the other documents, because Ilšu-ibnīšu, the son of Mār-erṣetim, is attested as a *rabiānum* of Kār-Šamaš elsewhere during Samsu-iluna's 30th year (see, e.g., YOS 12 536 and MHET I n° 2). The absence of a seal impression indicating the patronymic of the *rabiānum* in VAS 18 17 leaves it open whether he was the son of Bēlšunu or the son of Mār-erṣetim. Another name that appears twice is Marduk-nāṣir; in the first case (VAS 29 19) he is the son of Apil-ilīšu, and in the second case (YOS 13 491) his paternal filiation is omitted. He is listed right before the elders in the latter instance, and he might have been the *rabiānum* known from two other contracts from Kār-Šamaš during the reigns of Samsu-iluna (YOS 12 537) and Abī-ešuḫ (MHET II/4 n° 469).[13] This instance further supports the hypothesis that the *rabiānum* office originated not only from the elders but also from the city.

The two sale documents issued within one year have in common six men, namely, the son of Aḫum-waqar, Paluḫ-rigimšu and Bayaum, the sons of Ibni-Šamaš, Iddin-Sîn, the son of Anum-pîša, Mār-erṣetim, the son of Utu-maš-zu, and Ipiq-Ištar (VAS 29 19 and VAS 18 17). The co-occurrence of these men listed

[13] YOS 12 537 (Si 30) is the sale of a house located in Kār-Šamaš, and Marduk-nāṣir, the *rabiānum* of Kār-Šamaš, is the first witness. MHET II/4 n° 469, dated to Ae 'k' is a field lease in which the *rabiānum* seems to be both the lessor of the property and the first witness. In this contract, his title is not qualified by a city name.

between an official and the elders in contracts dealing with the sale of a 'house of the city' confirms, I think, that they were representatives of the institution that owned the property. The attestation of Nakarum, the son of Warad-Amurrum, Ilšu-ibnīšu, the son of Bēlšunu, and possibly also of Marduk-nāṣir over a period of at least 14 years might suggest that city membership was either a life-long appointment, or that the same man could be a member several times. Finally, it is worth highlighting that two brothers, Paluḫ-rigimšu and Bayaum, are listed among the city members, which may indicate that family ties were an important qualification in determining membership.

THE ACTIVITIES OF THE CITY

A close look at texts mentioning the city is necessary to understand the activities and functions of this institution. These tablets pertain to a number of different subjects including real estate dealings, agricultural affairs, legal issues, and the jurisdiction over criminal offences such as robbery. As was the case with the *rabiānum* and the elders, the city participated in real estate transactions. Several documents from northern Mesopotamia show that certain urban properties belonged to the city (MHET II/5 n° 706, VAS 18 17, VAS 29 19), and, in some cases, the city shared the ownership of plots of land with the *rabiānum* (MHET II/6 n° 871), and with the city elders (VAS 13 20).[14] An examination of the sellers of real estate belonging to the city reveals close collaboration among the *rabiānum*, the city, and the elders concerning the sale of properties often described as 'the house of the city'.

Thus, in a contract from the Sippar area issued at some point before Hammurabi's reign, the sellers of a 'house of the city' are Warad-Sîn, the *rabiānum*, six men, probably city representatives, and the elders (MHET II/5 n° 706). The *rabiānum*, the city, and the elders are once again the sellers of a property characterized likewise in a document from Kār-Šamaš dating to the 26th year of Samsu-iluna (VAS 18 17). Another tablet also from Kār-Šamaš issued one year earlier than the previous one has a nu–banda$_3$-official, city members, and the elders as the sellers of a city property (VAS 29 19). In a Sippar example from the time of Hammurabi, 'the house of the city and the elders' is sold jointly by the two institutions that owned the property to a Mār-Bayûm, the son of Iddin-Šamaš; while the *rabiānum* Ibni-Amurrum is the first witness (VAS 13 20). Also from Sippar comes a tablet dated to Samsu-iluna's 22nd year that has the *rabiānum* Awīl-ilī and the elders selling the house of the city and the *rabiānum*; and yet another *rabiānum*, Apil-Adad, is the fourth witness (MHET II/6 n° 871).

14 It is possible that MHET II/5 n°617, although broken, also records the sale of a property belonging to the city and the *rabiānum*.

The city appears, furthermore, as seller of properties apparently belonging to third parties. For instance, a fragmentary lawsuit from unknown provenance states that the city had previously sold the house of Šamaš-rabi to Mār-erṣetim (YOS 12 321, Si 10). Unfortunately, the contract does not mention the reasons why the city was the seller in this transaction. But we know that the house was later the object of a legal dispute when Ibni-Amurrum, the son of the original owner, seems to have claimed the property. In an earlier document from the Sippar area dating to the time of Sîn-muballiṭ, the city of Tuḫamum, acting as guarantor, sells a house to Munawwirtum, a *nadītum* of Šamaš (MHET II/1 n° 96). The lines describing the property are broken; nevertheless, since the city assumes the guarantee for the sale (*našî pūtīšu*), it is reasonable to assume that the property did not originally belong to the city. Moreover, in a tablet from the reign of Samsu-iluna, the city and the *rabiānum* sell a house to Amurrum-muballiṭ, although in this case the property is described as *ša bēlam lā īšu*, 'without owner' (YOS 12 194). Also from unknown provenance is a contract from the time of Hammurabi in which the city and the *rabiānum* sell real estate to Sîn-adallal (YBC 4207). These documents seem to suggest that alienation of property by the city was mainly undertaken in northern Mesopotamia during the reigns of Hammurabi and his successor Samsu-iluna, but the example from the time of Sîn-muballiṭ might indicate that these transactions occurred earlier as well.

The city was also engaged in the management of certain agricultural properties, including the rental and the assignment of fields, and in the administration of grain for the distribution of rations or for other purposes. An undated letter from Sippar, for example, mentions that the city had given a field to a man after the previous holder died without heirs (CT 6 27b). A similar case might be reported in a letter from Larsa, but the key lines are unfortunately missing (OECT 3 47). Moreover, the city members from Kār-Šamaš are among the lessors in a field lease from the time of Abī-ešuḫ (YOS 13 491). An early document possibly from Ḫalḫalla dated to king Sūmû-la-el implies, furthermore, that the city may occasionally have received grain of the king's land (CT 4 9b). The urban institution was presumably stocking local produce to be transferred later to the central authority or to be assigned to laborers.

A document from Sippar dated to the reign of Samsu-iluna shows that the city allocated barley in payment for the maintenance of irrigation canals (TCL 1 125). The city had received the grain from a certain Igmil-Sîn some two and a half months before this contract was issued, and it is probable that the barley was for the recruited workers (see Harris 1975: 59). Nevertheless, the document states that because the canal was not dug, the grain was collected again. Evidently, the city was acting here as an intermediary between the royal administration that provided the grain and the laborers hired to perform irrigation works. Although the function of Igmil-Sîn is unclear because he does not bear a title, it is likely that he was acting as a crown representative. This tablet is also a rare example of an interrupted redistribution cycle; the rations that the crown provided never reached the workers, for the state took the grain back from the city soon afterwards because the task had not been accomplished. This further shows that the city had limited control over the resources assigned by the crown. As already mentioned in the previous chapter, the elders and the *rabiānum* were similarly responsible for the recruitment of workers and the distribution of rations.

Inhabitants of urban centers resorted to the city to obtain evidence related to legal issues. It is clear from certain documents that the city had the power to certify the juridical situation of city dwellers. For instance, there is the case of a woman whom the Elamites brought to an unspecified city when she was still an infant and her wet-nurse purchased her (VAS 16 80). Although the letter is vague, it seems that this woman became later the property of a man from Mutiabalum, because this city denied her freedom and her master retained her. The first part of the letter, however, states that the woman in question (*awīltum*) is a citizen of Ida-Maraṣ and that her city will prove that she is a free woman (dumu-munus *awīlim*). Presumably, she regained freedom once her native city certified her status; this fact may consequently have cancelled the denial of the other city, Mutiabalum. The procedure possibly encompassed the issuing of a tablet, as becomes clear from other instances.[15] According to a document from Ur dated to Rīm-Sîn, the city of Zibnātum drew up a sealed tablet to prove that Ḫubbutum had infected Ms. Šāt-Sîn with the *li'bum* disease (UET 5 246). Ipquša, who approached the city to obtain the document on behalf of Šāt-Sîn, returned to Ur with the certification and, apparently, judicial procedures (*dayyānūtum*) were arranged for him (see Kraus 1955: 133).

As a local authority, the city had also jurisdiction over criminal offences committed within its domain. The 'Laws of Hammurabi' (§§23 and 24) hold the city and the *rabiānum* responsible for lost property in case the thief were not seized. Although there is a document where the *rabiānum* of Zaralulu has to pay a fine for a robbery committed by an inhabitant of his city (YOS 14 40), I have found no tablet where it is the city that pays the fine. Nevertheless, there are certain texts recording the city's involvement in the prosecution of robbery. On one occasion, for instance, the *rabiānum* and the elders report that the city set a thief free although the stolen goods were found in his possession (YOS 2 109). In a lawsuit from Iščhali, a thief pleaded guilty of having broken into the house of Ilšu-nāṣir. Because he was caught doing so and the stolen object was seized in his hands, the city and

15 This example resembles CT 48 44 (Si), where the city elders participate in the identification of a woman's status as *ugbabtum*.

the elders imposed a punishment on Tarībum, the culprit, after listening to the deposition of both parties (UCP 10/1 107). Moreover, the city's prerogative to question suspects is apparent from a letter mentioning that the city interrogated a slave who was seized and held for four days (TCL 17 90).

Lawsuits from different areas and periods record the role of the city in the settlement of legal disputes. In most of the extant examples, the city deals with those cases in collaboration with other authorities. The following combinations are attested: 1) city + elders, 2) city + elders + *rabiānum*, 3) city + *rabiānum* + judges, 4) city + judges, 5) city + elders + a royal official, and 6) the city alone but with the *rabiānum* as the first witness. The city and the elders are recorded alongside one another in several tablets from southern Mesopotamia from the time of Rīm-Sîn to the reign of Samsu-iluna. Thus, in a text from Lagaš (TCL 1 232, RS 28), both the city and the elders handled a case regarding a claim that Sîn-erībam and Aplum brought against the children of the chief *gudapsûm*. The object of the dispute was an orchard that was finally returned to the original owner. At least part of the process seems to have taken place at the temple of Nin-MAR.KI, probably because one of the parties was a relative of a *gudapsûm*, a reason that also accounts for the presence of several *pašīšum*-priests as witnesses to the transaction. It is important to recall that, similarly, the elders and the *rabiānum* participated in the assembly of the *pašīšum*-priests to investigate the theft of the vestment of Nin-MAR.KI's statue in an undated document from Larsa (TCL 11 245). In another document from Larsa, two men approached Nabû-mālik concerning a dispute over agricultural work (*JEOL* 25: 46, Ḫa 31). The royal official, however, did not deal with the issue himself but transferred the case to the city and the elders of Ḫarḫarrû; for that matter the parties were sent to Ḫarḫarrû in the company of a soldier.[16]

There are other tablets from southern Mesopotamia where the city and the elders are the adjudicating entities, whereas another local authority, the *rabiānum*, is the first witness. For instance, in Larsa during the time of Hammurabi, the parties engaged in a litigation regarding the dowry of Aḫāssunu approached Sîn-iddinam but, as was the case in the previous example, the royal governor of Larsa handed over the case to the city and the elders (Riftin 47). The fact that the *rabiānum* Aḫum was listed as a witness indicate that he was present during the process. Similarly, in a document from Ašduba also dated to Hammurabi, the city and the elders rendered a verdict, and Sîn-imguranni, the *rabiānum*, headed the list of witnesses (TS 58). This text is interesting because it records two related cases; one took place at some point during the reign of Rīm-Sîn, and the other in Hammurabi's 41st

16 Although Nabû-mālik does not have a title, the fact that the soldier is described as 'a soldier of Nabû-mālik' seems to be a clear indicator that the man was a royal official.

regnal year. The object of the dispute is a garden that Mār-Amurrim bought from Sîn-māgir, and the litigants are their children (see Charpin 1980a: 143). On the first occasion, Ilum-bāni, the adoptive son of Sîn-māgir raised a claim appealing to a royal edict of Rīm-Sîn. Consequently, the parties approached the judges and they confirmed the property for Ilum-bāni. Later, however, Sîn-muballiṭ, presumably the son of Mār-Amurrim, raised a claim over the same property.[17] The parties went back to the judges, but this time the judges sent them to the city and the elders and the case was decided once again in favor of Ilum-bāni. Kraus (1958: 207-208) has pointed out that this case illustrates the legal continuity in Larsa under Babylonian rule. Nevertheless, this does not explain the reasons why under Hammurabi the judges did not handle the case themselves, as they had done previously, but transferred it to the city and the elders. In view of the time elapsed between the two cases (at least ten years), it seems reasonable to think that the judges were not the same. Finally, as already mentioned, in a tablet from the environs of Nippur, the city and the elders of Pada handled a dispute between two brothers; while the *rabiānum* Nabi-ilīšu was the first witness (TIM 4 5/6, Si).

The city, the judges, and Marduk-nāṣir, the *rabiānum*, deal with a litigation concerning a field in a document from Sippar (MHET II/ 5 n° 837, *ca.* A-S-Sm). A certain Bēlšunu had sold a plot of land at the king's command to Sîn-iqīšam, and Erībam-Sîn raised a claim over this property. Unfortunately, the document is broken and some of the details are missing. This contract is the only example in the corpus recording the interaction of the city, the judges, and the *rabiānum*. The judges and the city, however, appear together in a document from Kutalla dating to the time of Hammurabi (*TS* 42). The text recounts that the city assembled and the judge(s) interrogated a certain Sîn-imguranni concerning a house.[18] Charpin (1980a: 98) has suggested that, although the tablet belongs to the archive of Ṣillī-Ištar from Kutalla, the deposition possibly took place in Larsa. Considering the various documents from Larsa issued roughly at the same period, it seems plausible that, in *TS* 42, the gathering of the city refers to the same institution that frequently acts in cooperation with other authorities. Another isolated example recording the interaction among Šamaš-ḫāzir, the city, and the elders is a letter referring to a dispute over a field in Larsa. We know from this text that a certain Šēp-Sîn claimed the field of Ibbi-Adad without any solid reasons and further expropriated the produce. The local authorities had convened to handle the case, but apparently one of the parties ignored their verdict. After the complaint of Ibbi-Adad, king Hammurabi himself wrote to his representative in Larsa, Šamaš-

17 Charpin (1980a: 144) has suggested that Sîn-muballiṭ could have tried to have the previous verdict cancelled by a new *mīšarum*, but, as Charpin himself has remarked, there is no *mīšarum* attested in Ḫa 42.

18 For an analysis of this document that differs from VAB 5 n° 285, see Charpin (1980a: 98-99).

ḫāzir, asking him, the city, and the elders to return the field and the rights over it to Ibbi-Adad, the righteous holder (TCL 7 40, Ḫa).

Finally, there are two contracts from the time of Sîn-muballiṭ where the city rendered a verdict by itself; in each case, a *rabiānum* is the first witness. In a tablet possibly from Kiš, a certain Warad-ilīšu raised a claim against two other persons. The city rendered a verdict and had the plaintiff issue a tablet of no further claim, whereas the *rabiānum* Riš-Zababa is the first witness (YOS 14 161). Similarly, in a document from Ḫalḫalla also from the time of king Sîn-muballiṭ, the city assembled and handled a case concerning a field belonging to a *nadītum* (CT 47 68a). Once again, the *rabiānum* of Ḫalḫalla is the first witness, and there are reasons to believe that at least some of the other men in the list were city members, because Imgur-Sîn, the son of Uqâ-ilān, bore the *rabiānum* title in a document from the time of Apil-Sîn, the previous ruler (CT 45 9). The role of the city in lawsuits, however, is not limited to adjudication, for a letter that Ibbi-Sîn sent to the *rabiānum* and the elders of Būlum mentions that the city raised a claim against Watar-Šamaš who had bought the garden five years earlier (VAS 16 142).

REASSESSING THE OLD BABYLONIAN CITY

When Walther wrote his *Das altbabylonische Gerichtswesen* in 1917, the number of Old Babylonian texts referring to the city as an institution of authority was very limited. Indeed, in addition to the two paragraphs of Hammurabi's laws, Walther had at his disposal only three documents explicitly mentioning the city. These sources included a letter (CT 6 27b) and a sale contract (VAS 13 20, Ḫa) both from Sippar, and a lawsuit from Lagaš (TCL 1 232, RS); in all of them, the city is mentioned alongside the elders. The interaction of the elders with the *rabiānum*, the joint attestation of the city with the elders, and the mention of the assembly of Dilbat (VAS 7 149) led Walther to assume that 'the city' encompassed the elders as well as other local authorities. Over the years, comparative studies of the role of the city as recorded in Old Assyrian tablets were used to strengthen Walther's conclusions on the Old Babylonian city. Therefore, the virtual identification of the city and the assembly became a fact. Most recent studies about the city are not so much concerned with the institution itself as they are with those legal cases that the city adjudicated. In juridical-oriented approaches, however, the city is ill defined because those studies very seldom include documents other than lawsuits. The inclusion of letters and economic records reveals aspects of the city that are not evident from legal texts.

Compared with the attestations for *rabiānum* and elders, the number of sources dealing with the city is small. Nevertheless, tablets mentioning the city in our corpus represent over ten times the records that Walther was able to gather. From the analysis of these texts, there are reasons to assume that the city was not a general label used to describe part or all of the smaller institutions included within the city. The elders, for instance, were not a section of the city body, which becomes apparent from several documents mentioning the city and the elders but not other institutions. Furthermore, if 'the city' (*ālum*) were equivalent to 'the assembly' (*puḫrum*), the reference to the elders would be redundant because the elders should be part of the assembly of local authorities. The fact that the city and the elders appear together in several but not all the documents shows that the elders and the city were not the same entity. This assumption finds confirmation in those tablets wherein the city is the owner and the seller of real estate. Although most of the examples come from northern Babylonia, two of them are of unknown provenance; and they are attested from the reign of Sîn-muballiṭ to the 26th year of Samsu-iluna. In five of these sale documents, the property belongs to the city, but the sellers vary. Thus, in three instances the sellers are the *rabiānum*, the city, and the elders, in another case the city and the elders, and finally there is one house sold by the *rabiānum* and the elders. These contracts originate from the Sippar region and cover a relatively brief period. Therefore, the presence or absence of 'the city' in these transactions cannot be attributed to regional usages. I assume that these variations were meaningful to the ancient scribe, even if we are still unable to understand subtleties pertaining to the functions of the city.

There are also cases showing that the interests and procedures of the city and the elders seem to conflict. For instance, the *rabiānum* and the elders handled a dispute concerning a house sold by the city (YOS 12 321). Although the text is partially broken, the fact that the adjudicating authorities make the parties reach an agreement without mentioning the city indicates that the elders and the *rabiānum* did not fully validate the original sale. This is particularly relevant in view of those real estate documents with a clause stating that, in case of conflict, the sellers will be responsible (see, e.g., MHET II/1 n° 96, and Stol 1998: 444). Similarly, Ibbi-Sîn instructed the *rabiānum* and the elders of Būlum to investigate a case where the city raised a claim concerning the ownership of a garden. Evidently, Ibbi-Sîn did not regard the *rabiānum* and the elders as part and parcel of the city; otherwise, he would have appointed another authority to arbitrate the conflict. A disagreement between the *rabiānum* and the elders on the one hand, and the city, on the other, seems also to be present in YOS 2 109. In this letter the *rabiānum* and the elders report on a robbery; their remarks on the fact that the city set the thief free show, I think, that they did not approve of the city's decision. These kinds of tensions, however, are difficult to trace because they are not the main topic of the documents. Nevertheless, being aware that conflicts existed among local authorities is also relevant to understanding that they might have represented different interests, as will be discussed in the last chapter.

Influential city dwellers constituted 'the city', but there is no evidence to sustain the hypothesis that the king presided over the 'city assembly' of the city-states during the early Old Babylonian period. Actually, there are very few attestations of the city as an institution of authority before the reign of Sūmû-la-el in the north. For the south, I have found no reference to the city before Rīm-Sîn (see table IV). Furthermore, the alleged collaboration between the king and the city during the prevalence of independent city-states is not restricted to an early stage. As we have seen, there are examples from the reign of Hammurabi showing that royal officials still interacted with local powers such as the city, the elders, and the *rabiānum* well after the constitution of territorial states. A similar cooperation is attested under Samsu-iluna, where the city is in charge of distributing barley rations among the workers. The interpretation that posits a deterioration of the power borne by the city and the elders is, as I see it, the result of an evolutionary approach to Mesopotamian political institutions. This view maintains that in early times political matters were openly debated in an assembly à la Gilgameš, a sort of imperfect or rather immature version of Greek democracy. This situation was then interrupted by a development towards authoritarian rulers who concentrated all power in their hands. Primitive democracy owes part of its existence to the literary assembly of the gods and, as such, has to be placed in time immemorial. These issues, however, will be discussed in the next chapter.

Table 4. **Dated city-documents chronologically arranged**[19]

Date	Provenance	Document
Ammī-ṣura x	ed-Dēr	*ED* II 27
Immerum (oath)	Sippar	Veenhof AOAT 267: 610
Sūmû-la-el	Sippar	CT 4 9b
Sîn-muballiṭ		
Sm 16	Kiš	YOS 14 161
Sm (oath)	Sippar	MHET II/ 1 n° 96
Sm (c.)	Ḫalḫalla	CT 47 68a
Sm (c.)	Sippar	MHET II/5 n° 837
Rīm-Sîn		
RS 28	Lagaš	TCL 1 232
RS	Unknown (south)	NBC 6757
RS	Ur	UET 5 246
Hammurabi		
Ḫa 14	Ašduba	*TS* 58
Ḫa 18	Unknown	YBC 4207
Ḫa 30	Sippar	VAS 13 20
Ḫa 31	Larsa	*JEOL* 25: 46
Ḫa 36	Kutalla	*TS* 42
Ḫa 41	Unknown	YBC 4496
Ḫa (lost)	Sippar	MHET II/5 n° 617
Ḫa (lost)	Larsa	Riftin 47
Samsu-iluna		
Si 7	Archive of Amurrum-muballiṭ	YOS 12 194
Si 8	Sippar	TCL 1 125
Si 10	environs of Nippur	TIM 4 5/6
Si 10	Unknown	YOS 12 321
Si 22	Sippar	MHET II/ 6 n° 871
Si 25	Kār-Šamaš	VAS 29 19
Si 26	Kār-Šamaš	VAS 18 17
Si (oath)	Lagaba	TLB I 141

19 Letters and undated documents are not included; however, when the date of a document can be estimated, the text was included.

6
*The Assembly (*puḫrum*)*

ON MESOPOTAMIAN ASSEMBLIES

The little description we have about Mesopotamian assemblies comes mostly from works depicting divine gatherings. There is also the frequently quoted composition known as 'Gilgameš and Akka', where the king of Uruk consults the elders and the guruš (usually translated as 'young men') before going to war against the rival city of Kiš. Aside from texts dealing with divine characters and mythological heroes, Mesopotamian sources such as letters and legal tablets mention human assemblies involved in the resolution of different issues. But these documents rarely describe the constituency and jurisdiction of the assemblies or the way they functioned.[1] There is no depiction of Mesopotamian governments similar to, let us say, Thucydides' 'Funeral Speech of Pericles' (*History* 2.37), or the detailed explanations and discussions that can be found in Plato's *The Republic*, or in Aristotle's *The Politics* and *The Constitution of Athens*. Nor do we have anything comparable to the humorous and mordant insights of Aristophanes' plays. The terse account of mundane cuneiform tablets clearly contrasts with the elaboration of Greek political treatises.

Not surprisingly then, the most vivid characterization of an ancient Near Eastern human debate comes from a Greek writer, Herodotus. When referring to certain Persian customs, Herodotus states that:

> [i]t is usual for them to be drunk when they are debating the most important issues. However, any decision they reach is put to them again on the next day, when they are sober, by the head of the household where the debate takes place; if they still approve of it when they are sober, it is adopted, but otherwise they forget about it. And any issues they debate when sober are reconsidered by them when they are drunk (*The Histories* 1.133).

Although this passage does not necessarily deal with Persian politics, associations are difficult to avoid. As is well known, *The Histories* abound with comments on the oddities of other peoples who are quite distinct from the Greeks, and Herodotus'

1 As an exception, one could mention the laconic and fragmentary tablets containing the so-called 'Statutes of the *kārum*' of the Assyrian merchants in Anatolia (see Larsen 1976: 183).

emphasis on 'alterity' renders his remark unbelievable. The alleged Persian way of debating would have taken place almost a thousand years after the Old Babylonian period, and in the early second millennium most Babylonians drank beer instead of wine. Yet, the drunkenness of Herodotus' Persians is reminiscent of certain episodes that occurred in the Mesopotamian assembly of the gods, where important decisions were made 'when the gods are in their cups' (Jacobsen 1943: 167).[2]

Due to the lack of narrative sources dealing with the role and constituency of the assembly in ancient Mesopotamia, early scholars resorted to literary compositions such as 'Gilgameš and Akka' and *Enūma eliš*, to scattered references to the assembly of the gods, and finally to comparisons based on Greek and Roman assemblies. Jacobsen (e.g. 1943 and 1957) undertook such an approach to trace early political development in Mesopotamia. Based on literary texts, he concluded that 'primitive democracy' was the form of government in prehistoric Mesopotamia, while 'autocratic' rule was the characteristic of historic times. Jacobsen's theory rests on two assumptions. First, that Sumerians and Akkadians regarded their gods as human in form, emotions, and ways of living. Therefore, since the world of the gods was politically organized along democratic lines, their domain was a reflection of older forms of human government (Jacobsen 1943: 167). Second, ancient myths telling stories about the gods are also sources for the earliest human political forms, namely, 'primitive democracy' (Jacobsen 1957: 99), while epic tales telling stories about human or semi-human heroes are sources for prehistoric political forms represented by 'primitive monarchy' (p. 112).

The early Mesopotamian assembly that Jacobsen (1943) reconstructed by means of combining fragments of different literary texts fulfilled three main functions. It worked as a court of law to settle conflicts, as exemplified by the exile that the 50 great gods and the seven gods who decide destinies imposed on Enlil in his youth for raping young Ninlil. The primitive assembly also decided important matters related to peace or war, as was the case in 'Gilgameš and Akka'. Finally, it could also grant supreme authority if need arose. Thus, in a literary text, the assembly of Kiš raised Ipḫur-Kiš to kingship (see Jacobsen 1978–79), while in *Enūma eliš* the gods gathered in the Ubšu-ukkinna granted Marduk supreme authority.[3] According to Jacobsen, only the judicial function of the assembly remained during the historic period, as becomes clear from tablets dealing with

2 Herodotus' passage ends a paragraph that explains the Persian custom regarding birthdays. In the Sumerian story 'The Birth of Man' (see Jacobsen 1987: 158–64), the gods have a party to celebrate man's birth where Enki and Ninmaḫ get drunk and create a series of men with physical disabilities. Similarly, in *Enūma eliš* the great gods in assembly ordained destiny for Marduk while drunk (III: 135–38, see Foster 1996: 370–73). For the assembly of gods see Cassin (1973a and 1973b).

3 Falkenstein (1954: 801) disagrees with this interpretation. For him, the importance of the assembly should not be overestimated, since it probably had only advisory powers. See also Finet (1973b: 16–17).

the Old Assyrian merchants in Anatolia and from documents dating to the Old Babylonian period. These judiciary assemblies were 'open to all citizens' and represented a 'stubborn survival' of democratic ideas rooted in earlier ages (Jacobsen 1943: 165).

Conclusions similar to those formulated by Jacobsen appear in the work of other scholars.[4] Such is the case, for instance, with Evans' (1958) analysis of Mesopotamian assemblies. In spite of the all-encompassing title, however, this study centers around the comparison between the assemblies at Uruk during the time of Gilgameš – 'Gilgameš and Akka' being the only source – and those at Kaneš during the Old Assyrian period. In order to establish the procedures and composition of Mesopotamian assemblies, the author relies on instances from Sparta and Rome in Classical Antiquity; other examples include the Roman Senate and the House of Commons. Although Evans does not question Jacobsen's methods or ideas about an alleged 'primitive democracy', he disagrees with Jacobsen regarding certain formal aspects of the assemblies. In both analyses, the conclusions are no more than educated guesses. As for the comparison between the assemblies at Uruk and Kaneš, Evans also believes that in later times the power of the assemblies deteriorated, and that jurisdiction was consequently restricted to judicial matters. Diakonoff (1969: 183–85) has proposed a similar decline in the power of the assemblies from the Early Dynastic to the Old Babylonian period. Thus, by the time of king Hammurabi, the community assemblies had become mere organs of the local administration (see Katz 1993: 22).

Another study specifically devoted to Mesopotamian assemblies is Szlechter's (1970) 'Les assemblées en Mésopotamie ancienne'. Some of the discussions and conclusions presented in this article had already appeared elsewhere (see Szlechter 1968). Like his predecessors, Szlechter traces the evolution and transformations of the institution from the pre-Sargonic period (c. 2380 BC) until the end of the First Dynasty of Babylon (c. 1595 BC). His analysis also rests upon literary texts, 'model court cases', legal documents, and letters, and it aims at understanding the composition and competence of the various assemblies attested throughout the centuries. For him the assembly consisted of the citizens and the elders, and he further maintains that terms such as 'elders', 'citizens' (*mār ālim*), and 'the city' (*ālum*) are all synonyms of the word 'assembly'. Since this article is a chronological presentation that relies on the conclusions of previous approaches, it is not surprising that the author also sees a restriction in the jurisdiction of the assembly. Thus, unlike its pre-Sargonic alleged forerunner, the Old Babylonian institution did not deal with political issues of the state such as war and peace but was

4 For a summary of different views regarding early governmental institutions and their historicity see Katz (1993: 21).

concerned only with judicial and administrative matters. Here again we encounter a deterioration of authority as a result of the centralization of power.

Interpretations of the development of political institutions in Mesopotamia interest us here because the conclusions of those studies have influenced the evaluation of Old Babylonian assemblies. The reconstruction of the role and functions of assemblies in early periods is problematic because it is based on literary sources dealing with the assembly of gods or fictitious characters. These compositions were written several centuries after the historical period to which they supposedly allude. Oppenheim (1960) has already emphasized the difficulties related to the use of literary texts for the study of political institutions. Besides this methodological problem, most of these approaches have produced a composite Mesopotamian assembly made out of examples from different periods and areas within the ancient Near East and elsewhere. Such interpretations seem to assume the existence of an original ruling assembly in every city-state. That kind of institution consisted of different bodies (elders, free men, and the like), which slowly transformed due to the growing pressure of autocratic regimes, and which survived over the millennia. During this process, the assembly lost most of its powers and was incorporated within the framework of territorial states as a judicial body of local authority. However, that the assemblies attested in the earliest tablets are the direct ancestors of the assemblies of the second millennium is, I think, a questionable assumption.

The attestation of the sign unken ('assembly') among the earliest written documents, does not necessarily guarantee that such a word had anything to do with the assembly as a community organ of self-government. Yoffee (2000: 56) has recently mentioned that in the earliest Uruk IV archaic administrative documents the sign gal + unken (to be read kingal) always relates to the administration of products in an institutional setting, although a literal translation could be 'chief of the assembly'. According to Yoffee, the titles gal-zu-unken-na, found in Ur III royal correspondence (see Michalowski 1976a: 41), and gal-unken-na (*mu'errum*), found in Early Dynastic and Old Babylonian documents, are completely unrelated to any kind of assemblies.[5] To the titles gal-zu-unken-na and gal-unken-na, we should now add ugula-unken, apparently a *hapax legomenon*, attested in the Ušumgal stele (Gelb *et al.* 1991: 44 and plate 15). This stele of unknown provenance, possibly from Umma, dates to the Early Dynastic I-II period, and it records a sale of land. The iconography that accompanies the text represents six figures; two of them are female, and those on sides A and B are larger. These people are distributed along four sides:

5 Yoffee (1977: 80–93) has studied the role of the gal-unken-na (*mu'errum*) during the Old Babylonian period. For a different interpretation regarding this title, see, e.g. Harris (1975: 65) and Charpin (1980b: 462).

Side A has a man: 'Ušumgal, the pab-šeš-priest of Šara(?)', probably the buyer.

Side B has a woman: 'Šara(?)-igizi-Abzu, the daughter of Ušumgal, the ÉŠ.A'.

Side C has a woman, 'IGI.RU(?).NUN, the ÉŠ.A, the daughter of Mesi, the pab-šeš-priest of the (temple) Enun'.

Side D has three men:
In the upper portion, one man: 'Ag, the **gal-unken**',
In the lower portion, two men: 'Nanna, the **ugula-unken**', and 'X.KU.EN, the **gal-nimgir**', the chief herald.

The editors of this text note that, although it might be tempting to do so, the three men on side D should not be considered co-sellers, that is, community members. This is so because even though the titles of two of them include the word unken, 'assembly', their titles indicate that they were actually state or temple officials who either authorized or witnessed the transaction.

Early documents from the Uruk IV and Early Dynastic I-II periods may not support the connection between the sign unken and the assembly, but they are still relevant to our discussion because they account for evidence that, together with archaeology, has usually been overlooked in those studies of the political stage depicted in 'Gilgameš and Akka'. Indeed, administrative documents and seals from the Uruk IV and Early Dynastic periods as well as the results of archaeological excavations at Uruk show the existence of a highly stratified and hierarchically structured society (see, e.g. Nissen 1988; Nissen *et al.* 1993 [1990]; Pollock 1999). If we are going to gather literary compositions to reconstruct the historical Gilgameš who might have ruled in Early Dynastic Uruk (i.e. c. 2900 BC; for this date see Nissen 1988: 95), we should also include the 'epic' of Gilgameš. This text was usually ignored in the reconstruction of early political developments, although it alludes to an assembly and some of the manuscripts at our disposal are Old Babylonian copies contemporaneous with those of 'Gilgameš and Akka'. From excavations at Uruk we know that the wall of Uruk attributed to Gilgameš existed, and that it dates to the Early Dynastic period. This wall was 9.5 km long, and enclosed an area of some 5.5 km^2. The city included, furthermore, large-scale buildings, for example the terrace to the west of the district of Eanna, and the enormous buildings of the precinct of Eanna itself (Nissen 1988: 95–103).

The organization of labor required to undertake these architectural projects indicate that whoever governed Uruk during the Early Dynastic period had already accumulated a considerable amount of power. This fact makes it unlikely that such a ruler (or ruling class) would have requested the advice of an assembly comprised of 'all free members' of the community. Let us not forget that Jacobsen's 'primitive democracy' pre-dated the origins of monarchic rule. Therefore, one might very well expect that, in case of a threat of war, strategies would be discussed within those powerful groups belonging to the state whose economic and political interests could be affected in case of war. In such a context, and granting that a consultation such as the one depicted in 'Gilgameš and Akka' ever took place, it seems reasonable to conclude that the assembly of Uruk was not necessarily a 'popular assembly'. Of course, this interpretation does not deny the existence of those community representatives and community assemblies traceable from sale documents from the pre-Sargonic and Sargonic periods (e.g. Diakonoff 1969 and Gelb 1969). It rather suggests the existence of multiple assemblies operating at different levels (e.g. royal and community assemblies), as will be seen from documents from the Old Babylonian period. If this line of reasoning is correct, then a comparison between Early Dynastic and Old Babylonian assemblies does not apply, nor does the explanation proposing the decline of the role of the assembly during the Old Babylonian period.

OLD BABYLONIAN ASSEMBLIES

The attestation of judicial assemblies during the Hammurabi dynasty attracted the attention of early researchers because before cuneiform documents became available the general assumption was that such assemblies were characteristic only of Greek cities (Cuq 1910: 89). Today it is possible to trace back the existence of the word 'assembly' to the third millennium (see Yoffee 2000: 56).[6] References to assemblies in texts other than literary compositions are few, but in Old Babylonian letters and economic and legal contracts the Akkadian term *puḫrum* and the Sumerian unken, meaning 'assembly', are relatively well documented, especially when compared with evidence from previous periods. Besides *puḫrum*, documents from the Mari region also record the word *tātamum*, which has a similar signification.[7] In certain Sumerian texts from the Ur III and early Old Babylonian

6 I could not find any references from economic or legal documents from the pre-Sargonic and Sargonic periods, although the Akkadian verb *paḫārum*, 'to assemble', is attested in Sargonic texts (see Gelb [1957] 1973: 212). A tablet from Early Dynastic Šuruppak records the geographical name unken[ki], as a district in course of formation (Pettinato 1977). Pomponio and Visicato (1994: 13) propose that the name of the site, meaning 'assembly', must have referred to the union of cities that brought it about. According to Durand (1989), in Ebla during the third millennium the logogram unken = *da-da-mu* (*tātamu*) means assembly, whereas the Sumerian word also appears in pre-Sargonic texts from Mari.

7 According to Durand (1989: 37), 'Le *tâtamum* que nous attestent les documents mariotes est de fait un collectif composé de personnes que l'on rassemble en un lieu pour discuter: a) d'affaires juridiques; b) d'affaires économiques; c) d'affaires politiques. Ses decisions enganget le peuple dans son entire.' See also Durand (1990: 48–50).

periods, 'assembly' is written syllabically as an Akkadian loanword pu-úḫ-ru-um (e.g. *NSGU* 3: 153; *Sumer* 20: 66; *JCS* 3: 168; *WO* 8/2: 160). The logogram unken is at present rather infrequently attested, since it appears only once in our corpus of economic and legal documents (TCL 18 151: 34).

Studies regarding the constituency and competence of the Old Babylonian assemblies date to the early twentieth century, and there are still disagreements about some of these issues. For Cuq (1910: 87–91), the assembly consisted of notables presided over by the *rabiānum*. It did not include the judges, but was controlled by the king, and apart from judicial matters, the *puḫrum* also dealt with private affairs and the administration of city property. The question of who exactly those notables were, however, does not become apparent from Cuq's analysis, but he seems to include the city elders. Walther (1917: 45–52) echoes Cuq about the distinction between the assembly and the judges, but he is uncertain about the equation of *puḫrum* with the elders, the city, and the *awīlû* ('notables'). Walther thinks it likely that the *bābtum* ('city ward') and the *kārum* ('the port authority') might have constituted the assembly. Nevertheless, whatever the differences might have been, Walther sees a close interconnection among all these institutions. Similarly, Driver and Miles (1952: 78) admit that it is not certain exactly what the assembly was, but they suggest that it might have consisted of the free burghers of a city, over whom the judges presided. They further pose that the *puḫrum* seems to have been identical with other assemblies such as that of the elders, the *kārum* ('the port authority'), and the *mārū bābtim* ('the inhabitants of the city ward'). Moreover, Driver and Miles reject Walther's interpretation that, in certain cases, *ina puḫrim* is simply a periphrasis for 'in public', a translation that is not unusual (see, e.g., Frankena 1974: 77; Stol 1981: 73). More recently, Dombradi (1996: 242–43) and Fortner (1996: 293–302) have summarized the judicial competence of the Old Babylonian assemblies considering new evidence.

Interpretations concerning the role of the assembly in Mesopotamian politics and society acquired new dimensions after Jacobsen's (1943) article on 'primitive democracy'. As already mentioned, for Jacobsen the Old Babylonian assembly represents the survival of an early governmental institution characteristic of prehistoric times. The tendency towards concentration of power and autocratic regimes in historic periods slowly diminished the functions and jurisdiction of the assembly until its competence was reduced to the local administration of justice. In Jacobsen's view, the *rabiānum* and the elders dealt with minor disputes, while the city as a whole, that is, the assembly, settled more difficult or important cases. Since Jacobsen believed that the city and the assembly are interchangeable terms, he inferred that participation in the assembly was not the exclusive prerogative of a 'small favored class or group', but that the institution must have included 'the citizenry at large' (p. 163), with the exception of women. Diakonoff's

(1969) study of the rise of despotic regimes in ancient Mesopotamia also begins with the Early Dynastic period and includes the Hammurabi dynasty. Diakonoff maintains that the first attempt to reduce community organs of self-government to the level of local administration took place under the Sargonic dynasty, in the 24th and 23rd centuries. During the Old Babylonian period, institutions such as the elders and the 'popular assemblages of the city' (*ālum, kārum,* and *puḫrum*) had still an important role, albeit reduced to local issues. Unlike Jacobsen, however, Diakonoff affirms that although these organs survived the 'pre-class community', in later times they were adapted to the needs of the ruling class and became part of the administration of class society.

CHARACTERISTICS AND FUNCTIONS OF THE OLD BABYLONIAN ASSEMBLY

The meager and fragmentary character of the documents is undoubtedly the greatest obstacle to understanding the constituency and competence of the Old Babylonian assembly. A starting point is to acknowledge the existence of multiple assemblies instead of a single institution in every city. Aside from the gatherings apparent from the use of the verb *paḫārum*, 'to assemble', the noun *puḫrum* appears in a variety of contexts with different modifiers. Thus, we encounter the assembly with no further specification, the assembly followed by a city-name, the city assembly, but also the assembly of the *awīlû*, the assembly of the *pašīšu*-priests, the assembly of the innkeepers, the assembly of the troops, the assembly of the land, the assembly of kings; finally the assembly of the 'nomads', and the assembly of the Amorites.[8] It seems from these examples that people of similar affiliations or belonging to the same profession used to gather to discuss issues pertaining to their trade. The membership of the assembly in other instances, however, is not self-evident. That is case with the assembly of the *awīlû*, the assembly simply, and the city assembly.

The attestation of a variety of specific gatherings all characterized as *puḫrum* challenges the assumption that during the Old Babylonian period the assembly was the feeble survivor of an earlier institution whose powers were restricted to judicial matters. Comparisons with the Greek assembly, on which that theory

8 I list here references to these various assemblies: assembly without specification (*LH* §§ 5 and 202, CT 8 19a, CT 45 60), assembly followed by a city-name (e.g. Nippur in *ARN* 36, Dilbat in VAS 7 149, and Isin in TCL 18 151), the city assembly (e.g. CT 52 87), the assembly of the *awīlû* (e.g. AbB 12 92, TCL 18 151), the assembly of the *pašīšu*-priests (e.g. TCL 11 254), the assembly of the innkeepers (e.g. AbB 12 89), the assembly of the troops (e.g. ARM 26 412), the assembly of the land (e.g. ARM 26 317), the assembly of kings (e.g. ARM 26 347), the assembly of the 'nomads' (e.g. AS 22 23), and the assembly of the Amorites (e.g. *Sumer* 23: 153; Stol 2004: 645).

rests, seem to have been made without considering the fact that in fifth and fourth-centuries Greece 'the assembly' coexisted with other collective decision-making groups involving the active participation of community members qualified as citizens. Thus, besides the assembly (*ecclesia*) where state affairs were discussed, there was the Council of 500 (*boule*), a representative body chosen by lot that, among its many public functions, draw legislation for consideration of the people (Kagan 1991: 54). There was also the Aeropagus, an old aristocratic council still influential at the time of Cleisthenes (c. 508 BC) whose power was reduced under Pericles in 458 BC, when small farmers (*zeugitai*) were allowed to join this body. The popular law courts (*dikasteria*) should be mentioned as another example. Jurors of the dikastic courts were selected by lot by means of an 'allotment machine' (*kleroterion*) and met daily (Dow [1939] 2004). Unlike the law courts, the fourth-century Athenian assembly (*ecclesia*) met four times per 'prytany', that is, each of the ten periods into which the official year was divided. There were 40 regular meetings and extraordinary sessions could be summoned if necessary (Hansen 1977, and Hansen and Mitchel 1984). We also know that voting procedures in the assembly and the courts were different, for the former voted by *cheirotonia,* 'show of hands', and the latter by *psephoi*, 'ballots' (Hansen 2004). It follows then that there seems to be no need to equate the elders, the city, and other collegiate Mesopotamian bodies with the assembly, or to regard these institutions as diminished in authority.

Although laconic in nature, Old Babylonian economic and legal documents often distinguished collective groups involved in the making of decisions using specific words such as *šībūtum*, *ālum*, *kārum*, *bābtum*, and so forth. However, in certain cases we find the generic word *puḫrum* without further specification. Of all the attestations mentioned above, the assembly that interests us here is the one concerned with the settlement of local disputes, and, as previous scholars have suggested, it is likely that this institution encompassed representatives from other local bodies, as for example the city elders, the city, the city ward, and other influential individuals. The recognition of the existence of multiple assemblies helps us in approaching 'the assembly' as a rather flexible institution, as an organ that might have been convoked for specific reasons on a relatively regular basis. This *puḫrum*, therefore, might have been constituted of different parties whose participation in an assembly session might have depended on the problem under consideration, although it is also possible that certain figures, for instance the judges and other authorities, might have held permanent 'membership' or had a binding responsibility to attend those meetings.

I. ASSEMBLY MEMBERS

Similar to other local collegiate groups such as the elders and the city, the assembly represents a collective institution, and, as such, Mesopotamian scribes considered it as a whole. Although there is no document listing all of the assembly members, certain texts allow us to identify individuals and institutions involved in proceedings that took place *ina puḫrim*, 'in the assembly'. Several documents mention the *awīlû*. This term is problematic because it has a wide semantic range. It can be rendered simply as 'men', it can denote a juridical status, 'free men', it can be used as an honorific title, 'gentlemen', or it could even be considered as a corporate body similar to the elders and related to the 'city ward', *bābtum*.[9] In our corpus, the assembly of the *awīlû* appears twice; one of the tablets mentions the *puḫri ša awīlê*, 'the assembly of the *awīlû*' (AbB 12 92), and the other has the assembly of the *awīlû* of Isin (TCL 18 151). In both letters, the context could suggest that *awīlû* encompasses a particular corporate entity, but the inference is not certain. There are other instances, however, where it becomes apparent that the *awīlû* refers to all the members of the assembly. That is the case with two letters recording the expression *ina puḫrim maḫar awīlê,* 'in the assembly before the *awīlû*' (AbB 3 114 and 13 64). A similar nuance is implied in yet another letter (AbB 12 2). Despite the various meanings that the word *awīlû* has in other texts, it seems safe to conclude that in assembly documents *awīlû*, 'the gentlemen', is an honorific title, especially because the available examples come from letters.

The judges appear as assembly members in several tablets. A letter from Sippar, for instance, mentions that Ipqu-ilīšu, the judge, has spoken against Ilšu-ibni in the assembly (AbB 12 2).[10] There are other instances in which the judges participate in the assembly together with other people. Thus, according to another letter, two men without title, namely, Ibbi-Enlil and Pî-Šamaš-rabi, the judges, and the 'shepherds' (sipa^{meš}) stood and spoke in the assembly before the *awīlû* (AbB 3 114). Similarly, in a letter from Sippar (CT 52 88 = AbB 7 88), among the people present in the assembly we find Sîn-aḫam-iddinam, the *mu'errum*-official, Ipqu-Nabium, the *gallābum*, 'barber', the judges of Sippar, and Ibni-Sîn, presumably the *waqil tamkārim*, 'overseer of the merchants' (see Harris 1975: 141 n. 98, and Charpin 1980b: 463 n. 9). It is worth noticing that this list is only partial, since it appears in a letter that Ibni-Sîn and the judges of Sippar sent to their superior, whose title is unspecified. The text mentions the speech of a certain Šamaš-bani in the assembly, and it further refers to the *ilkum*-service. This example clearly shows that the senders of the letter needed to identify the royal officials who participated in the assembly, namely, the gal-unken-na (*mu'errum*), and the šu-i (*gallābum*).

9 For a discussion of the *awīlû*, see Walther (1917: 67), Driver and Miles (1952: 343), Harris (1975: 65), Dombradi (1996: 245 § 320), Fortner (1996: 305–308).

10 Other examples include texts from Nippur, thus, *ARN* 59 (litigation, date lost, pre-Ḫa), and Lieberman 1992: 132 (a trial from the 'Manual of Sumerian Legal Forms', mentioning king Išme-Dagan).

Ipqu-Nabium, the *gallābum*, and a *mu'errum* are attested in another letter pertaining to the assembly from the time of king Ammī-ṣaduqa (AbB 12 2).[11] In this case, Ilšu-ibni, most probably the *wakil tamkārim* (see Charpin 1982: 61–62), had complained because the judge Ipqu-ilīšu spoke against him in the assembly; therefore, he required that the case be investigated. Ilūni, the writer of this message, informs Ilšu-ibni that he has taken care of the complaint and has spoken to the *awīlû*. He has also sent a letter of the *awīlû* to the *mu'errum* for Ipqu-Nabium, the *gallābum*, and he has further dispatched another letter to Sîn-rēmēni, the judge, and a tablet of the assembly to the judges. Finally, Ilūni states that the *awīlû* will reprimand Ipqu-ilīšu, they will send Ilūni a copy of their documents, and the *awīlû* will also inform the king concerning the litigation that will take place. These dealings reflect a network of connections within and outside the assembly session, and they also attest to manipulations and lobbying regarding the implementation of certain actions.

Yet another text from Sippar mentions the active participants in the assembly (AS 16: 235). Although undated, this letter was probably issued at some point during the span from the 15th year of king Sîn-muballiṭ to the 24th of Samsu-iluna (see Finkelstein 1965: 240).[12] This is the only assembly document from Sippar known to me that originates from a period other than the reign of Ammī-ṣaduqa (see Harris 1975: 64). In this case, a man took his tablets to the assembly and his documents were reviewed and sealed by three men, namely, Rīš-Šamaš, a resident of Sippar (*wāšib Sipparim*), Kudīya, the 'sedan bearer' (gu-za-lá), and Sîn-nādin-šumi, the 'registry secretary' (dub-sar zà-ga). Finkelstein (1965: 237) suggests that, since Rīš-Šamaš is associated with two persons bearing official titles, 'the appellation *wāšib Sipparim* implied a more positive function than that of "resident", "citizen" '. For Finkelstein, Rīš-Šamaš might have been the presiding officer of the assembly or the 'chairman' of the council that reviewed contracts affected by the *mīšarum*-edict. I will further propose that Rīš-Šamaš was a community representative and not necessarily a royal official. This man could well be the *rabiānum* of the same name attested during the reign of Samsu-iluna in a document pertaining to the sale of real estate (MHET II/6 869, Si 15). Because the exact date of this text (AS 16: 235) is unknown, and since the *rabiānum* office could be held more than once, it is impossible to ascertain whether Rīš-Šamaš was acting as the *rabiānum* or as a member of the body of the elders or the city. A document from Dilbat (VAS 7 149) recording a *rabiānum* in connection with the assembly supports the assumption that Rīš-Šamaš could be identified with the man who was or was going to be the *rabiānum* of Sippar in the 15th year of Samsu-iluna.

11 Ipqu-Nabium is also connected with the assembly proceeding in CT 8 19a, although in a broken passage.

12 For a date Si 24 see Kraus (1977: 131 n. h).

Indeed, in this tablet, Imgur-Sîn, the *rabiānum*, appears among a list of men including two who bore respectively the titles rá-gab, 'mounted messenger', and sanga-'priest' in a deposition that took place in the assembly of Dilbat.

Finally, a document usually dubbed 'Trial for Homicide' from early second millennium Nippur mentions certain men who participated in the assembly (PBS 8/2 173). When dealing with assembly membership in his study of city government, Van De Mieroop (1999c: 145–47) states that although there are several copies of this text probably used for teaching legal terminology, he sees 'no reason to assume that it does not reflect a real court case'. For Van De Mieroop this is as an exceptional document because it lists 'some of the professions of men who spoke out in the assembly: a bird-catcher, a potter, two gardeners, and a soldier', among others. He further states that this example shows that these workers had both the right and the time to sit in the assembly. However, as I interpret it, this court case is problematic for several reasons. It comes from the assembly of Nippur which, as will be discussed later in this chapter, may not have functioned the way other city assemblies did. In addition, it is important to recall that the homicide victim, Lu-Inanna, was a *nešakku*-official of the cult of the god Enlil in Nippur. Furthermore, since one of the men who addressed the assembly is characterized as soldier of the god Ninurta, the other men who were listed by their professions may very well have been temple personnel as well. If such was the case, their participation might not be representative of the situation of other city inhabitants who were not engaged in temple activities.

Although far from complete, documents other than model court cases allow us to identify some of the people who participated in the assembly. The attestation of the *awīlû* in assembly documents does not refer to a corporate body; rather, the term was used as a polite and generic expression, meaning simply 'the gentlemen'. It is also worth mentioning that when assembly members are enumerated or referred to by title, such a specification arises from the need of identifying the person responsible for a given act or decision. Thus, for instance, the fellow who took his tablets to the assembly thought it important to indicate precisely who were those persons who examined his documentation (AS 16: 235). Otherwise, there seems to have been no necessity of explaining what must have been obvious for the ancient Mesopotamians. The men mentioned by title in the texts analyzed in this section include the *mu'errum*-official, the *gallābum,* 'barber', the gu-za-lá, 'sedan bearer', and the dub-sar zà-ga, 'the registry secretary', all of them royal officials. We also encounter the judges and the *wakil tamkārim*, 'overseer of the merchants', whose precise connection with the crown is not yet completely clear, and finally community representatives, as for example the *rabiānum*. Unfortunately, I could not find any document where the elders, the city, or the *bābtum* appear in close connection with the assembly. The presence of the *rabiānum*, however, seems to guarantee the participation of those corporate bodies in the *puḫrum*. The evidence at our disposal shows, therefore, that active participants in 'the assembly' included both royal and community representatives.

II. CHARACTERISTICS OF THE ASSEMBLY

Most of the characteristics and ways of functioning of the assembly are difficult to trace due to the scarcity and details of the extant records. There is no certainty, for instance, about who acted as chair, and scholars have proposed a variety of answers to address this question. Despite different interpretations suggesting that the king, the *rabiānum*, or the judges presided over the assembly meetings, the available sources do not confirm or deny any of these hypotheses. Certain Nippur documents give the impression that the king must have fulfilled the role of assembly chair. Thus, a trial from the 'Manual of Sumerian Legal Forms' (Lieberman 1992: 132) mentions that king Išme-Dagan ordered the assembly of Nippur and its judges to gather in the Ubšu-ukkinna, a space located in the Ekur-sanctuary of that city. Based on this example, Lieberman maintains that the assembly of Nippur met on an *ad hoc* basis, and that the king had the prerogative of convoking this *puḫrum*. This interpretation, however, is not free from certain difficulties. The cases in the 'Manual', as well as other 'model court cases' from Nippur and elsewhere, had the pedagogical aim of teaching young scribes legal formulae (see, e.g., Roth 2001: 252–54), and, although these instances may have been inspired by real cases, they do not necessarily reflect an actual situation. Rather, the text studied by Stephen Lieberman seems to have carried a subliminal message: learning the technicalities of the scribal trade was not sufficient. It was equally important to know that it was Išme-Dagan of Isin and not a king from the rival city of Larsa who had control over Nippur. Furthermore, this assembly might not have been the same institution that dealt with local disputes in other cities, especially because Nippur was never a political capital or the permanent residence of kings.[13] These problems, however, will probably be clarified once 'model contracts' and 'model court cases' referring to the assembly are thoroughly studied.[14]

13 It is important to highlight that this trial seems to have taken place in the Ekur sanctuary of Nippur, since the Ubšu-ukkina was located in the courtyard of that temple (Lieberman 1992: 133). There is no mention, however, of the meeting-place of the assembly in other documents. Worth recalling is TCL 11 245, where the *pašīšum*-priests, the *rabiānum*, and the elders assembled in the courtyard of the temple of Nin -MAR.KI to deal with a case pertaining to the theft of the goddess's garments. The object of the dispute seems to explain why the meeting took place in a temple. Obviously, these examples do not mean that all assemblies of the local authorities gathered in temple courtyards.

14 According to M. Roth (2001: 254 note 21), Walter Bodine is studying model contracts and court cases. Roth (1983: 279) provides a list of 'model court records'.

Other 'model court cases' mentioning the king in connection with the assembly are the so-called 'Trial for Homicide' from Nippur (PBS 8/2 173), and the 'Adultery Trial' (*Sumer* 15: 22–24).[15] The latter text states that the verdict of the assembly was a decision of the king, whereas in the 'Trial for Homicide' king Ur-Ninurta of Isin ordered the submission of the case to the Nippur assembly. The second case parallels a document from Nippur dated to the 33rd year of Hammurabi (BE 6/2 10 + *ARN* 68), where king Hammurabi and a certain Adad-šarrum, the aga-uš lugal, 'royal soldier', wrote instructions that the case was to be presented in the assembly of Nippur. In these instances, however, the king does not seem to preside over the *puḫrum*, although he could have validated the decision of the assembly. The situation could have been diverse. There is the possibility that kings of relatively independent cities were the chairs of the assembly, but it could have been equally possible that royal officials represented the king. Interpretations regarding the central role of the monarch in the *puḫrum* seem to be based mainly on a comparison with the assembly of 'Gilgameš and Akka'. Nevertheless, the lack of evidence for comparing the Early Dynastic and the Old Babylonian periods makes it difficult to support the theory implying an alleged decline of the assembly activities during the predominance of territorial states.

Besides suggestions that the king, the *rabiānum*, or the judges presided over the assembly, yet another prospective candidate for that position is the gal-unken-na or *mu'errum*-official. This proposal rests on the etymology of the word, which could be translated literally as 'chief of the assembly'. Yoffee (1977: 81–93) has discussed the term as well as the activities of the gal-unken-na, and he concluded that this official had nothing to do with the chairmanship of the assembly (see also Yoffee 2000: 56). However, Charpin (1980b: 463) has opposed Yoffee's interpretation on the basis of a document in which, the gal-unken-na indeed appears as one of the assembly members (CT 52 88). More recently, Van De Mieroop (1992: 234) has adopted Charpin's view regarding the role of the *mu'errum* in that text, although he leaves his conclusions open to doubt. In the archaic lexical text known as 'The Titles and Professions List' (see Nissen *et al.* 1993: 111), the kingal (written with the signs gal-unken-na) appears in relation to the state or temple bureaucracy.[16] Similarly, on the Ušumgal stele dating from the Early Dynastic period, we find this title together with ugula-unken-na, in a context clearly related to the state or temple activities. This evidence seems to indicate that from the time of the early records the gal-unken-na might have been a state affiliate. The fact that during the Old Babylonian period the gal-unken-na appears in connection

15 For the 'Trial for Homicide', see the analyses by Jacobsen (1959) and Roth (1998). For different interpretations of the 'Adultery Trial', see van Dijk (1963) and Greengus (1969–70).

16 As Nissen *et al.* (1993: 110) pointed out, the oldest version from Uruk of the titles and professions list dates to the script phase Uruk IV.

with the assembly does not make him the chairman of the institution. Other officials such as the *gallābum*, the *guzallûm*, the *zazakkum*, the *wakil tamkārim*, and the *rabiānum* are also attested in similar contexts. This shows, as I have already suggested, the mixed character of the assembly in which royal officials and community representatives interacted.

Regarding its sessions, it is uncertain whether the assembly functioned on an *ad hoc* basis or whether it met periodically at regular times or daily as the Athenian *ecclesia* or the *dikasteria* respectively did. Since I think it likely that the *puḫrum* was the general gathering of royal officials and representatives of smaller community councils such as the elders, the city, and so forth, it is possible that the assembly gathered less frequently than the other institutions. This hypothesis, however, cannot be tested against any of the extant sources. Nevertheless, there is evidence to demonstrate that the convening of the assembly was not completely improvised. For example, there is a letter in which a man without title says *anāku annikīam ina puḫur ālim kussī nadiāku*, 'as for me, I am settled here in my seat in the city assembly' (TLB 4 35: 33–34).[17] This comment might imply that this person was a well-established assembly member, and that he attended the meetings regularly. Furthermore, two documents from Nippur (BE 6/2 53 and 54) record the otherwise unattested titles aga-uš pu-úḫ-ru-um, 'the pursuivant of the assembly' (Driver and Miles 1952: 78), and nimgir pu-úḫ-ru-um, 'the herald of the assembly'. The latter title is reminiscent of the public announcement of a lost seal that a herald carried out by blowing the horn according to the word of the assembly (see *Sumer* 20: 66–68).[18] That the *puḫrum* had an internal structure and hierarchy is also apparent from tablets issued by this institution, the *ṭuppī puḫrim*, 'the letters of the assembly' (e.g. AbB 12 2, AbB 13 64, and TIM 2 110), which implies the existence of an assembly bureaucracy.

The way in which claims and disputes were assigned to the assembly for arbitration can be inferred from certain documents, most of them from Nippur. According to these records, the assembly dealt with issues entrusted to it either by the king (e.g. PBS 8/2 173, Ur-Ninurta, Nippur; BE 6/2 10, Hammurabi, Nippur), the judges (e.g. PBS 5 100, Si 26, Nippur), or by the parties themselves (e.g. *ARN* 36, RS 48, Nippur; AS 16: 235, c. Sm-Si, Sippar). Although there are no remains of actual argumentative or demagogic speeches by influential individuals, occasionally

17 The lines of this passage are broken. Here I am following Frankena's (1968: 28) restoration: 33. *a-na-ku an-ni-ki-a-am i-na pu-ḫ*[*ur a-lim*] / 34. ^{giš}gu-za-*i na-di-a-*[*ku*]. He translates it as 'Ich habe hier in der Versammlung [der Stadt] meinen Sessel errichtet'. In a personal communication, Professor Martha Roth told me that she rather reads these lines *a-na-ku an-ni-ki-a-am i-na pu-ḫ*[*ur a-lim*] / 34. ^{giš}gu-za-*i na-di* to be translated simply as 'I am settled here in the city assembly'.

18 According to Roth (1983: 282), *Sumer* 20: 66 'is a "legal" document, which found its way into the scribal curriculum'.

disagreements involved heated debates. Discussions and verbal aggression in the midst of the assembly were common, and we know about some of those episodes because they were recorded in letters. Ilšu-ibni, for instance, grumbles because the judge Ipqu-ilīšu has spoken at length against him in the assembly. But he does not seem to have reacted passively, for a third party mentions that both Ilšu-ibni and Ipqu-ilīšu spoke against each other (AbB 12 2). Similarly, a certain Rabiat-šalummassa states that another fellow slandered him in the assembly (*ina puḫri šillati idbuba*, VAS 16 124: 17), whereas the writer of another letter encourages his addressee to complain time and again in the assembly (*ina puḫrim nēmettam ritašši*) that the plowing of a field is not being done (AbB 13 64).

III. COMPETENCE AND FUNCTIONS OF THE ASSEMBLY

A number of Nippur documents show that the assembly dealt with cases related to family issues and sexual offenses, among other things. Most of these instances, however, come from texts used for pedagogical instruction, and some of them clearly correspond to what Marthe Roth (2001: 254) characterizes as 'atypical and extreme (or "bright-line")' cases. The 'trial for adultery' (*Sumer* 15:12-14) records the case of a husband seizing his wife who was lying on the bed with another man (see Greengus 1969–70), although according to the unlikely interpretation of J. J. van Dijk (1963), it was the wife who seized her husband lying with another man. In any event, the culprits were carried to the assembly, where the matter was decided. The verdict resulted in divorce, and the punishment imposed on the unfaithful spouse consisted of the shaving of her pudendum, the piercing of her nose with an arrow, and public exposure. The assembly mediated in the dispute, but it did not issue the divorce contract. A different example, also pertaining to a sexual offense, appears in a 'Sammeltafel' possibly copied during the reign of Samsu-iluna (*JAOS* 86: 359). In this document, Lugalmelam deflowered the slave girl of Kuguzana. The slave owner approached the assembly, which after listening to the parties imposed a fine of half a mina of silver upon Lugalmelam. As Finkelstein (1966b: 360) remarked, the trial does not mention whether the slave-girl consented to have sex, or whether she was raped.

The assembly also dealt with family problems of a different nature. According to another 'model court case', the well-known 'Trial for Homicide' from Nippur (PBS 8/2 173), three men killed Nanna-sig, and his own wife was suspected of covering up the murder. The case was first taken to Isin, to king Ur-Ninurta. Then the king delegated the affair to the assembly of Nippur, and the assembly sentenced the assassins and the widow Nin-Dada to the death penalty. The fact that the deceased man was a *nešakku*-official of the Enlil cult in Nippur (see Roth 1998: 176) might indicate that this assembly of Nippur is closer to the one mentioned in the text that Lieberman (1992: 132) quotes than to those assemblies attested elsewhere. In another tablet from Nippur dated to the 26th year of king Samsu-iluna (PBS 5 100), the assembly participates in the procedures to clarify a case (see Leichty 1989). Even though previous scholars regarded this text as a record of paternity, Roth (2001: 260) has recently argued that it is actually a confirmation of filiation. Roth's important contribution to the understanding of this source resides in the recognition of the fact that the text is not a dispute or litigation but that it rather narrates a series of testimonies. It is precisely in the context of hearing these depositions that the assembly appears in this case. Another tablet also from Nippur, refers to a similar issue, although this example could be dubbed a record of maternity (*ARN* 59, date lost). Here, a woman approached the assembly of Nippur because another woman abducted her daughter. The judges listened to the testimonies, and they ordered that the infant should be returned to her mother.

There are other examples where the assembly mediates in inheritance disputes. According to a document from Nippur (*ARN* 36 + PBS 8/I 47, RS 48), a certain Rīm-Adad broke his inheritance tablet in front of Nannatum, his father. Nannatum approached the Nippur assembly, and the assembly prevented Rīm-Adad and his children from inheriting. The tablet further states that Rīm-Adad and his heirs should not raise a claim against Nannatum for inheritance of house, field, garden or any property. A new 'model court case' from early Old Babylonian Nippur without known duplicates was recently published (Hallo 2002: 146–54). The tablet deals with a claim over family inheritance brought to the assembly of Nippur and handled by the judges, and it presumably involved temple prebends and the guda-priest office of the goddess Ninlil. In another tablet from the same city dated to king Hammurabi, the children of Adad-rabi had a dispute with Ududu, their paternal uncle (BE 6/2 10 + *ARN* 68). Consequently, the heirs of Adad-rabi approached king Hammurabi. Ududu was a *pašīšum*-priest of Ninlil, and the property at issue was a field that Ududu had given to his brother; such a property was equivalent in value to the *pašīšum* prebend of Ninlil. Hammurabi transferred the case to the assembly of Nippur, most likely because the objects of the dispute comprised temple prebends. The assembly offered them a solution and, on the basis of that agreement, the heirs of Ududu gave some properties to the heirs of Adad-rabi. In other words, here the decision of the assembly belongs to the history of the litigation, and it is not necessarily connected to the tablet on which the dispute is finally settled.

Several documents mention the assembly as the place where people made claims and gave testimonies concerning different issues. In addition to the trials already cited, other examples include a fragmentary letter reporting that in the assembly a man enumerated a list of goods that he purchased for a certain Sîn-nādin-šumi (AbB 3 114). The statement probably originates from the fact that Sîn-nādin-šumi did not reimburse the one talent of silver that he owed to the middleman. A tablet from Sippar (CT 45 60, Aṣ 17) relates the exchange of fields between Adad-mušallim, the *iššiakkum*-official of the *gagûm*-'cloister', and Utu-šumundib, the judge. For unknown reasons, after one year Utu-šumundib changed his mind and wanted his field back. In the assembly, he declared that he was unable to produce Adad-mušallim's document of ownership because he had sent it to Babylon. The parties finally reached an agreement, which is the object of this contract (see Charpin 1986c: 130). In another document, Apil-ilīšu and Erībam made a declaration in the assembly of Dilbat about lost possessions that were finally found (VAS 7 149, Ḫa). An interesting record from Nippur dated to the reign of Enlil-bāni of Isin (*WO* 8/2: 160) shows that the Nippur assembly dealt with a case involving the silver of a business partnership. The assembly heard the parties and gave a decision favoring the plaintiffs. The assembly might also have been a place to validate or confirm economic transactions, since in a letter a man states that he will pay the silver in the assembly of Isin (TCL 18 151). Finally, article five of the 'Laws of Hammurabi' states that the judge who reverses his verdict will be deposed from his office in the assembly, thus implying that assembly members had the prerogative of removing incompetent or even corrupt officials.

TOWARDS AN UNDERSTANDING OF THE OLD BABYLONIAN ASSEMBLY

When compared with those texts mentioning the *rabiānum* or the elders, assembly documents are few. Besides the scarcity of primary sources, an additional problem resides in the fact that, in most cases, the assembly appears as an indirect reference in letters where people report what happened there, or in contracts that include a summary of previous proceedings related to the case under consideration. A look at the type of assembly documents shows that almost half of them are letters, while a considerable number of the texts from Nippur are either fragments or pedagogical tools, that is, artificial economic and legal contracts (see Table V).[19] Documents referring to the assembly of Nippur are problematic because it is sometimes difficult to decide what exactly this institution represents. One could argue that in 'model court cases', the assembly of Nippur is a sort of paradigm used to refer to any judicial authority and, as such, it is an empty category, but this explanation is hardly convincing. In certain cases, it is clear that the assembly of Nippur is a collegium closely connected with the temple of Enlil. Thus, the fragment that Lieberman (1992: 132) quotes mentions the courtyard of the Ekur-sanctuary, while in the 'Trial for Homicide'

[19] Letters mentioning the assembly include: AbB 3 114, AbB 12 2, AbB 12 92, AbB 13 60, AbB 13 64, AS 16 235 (= AbB 7 152), CT 52 87 (= AbB 7 87), CT 52 88 (= AbB 7 88), TCL 18 151, TIM 2 110 (= AbB 8 110), TLB 4 35 (= AbB 3 35), VAS 16 124 (= AbB 6 124), YBC 6380, and YOS 2 111 (= AbB 9 111).

(PBS 8/2 173) the victim is an official of the Enlil temple in Nippur. Moreover, in an inheritance contract from that city, at least one of the parties seems to have been a temple official (Hallo 2002: 146–54). Similarly, in a text dated to the 33rd year of Hammurabi (BE 6/2 10 + ARN 68), the king transfers the case to the assembly of Nippur, most probably because the object of the dispute includes the *pašīsum* prebend of the goddess Ninlil. In other cases, however, the Nippur assembly might not be connected to cases pertaining to temple personnel (e.g. *ARN* 38 + PBS 8/I 47, PBS 5 100). The role of the assembly of Nippur attested in these contracts may have been an organ restricted mostly to disputes involving people related to the temple.

Nippur texts provide us with the best sequence of assembly documents from a single city, which currently amount to some 14 examples; most of them are school texts. These tablets mention kings and dates from the dynasties of Isin, Larsa, and the First Dynasty of Babylon, although it should be noticed that the text recording the earliest king of the corpus – i.e. Išme-Dagan – is a 'model court case' tablet. Other Mesopotamian cities are not nearly as well documented. Despite the huge amount of tablets excavated at Sippar, only six of them refer to the assembly; of these six, one dates from the reign of Samsu-iluna and the rest are from the time of Ammī-ṣaduqa. The remaining examples come from Dilbat, Isin, Larsa (?), or are of unknown provenance. The assembly is currently not attested in texts from important cities such as Ur (see Van De Mieroop 1992: 233). In view of the scarcity of the extant evidence, the question is how to explain or, better, how to interpret such a minimal amount of assembly documents.

I think that the answer to this question is to be found in the type of assembly documents and in the kind of activities that the assembly performed. As already mentioned, these texts generally refer to the assembly rather indirectly. It is remarkable that in the assembly documents at our disposal we do not find expressions such as 'the parties approached the assembly and the assembly rendered a verdict', while analogous wording is common, for instance, in litigations handled by the elders. Fortner (1996: 296) has already noted that in lawsuits from Sippar the litigants do not come before an adjudicatory body termed 'the assembly'. Indeed, in texts dealing with disputes, the assembly is generally mentioned in the history of the litigation. When the assembly decides a dispute (e.g. *WO* 8/2: 160), it does not involve real estate. An exception to this is clearly BE 6/2 10, but this case pertains to temple prebends, and Hammurabi handed it over to the assembly of Nippur. Another exception is the inheritance contract from Nippur (Hallo 2002: 146–54), but here again temple prebends are at issue. In most other instances, it seems that the main role of the assembly is the hearing of cases.

I propose, then, that the reason why the assembly is poorly documented is because it did not participate directly in the issuing of written documents or in the direct decision of cases that could result in a written tablet. That the *ṭuppī puḫrim* were letters and not contracts is confirmed by one of the sources (TIM 2 110). The assembly seems to have been the place where problems or disputes were brought and sorted out, and only certain decisions were rendered. As brief passages from letters let us know, the assembly was the arena where oral discussions took place, where people complained and argued about their economic and legal problems. In the aural and oral nature of assembly disputes resides the scarcity of documents mentioning this institution. It is possible that, after considering the requests, assembly members transferred some of these cases to the pertinent authority, be it palace officials, the elders, the *kārum*, and so forth. This hypothesis is based on a letter from Sippar (AS 16: 235). In this instance, an unnamed man took his tablet to the assembly to be inspected because the king had issued a *mīšarum*-edict. Three assembly members, namely, a *rabiānum* and two royal officials, reviewed and confirmed (literally sealed) the tablets. The officials further upheld the documents and sent them to the house of Šalim-ṭeḫḫušu, the ugula šu-i^{meš}, 'overseer of the barbers', who arbitrarily broke the tablets. The man then went back to the three officials to complain but they answered: 'What can we say to the overseer of the barbers?' Finally, frustrated by the proceedings of corporate and official bureaucracies, the man writes a letter to the king. I think that the assembly comprised royal officials and community representatives to avoid conflicting interests of royal and customary uses and common laws. In previous chapters we have seen that the elders and the *rabiānum* had reassigned land that was supposedly under state control. That the assembly mechanisms must not have been fully effective is clear from those few examples, but joint procedures must have reduced the number of disputes significantly.

FINAL REMARKS

The assembly of the gods, at least in the mundane version that has reached us through literary texts, was a place where deities made important decisions, but it was also the place where the gods socialized. Many important issues pertaining to the fate of humans were planned in these meetings under the effect of alcohol. According to *Enūma eliš*, the fortune of the universe was decided in an assembly where the gods, inspired by drink, granted Marduk supreme powers. Another myth explains that disabled human beings came into existence because two gods had an intellectual dispute after getting drunk during the celebration of the birth of humankind. The meetings of Mesopotamian gods recall Herodotus' Persians, who debated important issues while drunk. This parallel regarding the connection between assembly and banquets has been further strengthened with examples from the Greek assemblies in Homeric times and Classical Athens. Thus, the literary assemblies of gods and (semi)-humans alike were utilized to analyze not only early Mesopotamian political institutions but also Sumerian behavior.[20]

Allegorical readings of literary texts have furnished us with interpretations of Mesopotamian institutions that, albeit transfigured, made their way into historical periods. One of the texts subject to those approaches is 'Gilgameš and Akka', which has been used to fine-tune the chronology of Early Dynastic rulers of Uruk and Kiš, and it has also served as a source for the study of the role of the elders and the assembly in Mesopotamian politics. These interpretations, however, rely heavily on a too literal – and I shall add too serious – reading of literary texts. Michalowski (2003) has recently argued that 'Gilgameš and Akka' was actually 'a later parody of the Ur III poems about the legendary Uruk king'. To do justice to earlier interpretations, however, we should acknowledge that comparisons of the assembly recorded in Old Babylonian documents with the one attested in literary texts and with Greek institutions originate in the need to explain the role and competence of an entity poorly documented in economic and legal documents. A conclusion results from this study: we cannot affirm that Old Babylonian assemblies were the feeble survivors of a more powerful earlier institution which had counted among its functions decisions pertaining to war and peace or the appointment of rulers. Many assemblies with different prerogatives and characteristics are attested in the ancient Near East. Among them we find city assemblies, the assemblies of the Amorites (e.g. *Sumer* 23: 153), royal assemblies (e.g. ARM 26 347), and assemblies of the state bureaucracy (see Beckman 1982: 442). In view of such diversity, it seems impossible to establish a direct connection between Old Babylonian assemblies and their alleged Early Dynastic forerunners.

The assembly studied in this chapter represents the gathering of different royal and local authorities that mediated disputes involving community members, including those with connections to the state. Because people reported having approached the assembly, it is possible that the institution gathered on a relatively regular basis. The assembly also seems to have had an internal structure and personnel in charge of certain functions, as for instance heralds and scribes. But, as I see it, the assembly should not be considered as a rigidly regulated body. Rather, it was the result of the gathering of different local institutions of authorities encompassing royal and community representatives. This will explain the scarcity of assembly documents. Because the assembly was a collective body constituted of different authorities, cases were publicly exposed in the assembly. However, the resolution of problems that required the issuing of a contract was

20 According to Jacobsen (1943: 167), 'Here, as so often in Mesopotamian mythology, the important decisions originate when the gods are in their cups. In the toilsome earthbound life of the primitive Sumerians wine and beer were evidently necessary to lift the spirit out of the humdrum existence of everyday cares to original thought and perspective.'

transferred to the pertinent authority that would adjudicate the case. If one of the parties was not satisfied with the verdict given in this instance, s/he could appeal to a higher authority, including the king himself. Since some of the issues brought to the assembly involved royal affairs, the state has its own officials in the assembly. These representatives participated and supervised those cases where community members were engaged in state activities or had disputes with state affiliates. The Old Babylonian assembly, then, was the arena where different sectors of society came together to argue about their economic and legal problems. It was, in brief, a place of negotiation.

Table 5. The assembly of Nippur[21]

Date	**Document**	
Isin Dynasty		
Išme-Dagan	Lieberman 1992: 132 'model court case'	Trial
Ur-Ninurta (n.d.)	PBS 8/2 173 'model court case'	Trial for homicide
Būr-Sîn (n.d.)	*JCS* 3: 168 = Ni 4551	Legal case (fragment)
Enlil-bāni (n.d.)	*WO* 8/2: 160	Litigation
Larsa Dynasty		
Rīm-Sîn 48	*ARN* 36 + PBS 8/I 47	Inheritance
First Dynasty of Babylon		
Hammurabi 33	BE 6/2 10 + *ARN* 68	Litigation
Samsu-iluna 26	PBS 5 100 'model court case'	Confirmation of filiation
(c. Si, n.d., copy)	*JAOS* 86: 359 'model court case'	Trial
(c. Ḫa? or Si?)	*ARN* 127	Fragment
No date or date lost		
n.d. (early O.B.)	*Sumer* 15 'model court case'	Case of adultery
n.d. (early O.B.)	Hallo 2002: 146–54 'model court case'	Inheritance
lost (pre-Ḫa ?)	*ARN* 59	Litigation
lost ?	*JCS* 3: 168 = Ni 2006	Legal case (fragment)
	JAOS 103: 282 'model court case'	Legal dispute

21 This list is based on published documents. The publication of the 'Manual of Sumerian Legal Forms' will probably provide further attestations of the assembly.

7

Local Power and the Writing of Old Babylonian History

BRIDGING THE GAP

Cuneiform writing was invented in southern Mesopotamia around 3200 BC (e.g. Michalowski 1994; Cooper 1996), and the last dated cuneiform tablet is an astronomical almanac written in 75 AD (Sachs 1976). But evidence from the Graeco-Babyloniaca texts and classical sources shows that the cuneiform writing system and the languages it conveyed were still read in the third century AD (Geller 1997). After being abandoned as *lingua franca* in the years following 1200 BC, the use of Akkadian was in gradual decline. Administrative and legal documents in that language continued to be written under Cyrus and his successors after the Persian conquest of Babylon in 539 BC. Under Parthian domination in 126 BC, cuneiform was definitely restricted to temple communities (Baines *et al.* 2003). It is difficult to ascertain the proficiency in Sumerian and Akkadian of those priests still learning the skill in Mesopotamian temples during the Parthian and Sasanian periods, but it is likely that both languages were preserved mostly as relics. Questions about the exact date the last wedge was written belong to the domain of the antiquarian (see Rempel and Yoffee 1999: 385), what is important is the fact that after the third century AD, cuneiform became simply unintelligible.

Judging from the surviving examples, in its very final stages cuneiform writing seems to have been confined to technical knowledge related to astronomical observation and calculation. This could have contributed to the reputation of Babylonians as the masters of astronomy and magic. Already by the second century AD, the Greek writer Lucian has Babylon, its priests, and language as the setting, mediums, and tools for Menippos' visit to the Netherworld (Geller 1997: 58–60). This connection among Babylonian priests, cuneiform scriptures, and magic seems to have made its way to certain medieval traditions related to Hermes Trismegistus. Thus, for instance, the *General Estoria* of Alfonso the Learned of Castille contains a story about a certain Asclepius who resorted to a niece of Nimrod to read a book by Hermes written in incomprehensible characters. The old woman mentions that those figures were written by her own people and that they actually resemble the patterns made by stars in the sky (see Fraker 1996: 190–98), which seems to me an allusion to cuneiform writing. This is not surprising because Latin authors were quite familiar with Berossos' work dating to around 290 BC, and fragments preserved from the manuscripts of Syncellus' *Ecloga Chronographica* and Pliny's *Naturalis Historia* emphasize Mesopotamian astrological or astronomical knowledge (see Verburgghe and Wickersham 2000). This, together with the Bible and classical writings, was the kind of Babylonian material at the disposal of writers of universal history, one of whose later exponents was François Lenormant.[1]

Although references to Babylonian writings appear in several excerpts of Berossos, in the early 1880s Hegel commented on the absence of 'canonical books or indigenous works' of Assyrians, Babylonians, Medes, and Persians. Indeed, at that time the inaccessibility of cuneiform records represented a gap of some 1600 years, that is, from the third century AD until cuneiform writing was deciphered in the second half of the nineteenth century. The decipherment of cuneiform, officially acknowledged in 1857, offered the possibility of writing history from primary sources and early Assyriologists did not hesitate to claim that their works rested on native accounts. But those approaches needed per force to rely on tradition, for the first inscriptions that came to light were but the scattered and arbitrary pieces of a mosaic whose whole picture was blurred by oblivion. This was the method that prevailed for a few decades until cuneiform texts spoke for themselves, and historical facts other than those preserved in Western traditions were recovered.

A look at the ways in which Mesopotamian history has been written since the decipherment of cuneiform writing shows certain tendencies that correspond, at times anachronistically, with main trends in Western historiography. The availability of cuneiform records coincided with the development of positivism as a novel historical method that relied on archival sources, and it focused on political history, the history of the state, kings, and statesmen. In Assyriological studies, however, positivistic methods coexisted with a variety of approaches rooted in other traditions including humanism, the Enlightenment, historicism, and social evolutionism, while several studies were definitely inspired by religious curiosity. It was only since the second half of the twentieth century that questions about historiographic practices unevenly permeated Assyriological studies. The authors of the earliest reconstructions of Mesopotamian history made an effort to identify characters and events from Biblical and Greek traditions with the information coming from native sources. But this initial methodology was rapidly superseded by the overwhelming quantity of documents that came to light in succeeding years. New characters, new names, and new historical facts supplemented the old ones. At the same time, the discovery of previously unknown rulers and their deeds slowly changed the focus from religious and classical topics to other areas.

1 Unlike writers of universal history, Lenormant's study only reaches the war of the Medes. But his parameters for writing history follow those of universal historians.

ON THE WRITING OF OLD BABYLONIAN HISTORY

Certain Old Babylonian kings and their inscriptions were already known from the dawn of Assyriology in the late nineteenth century, even when knowledge of Old Babylonian political history was still rudimentary. That was certainly the case with Hammurabi and some of his achievements, although his reign gained a central position in Mesopotamian history after the recovery of the stele inscribed with the 'Laws of Hammurabi' in 1901/2. This discovery prompted the development of a new specialty, namely, the study of Mesopotamian legal systems. In this new field, and for many years, comparisons with Roman laws buttressed Greek and biblical examples as the referents – or even standards – for the analysis of Babylonian and Assyrian legislation. Old Babylonian scholars have studied Hammurabi's law collection in close connection with those tablets recording legal disputes. Only two years after the publication of Hammurabi's stele, German scholars started publishing the six-volume compilation of legal documents entitled *Hammurabis Gesetz*, in which texts were arranged under categories following Roman legal theory (Roth 2001: 245).[2] Aside from legal history, historians have used Hammurabi's laws to study social stratification, social sanctions and taboos, and they have resorted to legal records mainly to understand judicial procedures. Hammurabi's centrality and permanence in history are apparent from the publication of three recent books devoted to this ruler (Klengel 1991; Charpin 2003; Van De Mieroop 2005).

Studies on the economic history of the Old Babylonian period reflect a variety of theoretical frameworks that mostly follow versions of either Weberian or Marxist analysis. Since the use of different models influences the evaluation of written and archaeological evidence, there are disagreements regarding major socio-economic problems. Dissent revolves around the existence and effective economic significance of private land ownership. Although some scholars have employed Roman law to explain the lack of fully private property that included not only the right of use, but also the right of alienating arable land, such an explanation conflicts with the existence of ownership rights in the case of orchards and houses, which were indeed sold. Related to this problem are the debates about the existence or non-existence of communities and communal exploitation of land, markets, and market mechanisms. Interpretations regarding these issues determine the role and real control of the state in economic affairs as well as the role and importance of the private sector in Old Babylonian economy and society. Despite the many disagreements, however, all these interpretations are fundamentally focused on the role of the state, although for different reasons. Those

2 See Kohler and Peiser (1904), Kohler and Ungnad (1909a, 1909b, 1910; 1911), and Koschaker and Ungnad (1923).

who categorically deny the relevance of a communal and a private sector of the economy concentrate on the role of the state because for them little exists outside the state. Similarly, those who acknowledge the existence of communities and of a private sector of the economy end up studying the state because it is impossible to deal with the communities due to the nature of the written documents. In the latter approaches, private activities have been analyzed in individual articles, but there is still no study aimed at interrelating the private and state spheres.

As I see them, debates concerning Old Babylonian economic and social history have reached stalemate, since any attempt to pursue these problems further seems to rely on the acceptance of the general premises of one interpretation or the other. Reflection on these matters led me to seek alternative ways of thinking about Old Babylonian history. My aim was to approach history from a place other than the state, but I also wanted to account for the ways in which the state, the elite members of the private sector, and the rest of society interacted. The impossibility of studying communities from written documents made me skeptical of the usual dichotomy of 'history from above' or 'history from below'; instead I tried a history 'from in-between'. That is, a history of the Old Babylonian period starting from relatively independent local institutions of authority, for they dealt with economic and legal disputes of city inhabitants, and they also represented the urban community in its dealings with the state. In the strict sense, however, such an approach is closer to the history of the upper classes in terms of economic power. Nevertheless, my research allowed me to explore mechanisms of control outside the jurisdiction of the state. Albeit limited in scope, such a perspective may help in understanding certain mechanisms pertaining to the functioning of the economy and society. Before turning to my conclusions regarding local authorities, however, I shall mention certain concerns about the use of written sources, a topic that is narrowly connected with historiography and the writing of history.

CUNEIFORM SOURCES AND HISTORY WRITING

The earliest attempts at recording the past in narrative units – whether we have Herodotus or the Israelites in mind – were a mixture of both ethnocentric accounts and 'heterologies'. The familiar, that is knowledge of one's own past and traditions, was the starting-point to explain and make sense of 'the other', be it the Persians or the Assyrians. Up until the fifteenth century there was a sense of familiarity in history writing: alterity was not as different as it must have appeared. The discovery of the New World was a rupture; practically nothing was known about those 'new' subjects of history, although they were originally taken as the inhabitants of Cathay and Xipango. Something similar happened in the domain of ancient history when cuneiform writing was deciphered, because these new records revealed an almost completely forgotten past. For contemporary historians, classical antiquity is so far away and yet so close, for it belongs to the putative ancestry of 'Western civilization'. Although ancient Greek and Latin are dead languages, scholarly tradition made an effort to keep them alive, and with them old institutions and ideas survived. I really doubt that any classical historian would ever start a study of the Greek assembly by compiling all attestations s/he can find of the word 'assembly'.

The peculiarities of every field, however, impose on the historian the necessity of resorting to particular methodologies. Mesopotamian languages were buried for two millennia and with them institutions and visions of the world. Cuneiform tablets and the information that they preserve have been recovered for only a century and a half. Ancient scribes did not describe or write about their institutions, and they never produced writings similar to the works of Plato, Aristotle, Homer, or Cicero. The characteristics of Mesopotamian sources together with the two-millennia cleavage that separates the extinction of the cuneiform world from its subsequent recovery require different methods for the writing of history. Aside from the temporal and cultural gap, the sources that the historian of ancient Mesopotamia utilizes differ from those of the classical historian. I think that these differences partially account for the Assyriologist's obsession with written records and philology. I studied words and included philological discussions because the authorities I have analyzed appear in texts that were not originally meant to explain the characteristics and functions of these institutions. In that sense, words are the only remains we have to trace their attestations and access information. This is perhaps most apparent not only in my treatment of the *rabiānum* but also in the chapter dealing with elders.

Tablets mentioning the local powers encompassed in this book have come to us through different avenues. Some were unearthed when archeology was still in its infancy and there is no thorough report of those findings. Others come from illegal diggings and contextual information is completely missing. Internal evidence such as prosopography and paleography is undoubtedly helpful, but it cannot answer questions related, for instance, to the exact building housing the tablets. Under those circumstances, whether documents originate from official institutions or private houses may remain unknown. Only a few cities were properly excavated, but even in these cases large areas of the sites were left untouched by professionals and explored by looters. Moreover, the ancient Mesopotamian did not record all transactions, and certain contracts were discarded in antiquity once they had fulfilled their purpose. Additional heuristic problems relate to the classification of sources. Although taxonomies could be regarded as mere formal aspects, they play a role when texts belonging to different genres are employed for the writing of history. In view of these issues, the historian has to make decisions, and I have made mine. My study is mostly based on economic and legal documents as well as letters, but I also took into account royal inscriptions to address certain problems pertaining to the *rabiānum* office. I have also considered literary texts, even if I am critical about the historical information that they convey. My approach to 'model court cases', usually regarded as school exercises, was also cautious. And I have excluded omens because I think that they do not contribute to the historical enquiries I wanted to undertake. Throughout the book, textual problems were discussed when I considered it pertinent.

Since the first decades of the twentieth century, historians have been arguing against the uncritical use of sources, as well as against the alleged objectivity that positivist historians claimed that facts convey. Vehement statements against 'the real' and the use of facts in history writing took a new turn, 'the linguistic turn', from the late 1960s. This new challenge came from the pen of certain literary critics who ventured into the domain of history writing (e.g. Barthes 1967), and from historians interested in the nature of historical writing (e.g. Veyne 1971; White 1973; de Certeau [1975] 1988). For the sympathizers with the 'linguistic turn', history has the status of a peculiar discourse, a narrative that produces signifiers and meanings, and, as such, history is a form of fiction. For many historians, the interest in the writing of history seems to have shifted from the use of sources to the use of narrative. Dominick LaCapra (1985: 12) has put it plainly: 'Historians ... continue to confide in a "documentary" or "objectivist" model of knowledge that is typically blind to its own rhetoric.' In its extreme versions, this theory implies that in the end sources and facts matter little because the historian produces a knowledge identical to that provided by fiction (see Chartier 1997: 35). In the words of C. Ginzburg (1999: 101):

> I find the current approach to historical narratives highly simplistic, since it usually focuses on the final literary product, disregarding the research (archival, philological, statistical, and so forth) that made it possible.

No remark could be more suitable to do justice to the painstaking research involved in the writing of Mesopotamian history. Sometimes I have the impression that the 'metahistorical' approach has succeeded in undermining the importance of the use of documents in history writing. In the case of ancient Mesopotamian history, archaeology and texts (with all their linguistic problems) are the historian's basic raw material. What really differentiates a historian from an antiquarian is a question of methods and goals: the former compiles evidence in order to analyze what happened in the past, while the latter gathers objects and facts for the sake of curiosity.

I shall explain, then, my research criteria and motivations. The institutions included in this study have been known for many years, but they have been studied mainly in works dealing with the administration of justice. Those approaches rarely include sources other than legal texts. Since I was interested in the role of these authorities beyond the administration of justice, I decided to compile as many documents as I could find, including not only legal records but also letters and economic texts. In order to do so, I traced those words referring to the local powers here discussed. This has proven to be effective in establishing the jurisdiction and activities of these authorities. We may have translations for words, but the distance between Old Babylonian institutions and those familiar to the contemporary historian often gives the impression that we are dealing with empty shells. Time has drained words of their semantic richness, while etymology alone does not suffice to explain institutions. Realities hidden behind written words have to be recovered by crisscrossing and comparing data. Comparisons and contrasts have allowed me to differentiate institutions or authorities that were called by identical or similar terms. Such is the case, for instance, with the title *rabiānum*, which generally designated the chief of the city, but which was also used during the early Old Babylonian period as a royal title, usually combined with a gentilic. Similarly, the word 'elders' denoted different institutions in Babylonia and in the Mari region, and it possibly had yet another nuance in the Ur III period. Thus, according to Van De Mieroop (1997: 124), in Ur III administrative documents, 'elders' seems to have been used to differentiate high officials from common personnel.

ON LOCAL POWERS

A number of authorities coexisted in Old Babylonian cities. Some of them were royal officials, while others were elite representatives of urban communities with no formal dependence on the state. The latter are what I call 'relatively independent' institutions of authority. The local powers analyzed in this study comprised the *rabiānum*, 'the chief of the city', the *šībūt ālim*, 'the city elders', the *ālum*, 'the city', and the *puḫrum*, 'the assembly'. Of these, the *rabiānum*, the elders, and the city belong to the group of relatively independent local powers, and they appear together in a number of documents, whereas the assembly had a mixed character because it also included royal officials. I have excluded other similar local institutions, for example the *bābtum*, 'the city ward', the *kārum*, 'the port authority', and local judges, for different reasons. Thus, although the city ward was probably a relatively independent authority, it rarely appears with the local powers considered in this study. The exceptions are two ration lists and a lawsuit, where *bābtum* is attested together with the elders. In the case of the *kārum*, its actual connection with the state is not immediately apparent. Similarly, the constitution and level of independence of local judges is not certain and needs further investigation.

When referring to the relative independence of the *rabiānum*, the elders, and the city from the royal sphere, it is important to bear in mind the complex character of Old Babylonian society. In that sense, the existence of completely autonomous local powers was impossible. The functioning of economy and society relied on the interaction between the royal administration and community representatives, as well as on their mutual interdependence. There are, nevertheless, certain features that can be traced to establish the degree of independence from the state. That the *rabiānum* was not a royal official becomes apparent from seal legends, in which the *rabiānum* is the 'servant' of a deity instead of the king. As one might have expected, there were certain exceptions, as is the case with the *rabiānum* Ibni-Eraḫ of Šaduppûm, who was 'servant of Dāduša' on his seal, and bears the title of *rabiānum* in a document issued under the reign of Ibāl-pî-el II, Dāduša's successor. It should be stressed, however, that this is the only example that I was able to find among the extant seal impressions.

The close connection of the *rabiānum*, the elders, and the city becomes apparent not only from their joint participation in various documents, but also from the fact that the *rabiānum* office originated from the elders and the city. The mechanisms of this selection and the duration of the appointment cannot be inferred from the available sources, but it is certain that the *rabiānum* as well as the elders and the city members specifically listed in the sources were urban elites. It is also worth recalling that we know of *nadītum*-women who were the daughters of the *rabiānum*. The privileged economic and social position that members of these local authorities held in society may account for their multifarious connections with the state. As is usually the case, negotiation strategies required concessions from both sides. It should not surprise us then, that under certain circumstances, the state had attempted to fill the *rabiānum* position with its own men, and that this could have been the case with Ibni-Eraḫ in Šaduppûm. It seems reasonable to assume that different interests and conjunctures conditioned the rapprochements and withdrawals between royal authorities and community representatives.

ACTIVITIES AND INTERACTION OF THE LOCAL POWERS

The huge number of *rabiānum* documents clearly contrasts with the scanty attestation of the elders, the city, and the assembly. Interestingly, in 60 per cent of the tablets mentioning the *rabiānum*, he appears as a witness, usually the first one. These contracts encompass real estate transactions (sale, rental, and exchange), labor contracts, family issues (including inheritance, marriage, adoptions), loans, sales of cattle, and legal cases. Most of these documents pertain to objects or situations that the parties could potentially contest in the future. This suggests that the local official who witnessed the transaction needed to be an easily identifiable person, instead of a collective body such as the elders or the city. When the elders appear as a group in the list of witnesses they are headed either by the *rabiānum*, or by a man with no title who was presumably the *rabiānum*. There are also instances where 'the elders' without further specification are mentioned after a list of other men. Evidently, it was necessary for corporate institutions to appoint a representative who could be held responsible for the participation of local authorities as guarantors and witnesses of certain transactions. It is also possible that the *rabiānum* was in charge of other organizational activities related to the functioning of local institutions. The rotation of the *rabiānum*-ship among the elders and the city implies that at least some – if not all – of the members periodically shared the responsibilities of the *rabiānum* office with a certain equity.

These local authorities had an active role in real estate transactions. Documents from northern cities such as Sippar, Kār-Šamaš, Dilbat, and Ḫarbānu show that the *rabiānum*, the city, and the elders sold houses belonging to themselves or to third parties; the extant examples span from Sîn-muballiṭ to Ammī-ṣaduqa. Unfortunately, this kind of contract gives no detail regarding the use of the proceeds coming from the sale of these properties. In addition, the *rabiānum* also participated – at least in certain cases – in the assignment of *biltum*-land for corvée workers, and in the rental of fields and orchards. Although in several instances he is the only authority, in other cases the *rabiānum* is attested together with the elders in the management of agricultural affairs involving the rental of fields for cultivation, the estimated yield of gardens, the exchange of houses, and in the settlement of neighbors' disputes over the control of irrigation canals. Furthermore, there are examples in which the elders not only assigned fields but also expropriated and reassigned the land of certain individuals. Most of these references come from letters, but there are also a number of contracts in which the elders participate in the assignment of fields in concert with other men, some of whom were royal officials. The earliest of these texts date from the reign of Rīm-Sîn of Larsa, and they originate from both northern and southern Mesopotamia. The city was also involved in agricultural affairs pertaining to the rental and assignment of fields, and a document from the time of Sūmû-la-el suggests that the city may have also received the produce of the king's land.

The *rabiānum*, the elders, and the city also had a certain control over the local labor force. In several tablets from northern Mesopotamia issued under the last kings of the First Dynasty of Babylon, the *rabiānum* acts as middleman or witness in the hiring of laborers for the crown. In these documents, the contracting party looking for harvesters is always a royal official. In other cases the *rabiānum* and the elders are reported to have received grain to be distributed as food rations for hired laborers, but unfortunately these references come from undated letters. In view of these examples, the attestation of the elders as recipients of rations in two lists from Dilbat dating from Ammī-ṣaduqa seems to indicate that the elders would use the grain for feeding workers. There is finally one document from Sippar from the reign of Samsu-iluna in which the city allocated grain for men working on the maintenance of the irrigation canals. The text clearly states that the city will distribute the barley among the recruited workers.

Economic documents and letters show that the activities of the relatively independent institutions of authority were not merely restricted to the local administration of justice. These local powers also had an active participation in the distribution of resources, in the management of land including urban property, and in the recruitment of the labor force. It is worth noticing, however, that we know about some of these economic activities because they are mentioned in letters. The characteristics of the sources seem to account for the fact that certain transactions were either unrecorded in economic contracts or that those documents have not survived. It becomes apparent then that the prominent role that the local authorities played as adjudicating entities in lawsuits correlates with the nature of the written records and with the exclusively judicial approaches to those sources. Of course, this remark is not aimed at underestimating the importance of legal documents or legal history. It rather attempts to explain the reasons why the economic role of the *rabiānum*, the elders, and the city has received little or no attention in previous studies.

Interactions among local powers are traceable from different records encompassing a number of activities. In litigations and lawsuits the *rabiānum*, the elders, and the city function as adjudicating entities in the settlement of a number of disputes that include various kinds of real estate and family issues as for instance division of property and dowries. The *rabiānum* and the elders, or the city and the elders also act in concert in certain cases concerning robbery. Although in most of the extant examples local authorities collaborate in the solution of those problems brought to them by royal officials or common people, there are also records showing that occasionally the interests and procedures of these powers conflicted. Interestingly, in the few available instances it is the coalition of the *rabiānum* and elders which disagrees with the city. As will be seen later, in a number of cases decisions taken by the *rabiānum* and the elders also oppose royal interests; the 'city' however, does not seem to have contradicted the state. The dissensions between the state and the *rabiānum* and the elders, together with the fact that the 'city' is not involved in them, suggest the hypothesis that the 'city', might have been instituted by the state to counterbalance the role of the elders. The 'city', which also included members of the urban elite, possibly mimicked the constitution and functioning of the elders since it seems to have been a community organ sponsored by the state, although its members were not royal officials. However, until more 'city' documents come to light this explanation remains hypothetical.

INTERACTION BETWEEN LOCAL POWERS AND THE STATE

The dealings between local powers and the state are characterized by both collaboration and conflict. The diversity of these interactions is a clear indicator of the complex political, economic, and social networks operating in Old Babylonian society, a fact that bipolar models and evolutionary approaches usually overlook. There are a number of cases where the king himself sent letters to the *rabiānum* and the elders with instructions on how to proceed regarding various issues. In most instances, however, the contacts take place through the mediation of royal officials who delegate certain responsibilities to the local powers. Thus, in several lawsuits, the parties approach royal authorities, but instead of arbitrating, these officials have the elders and the city convene to clarify the matter. The same delegation of authority is attested in the case of judges who transfer to the city and the elders certain claims that had previously been brought to them. Since local institutions knew the city inhabitants and were aware of their problems, they gave testimony before the judges to help solve litigations. This cooperation is also apparent from those documents in which local authorities and royal officials interact not only in disputes but also in transactions pertaining to real estate. Moreover, from the time of Abī-ešuḫ onwards, there is evidence that the *rabiānum* and the elders participated in the collection of taxes.

Collaboration, however, does not necessarily imply dependence or submission. Tensions among relatively independent local institutions and royal policies are difficult to detect because documents mention them only indirectly. It seems possible to maintain, however, that disputes over the management of resources existed in all periods, although they tend to be more frequent – and therefore more visible – in times of political turmoil. One of the earliest examples known to me dates from the time of Hammurabi. In this case a *rabiānum* not only claimed a field that the palace had assigned to a miller, but he went so far as to take the produce of the field. In addition there are examples where the *rabiānum* and the elders reassigned properties belonging to soldiers who were absent because of their military duties; one of these cases comes from the reign of Samsu-iluna. These instances imply that local authorities reassigned royal lands arbitrarily to secure their own clients. When the mechanisms of the state machinery worked properly, the royal bureaucracy was able to fix those disruptions that originated from the transgressions of jurisdiction by local authorities. But in periods of increasingly weakened central government the situation became rather difficult to manage. Thus, from the time of Abī-ešuḫ onwards, we see the *rabiānum* and the elders involved in apparently fraudulent maneuvers concerning the collection of taxes, which include appropriation and concealment. These strategies, together with the control of the labor force, show that local authorities grew stronger under debilitated regimes with a failing bureaucracy. These cases clearly contradict theories that see a progressive decline in the power of local authorities until they were reduced to mere organs of local justice.

As is the case everywhere else, during the Old Babylonian period people used to gather to deal with various affairs related to their activities or trades. Indeed, tablets record a number of different assemblies, for example the assembly of innkeepers, the assembly of the troops, the assembly of kings, and the assembly of the Amorites, among others. Similarly, royal officials and local authorities had separate meetings. Those gatherings are usually recorded in legal documents mentioning that officials and institutions convened to listen to complaints brought forward by the parties, to investigate given cases, and to render verdicts. Aside from these partial meetings, there is evidence of a local assembly constituted of royal officials and a number of community representatives including the *rabiānum*, the city, the elders, but also members of the *bābtum*, the *kārum*, and the judges. The characteristics of this assembly, however, are difficult to trace because our evidence consists mainly of indirect references in letters or legal documents. Nevertheless, oblique references are also telling. Thus, according to the extant data, the assembly did not issue contracts nor did it render verdicts that could directly result in a written document. The assembly was rather a place where people coming from different sectors of society expressed their claims and complaints. For the historian interested in social history, the importance of the assembly resides in the fact that it was a place of negotiation articulating disparate sectors of the Old Babylonian society.

CONFLICTS AND NEGOTIATIONS

Interpretations regarding Mesopotamian political regimes as despotic systems prevailed for a long time. Even scholars who were not much concerned with political theory seem to have accepted the totalitarian and authoritarian character of Mesopotamian kings. This is particularly clear from those economic approaches suggesting that nothing escaped the state control, and that little – if anything – existed beyond the state. In recent years, however, studies addressing Near Eastern and Mesopotamian governments from different perspectives have questioned the despotic theory (see, e.g., Liverani 1993). The origins of the putative despotic nature of Mesopotamian rulers are manifold, and can be traced to the Bible, to classical literature, and to Western political treatises of the eighteenth and nineteenth centuries. Adulations of kings as they appear in royal inscriptions played no small role in the almighty perception of Mesopotamian monarchs. When criticizing Finley's description of ancient Near Eastern politics as 'government by antechamber', Van De Mieroop (1999c: 143–44) attributes such a view to orientalist stereotypes. For him most decisions were taken communally and were not documented; as a result he maintains that 'government was thus a very decentralized affair' (p. 161). Collective decision-making groups in the Mari region have recently been studied by Fleming (2004), who regards these institutions as survivors of earlier forms of government. Yoffee (2005: 100–112) has now offered a new refutation of 'oriental despotism', framed within his criticism of neo-evolutionist theories of anthropologists and archaeologists. Yoffee argues against the myth of 'monopoly on law' usually ascribed to the earliest states, and refers to constant tensions among local groups and the central authority.

It should be clear at this point that I also disagree with the monolithic and authoritarian appreciation of Mesopotamian rule. The scope of my study, however, differs from others in methods and goals. I focused only on the Old Babylonian period without pursuing the research of earlier and later epochs. When I eventually refer to previous situations it is for the most part to argue that we cannot trace a straightforward progression from Early Dynastic to Old Babylonian local institutions of authority. Such a perspective supports the gradual decline of local councils that were reduced to becoming the feeble survivors of their stronger forerunners. This evolution presupposes the assumption of either a 'primitive democracy' or a 'primitive communism', to borrow Liverani's (1993: 11) set of oppositions. Corporate bodies, I think, existed in all periods, even if our sources are scanty. But it has yet to be proven that those councils that supposedly participated in state decisions – such as peace and war or the installation of a ruler – were the same that survived in later periods. Things were further complicated by suggestions that in case of dynastic crisis the elders managed the situation. These arguments rested upon a letter that the elders of Talḫayûm wrote to the king of Mari because their king died. But as I hope I have shown, the elders of the Mari area cannot be equated with those from other Mesopotamian cities who constituted a relatively independent local collegium. Mari elders indeed participated in state affairs, while the council of city elders from elsewhere did not. Other instances to illustrate the participation of the *rabiānum* and the elders in state politics come from omen literature, but those omens are a-historical. Using them for historical analysis will suppose to undertake a sort of 'archaeology of text', that will not necessarily secure a positive result. I pursued a thorough research of Old Babylonian documents because I wanted to see how local powers operated. And I also wanted to figure out what kind of decisions the *rabiānum*, the city, the elders, and the assembly made, and how these decisions influenced people's life. In the documents that I have analyzed, I could not find any trace of 'sovereign power' held by these authorities. This fact, however, does not make them less interesting.

Most scholars now acknowledge that it is impossible to rule by pure force, and that a certain consensus is needed to run a kingdom. Thus, alongside those who emphasize the authoritarian features of monarchs and regard royal inscriptions as mere propaganda, there are others who remark on the efforts of kings to present themselves as just rulers. For the Old Babylonian period, Hammurabi has undoubtedly become the epitome of the fair ruler. His inscriptions portray him as the one who cares for the widow and the orphan, who secures prosperity for the people by digging canals and building defensive walls and temples, and who maintains the cosmic order by performing religious ceremonies. Very few Assyriologists will nowadays take those claims at face value. The purpose of those texts, some have argued, is to build consensus by means of an exchange of real and imaginary services (see, e.g., Childe [1936] 1956; Godelier 1983). While the king and his priests secure the continuation of celestial and terrestrial laws, people work to support the ruling class whose members are the ideologues of their society. Everybody thus performs duties to keep social stability. I share parts of this explanation, but I also think that it offers a vision that is too harmonious. The ideological foundations of any political regime are fundamental. We should acknowledge, however, that ideologies tend to suppress conflicts. Society does not exist without conflicts, but where do we look for them?

There are different avenues to approach that question. Various political crises can be identified in royal literature. Kings conquer cities and subjugate entire populations, palace intrigues emerge and are sometimes suffocated, and individuals with monarchic aspirations revolt. Most of the Old Babylonian period evidences this kind of political turmoil. These problems have been researched and further investigations to clarify certain aspects are needed. Social conflicts that do not necessarily result from political crises are less apparent, but I think that they should be sought in the activities of local authorities such as those that I have studied. These documents are terse, and they do not charm us with the sophisticated language of royal narratives. They do tell us, nonetheless, about earthly social conflicts and negotiation strategies. Economic conflicts concerning the strife to secure one's belongings or means of subsistence cover a wide range of examples. Family tensions about properties and goods pertain to inheritance, disinheritance, bequests, division of property, and dowries. Silver and real estate are also among the frequent disputes of neighbors and partners. The assignment or re-assignment of arable land for sustenance is similarly a commonplace and usually involve palace affiliates such as soldiers and city inhabitants not directly dependent on the state. Houses were robbed. Silver, grain, and cattle were stolen. Debts were not paid. Servants and slaves were abducted. Problems of this kind were brought to local authorities, and even a shepherd who needed to complain about the size of the temple flock in his charge approached those institutions.

Mesopotamian cities housed a wide spectrum of social actors. Wealthy and prosperous people lived alongside poor fellows and impoverished inhabitants, slaves and free citizens. Temple and palace personnel interacted with those who had other private means of living. This constellation of characters and their trades explains, I think, why in legal and economic documents we usually find a variety of officials witnessing the transaction or participating in the making of decisions. What was important at the time of seeking the intervention of the authorities was the filiation of the parties. Hence the presence of the *rabiānum* together with royal officials, priests, or merchants in many documents. Letters show that royal and relatively independent local powers communicated by written messages when circumstances so required. But as I have argued, these authorities further convene in the local assembly to deal with claims and disputes of city inhabitants. Most likely certain disputes did not involve the issuing of a contract, and references to those instances are only indirectly mentioned in letters. The mechanism of assigning jurisdiction in certain cases was complex. Evidence shows that a person could bring a complaint to the local authorities, and they delegated the case to the judges. In other instances, it is a royal official or even the king himself who transferred the settlement of the matter to the *rabiānum*, the elders, and the city. Therefore, city inhabitants unsatisfied by a verdict had several other avenues to appeal.

The role of these authorities in city government is not only apparent from the fact that city inhabitants resort to them when in trouble. Kings and crown officials also rely on relatively independent local powers for economic and legal purposes. Examples are again diverse and abundant. *Rabiānums* and elders, for instance, participated in the collection of taxes for the crown. During the late Old Babylonian period, certain *rabiānums* provided the crown with harvesters. And king Samsu-iluna asked the *rabiānum* and the elders to protect the house that he bought from a dream interpreter so that nobody will get away with a load of bricks. These are only a few instances drawn from the previous pages. I maintain that the *rabiānum*, the elders, and the city acted as intermediaries between the state and the rest of society. In this function, however, they were neither grassroots leaders nor royal servants. Their role, nevertheless, was instrumental to both community members and the crown. The central authority was aware that those local powers will not hesitate to trespass on royal jurisdiction when opportunity arose; likewise city inhabitants knew that a goat for the *rabiānum* will be the right bribe to stop him interfering in the digging of earth. When local powers did not obstruct the king's interest, royal officials seem to have taken a *laisser faire* policy. Local institutions were both the mediators and the sources of conflicts. These tensions and negotiations are vital to our understanding of Old Babylonian society.

I conclude by referring to the second question that I posed at the beginning of this study, that is, how is it possible with the available sources to go beyond the royal domain and study other spheres of society? I am aware that in my attempt to do so I have taken only a few steps down from the state sector, because I have researched the activities and functions of Old Babylonian local elites. Yet, this approach allowed me to trace a system of relationships functioning at both a vertical and a horizontal level. I further believe that tracing networks of interaction between the state and community representatives helps us to understand complexities that are not self-evident from studies focused only on the state. Historians of the ancient Near East usually discuss the ideas of history in antiquity and the ways in which the ancients perceived their past, but there has been little or no debate around the ways in which historians write about ancient Near Eastern history. This is a difficult task indeed, and the formulation of research problems is tied to new methods, sources, and theories. But I think that reflecting on history writing will assist us in asking new questions of old sources.

Bibliography

Abusch, T. *et al.* (eds) 2001, *Historiography in the Cuneiform World.* Proceedings of the XLVe Rencontre Assyriologique Internationale. Bethesda, Maryland: CDL Press.

Adams, R. McC. 1965, *Land Behind Baghdad.* Chicago: University of Chicago Press.

—, 1981, *Heartland of Cities. Surveys of Ancient Settlements and Land Use on the Central Floodplain of the Euphrates.* Chicago: University of Chicago Press.

Al-Rawi, F. N. H. 1994, 'Texts from Tell Haddad and Elsewhere'. *Iraq* 56: 35–44.

Al-Zeebari, A. 1964, Altbabylonische Briefe des Iraq-Museum. Doctoral dissertation, Westfälischen Wilhelms-Universität zu Münster, Mosul, University of Baghdad.

Albenda, P. 1987, 'Woman, Child, and Family: their Imagery in Assyrian Art'. In J.-M. Durand (ed.), *La femme dans le Proche-Orient antique*, 17–21. Paris: Éditions Recherche sur les Civilisations.

Ali, F. 1964, 'Blowing the Horn for Official Announcement'. *Sumer* 20: 66–68.

Anbar, M. 1975, 'Textes de l'époque babylonienne ancienne'. *RA* 69: 109–36.

—, 1991, *Les tribus amurrites de Mari.* OBO 108. Göttingen: Universitatsverlag Freiburg, Schweiz: Vandenhoeck and Ruprecht.

Anderson, P. 1974, *Lineages of the Absolutist State.* London: NLB.

Archi, A. 2001, 'The King-lists from Ebla'. In T. Abusch *et al.* (eds), *Historiography in the Cuneiform World*, Part I. Proceedings of the XLVe Recontre Assyriologique International, 1–13. Bethesda, Maryland: CDL Press.

Armstrong, G., and Brandt, M. 1994, 'Ancient Dunes at Nippur'. In H. Gasche *et al.* (eds), *Cinquante-deux réflexiones sur le Proche-Orient ancien offertes à Léon De Meyer.* Mesopotamian History and Environment. Occasional Publications vol. 2, 255–63. Leuven: Peeters.

Åström, P. (ed.) 1987, *High, Middle or Low? Acts of an International Colloquium on Absolute Chronology Held at the University of Gothenburg, 20th-22nd August 1987.* Part I. Gothenburg: P. Åströms Förlag.

Bahrani, Z. 2001, *Women of Babylon: Gender and Representation in Mesopotamia.* London and New York: Routledge.

Baines, J., Cooper, J., and Houston, S. 2003, 'Last Writing: Script Obsolescense in Egypt, Mesopotamia, and Mesoamerica'. *Comparative Studies in Society and History* 45/3: 430–79.

Bardet, G. *et al.* 1984, *Archives administratives de Mari I.* ARM 23. Paris: Éditions Recherches sur les Civilisations.

Barthes, R. 1967, 'Le discours de l'histoire'. *Social Science Information* 6/4: 65–75.

Beaulieu, P. A. 1993, 'Women in Neo-Babylonian Society'. *Canadian Society for Mesopotamian Studies Bulletin* 26: 7–14.

Beckman, G. 1982, 'The Hittite Assembly'. *JAOS* 102: 435–42.

—, 1995, *Old Babylonian Archival Texts in the NIES Babylonian Collection*. Bethesda: CDL Press.

Birot, M. 1960, *Textes administratifs de la salle 5 du palais.* ARM 9. Paris: Imprimerie Nationale.

—, 1968, 'Découvertes épigraphiques à Larsa'. *Syria* 45: 241–47.

—, 1974, *Lettres de Yaqqim-Addu, gouverneur de Sagarātum.* ARM 14. Paris: Librairie Orientaliste Paul Geuthner.

—, 1993, *Correspondance des gouverneurs de Qaṭṭunân*. ARM 27. Paris: Éditions Recherches sur les Civilisations.

Bloch, M. 1993, *Apologie pour l'histoire ou métier d'historien.* Paris: Armand Colin (First edition 1949).

Bobrova, L., and Koshurnikov, S. 1989, 'On Some New Works in the Social History of the Old Babylonian Period'. *AfO* 16: 51–60.

Böhl, F. M. T. De Liagre 1951, 'Ein Brief des Königs Samsu-iluna von Babylon (± 1685 – 1648 v. Chr.)'. *BiOr* VIII n° 2/3: 50–56.

Boson, G. 1942, 'Un contrato babylonese dell'epoca di Hammurabi'. *Aegyptus* n° 3–4: 265–69.

Bottéro, J. 1957, *Textes économiques et administratifs.* ARM 7. Paris: Imprimerie Nationale.

—, 2001, *Ancient Mesopotamia: Everyday Life in the First Civilization*. Edinburgh: Edinburgh University Press.

Bottéro, J., and Kramer, S. 1989, *Lorsque les dieux faisaient l'homme*. Paris: Gallimard.

Bottéro, J., and Monsacré, H. 1994, *Babylone et la Bible. Entretiens avec Hélène Monsacré.* Paris: Les Belles Lettres.

Boyer, G. 1928, *Contribution à l'histoire juridique de la 1re. dynastie babylonienne*. Paris: Librairie Orientaliste Paul Geuthner.

—, 1958, *Textes juridiques*. ARM 8. Paris: Imprimerie Nationale.

Braudel, F. 1949, *La Méditerranée et le monde méditerranéen à l'epoque de Philippe II*. Paris: Colin.

Breckwoldt, T. 1995, 'Management of Grain Storage in Old Babylonian Larsa'. *AfO* 42/43: 64–88.

Breisach, E. 1994, *Historiography: Ancient, Medieval, and Modern*. Chicago and London: University of Chicago Press.

Brinkman, J. 1997, 'Mesopotamian Chronology of the Historical Period'. Appendix to A. L. Oppenheim's *Ancient Mesopotamia. Portrait of a Dead Civilization*, 335–38. Chicago: University of Chicago Press

Buccellati, G. 1966, *The Amorites of the Ur III Period*. Naples: Instituto Orientali di Napoli.

—, 1976, 'The Case against the Alleged Akkadian Plural Morpheme -*ānū*'. *Afro-asiatic Linguistics* 3/2: 28–30.

—, 1998, 'Urkesh as Tell Mozan: Profiles of the Ancient City'. In G. Buccellati and M. Kelly-Buccellati (eds), *Urkesh and the Hurrians Studies in Honor of Lloyd Cotsen*, 11–34. Bibliotheca Mesopotamica vol. 26. Malibu: Undena Publications.

Buchanan, B. 1981, *Early Near Eastern Seals in the Yale Babylonian Collection*. New Haven: Yale University Press.

Burke, P. 1993, *History and Social Theory*. Cambridge: Polity Press.

Burke, P. (ed) 1995, *New Perspectives on Historical Writing*. Pennsylvania: The Pennsylvania State University.

Cagni, L. 1980, *Briefe aus dem Iraq Museum*. AbB 8. Leiden: E. J. Brill.

Campbell, E. 1961, 'The Ancient Near East: Chronological Bibliography and Charts'. In G. Wright (ed), *The Bible and the Ancient Near East. Essays in Honor of William F. Albright*, 214–19. Garden City, NY: Doubleday.

Cassin, E. 1973a, 'La contestation dans le monde divin'. In A. Finet (ed.), *La voix de l'opposition en Mesopotamie. Colloque organisé par l'Institut des Hautes Études de Belgique*, 89–110. Bruxelles: Institute des Hautes Études de Belgique.

—, 1973b, 'Note sur le "puḫrum" des dieux'. In A. Finet (ed.), *La voix de l'opposition en Mesopotamie. Colloque organisé par l'Institut des Hautes Études de Belgique*, 111–18. Bruxelles: Institute des Hautes Études de Belgique.

Certeau, M. de 1988, *The Writing of History*. New York: Columbia University. (First French edition: 1975)

Charpin, D. 1978, 'Recherches sur la dynastie de Mananâ (I): essai de localization et de chronologie'. *RA* 72: 13–40.

—, 1979, 'Review of *Early Old Babylonian Documents: YOS 14*, by S. Simmons'. *BiOr* 36: 188–200.

—, 1980a, *Archives familiales et propriété privée en Babylonie ancienne: étude des documents de Tell Sifr*. Genève: Librairie Droz.

—, 1980b, 'Remarques sur l'administration paléobabylonienne sous les successeurs d'Ḫammurapi'. *JAOS* 100: 461–71.

—, 1982, 'Marchand du palais et marchands du temple à la fin de la Ier. dynastie de Babylone. *Journal Asiatique* 270: 25–65.

—, 1983–84, 'Review of *altbabylonische Briefe aus dem Iraq Museum*, by L. Cagni'. *AfO* 29–30: 103–108.

—, 1985a, 'Données nouvelles sur la chronologie des souverains d'Ešnunna'. In J.-M. Durand and J. Kupper (eds), *Miscelanea babylonica. Mélanges offertes à Maurice Birot*, 51–66. Paris: Éditions Recherches sur les Civilisations.
—, 1985b, 'Le sceau d'un *rabiānum*'. *RA* 79: 191.
—, 1985c, 'Un quartier de Babylone et ses habitants sous les successeurs d' Ḫammurabi'. *BiOr* 42: 265–78.
—, 1986a, *Le clergé d'Ur au siècle d'Hammurabi*. Genève: Librairie Droz.
—, 1986b, 'Les elamites a Šubat-Enlil'. In L. de Meyer *et al.* (eds), *Fragmenta historiae elamicae mélanges offerts à M.-J. Steve*, 129–37. Paris: Éditions Recherches sur les Civilisations.
—, 1986c, 'Transmission des titres de proprieté et constitution des archives privées en Babylonie ancienne'. In K. Veenhof (ed.), *Cuneiform Archives and Libraries. Papers Read at the 30e. Rencontre Assyriologique Internationale. Leiden, 4-8 July 1983*, 121–40. Leiden: Nederlands Historisch-Archaeologisch Instituut te Istanbul.
—, 1987, 'Šubat-Enlil et le pays d'Apum'. *MARI* 5: 129–40.
—, 1991, 'Un traité entre Zimri-Lim de Mari et Ibāl-pî-el d'Ešnunna'. In D. Charpin and F. Joannès (eds), *Merchands, diplomats et empereurs. Études sur la civilisation mésopotamienne en l' honneur de Paul Garelli*, 139–66. Paris: Éditions Recherches sur les Civilisations.
—, 1992, 'Mari entre l'Est et l'Ouest'. *Akkadica* 79: 1–10.
—, 1993a, 'Un souverain éphémère en Ida-Maraṣ: Išme-Addu d'Ašnakkum'. *MARI* 7: 165–91.
—, 1993b, 'Données nouvelles sur la poliorcétique à l'époque paléo-babylonienne'. *MARI* 7: 193–203.
—, 1999, 'Hagalum, šakkanakkum de Râpiqum, et ses serviteurs'. In B. Böck *et al.* (eds), *Minuscula Mesopotamica. Festschrift für J. Renger*. AOAT 267, 95–108. Münster: Ugarit-Verlag.
—, 2000, 'Lettres et process paléo-babyloniens'. In F. Joannès (ed.), *Rendre la justice en Mésopotamie. Archives judiciaries du Proche-Orient ancien (IIIe – Ier. millénaires avant J.C.)*, 69–111. Saint-Denis: Presses Universitaires de Vincennes.
—, 2003, *Hammu-rabi de Babylone*. Paris: Presses Universitaires de France.
—, 2004, 'Histoire politique du Proche-Orient amorrite (2002–1595)'. In D. Charpin *et al.*, *Mesopotamien: die altbabylonische Zeit*. OBO 160/4, 25–480. Fribourg and Göttingen: Academic Press/Vandenhoeck and Ruprecht.
Charpin, D., and Durand, J.-M. 1981, *Documents cunéiformes de Strasbourg conservés à la Bibliothèque Nationale et Universitaire*, Tome I: Authographies. Paris: Éditions ADPF.
—, 1985, 'La prise du pouvoir par Zimri-Lim'. *MARI* 4: 293–344.
—, 1986, '"Fils de sim'al": les origines tribal des rois de Mari'. *RA* 80: 141–83.
—, 1991, 'La suzeraineté de l'empereur (sukkal-maḫ) d'Élam sur la Mésopotamie et le "nationalisme" Amorite'. In *Mésopotamie et Élam*, Actes de la XXXIV RAI,

Gand 1989, 59–66. Gand: Mesopotamian History and Environment Occasional Publications.
Chartier, R. 1997, *On the Edge of the Cliff. History, Language, and Practices*. Baltimore and London: Johns Hopkins University Press.
Chiera, E. 1922, *Old Baylonian Contracts*. Publications of the Babylonian Section, vol. 8/2. Philadelphia: The University Museum.
Childe, V. G. 1956, *Man Makes Himself*. London: Watts & Co (First edition 1936).
Çiğ, M. *et al.*, 1952. *Altbabylonische Rechtsurkunden aus Nippur*. Istanbul: Milli Eğitim Basimevi.
Civil, M. 1974, 'Lexicography'. AS 16: 123–57.
—, 1980, 'L'information textuelle et ses limites'. In M. T. Barrelet, (ed.), *L'archéologie de l'Iraq du début de l'époque néolitique a 333 avant notre ère*, 225–32. Paris: CNRS.
Clay, A. 1919, *The Empire of the Amorites*. New Haven: Yale University Press.
Cocquerillat, D. 1967, 'Aperçue sur la phéniciculture en Babylonie à l'époque de la 1ère dynastie de Babylone'. *JESHO* 10: 161–223.
Contenau, G. 1954, *Everyday Life in Babylonia and Assyria*. New York: St. Martin's Press.
Cooper, J. 1973, 'Sumerian and Akkadian in Sumer and Akkad'. *Or* 42: 239–46.
—, 1996, 'Sumerian and Akkadian'. In P. Daniels and W. Bright (eds), *The World's Writing Systems*, 37–57. Oxford: Oxford University Press.
Cuq, É. 1910, 'Essai sur l'organization judiciaire de la Chaldée à l'époque de la première dynastie babylonienne'. *RA* 7: 65–101.

Dalley, S. 1979, *A Catalogue of the Akkadian Cuneiform Tablets in the Collections of the Royal Scottish Museum, Edinburgh, with Copies of the Texts*. Art and Archaeology 2. Edinburgh: Royal Scottish Museum.
Dalley, S. *et al.* 1976, *The Old Babylonian Tablets from Tell al Rimah*. Hertford: British School of Archaeology in Iraq.
Deimel, A. 1931, *Šumerische Tempelwirtschaft zur Zeit Urukaginas und seiner Vorgänger*. Roma: Pontifici Instituti Biblici.
—, 1950, *Šumerisches Lexikon. Pantheon Babylonicum*, IV. Teil, Band I. Rome: Verlag des Päpstl. Bibelinstituts.
Dekiere, L. 1994a, *Old Babylonian Real Estate Documents from Sippar in the British Museum. Part I, Pre-Hammurabi Documents*. Mesopotamian History and Environment Series III: Texts, vol. 2. Ghent: University of Ghent.
—, 1994b, *Old Babylonian Real Estate Documents from Sippar in the British Museum. Part II, Documents from the Reign of Hammurabi*. Mesopotamian History and Environment Series III: Texts, vol. 2. Ghent: University of Ghent.
—, 1995a, *Old Babylonian Real Estate Documents from Sippar in the British Museum.*

Part III, Documents from the Reign of Samsu-iluna. Mesopotamian History and Environment Series III: Texts, vol. 2. Ghent: University of Ghent.

—, 1995b, *Old Babylonian Real Estate Documents from Sippar in the British Museum. Part IV, Post-Samsu-iluna Documents*. Mesopotamian History and Environment Series III: Texts, vol. 2. Ghent: University of Ghent.

—, 1996, *Old Babylonian Real Estate Documents from Sippar in the British Museum. Part V, Documents without Date or with Date Lost*. Mesopotamian History and Environment Series III: Texts, vol. 2. Ghent: University of Ghent.

—, 1997, *Old Babylonian Real Estate Documents. Documents from the series 1902-10-11 (From Zabium to Ammi-ṣaduqa), Part VI*. Mesopotamian History and Environment Series III: Texts, vol. 2. Ghent: The University of Ghent.

De Meyer, L. 1978, 'Documents épigraphiques paléo-babyloniens provenant des sondages A, B et D'. In L. De Meyer (ed), *Tell ed-Dēr II*, 147–84. Leuven: Editions Peeters.

Dentan, R. (ed.) 1955, *The Idea of History in the Ancient Near East*. New Haven and London: Yale University Press.

Dercksen, J. 2000, 'Institutional and Private in the Old Assyrian Period'. In A. Bongenaar (ed.), *Interdependency of Institutions and Private Enterpreneurs. MOS Studies 2. Proceedings of the Second MOS Symposium. Leiden 1998*, 135–52. Leiden: Nederlands Historisch-Archaeologisch Institut te Istanbul.

Desrochers, M. 1978, Aspects of the Structure of Dilbat during the Old Babylonian Period. Doctoral dissertation, Los Angeles, University of California.

Dhorme, E. 1914, 'La fille de Nabonide'. *RA* 11: 105–17.

—, 1947, 'La mère de Nabonide'. *RA* 41: 1–21.

Diakonoff, I. 1963, 'The Commune in the Ancient Near East as Treated in the Works of Soviet Researchers'. *Soviet Anthropology and Archaeology* 2: 32–46.

—, 1969, 'The Rise of the Despotic State in Ancient Mesopotamia'. In I. Diakonoff (ed.), *Ancient Mesopotamia*, 173–203. Moscow: Nauka.

—, 1975, 'The Rural Community in the Ancient Near East'. *JESHO* 18: 121–33.

—, 1985, 'Extended Families in Old Babylonian Ur'. *ZA* 75: 47–65.

—, 1986, 'Women in Old Babylonian not under Patriarchal Authority'. *JESHO* 29: 225–38.

—, 1995, 'Old Babylonian Ur. A Review Article of Marc Van de Mieroop, *Society and Enterprise in Old Babylonian Ur*'. *JESHO* 38: 91–4.

Dobb, M. 1959, *Studies in the Development of Capitalism*. London: Routledge and Sons.

Dombradi, E. 1996, *Die Darstellung des Rechtsaustrags in den altbabylonischen Prozessurkunden*. FAOS 20. Stuttgart: Franz Steiner Verlag.

Donbaz, V., and Yoffee, N. 1986, *Old Babylonian Texts from Kish Conserved in the Istanbul Archaeological Museums*. Malibu: Undena Publications.

Dossin, G. 1933, *Lettres de la première dynastie babylonienne I. Textes cunéiformes du Louvre*. TCL XVII. Paris: Librairie Orientaliste Paul Geuthner.

—, 1938, 'Les archives épistolaires du palais de Mari'. *Syria* 9: 105–26.

—, 1951, *Correspondance de Šamši-Addu*. ARM 4. Paris: Imprimerie Nationale.

—, 1955, 'L'inscription de fondation de Iaḫdun-Lim, roi de Mari'. *Syria* 32: 1-28.

—, 1956, 'Une lettre de Iarîm-Lim, roi d'Alep, à Iašub-Iaḫad, roi de Dîr'. *Syria* 33: 63–9.

Dosin, M. and Finet, A. 1978, *Correspondance féminine*. ARM 10. Paris: Librairie Orientaliste Paul Geuthner.

Dosin, M. *et al.* 1964, *Textes diverses. A l'occasion du XXXe. anniversaire de la découverte de Mari*. ARM 13. Paris: Librairie Orientaliste Paul Geuthner.

Dow, S. 2004, 'Aristotle, the *Kleroteria* and the Courts'. In P. J. Rhodes (ed.), *Athenian Democracy*, 62–94. Oxford: Oxford University Press.

Driver, G. and Miles, J. 1952/5, *The Babylonian Laws*, 2 vols. Oxford: Clarendon Press.

Durand, J.-M. 1983, *Textes administratifs des salles 134 et 160 du palais de Mari*. ARM 21. Paris: Librairie Orientaliste Paul Geuthner.

—, 1986, 'Fragments rejoints pour une histoire elamite'. In L. de Meyer *et al.* (eds), *Fragmenta Historiae Elamicae Mélanges Offerts à M.-J. Steve*, 111–28. Paris: Éditions Recherches sur les Civilisations.

—, 1988a, *Archives épistolaires de Mari* I/1. ARM 26. Paris: Éditions Recherches sur les Civilisations.

—, 1988b, 'Les anciens de Talḫayûm'. *RA* 82: 97–113.

—, 1989, 'L'assemblée en Syrie à l'époque pré-amorite', *Quaderni di Semitistica* 16: 27–44.

—, 1990, 'La cité-état d'Imâr à l'époque des rois de Mari'. *MARI* 6: 39–92.

—, 1992, 'Unité et diversité au Proche-Orient à l'époque amorrite'. In D. Charpin and R. Joannès (eds), *La circulation des biens, des personnes et des idées dans le Proche-Orient ancien*, 97–128. XXXVIIIe. RAI. Paris: Éditions Recherches sur les Civilisations.

—, 1997, *Les documents épistolaires du palais de Mari*, v. I, LAPO 16. Paris: Les Éditions du Cerf.

—, 1998, *Les documents épistolaires du palais de Mari*, v. II, LAPO 17. Paris: Les Éditions du Cerf.

—, 1999–2000, 'Apologue sur des mauvaises herbes et un coquin'. *AuOr* 17–18: 191–96.

—, 2000, *Les documents épistolaires du palais de Mari*, v. III, LAPO 18. Paris: Les Éditions du Cerf.

Durand, J.-M. (ed.) 1987, *La femme dans le Proche-Orient antique*. Paris: Éditions Recherche sur les Civilisations.

Dyckhoff, C. 1998, 'Balamunamḫe von Larsa – eine altbabylonische Existenz zwischen Ökonomie, Kultus und Wissenschaft'. In J. Prosecky (ed.), *Intellectual Life of the Ancient Near East*, RAI 34, 117–24. Prage: Prague Oriental Institute.

Ebeling, 1928, 'Aḫut', *RlA* 1: 60.
Edzard, D. O. 1957, *Die 'zweite Zwischenzeit' Babyloniens*. Wiesbaden: O. Harrassowitz.
Eidem, J. 1994, 'Raiders of the Lost Treasure of Samsī-Addu'. In D. Charpin and J.-M. Durand (eds), *Florilegium Marianum II. Recueil d'études à la mémoire de M. Birot*. 201–208. Mémoires de NABU 3. Paris: Société pour l'Étude du Proche-Orient Ancien.
Ellis, M. de Jong 1974, 'The Division of Property at Tell Harmal'. *JCS* 26: 133–53.
Ellis, R. 1968, *Foundation Deposits in Ancient Mesopotamia*. New Haven: Yale University Press.
Evans, G. 1958, 'Ancient Mesopotamian Assemblies'. *JAOS* 78: 1–11.

Falkenstein, A. 1954, 'La cité-temple sumérienne'. *Cahiers d'Histoire Mondiale I*: 784–814.
—, 1956–57, *Die neusumerischen Gerichtsurkunden*. München: Verlag der Bayerischen Akademie der Wissenschaften.
—, 1963, 'Zu den Inschriftfunden der Grabung in Uruk-Warka 1960-1961', *Baghdader Mitteilungen* 2: 1–82.
Farber, H. 1978, 'A Price and Wage Study for Northern Babylonia during the Old Babylonian Period'. *JESHO* 21: 1–51.
Faust, D. 1941, *Contracts from Larsa Dated to the Reign of Rīm-Sîn*. YOS 8. New Haven: Yale University Press.
Feigin, S. 1979, *Legal and Administrative Texts of the Reign of Samsu-iluna*. YOS 12. New Haven and London: Yale University Press.
Figula, H. 1929, 'Ein Kaufvertrag mit einem noch nicht vollständig bekannten Datum Ammiditanas'. *MAOG* IV: 290–93.
Finet, A. 1973a, *Le code de Hammurapi. Introduction, traduction et annotation de André Finet*. Paris: Les Éditions du Cerf.
—, 1973b, 'Le trône et la rue en Mésopotamie: L'exaltation du roi et les techniques de l'opposition'. In A. Finet (ed), *La voix de l'opposition en Mésopotamie*. Colloque organisé par l'Institut des Hautes Études de Belgique 19 et 20 mars 1973, 2–27. Bruxelles: Institut des Hautes Études de Belgique.
—, 1982, 'Les autorités locales dans le royaume de Mari'. *Akkadica* 26: 1–16.
Finet, A. (ed.) 1982, *Les pouvoirs locaux en Mesopotamie et dans les régions adjacents*. Colloque organisé par l'Institut des Hautes Études de Belgique 26 et 29 janvier 1980. Bruxelles: Institut des Hautes Études de Belgique.
Finkelstein, J. 1963, 'Mesopotamian Historiography'. *PAPS* 107: 461–72.

—, 1965, 'Some New *misharum* Material and its Implications', Assyriological Studies 16. Chicago: University of Chicago Press.

—, 1966, 'The Genealogy of the Ḫammurapi Dynasty'. *JCS* 19: 95–118.

—, 1966a, 'Sex Offenses in Sumerian Laws'. *JAOS* 86: 355–72.

—, 1967, 'A Late Old Babylonian Copy of the Laws of Ḫammurapi'. *JCS* 21: 39–48.

—, 1972, *Late Old Babylonian Documents and Letters.* YOS 13. New Haven: Yale University Press.

Fish, T. 1936, *Letters of the First Babylonian Dynasty in the John Rylands Library, Manchester*. Manchester: The Manchester University Press.

Fitzgerald, M. 2002, The Rulers of Larsa. Doctoral dissertation, New Haven, Yale University.

Fleming, D. 2004, *Democracy's Ancient Ancestors. Mari and Early Collective Government*. Cambridge: Cambridge University Press.

Fortner, J. 1996, Adjudicating Entities and Levels of Legal Authority in Lawsuit Records of the Old Babylonian Era. Doctoral dissertation, Cincinnati, Hebrew Union College.

Foster, B. 1981, 'A New Look at the Sumerian Temple State'. *JESHO* 24: 225–41.

—, 1982, *Administration and Use of Institutional Land in Sargonic Sumer*. Mesopotamia 9. Copenhagen: Akademisk Forlag.

—, 1996, *Before the Muses. An Anthology of Akkadian Literature*, 2 vols. Bethesda, MD: CDL Press.

Fraker, C. 1996, *The Scope of History. Studies in the Historiography of Alfonso el Sabio*. Ann Arbor: University of Michigan Press.

Franke, J. 1977, 'Presentation in Seals of the Ur III/ Isin-Larsa Period'. In M. Gibson and R. Biggs (eds), *Seals and Sealings in the Ancient Near East*, 63. Bibliotheca Mesopotamica 6. Malibu: Undena Publications.

Frankena, R. 1966, *Briefe aus dem British Museum: LIH und CT 2 – 33*. AbB 2. Leiden: E. J. Brill.

—, 1968, *Briefe aus der Leidener Sammlung: TLB IV.* AbB 3. Leiden: E. J. Brill.

—, 1974, *Briefe aus den Berlin Museum: VAS 16, 7 und 9.* AbB 6. Leiden: E. J. Brill.

Frankfort, H. 1948, *Kingship and the Gods*. Chicago: University of Chicago Press.

Frayne, D. 1990, *The Old Babylonian Period (2003–1595 B.C.)*. Royal Inscriptions of Mesopotamia, vol. 4. Toronto-Buffalo-London: University of Toronto Press.

Fukuyama, F. 1992, *The End of History and the Last Man*. New York: Free Press.

Gadd, C. 1951, 'En-an-e-du'. *Iraq* 13: 27–39.

Gallery, M. 1979, 'Recent Contributions to Old Babylonian Studies'. *JAOS* 99: 73–80.

Gasche, H. *et al.* 1989, *La Babylonie au 17e siècle avant notre ère: approche archéologique, problèmes et perspectives*. Mesopotamian History and Environment Series II: Memoires I. Ghent: University of Ghent.

—, 1998, *Dating the Fall of Babylon. A Reappraisal of Second-Millennium Chronology (A Joint Ghent-Chicago-Harvard Project)*. Mesopotamian History and Environment Series II: Memoirs IV. Ghent-Chicago: University of Ghent and the Oriental Institute of Chicago.

Gelb, I. 1961, 'The Early History of the West Semitic Peoples'. *JCS* 14: 27–47.

—, 1968, 'An Old Babylonian List of Amorites'. *JAOS* 88: 39–46.

—, 1969, 'On the Alleged Temple and State Economies in Ancient Mesopotamia'. In *Studi in onore di Edoardo Volterra*, 138–54. Milan: A. Giuffrè.

—, 1973, *Glossary of Old Akkadian*. Materials for the Assyrian Dictionary 3. Chicago: University of Chicago Press (First edition 1957).

—, 1984, '*šibūt kušurrā'im*, "Witnesses of the Indemnity"'. *JNES* 43: 263–76.

—, 1992, 'Mari and the Kish Civilization'. In G. Young (ed.), *Mari in Retrospect. Fifty Years of Mari and Mari Studies*, 121–202. Winona Lake, IN: Eisenbrauns.

Gelb, I. *et al.* 1991, *Earliest Land Tenure Systems in the Near East: Ancient Kudurrus*. Chicago: The Oriental Institute.

Geller, M. 1997, 'The Last Wedge'. *ZA* 87: 43–95.

George, A. 1999, *The Epic of Gilgamesh. The Babylonian Epic Poem and Other Texts in Akkadian and Sumerian*. New York: Barnes and Noble.

Gibson, McG. 1980, 'Current Research at Nippur: Ecological, Anthropological and Documentary Interplay'. In *L'archéologie de l'Iraq au début de l'époque néolithique à 333 avant notre ère*. Colloques internationaux du Centre National de la Recherche Scientifique n° 580, 193–205. Paris: Éditions du Centre National de la Recherche Scientifique.

Ginzburg, C. 1976, *Il formaggio e i vermi: il cosmo di un mugnaio del '500*. Torino: G. Einaudi.

—, 1999, *History, Rhetoric, and Proof*. Hanover and London: University Press of New England.

Gledhill, J., and Larsen, M. 1982, 'The Polanyi Paradigm and a Dynamic Analysis of Archaic States. In C. Renfrew *et al.* (eds), *Theory and Explanation in Archaeology: The Southampton Conference*, 197–229. New York: Academic Press.

Goddeeris, A. 2002, *Economy and Society in Northern Babylonia in the Early Old Babylonian Period (ca. 2000 – 1800 B.C.)*. Orientalia Lovaniensia Analecta 109. Leuven-Paris-Sterling, Virginia: Uitgeverij Peeters and Departement of Oosterse Studies.

Godelier, M. 1983, 'Procesos de la constitución, la diversidad y las bases del estado'. *Revista de Ciencias Sociales*, México, 666–83.

Goetze, A. 1965, 'Tavern Keepers and the like in Ancient Babylonia'. AS 16: 211–15.

—, 1958, 'Fifty Old Babylonian Letters from Harmal'. *Sumer* 14: 3–78.

Grant, E. 1917, 'Balamunamḫe, the Slave Dealer'. *AJLS* 34: 119–204.

Greengus, S. 1969–70, 'A Textbook Case of Adultery in Ancient Mesopotamia'. *HUCA* 40–41: 35–44.

—, 1979, *Old Babylonian Tablets from Ishchali and Vicinity*. Leiden: Nederlands Historisch-Archaeologisch Institut te Istanbul.

Groneberg, B. 1980, *Die Orts- und Gewässernamen der altbabylonischen Zeit*. Répertoire géographique des textes cunéiformes III. Wiesbaden: Dr. Ludwing Reichert Verlag.

Guichard, M. 1994, 'Au pays de la dame de Nagar'. In D. Charpin and Durand J.-M. (eds), *Florilegium Marianum II, recueil d'études à la mémoire de Maurice Birot*. Mémoires de NABU 3, 235–72. Paris: Société pour l'Étude du Proche-Orient Ancien.

Hallo, W. 1957, *Early Mesopotamian Royal Titles: a Philologic and Historical Analysis*. New Haven: American Oriental Society.

—, 2002, 'A Model Court Case Concerning Inheritance'. In T. Abusch (ed.), *Riches Hidden in Secret Places. Ancient Near Eastern Studies in Memory of Thorkild Jacobsen*, 141–54. Winona Lake, Indiana: Eisenbrauns.

Hansen, M. 1977, 'How Often did the *Ecclesia* Meet?' *Greek, Roman and Byzantine Studies* XVIII: 43–70.

—, 2004, 'How did the Athenian *Ecclesia* Vote?' In P. J. Rhodes (ed.), *Athenian Democracy*, 40–61. Oxford: Oxford University Press.

Hansen, M., and Mitchel, F. 1984, 'The Number of Ecclesiai in Fouth-century Athens'. *Symbolae Osloenses* LIX: 13–19.

Harris, R. 1962, 'Bibliographical Notes on the *nadītu* Women of Sippar'. *JCS* 16: 1–12.

—, 1964, 'The Nadītu Woman'. In J. Brinkman (ed.), *Studies Presented to A. L. Oppenheim*, 106–35. Chicago: University of Chicago Press.

—, 1965, 'The Journey of the Divine Weapon'. *AS* 16: 217–24.

—, 1970, 'Review of *CT XLVIII Old Babylonian Legal Documents* by J. J. Finkelstein'. *JESHO* 13: 315–18.

—, 1972, 'Notes on the Nomenclature of Old Babylonian Sippar'. *JCS* 24: 102–104.

—, 1975, *Ancient Sippar. A Demographic Study of an Old Babylonian City (1894–1595)*. Leiden: Nederlands Historisch-Archaeologisch Instituut te Istanbul.

—, 1976, 'On Foreigners in OB Sippar'. *RA* 70: 145–52.

Hegel, G. 1942, *The Philosophy of History*. Ann Arbor: Edwards Brothers, Inc.

Herodotus 1998, *The Histories*. Translated by R. Waterfield. Oxford: Oxford University Press.

Hobsbawm, E. 1997, *On History*. New York: The New Press.

Holma, H. 1914, *Zehn altbabylonischen Tontafeln in Helsingfors*. Acta Societatis Scientiarum fennicæ 45/3. Helsinfors: Druckerei der Finnishen litteraturgesellschaft.
Hommel, F. 1885, *Geschichte Babyloniens und Assyriens*. Berlin: G. Grotes'sche Verlagsbuchhandlung.
Huber, P. *et al.* 1982, *Astronomical Dating of Babylon I and Ur III*. Monographic Journals of the Near East, Occasional Papers on the Near East 1/4. Malibu: Undena Publications.
Hudson, M. 1996, 'Privatization: A Survey of the Unresolved Controversies'. In M. Hudson and B. Levine (eds.), *Privatization in the Ancient Near East and the Classical World*, 1–32. Cambridge, MA: Harvard University.
Hudson, M. and Levine, B. (eds) 1996, *Privatization in the Ancient Near East and Classical World*. Cambridge, MA: Harvard University.
Hughes-Warrington, M. 2003, *Fifty Key Thinkers on History*. London and New York: Routledge.

Iggers, G. 1997, *Historiography in the Twentieth Century. From Scientific Objectivity to the Postmodern Challenge*. Hanover and London: Wesleyan University Press.

Jacobsen, T. 1939, *The Sumerian King List*, Assyriological Studies 11. Chicago: University of Chicago Press.
—, 1940, 'Historical Data'. In H. Frankfort *et al.* (eds), *The Gimilsin Temple and the Palace of the Rulers at Tell Asmar*, Oriental Institute Publications v. 43, 116–200. Chicago: University of Chicago Press.
—, 1943, 'Primitive Democracy in Ancient Mesopotamia'. *JNES* 2: 159–72.
—, 1957, 'Early Political Development in Mesopotamia'. *ZA* 18 (52): 91–140.
—, 1959, 'An Ancient Mesopotamian Trial for Homicide'. *Studia Biblica et Orientalia III, Analecta Biblica et Orientalia* XII: 130–50.
—, 1978–9, 'Iphur-Kish and His Times'. *AfO* 26: 1–14.
—, 1987, *The Harps that Once... Sumerian Poetry in Translation*. New Haven and London: Yale University Press.
Jakobson, V. 1971, 'Some Problems Connected with the Rise of Landed Property (Old Babylonian Period)'. In H. Klengel (ed.), *Beiträge zur sozialen Struktur des alten Vorderasien*, 33–37. Berlin: Akademie-Verlag.
Janssen, C. 1991, 'Samsuiluna and the Hungry Naditums'. *Mesopotamian History and Government, Series 1, Northern Akkad Project Reports* 5: 3–39.
—, 1992, 'Inanna-mansum et ses fils: relation d'une succession turbulente dans les archives d'Ur-Utu'. *RA* 86: 19–52.
Jastrow, M. 1980, *The Civilization of Babylonia and Assyria*. New York: Arno Press (First edition 1915).
Jean, C.F. 1929, 'Larsa d'après les textes cunéiformes (2187-1901)'. *Babyloniaca* 11: 1–64.

—, 1931, *Tell Sifr textes cuneiforms conserves au British Museum, réédités par Charles-F. Jean*. Paris: Librairie Orientaliste Paul Geuthner.

—, 1950, *Lettres diverses.* ARM 2. Paris: Imprimerie Nationale.

Jeyes, U. 1983, 'The Naditu Women of Sippar'. In A. Cameron and A. Kuhrt (eds), *Images of Women in Antiquity*, 260–72. London: Routledge.

Joannès, F. 1991, 'L'étain, de l'Élam à Mari'. In *Mésopotamie et Élam*, Actes de la XXXIV R.A.I., Gand 1989, 67–76. Gand: MHE Occasional Publications.

—, 1992, 'Histoire de Ḫarādum à l'époque paléo-babylonienne'. In C. Kepinski-Lecomte (ed.), *Ḫarādum I. Une ville nouvelle sur le Moyen-Euphrate (XVIIIe-XVIIe siècles av. J.-C.)*, 30–36. Paris: Éditions Recherches sur les Civilisations.

Kagan, D. 1991, *Pericles of Athens and the Birth of Democracy*. New York: The Free Press.

Kalla, G. 1999, 'Die Geschichte der Entdeckung der altbabylonischen Sippar-Archive'. *ZA* 89: 201–26.

Kamp, K. and Yoffee, N. 1980, 'Ethnicity in Ancient Western Asia During the Early Second Millennium B.C.: Archaeological Assessments and Ethnoarchaeological Prospectives'. *BASOR* 237: 85–105.

Kang, S. 1972, *Sumerian Economic Texts from the Drehem Archive. Sumerian and Akkadian Cuneiform Texts in the Collection of the World Heritage Museum of the University of Illinois*, vol. 1. Urbana, Chicago and London: University of Illinois Press.

Katz, D. 1993, *Gilgamesh and Akka*, Library of Oriental Texts vol. 1. Groningen: Styx Publications.

Keith, K. 1999, Cities, Neighborhoods, and Houses: Urban Spatial Organization in Old Babylonian Mesopotamia. Doctoral dissertation, Ann Arbor, University of Michigan.

Kelley, D. 1991, *Versions of History from Antiquity to the Enlightenment*. New Haven: Yale University Press.

Kienast, B. 1978, *Die altbabylonischen Briefe und Urkunden aus Kisurra*. Freiburger altorientalische Studien (FAOS 2). Wiesbaden: Franz Steiner Verlag.

King, L. 1900, *The Letters and Inscriptions of Hammurabi, King of Babylon about 2000 B.C.*, 2 vols. London: Luzac and Co.

—, 1915, *A History of Babylon. From the Foundation of the Monarchy to the Persian Conquest*. London: Chatto and Windus.

Klengel, H. 1960, 'Zu den *šībūtum* in altbabylonischer Zeit', *OrNs* 29: 357–75.

—, 1971, 'Soziale Aspekte der altbabylonischen Dienstmiete'. In H. Klengel (ed.), *Beiträge zur Sozialen Struktur des Alten Vorderasien*. Schriften zur Geschichte und Kultur des alten Oriens I, 39–52. Berlin: Akademie-Verlag.

—, 1976, 'Untersuchungen zu den sozialen Verhältnissen im altbabylonischen Dilbat'. *AfO* 4: 63–110.

—, 1983, 'Bermerkungen zu den altbabylonischen Rechtsurkunden und Wirtschaftstexten aus Babylon (*VS* 22: 1-82)'. *AoF* 10: 5–48.
—, 1989, '"Älteste" in den Texten aus Ebla und Mari'. In M. Lebeau and Ph. Talon (eds), *Reflets des deux fleuves. Volume de mélanges offertes à André Finet*, 61–65. Leuven: Peeters.
—, 1991, *König Hammurapi und Alltag Babylons*. Zurich: Artemis and Winkler.
Klengel, H., and Klengel-Brandt, E. 2002, *Spät-altbabylonische Tontafeln Texte und Siegelabrollungen*. VAS 29. Mainz am Rheim: Verlag Philipp von Zabern.
Klíma, J. 1983, 'La communauté rurale dans la Babylonie ancienne'. In *Recueil de la Societé Jean Bodin pour l'histoire comparative des institutions*, XLI/2, 106–32. Paris: Dessaint et Tolra.
Kohler, J., and Peiser, F. 1904, *Hammurabis Gesetz*, vol. 1. Leipzig: E. Pfeiffer.
Kohler, J., and Ungnad, A. 1909a, *Hammurabis Gesetz*, vol. 2. Leipzig: E. Pfeiffer.
—, 1909b, *Hammurabis Gesetz*, vol. 3. Leipzig: E. Pfeiffer.
—, 1910, *Hammurabis Gesetz*, vol. 4. Leipzig: E. Pfeiffer.
—, 1911, *Hammurabis Gesetz*, vol. 5. Leipzig: E. Pfeiffer.
Koschaker, P., and Ungnad, A. 1923, *Hammurabis Gesetz*, vol. 6. Leipzig: E. Pfeiffer.
Koshurnikov, S. 1996, 'Prices and Types of Constructed City Lots in the Old Babylonian Period'. In K. Veenhof (ed.), *Houses and Households in Ancient Mesopotamia*. XLe R.A.I. Leiden, 257–60. Leiden: Nederlands Historisch-Archaeologisch Instituut te Istanbul.
Kozyreva, N. 1999, 'Sellers and Buyers of Urban Real Estate in Southern Mesopotamia at the Beginning of the Second Millennium B.C'. In M. Hudson and B. Levine (eds), *Urbanization and Land Ownership in the Ancient Near East*, 335–61. Peabody Museum of Archeology. Cambridge, MA: Harvard University.
Kraus, F. R. 1954, 'Le rôle des temples depuis la troisième dynastie d'Ur jusqu'à la première dynastie de Babylone'. *Cahiers d'Histoire Mondiale* I: 518–45.
—, 1955, 'Neue Rechtsurkunden der altbabylonischen Zeit. Bermerkungen zu *Ur Excavations Texts 5*'. *WO* 2: 120–36.
—, 1958, *Ein Edikt des Königs Ammi-ṣaduqa von Babylon.* Studia et Documenta ad Iura Orientis Antiqui Pertinentia, vol. 5. Leiden: E. J. Brill.
—, 1964, *Briefe aus den British Museum: CT 43 und 44*. AbB 1. Leiden: E. J. Brill.
—, 1970, *Sumerer und Akkader: Ein Problem der altmesopotamischen Geschichte*. Amsterdam: North-Holland Publishing.
—, 1972, *Briefe aus dem Istanbuler Museum.* AbB 5. Leiden: E. J. Brill.
—, 1974, 'Das altbabylonische Königtum'. In P. Garelli (ed.), *Le palais et la royauté (archéologie et civilisation)*, XIXe Rencontre Assyriologique Internationale, 235–61. Paris: Librairie Orientaliste Paul Geuthner.
—, 1977, *Briefe aus dem British Museum: CT 52*. AbB 7. Leiden: E. J. Brill.
—, 1982, '*kārum* ein Organ städtischer Selbstverwaltung der altbabylonischen

Zeit'. In A. Finet (ed.), *Les pouvoirs locaux en Mésopotamie et dans les régions adjacents*, 29–42. Bruxelles: Institut des Hautes Études de Belgique.

—, 1985, *Briefe aus kleineren westeuropäischen Sammlungen.* AbB 10. Leiden: E.J. Brill.

Kuhrt, A. 1995, *The Ancient Near East c. 3000–333 B.C.*, vol. 1. London and New York: Routledge.

Kupper, J. R. 1950, *Correspondance de Kibri-Dagan, gouverneur de Terqa.* ARM 3. Paris: Imprimerie Nationale.

—, 1954, *Correspondance de Bahdi-Lim.* ARM 6. Paris: Imprimerie Nationale.

—, 1957, *Les nomades en Mésopotamie au temps des rois de Mari.* Bibliothèque de la Faculté de Philosophie et Lettres de l'Université de Liège n° 142. Paris: Société d'Édition 'Les Belles Lettres'.

—, 1973, 'La voix de l'opposition à Mari'. In A. Finet (ed.). *La voix de l'opposition en Mésopotamie. Colloque organisé par l'Institut des Hautes Études de Belgique 19 et 20 mars 1973.* Bruxelles: Institut des Hautes Études de Belgique.

—, 1982, 'Les pouvoirs locaux dans le royaume de Mari'. In A. Finet (ed.), *Les pouvoirs locaux en Mésopotamie et dans les regions adjacentes*, 43–53. Bruxelles: Institut des Hautes Études de Belgique.

—, 1983, *Documents administratifs de la salle 135 du palais de Mari.* ARM 22. Paris: ERC.

—, 1985, 'La cité et le royaume de Mari. L' organization urbaine à l'époque amorite'. *MARI 4*: 463–66.

—, 1990, 'Les formules de malédiction dans les inscriptions royales de l'époque paléo-babylonienne'. *RA* 84: 157–63.

—, 1998, *Lettres royales du temps de Zimri-Līm.* ARM 28. Paris: Éditions Recherche sur les Civilisations.

LaCapra, D. 1985, *History and Criticism.* Ithaca and London: Cornell University Press.

Lackenbacher, S. 1988a, 'Abimekim'. In D. Charpin *et al.* (eds), *Archives épistolaires de Mari* I/2. ARM 26, 371–99. Paris: Éditions Recherche sur les Civilisations.

—, 1988b, 'Les lettres de Buqâqum'. In *Archives épistolaires de Mari* I/2. ARM 26, D. Charpin *et al.* (eds), 401–10. Paris: Éditions Recherche sur les Civilisations.

Lafont, B. 1994, 'L'admonestation des anciens de Kurdâ à leur roi'. In D. Charpin and J.-M. Durand (eds), *Florilegium Marianum II. Recueil d'études à la mémoire de M. Birot*, 209–19. Mémoires de NABU 3. Paris: Société pour l'Étude du Proche-Orient Ancien.

Lambert, W. 1968, 'Another Look at Hammurabi's Ancestors'. *JCS* 22: 1–2.

—, 1977, 'Kakkala', *RlA* 5: 288.

Lambert, W., and Millard, A. 1999, *Atra-ḫasīs. The Babylonian Story of the Flood.* Winona Lake, IN: Eisenbrauns (First edition 1969).

Landsberger, B. 1924, 'Über die Völker Vorderasiens im dritten Jahrtausend', *ZA* 1 (XXXV): 213–38.

—, 1937, *Die Series ana ittišu*, MSL I. Rome: Pontifici Instituti Biblici.

—, 1955, 'Remarks on the Archive of the Soldier Ubarum'. *JCS* 9: 121–31.

—, 1957, *The Series* ḪAR-ra = *ḫubullu*, MSL V. Roma: Pontificium Institutum Biblicum.

Landsberger, B., and Civil, M. 1967, *The Series* ḪAR-ra = *ḫubullu*, tablet XV and related texts, MSL IX. Roma: Pontificun Institutum Biblicum.

Langdon, S. 1924, *Excavations at Kiš*, vol. 1. Paris: Librairie Orientaliste Paul Geuthner.

Larsen, M. 1976, *The Old Assyrian City-state and its Colonies*. Copenhagen: Akademisk Forlag.

—, 1995, 'The Babel/Bible Controversy and its Aftermath'. In J. Sasson (ed.), *Civilizations of the Ancient Near East*, vol. I-II, 95–106. Peabody, MA: Hendrickson Publishers.

—, 1996, *The Conquest of Assyria. Excavations in an Antique Land 1840–1860*. London: Routledge.

Launderville, D. 2003, *Piety and Politics: The Dynamics of Royal Authority in Homeric Greece, Biblical Israel, and Old Babylonian Mesopotamia*. Grand Rapids, MI: William B. Eerdmans Publishing Company.

Lautner, J. 1922, *Die richterliche Entscheidung und die Streitbeendigung im altbabylonische Prozessrechte*. Leipziger rechtswissenschaftliche Studien. Leipzig: Verlag Th. Weicher.

—, 1933, *Altbabylonische Personenmiete und Entarbeiterverträge*. Leiden: E. J. Brill.

Le Roy Ladurie, E. 1978, *Montaillou. The Promised Land of Error*. New York: George Braziller, Inc.

Leemans, W. F. 1957, 'Some Aspects of Theft and Robbery in Old Babylonian Documents'. *RSO* 32: 661–66.

—, 1959, 'Quelques remarques au sujet des tablettes de l'époche vieux-babylonienne du musée de Genève'. *JESHO* 2: 324–33.

—, 1968, *The Old Babylonian Merchant: His Business and his Social Position*. Leiden: E. J. Brill.

—, 1983, 'Trouve-t-on des communautés rurales dans l'ancienne Mésopotamie?' In *Recueils de la societé Jean Bodin pour l'histoire comparative des institutions*, XLI/2: 43–106. Paris: Dessaint et Tolra.

Leichty, E. 1975, 'A. Leo Oppenheim, 1904–1974'. *JAOS* 95: 369–70.

—, 1989, 'Feet of Clay'. In H. Behrens *et al.* (eds), *DUMU-E$_2$-DUB-BA-A. Studies in Honor of Åke Sjöberg*, 349–56. Philadelphia: Occasional Publications of the Samuel Noah Kramer Fund.

Leick, G. 2002, *Mesopotamia. The Invention of the City*. London: Penguin Books.

Lenormant, F. 1881, *Histoire ancienne de l'Orient jusqu'aux guerres médiques.* 9ème. édition, 6 volumes. Paris: A. Levy-Librarie-Editeur (First edition 1868).

Lieberman, S. 1992, 'Nippur: City of Decisions'. In M. de J. Ellis (ed.), *Nippur at the Centennial*, 127–36. Philadelphia: Occasional Publications of the S. N. Kramer Fund.

Limet, H. 1986, *Textes administratifs relatifs au métaux*. ARM 25. Paris: ERC.

Liverani, M. 1973, 'Memorandum on the Approach to Historiographic Texts'. *OrNS* 42: 178–94.

—, 1975, 'Communautés de village et palais royal dans la Syrie du IIème. millénaire'. *JESHO* 18: 146–64.

—, 1979, 'The Ideology of the Assyrian Empire'. In M. T. Larsen (ed.), *Power and Propaganda*, 297–318. Copenhagen: Akademisk Forlag.

—, 1981, 'Critique of Variants and the Titulary of Sennacherib'. In F. M. Fales (ed.), *Assyrian Royal Inscriptions: New Horizons*, 225–57. Rome: Instituto per l'Orient.

—, 1992, *Studies in the Annals of Ashurnasirpal II 2: Topographical Analysis*. Rome: La Sapienza.

—, 1993, 'Nelle pieghe del despotismo. Organismi rappresentative nell'antico Oriente'. *Studi Storici* 34: 7–33.

—, 1995, 'The Deeds of Ancient Mesopotamian Kings'. In J. Sasson (ed.), *Civilizations of the Ancient Near East*, vol. 3, pp. 2353–66. Peabody, MA: Hendrickson Publishers Inc.

—, 1997, 'The Ancient Near Eastern City and Modern Ideologies'. In *Die Orientalische Stadt: Kontinuität, Wandel, Bruch*. Berlin: Saarbrücker Druckerei un Verlag.

Luke, J. 1965, Pastoralism and Politics in the Mari Period. Doctoral dissertation, Ann Arbor, University of Michigan.

Maekawa, K. 1980, 'Female Weavers and their Children'. *ASJ* 2: 81–125.

Marx, K. 1964, *Pre-Capitalist Economic Formations*. Edited and with an introduction by E. Hobsbawm. London: Lawrence and Wishart.

Meissner, B. 1893, *Beiträge zum altbabylonischen Privatrecht*, Leipzig: J. C. Hinrichs'sche Buchhandlung.

Michalowski, P. 1976a, The Royal Correspondence of Ur. Doctoral dissertation, New Haven, Yale University.

—, 1976b, 'Royal Women of the Ur III Period Part I: The Wife of Šulgi'. *JCS* 28: 169–72.

—, 1978, 'Royal Women of the Ur III Period Part II: Geme-Ninlila'. *JCS* 31: 171–76.

—, 1982, 'Royal Women of the Ur III Period Part III'. *ASJ* 4: 129–39.

—, 1983, 'History as Charter. Some Observations on the Sumerian King List', *JAOS* 102: 237–48.

—, 1989, *Lamentation over the Destruction of Sumer and Akkad*. Winona Lake, IN: Eisenbrauns.
—, 1993, 'Memory and Deed: the Historiography of the Political Expansion of the Akkad State'. In M. Liverani (ed.), *Akkad: First World Empire*, 69–90. Padova: Sargon srl.
—, 1994, 'Writing and Literacy in Early States: A Mesopotamianist Perspective'. In D. Keller-Cohen (ed.), *Literacy: Interdisciplinary Conversations*, 49–70. Cresskill, NJ: Hampton Press.
—, 1999, 'Commemoration, Writing, and Genre in Ancient Mesopotamia'. In C. Shuttleworth Kraus (ed.), *The Limits of Historiography. Genre and Narrative in Ancient Historical Texts*, 69–90. Brill: Leiden-Boston-Köln.
—, 2003, 'A Man Called Enmebaragesi'. In *Literatur, Politik, und Recht in Mesopotamien*. Orientalia Biblica et Christiana. Heidelberg: Harrasowitz.
Mitchell, T. 1991, *Colonizing Egypt*. Berkeley, Los Angeles, and London: University of California Press (First edition 1988).
Momigliano, A. 1990, *The Classical Foundations of Modern Historiography*. Berkeley, Los Angeles, and London: University of California Press.
Moorey, P. *et al.* 1988, 'New Analyses of Old Babylonian Metal Work from Tell Sifr'. *Iraq* 50: 39–48.
Morley, N. 1999, *Writing Ancient History*. New York: Cornell University Press.
Murra, J. 1975, *Formaciones económicas y políticas del mundo andino*. Lima: Instituto de Estudios Peruanos.

Nakata, I. 1989, 'A Further Look at the Institution of *sugāgūtum* in Mari'. *JANES* 19: 113–18.
Nemet-Nejat, K. 1998, *Daily Life in Ancient Mesopotamia*. Westport, Connecticut and London: Greenwood Press.
Nissen, H. 1988, *The Early History of the Ancient Near East 9000–2000 BC*. Chicago and London: University of Chicago Press.
Nissen, H. *et al.* 1993, *Archaic Bookkeeping. Early Writing Techniques of Economic Administration in the Ancient Near East*. Chicago and London: University of Chicago Press (First German edition: 1990).

Oppenheim, A. L. 1936, 'Zu keilschriftlichen Omenliteratur'. *OrNS* 5: 199–228.
—, 1960, 'Assyriology – Why and How?' *Current Anthropology* 1: 409–23.
—, 1967, 'A New Look at the Structure of Mesopotamian Society'. *JESHO* 10: 1–16.
—, 1969, 'Mesopotamia – Land of Many Cities'. In I. Lapidus (ed.), *Middle Eastern Cities: A Symposium on Ancient, Islamic and Contemporary Middle Eastern Urbanism*, 1–18. Berkeley: University of California Press.

—, 1997, *Ancient Mesopotamia. Portrait of a Dead Civilization*. Chicago: University of Chicago Press (First edition 1964).

Owen, D. 1981, 'Tax Payments from Some City Elders in the Northeast'. *ASJ* 3: 63–76.

Parayre, D. 1985, 'Un cylindre inédit de la collection Vendryès'. In J.-M. Durand and J. Kupper (eds), *Miscelanea Babylonica. mélanges offertes à Maurice Birot*, 233–35. Paris: Éditions Recherches sur les Civilisations.

Pettinato, G. 1979, *Catalogo dei testi cuneiformi di Tell Mardikh – Ebla. Materiali epigrafici di Ebla 1* (MEE 1). Napoli: Istituto Universitario Orientale di Napoli.

—, 1977, 'Fondazione della città UNKEN^{KI}', *Oriens Antiquus* 16: 173–76.

—, 1986, *Ebla. Nuovi orizzonti della storia*. Milano: Rusconi.

Pientka, R. 1998, *Die Spätaltbabylonische Zeit: Quellen, Jahresdaten, Geschichte*. Münster: Rhema.

Pinches, T. 1915, *The Babylonian Tablets of the Berens Collections*. Asiatic Society Monographs vol. XVI. London: Royal Asiatic Society.

Polanyi, K. 1957, 'Marketless Trading in Hammurabi's Time'. In C. Arensberg and H. Pearson (eds), *Trade and Market in Early Empires*, 12–26. Chicago: Free Press.

—, 1977, *The Livelihood of Man*. New York: Academic Press.

Pollock, S. 1999, *Ancient Mesopotamia. The Eden that Never Was*. Cambridge: Cambridge University Press.

Pomponio, F., and Visicato, G. 1994, *Early Dynastic Administrative Tablets of Šuruppak*. Napoli: Istituto Universitario Orientale di Napoli.

Postgate, N. 1992, *Early Mesopotamia. Society and Economy at the Dawn of History*. London and New York: Routledge.

Powell, M. 1999, '*Wir müssen alle unsere Nische nutzen*: Monies, Motives, and Methods in Babylonian Economics'. In J. Deckersen (ed.), *Trade and Finance in Ancient Mesopotamia (MOS I). Proceedings of the First MOS Symposium (Leiden 1997)*, 5–23. Leiden: Nederlands Historisch-Archaeologisch Instituut te Istanbul.

Rawlinson, G. 1871, *A Manual of Ancient History. From the Earliest Times to the Fall of the Western Empires*. New York: Harper & Brothers.

Rawlinson, H. 1852, 'Outlines of Assyrian History Collected from the Cuneiform Inscriptions'. *29th Annual Report of the Royal Asiatic Society of Great Britain*, London, 15–42.

Rempel, J., and Yoffee, N. 1999, 'The End of the Cycle? Assessing the Impact of the Hellenization on Mesopotamian Civilization'. In B. Böck *el al.* (eds), *Minuscula Mesopotamica: Festschrift für Johannes Renger*, Alter Orient und Altes Testament 267, 384–98. Münster: Ugarit-Verlag.

Renger, J. 1967, 'Untersuchungen zum Priestertum in der altbabylonischen Zeit. 1. Teil'. *ZA* 58: 110–88.

—, 1969, 'Untersuchungen zum Priestertum in der altbabylonischen Zeit. 2. Teil'. *ZA* 59: 104–230.

—, 1977, 'Wrongdoing and its Sanctions: on "Criminal" and "Civil" Law in the Old Babylonian Period'. *JESHO* 20: 56–77.

—, 1979, 'Interaction of Temple, Palace, and "Private Enterprise" in the Old Babylonian Economy'. In E. Lipinski (ed.), *State and Temple Economy in the Ancient Near East I*, 249–56. Leuven: Departement Oriëntalistiek.

—, 1984, 'Patterns of Non-Institutional Trade and Non-Commercial Exchange in Ancient Mesopotamia at the Beginning of the Second Millennium BC'. In A. Archi (ed.), *Circulation of Goods in Non-Palatial Contexts in the Ancient Near East*, 31–123. Rome: Edizioni dell'Ateneo.

—, 1990, 'Different Economic Spheres in the Urban Economy of Ancient Mesopotamia. Traditional Solidarity, Redistribution and Market Elements as the Means of Access to the Necessities of Life'. In E. Aerts and H. Klengel (eds), *The Town as Regional Economic Centre in the Ancient Near East*, 20–28. Leuven: Leuven University Press.

—, 1995, 'Institutional, Communal, and Individual Ownership or Possession of Arable Land in Ancient Mesopotamia from the End of the Fourth to the End of the First Millennium BC'. *Chicago-Kent Law Review* 71: 269–319.

Richardson, S. 2002, The Collapse of a Complex State: A Reappraisal of the End of the First Dynasty of Babylon, 1683-1597 B.C. Doctoral dissertation, New York, Columbia University.

Riftin, A., 1937. *Staro-Vavilonskie iuridicheskie i administrativnye dokumenty v sobraniiakh SSSR*. Moscow and Leningrad: Nauka.

Röllig, W. 1976, 'Die altmesopotamische Markt'. *WO* 8: 286–95.

Roth, M. 1983, 'The Slave and the Scoundrel'. *JAOS* 103: 275–86.

—, 1997, *Law Collections from Mesopotamia and Asia Minor*. Society of Biblical Literature Writings from the Ancient World Series. Atlanta: Scholars Press.

—, 1998, 'Gender and Law: A Case Study from Ancient Mesopotamia'. In V. Matthews *et al.* (eds), *Gender and Law in the Hebrew Bible and the Ancient Near East*, 173–84. Sheffield: Sheffield Academic Press.

—, 1999, 'The Priestess and the Tavern: LH § 110'. In B. Böck *et al.* (eds), *Munuscula Mesopotamica Festschrift für J. Renger*. AOAT 267, 445–64. Münster: Ugarit Verlag.

—, 2000, 'The Law Collection of King Hammurabi: Toward an Understanding of Codification and Text'. In E. Lévy (ed.), *La codification des lois dans l'antiquité*. Actes du Colloque de Strasbourg 27–29 novembre 1997, 9–31. Paris: Diffusion De Boccard.

—, 2001, 'Reading Mesopotamian Law Cases. *PBS* 5 100: A Question of Filiation'. *JESHO* 44: 243–92.

Rowton, M. 1967, 'Watercourses and Water Rights in the Official Correspondence from Larsa and Isin'. *JCS* 21: 267–74.

—, 1970, 'Chronology II. Ancient Western Asia'. In I. Edwards *et al.* (eds), *The Cambridge Ancient History* I/1, 193–239. Cambridge: Cambridge University Press.

Sachs, A. 1976, 'The Latest Datable Cuneiform Tablets'. In B. Eichler *et al.* (eds), *Kramer Aniversary Volume*. Alter Orient und Altes Testament 25, 379–98. Kevelaer/Neukirchen-Vluyn: Butzon & Bercker/Neukirchen Verlag.

Said, E. 1994, *Orientalism*. New York: Vintage Books (First edition 1978).

Sasson, J. 1969, *The Military Establishments at Mari*, Studia Pohl 3. Rome: Pontifical Biblical Institute.

—, 1981, 'On Choosing Models for Recreating Israelite Pre-Monarchic History'. *Journal for the Study of the Old Testament* 21: 3–24.

—, 1985, 'Yarim-Lim's War Declaration'. In J.-M. Durand and J. Kupper (eds), *Miscelanea babylonica. Mélanges offertes à Maurice Birot*, 237–53. Paris: Éditions Recherches sur les Civilisations.

—, 1995, 'King Ḫammurabi of Babylon'. In J. Sasson (ed.), *Civilizations of the Ancient Near East*, vol. 1, 901–15. Peabody, MA: Hendrickson Publishers.

Sayce, A. H. 1899, *Babylonians and Assyrians. Life and Customs*. New York: Charles Scribner's sons.

Scheil, V. 1928, 'Sparsim: 5 babtum'. *RA* 25: 43.

—, 1930, 'Nouveaux présages tirés du foie'. *RA* 27: 141–54.

Schneider, A. 1920, *Die Anfänge der Kulturwirtschaft: Die sumerische Tempelstadt*. Essen: G. D. Bädeker.

Schneider, H. 1990, 'Die Bücher-Meyer Kontroverse'. In W. Calder and A. Demondt (eds), *Eduard Meyer. Leben und Leistung eines Universalhistoriker*, 417–45. Leiden: E.J. Brill.

Schorr, M. 1971, *Urkunden des altbabylonischen Zivil-und Prozessrechts*. *VAB* 5. New York: George Olms Verlag (First edition 1913).

Seri, A. 2004, 'Review of *Spät-altbabylonische Tontafeln Texte und Siegelabrollungen*. (*VAS* 29), by H. Klengel and E. Klengel-Brandt'. *JCS* 56: 129–34.

—, 2005, 'Review of *Il regolamento degli scambi nell'antichità (III – I millennio a.C.)*, by L. Milano and N. Parise (eds)'. *JESHO* 48 (forthcoming).

Sigrist, M. 1990, *Old Babylonian Account Texts in the Horn Archaeological Museum*, Andrews University Cuneiform Texts vol. IV. Berrien Springs, MI: Andrews University Press.

Simmons, S. 1959, 'Early Old Babylonian Tablets from Ḫarmal and Elsewhere'. *JCS* 13: 71–93.

—, 1960, 'Early Old Babylonian Tablets from Ḫarmal and Elsewhere (continued)'. *JCS* 14: 23–32.

—, 1978, *Early Old Babylonian Documents*, Yale Oriental Series, Babylonian Texts, vol. 14. YOS 14. New Haven: Yale University Press.

Smith, G. 1877, *The History of Babylonia*. London, Society for Promoting Christian Knowledge. New York: Young & Co.

Smith, S. 1946, 'Excavations at Tell Harmal I. Diniktim'. *Sumer* 2: 19–21.

Snell, D. 1997, *Life in the Ancient Near East 3100–332 BC*. New Haven and London: Yale University Press.

Sollberger, E. 1965, 'Three Ur Dynasty Documents'. *JCS* 19: 26–30.

Sommerfeld, W. 1982, *Der Aufstieg Marduks: Die Stellung Marduks in den babylonischen Religion des zweiten Jahrtausends v. Chr.* AOAT 213. Neukirchen–Vluyn: Neukirchener Verlag.

Spar, I. (ed.) 1988, *Cuneiform Texts in the Metropolitan Museum of Art*, vol. 1. New York: The Metropolitan Museum of Art.

Steinkeller, P. 1989, *Sale Documents of the Ur III Period*. FAOS 17. Stuttgart: Franz Steiner Verlag.

—, 1999, 'Land-Tenure Conditions in Third Millennium Babylonia: The Problem of Regional Variation'. In M. Hudson and B. Levine (eds), *Urbanization and Land Ownership in the Ancient Near East*, 289–321. Cambridge, MA: Peabody Museum of Archaeology Harvard University.

—, 2004a, 'A History of Mashkan-shapir and its Role in the Kingdom of Larsa'. In E. Stone and P. Zimansky, *The Anatomy of a Mesopotamian City: Survey and Soundings at Mashkan-shapir*, 26–42. Winona Lake, IN: Eisenbrauns.

—, 2004b, 'A Building Inscription of Sin-iddinam and Other Inscribed Materials from Abu Duwari'. In E. Stone and P. Zimansky, *The Anatomy of a Mesopotamian City: Survey and Soundings at Mashkan-shapir*, 135–52. Winona Lake, IN: Eisenbrauns.

—, 2004c, 'Studies in Third Millennium Paleography, 4; Sign Kiš'. *ZA* 94: 175–85.

Stol, M. 1976a, *Studies in Old Babylonian History*. Leiden: Nederlands Historisch-Archaeologisch Instituut te Istanbul.

—, 1976b, 'On Ancient Sippar'. *BiOr* 33: 146–54.

—, 1981, *Letters from Yale*. AbB 9. Leiden, E. J. Brill.

—, 1982a, 'State and Private Business in the Land of Larsa'. *JCS* 34: 127–55.

—, 1982b, 'A Cadastral Innovation by Ḫammurabi'. In G. van Driel *et al.* (eds), *Zikir Šumim: Assyriological Studies Presented to F. Kraus on the Occasion of his Seventieth Birthday*, 351–58. Leiden: E. J. Brill.

—, 1991, 'Old Babylonian Personal Names'. *Studi epigraphici e linguistici sul Vicino Oriente antico* 8: 191–212.

—, 1995, 'Old Babylonian Corvée (*tupšikkum*). In T. van den Hout and J. de Roos (eds), *Ancient Near Eastern Studies Presented to Philo H. J. Houwink ten Cate*

on the Occasion of his 65th Birthday, 294–309. Leiden: Nederlands Historisch-Archaeologisch Instituut te Istanbul.
—, 1998, 'Die altbabylonische Stadt Ḫalḫalla'. In E. Balke *et al.* (eds), *Dubsar antamen. Studien zur altorientalistik. Festschrift Römer*. AOAT 253. 415–45. Münster: Ugarit-Verlag.
—, 2004, 'Wirtschaft und Gesellschaft in altbabylonischer Zeit'. In D. Charpin *et al.*, *Mesopotamien: die altbabylonische Zeit.* OBO 160/4, 643–975. Fribourg and Göttingen: Academic Press/Vandenhoeck and Ruprecht.
Stolper, M. 1982, 'On the Dynasty of Šimaški and the Early Sukkalmaḫs'. *ZA* 72: 42–67.
—, 1992, 'On Why and How'. *Culture and History* 11: 13–22.
Stone, E. 1977, 'Economic Crisis and Social Upheaval in Old Babylonian Nippur'. In L. Devine and T. Young (eds), *Mountains and Lowlands: Essays in the Archaeology of Greater Mesopotamia*, 267–89. Bibliotheca Mesopotamica vol. 7. Malibu: Undena Publications.
—, 1987, *Nippur Neighborhoods*. Studies in Ancient Oriental Civilization n° 44. Chicago: The Oriental Institute.
Stone, L. 1979, 'The Revival of Narrative: Reflections on a New Old History'. *Past and Present* 85: 3–24.
Strassmaier, J. 1882, *Die altbabylonische Verträge aus Warka Verhandlung des 5. internationalen orientalischen Congresses*, 2 Teil, I Halfte. Berlin.
Szlechter, E. 1958, *Tablettes juridiques de la 1re dynastie de Babylone conservées au Musée d'Art et d'Histoire de Genève*. Paris: Recueil Sirey.
—, 1963, *Tablettes juridiques et administratives de la IIIe dynastie d'Ur et de la Ire. dynastie de Babylone conservées au Musée de l'Université de Manchester et à Cambridge, au Musée Fitzwilliam à l'Institut d'Études Orientales et à l'Institut d'Egyptologie*, Tome I, Planches. Paris: Recueil Sirey.
—, 1968, 'Gouvernés et gouvernants en Mésopotamie, depuis les origines jusqu'a la fin de la Ière dynastie de Babylone'. In *Gouvernés et gouvernants. Deuxième partie: antiquité et haut moyen age*, 73–86. *Recueils de la société Jean Bodin pour l'histoire comparative des institutions*. Bruxelles: Éditions de la Librairie Encyclopédique.
—, 1970, 'Les assemblées en Mésopotamie ancienne'. In *Liber Memorialis Georges de Lagarde. 'Études présentées à la commission internationale pour l'histoire des assemblées d'états*, 3–21. Louvain and Paris: Éditions Nauwelaerts.

Tadmor, H., and Weinfeld, M. (eds) 1984, *History, Historiography, and Interpretation. Studies in Biblical and Cuneiform Literatures*. Jerusalem: The Hebrew University of Jerusalem.
Talon, P. 1985, *Textes administratifs de salles 'Y et Z' du palais de Mari*. ARM 24. Paris: ERC.

Thompson, E. P. 1963, *The Making of the English Working Class*. New York: Vintage Books.

Thureau-Dangin, F. 1972, *Die sumerischen und akkadischen Königsinschriften*. VAB I. Leipzig: Zentralantiquariat der Deutschen demokratischen Republic.

Ungnad, A. 1914, *Babylonische Briefe aus der Zeit der Hammurapi-Dynastie*. Leipzig: J.C. Hinrichs.

Van De Mieroop, M. 1987a, *Crafts in the Early Isin Period: A Study of the Isin Archive from the Reigns of Išbi-Erra and Šū-ilīšu*. Orientalia Lovaniensie Analecta 24. Leuven: Departement Oriëntalistiek.

—, 1987b, 'The Archive of Balamunamḫe'. *AfO* 34: 1–29.

—, 1992, *Society and Enterprise in Old Babylonian Ur*. Berlin: Dietrich Reimer Verlag.

—, 1993, 'The Reign of Rīm-Sîn'. *RA* 87: 47–69.

—, 1997, *The Ancient Mesopotamian City*. Oxford: Clarendon Press.

—, 1999a, *Cuneiform Texts and the Writing of History*. London and New York: Routledge.

—, 1999b, 'Thoughts on Urban Real Estate in Ancient Mesopotamia'. In M. Hudson and B. Levine (eds), *Urbanization and Land Ownership in the Ancient Near East*, 253–87. Cambridge, MA: Harvard University.

—, 1999c, 'The Government of an Ancient Mesopotamian City'. In K. Watanabe (ed.), *Priests and Officials in the Ancient Near East*, 139–61. Heidelberg: Universitätsverlag C. Winter.

—, 2005, *Hammurabi of Babylon*. Oxford: Blackwell Publishing.

van Dijk, J. 1959, 'Textes divers du Musée de Bagdad'. *Sumer* 15: 5–14.

—, 1963, 'Neusumerische Gerichtsurkunden in Bagdad'. *ZA* 55: 70–90.

—, 1965, 'Une insurrection general au pays de Larša avant l'avènement de Nūr-Adad'. *JCS* 19: 1–25.

—, 1978, 'Išbi'erra, Kindatu, l'homme d'Elam et la chute de la ville d'Ur'. *JCS* 30: 189–208.

Van Driel, G. 1969, 'Review of *Épithètes royales akkadiennes et sumériennes* by M. J. Seux'. *BiOr* 26: 77–81.

—, 1998, 'Land in Ancient Mesopotamia: "that what Remains Undocumented does not Exist"'. In B. Harring and R. de Maaijer (eds), *Landless and Hungry? Access to Land in Early and Traditional Societies*, 19–49. Leiden: Research School CNWS, School of Asian, African and Amerindian Studies.

—, 2001, 'On Villages'. In W. H. van Soldt (ed.), *Veenhof Anniversary Volume. Studies Presented to Klaas R. Veenhof on the Occasion of his Sixty-five Birthday*, 103–18. Leiden: Instituut voor het Nabije Oosten.

Van Soldt, W. 1990, *Letters in the British Museum*. AbB 12. Leiden: E. J. Brill.

—, 1994, *Letters in the British Museum*. AbB 13. Leiden: E. J. Brill.

Vanstiphout, H. 1987, 'Towards a Reading of 'Gilgameš and Agga'. *AuOr* 5: 129–41.

Veenhof, K. 1986, 'Cuneiform Archives'. In K. Veenhof (ed.), *Cuneiform Archives and Libraries. Papers Read at the 30e Rencontre Assyriologique Internationale. Leiden, 4-8 July 1983*, 1–36. Leiden: Nederlands Historisch-Archaeologisch Instituut te Istanbul.

—, 1991, 'Assyrian Commercial Activities in Old Babylonian Sippar – Some New Evidence'. In D. Charpin and F. Joannès (eds), *Marchands, diplomats et empereurs. Études sur la civilisation mésopotamienne offertes à Paul Garelli*, 287–303. Paris: ERC.

—, 1995a, 'Kanesh: An Assyrian Colony in Anatolia'. In J. Sasson *et al.* (eds), *Civilizations of the Ancient Near East*, vol. II, 859–72. New York: Simon & Schuster Macmillan.

—, 1995b, "In Accordance with the Words of the Stele': Evidence for Old Assyrian Legislation'. *Chicago-Kent Law Review* 70: 1717–44.

—, 1997–2000, 'The Relation between Royal Decrees and Law Collections in the Old Babylonian Period', *Ex Oriente Lux* 35/6: 49–83.

—, 1999, 'Redemption of Houses in Assur and Sippar'. In B. Böck *et al.* (eds), *Munuscula Mesopotamica: Festschrift für Johannes Renger*. AOAT 267, 599–616. Münster: Ugarit-Verlag.

Veenker, R. 1974, 'An Old Babylonian Legal Procedure for Appeal Evidence from *ṭuppi lā ragāmim*'. *HUCA* 45: 1–15.

Verbrugghe, G., and Wickersham, J. 2000, *Berossos and Manetho, Introduced and Translated: Native Traditions in Ancient Mesopotamia and Egypt*. Ann Arbor: University of Michigan Press.

Veyne, P. 1971, *Comment on écrit l'histoire: essai d'épistémologie*. Paris: Éditions du Seuil.

Visicato. G. 1995, *The Bureaucracy of Šuruppak. Administrative Centres, Central Offices, Intermediate Structures and Hierarchies in the Economic Documentation of Fara*. Münster: Ugaritic-Verlag.

—, 2001, 'The Organization of Ancient Šuruppak'. In H. Martin *et al.* (eds), *The Fara Tablets in the University of Pennsylvania Museum of Archaeology and Anthropology*, 115–24. MD: CDL Press.

von Soden, W. 1986, 'Review of *VAS* 22 by H. Klengel'. *Orientalistische Literaturzeitung* 81: 245–47.

—, 1995, *Grundriss der akkadischen Grammatik*. Roma: Editrice Pontificio Istituto Biblico.

Walker, C. 1980, 'Some Assyrians at Sippar in the Old Babylonian Period'. *Anatolian Studies* 30: 15–22.

Walther, A. 1917, *Das altbabylonische Gerichtswesen*, Leipziger Semitistische Studies, VI. Band, Heft 4–6. Leipzig: J. Hinrichs.

Walters, S. 1970, *Water for Larsa: An Old Babylonian Archive Dealing with Irrigation*. New Haven and London: Yale University Press.

Waterman, L. 1916, *Business Documents of the Hammurapi Period from the British Museum*. *AJSL* 24: 145–204.

Weitmeyer, M. 1962, *Some Aspects of the Hiring of Workers in the Sippar Region at the Time of Hammurabi*. Copenhagen: Munksgaard.

Westbrook, R., and Wilcke, C. 1974/7, 'The Liability of an Innocent Purchaser of Stolen Goods in Early Mesopotamian Law'. *AfO* 25: 111–21.

White, H. 1973, *Metahistory: The Historical Imagination in Nineteenth-Century Europe*. Baltimore: Johns Hopkins University Press.

Whiting, R. 1985, 'The Reading of the Divine Name ^{d}Nin-MAR.KI'. *ZA* 75: 1–3.

—, 1987, *Old Babylonian Letters from Tell Asmar*. AS 22. Chicago: The Oriental Institute.

Wilcke, C. 1976, 'Zu den spät-altbabylonischen Kaufverträgen aus Nordbabylonien'. *WO* 8: 254–85.

—, 1990, 'Review of VAS 22 by H. Klengel'. *ZA* 80: 297–306.

—, 1992, 'Diebe, Räuber und Mörder'. In V. Haas (ed.), *Außenseiter und Randgruppen. Beiträge zu einen Sozialgeschichte des Alten Orients*. Xenia 32, 53–78. Konstanz: Universitätsverlag.

Wiseman, D. 1962, *The Expansion of Assyrian Studies. An Inaugural Lecture Delivered on 27 February 1962*. Oxford: Oxford University Press.

Wittfogel, K. 1957, *Oriental Despotism. A Comparative Study of Total Power*. New Haven: Yale University Press.

Wu, Y., and Dalley, S. 1990, 'The Origins of the Mananâ Dynasty at Kish, and the Assyrian King List'. *Iraq* 52: 159–63.

Yoffee, N. 1977, *The Economic Role of the Crown in the Old Babylonian Period*. Bibliotheca Mesopotamica, vol. 5. Malibu: Undena Publications.

—, 1978, 'On Studying the Old Babylonian Period'. *JCS* 30: 18–32.

—, 1988a, 'Orienting Collapse'. In N. Yoffee and G. Cowgill (eds), *The Collapse of Ancient States and Civilizations*, 1–9. Tucson: Arizona Press.

—, 1988b, 'The Collapse of Ancient Mesopotamian States and Civilizations'. In *The Collapse of Ancient States and Civilizations*, N. Yoffee and G. Cowgill (eds), 44–68. Tucson: Arizona Press.

—, 1988c, 'Aspects of Mesopotamian Land Sales'. *American Anthropologist* 90: 119–30.

—, 1995, 'Political Economy in Early Mesopotamian States'. *Annual Review of Anthropology* 24: 281–311.

—, 1997, 'Review of *The Ancient Near East c. 3000 – 330 B.C.*, by A. Kuhrt'. *ZA* 87: 297–99.

—, 1998, 'The Economics of Ritual at late Old Babylonian Kiš'. *JESHO* 41: 312–43.

—, 1999, 'Review of *Die Darstellung des Rechtsaustrags in den altbabylonischen Prozess-urkunden*, by E. Dombradi'. *JCS* 51: 142–44.

—, 2000, 'Law Courts and the Mediation of Social Conflict in Ancient Mesopotamia'. In J. Richards and M. van Buren (eds), *Order, Legitimacy, and Wealth in Ancient States*, 46–63. Cambridge: Cambridge University Press.

—, 2005, *Myths of the Archaic State. Evolution of the Earliest Cities, States, and Civilizations*. Cambridge: Cambridge University Press.

Yokoyama, M. 1994, The Administrative Structure and Economic Function of Public Service (ilkum) of the Old Babylonian State in the Old Babylonian Period. Doctoral dissertation, Los Angeles, University of California.

Zaccagnini, C. 1981, 'Modi di produzione asiatico e Vicino Oriente antico. Appunti per una discussione'. *Dialoghi di Archeologia NS* 3: 3–65.

Index

NAMES AND SUBJECTS

Febvre, Lucien 17, 19
Finet, André 46
Finkelstein, Jacob 24, 38, 53, 169, 174
Finley, Moses 23, 193
First Dynasty of Babylon 30, 31, 3–8, 49, 58, 94, 95, 100, 177, 180, 189
Fitzgerald, Madeleine 66
Fleming, Daniel 31, 48, 115, 193
Flood story 12, 97
Fortner, John 47, 75, 142, 165, 177
Frankena, Rintje 80
Frayne, Douglas 57, 60
Fukuyama, Francis 22

Gallery, Maureen 78
Gelb, Ignace 17, 18, 42, 64
'Genealogy of Hammurabi' 37, 38
Ginzburg, Carlo 23, 186
Goddeeris, Anne 144, 146
Goetze, Albrecht 76, 77
Grant, Elihu 40

Ḫaneans 100, 105
Harris, Rivkah 24, 47, 62–4, 74, 142
Hegel 9, 17, 182
Hermes Trismegistus 181
Herodotus 9, 13, 159, 178, 184
Hincks, Edward 9
histoire sérielle 22
historiography 19, 24–5, 182
history from below 22, 23
history of political thought 23
history of the body 23
history of the event 23
Homer 185
Hommel, Fritz 14, 15

Igger, Georg 23

Jacobsen, Thorkild 49, 142, 160, 165–6
Jakobson, Vladimir 41, 44

King, Leonard 53
Keith, Kathryn 140
Klengel, Horst 48, 75, 101
kleroterion 167
Koshurnikov, Sergej 44–5
Kozyreva, Nelli 45
Kraus, Fritz R. 17, 67, 69
Kupper, Robert 100

LaCapra, Dominick 186
Lafont, Bertrand 114
Lamprecht, Karl 18
Landsberger, Benno 74–6, 141
Langdon, Stephen 64
'Larsa King List' 66
Larsen, Mogens 39, 141
'Laws of Ešnunna' 68
'Laws of Hammurabi' 31–2, 37, 48, 53, 85, 151, 176, 183
Layard, Austen H. 39
Le Roy Ladurie, Emmanuel 23
Leick, Gwendolyn 23
Leemans, W. F. 27, 40
Lenormant, François 11–13, 182
Lieberman, Stephen 171, 176
linguistic turn 22
Liverani, Mario 24, 193
Lucian 181

Maekawa, Kazuya 25
market economy 26, 43, 45–6
Marx, Karl 17, 26
Marxist theory 22
Meissner, Bruno 53
Menocchio 23
Meyer, Edward 43
Michalowski, Piotr 24–5, 123, 179
microhistory 22
Mitchell, Timothy 17
Momigliano, Arnaldo 20
Montesquieu 14, 17
Morley, Neville 13

Naturalis Historia 182
new economic history 22
Nimrod 181
nomadism 16, 47–9, 56, 65, 70, 100, 102

oikos economy 43
Oppenheim, A. Leo 20, 21, 43, 162

MESOPOTAMIAN DIVINE, PERSONAL, GEOGRAPHIC NAMES, AND WORDS

CUNEIFORM TEXTS

www.ingramcontent.com/pod-product-compliance
Lightning Source LLC
Chambersburg PA
CBHW050348270326
41926CB00016B/3644
9781908049001